Understanding and Teaching Religion in US History

The Harvey Goldberg Series
for Understanding and Teaching History

The Harvey Goldberg Series for Understanding and Teaching History gives college and secondary history instructors a deeper understanding of the past as well as the tools to help them teach it creatively and effectively. Named for Harvey Goldberg, a professor renowned for his history teaching at Oberlin College, Ohio State University, and the University of Wisconsin from the 1960s to the 1980s, the series reflects Goldberg's commitment to helping students think critically about the past with the goal of creating a better future. For more information, please visit www.GoldbergSeries.org.

Series Editors

John Day Tully is a professor of history at Central Connecticut State University and was the founding director of the Harvey Goldberg Center for Excellence in Teaching at Ohio State University. He has coordinated many Teaching American History grants and has received the Connecticut State University System's Board of Trustees Teaching Award.

Matthew Masur is a professor of history at Saint Anselm College, where he has served as codirector of the Father Guerin Center for Teaching Excellence. He has also been a member of the Teaching Committee of the Society for Historians of American Foreign Relations.

Brad Austin is a professor of history at Salem State University. He has served as chair of the American Historical Association's Teaching Prize Committee and has worked with hundreds of secondary school teachers as the academic coordinator of many Teaching American History grants.

Advisory Board

Leslie Alexander Associate Professor of History, University of Oregon
Kevin Boyle William Smith Mason Professor of American History, Northwestern University
Ross Dunn Professor Emeritus, San Diego State University
Leon Fink UIC Distinguished Professor of History, University of Illinois at Chicago
Kimberly Ibach Principal, Fort Washakie High School, Wyoming
Alfred W. McCoy J.R.W. Smail Professor of History, Director, Harvey Goldberg Center for the Study of Contemporary History, University of Wisconsin–Madison
David J. Staley Associate Professor of History, Director, Center for the Humanities in Practice, Ohio State University
Maggie Tran Chair of Social Studies, McLean High School, Virginia
Sam Wineburg Margaret Jacks Professor of Education and (by courtesy) of History, Director, Stanford History Education Group, Stanford University

Understanding and Teaching Religion in US History

Edited by

KAREN J. JOHNSON AND
JONATHAN M. YEAGER

The University of Wisconsin Press

The University of Wisconsin Press
728 State Street, Suite 443
Madison, Wisconsin 53706
uwpress.wisc.edu

Printed in the United States of America

This book may be available in a digital edition.

Library of Congress Cataloging-in-Publication Data

Names: Johnson, Karen J., 1981– editor. | Yeager, Jonathan M., editor.
Title: Understanding and teaching religion in US history / edited by
    Karen J. Johnson and Jonathan M. Yeager.
Other titles: Harvey Goldberg series for understanding and teaching
    history.
Description: Madison : The University of Wisconsin Press, [2024] |
    Series: The Harvey Goldberg series for understanding and teaching
    history | Includes bibliographic references and index.
Identifiers: LCCN 2023040964 | ISBN 9780299346300 (hardcover)
Subjects: LCSH: United States—Religion—History—Study and
    teaching. | United States—History—Religious aspects—Study and
    teaching.
Classification: LCC E175.8 .U535 2024 | DDC 200.973—dc23/
    eng/20231024
LC record available at https://lccn.loc.gov/2023040964

To Eric, a master teacher, and to my students who will teach the next generation.

—K. J. J.

To my students at UTC who make teaching American religious history meaningful.

—J. M. Y.

Contents

Contents

Contents

Acknowledgments

Quite simply, we are grateful first and foremost to the outstanding historians who worked on chapters for this book. They brought together their historical expertise with teaching in such helpful ways. It has been an honor to work with them.

We are also especially grateful to Brad Austin, who worked closely with us on this volume. Brad's enthusiasm, teaching wisdom, and editorial support have been immense. Thank you to Nathan MacBrien from the University of Wisconsin Press for his support. Thank you to Tim Larsen, who helped the two of us find one another and start collaborating on the book. Edward Blum, Kevin Schultz, and Douglas Sweeney—all excellent historians—gave early feedback on the scope of material covered. The reviewers offered helpful feedback that strengthened the volume.

Understanding and Teaching Religion in US History

Introduction

Why Religion Matters in Teaching US History

KAREN J. JOHNSON AND

JONATHAN M. YEAGER

Religion is deeply embedded in American history, and one cannot understand American history's broad dynamics without accounting for religion. Without it, teachers cannot rightly explain key themes in our US surveys, such as gender, race, class, politics, and social dynamics. From the Native American religions to the earliest European explorations of the New World to recent presidential elections, religion has been a significant feature of the American story. Navigating our current polarized context—and more than that, living in a pluralistic nation whose diversity will only increase in coming years—requires understanding religion. Understanding religion historically does not mean teaching students to practice different religions, or to adhere to a set of beliefs about the divine. It does mean accounting for religion—what people believe and how they practice their beliefs—as a historical force. It means asking questions about how people's systems of faith shaped the meaning they ascribed to the world; pondering how religious institutions influenced American politics and culture; wondering how worship and gender, race, or class intersected. Teaching the subject historically can foster humility and provide context for religion's role in American life.

Religion, as the chapters in this book show, shaped and was shaped by major periods and themes in United States history. It was also never monolithic—while Protestant Christianity, in all its diverse forms, was the dominant expression of religion throughout much of US history, Islam, Judaism, Catholicism, and Native American religions have also shaped the religious landscape from the beginning. Throughout America's history, it is undeniable that religion has played a major role in influencing the culture and political climate of the United States. These chapters collectively argue that teachers must consider religion to understand key dynamics in American history, and that this accounting offers a better understanding of that history and the power of the stories we tell in contemporary society.

Examining the religious aspects of US history, for instance, helps us become better informed about contentious debates, such as the role of pluralism in American life and whether America was founded as a Christian nation. Did the Puritans travel to the New World to seek religious freedom? Did they try to form a theocracy, in which God would rule their towns and colonies, or did they simply want to incorporate moral and ethical guidelines within the local governments that they established? Origins stories are central to national identity, and students would benefit from engaging these questions thoughtfully.

Some of the most heated intellectual battles for whether America was founded as a Christian nation are fought over the opinions of the Founders. Secular and faith-based scholars and laypeople have intensely examined the religious intent of men such as George Washington, John Adams, Benjamin Franklin, and Thomas Jefferson, when they established the laws of the new nation, and as they forged important documents such as the Declaration of Independence and the US Constitution. Did the Founders purposely design America to be a Christian nation, or did they want its citizens to allow their individual consciences to guide them in matters of faith?

Even for moments in US history that have few overt religious overtones when they are normally taught, such as the Great Depression, religion played a significant role. In the 1930s, the US government began shaping Americans' lives in new ways as they grappled with the widespread suffering. Why did everyday Americans, farmers, housewives, and factory workers who considered themselves as self-sufficient, independent people welcome the federal government's increasing involvement in their everyday lives? Weighing the limits of religious institutions to address the suffering and the rhetoric of religious leaders—including evangelicals whose descendants would advocate for smaller government fifty years later—shows how religious shifts facilitated the state's expansion.

Many teachers will be familiar with the faith of Martin Luther King Jr., steeped in the theologies of Black churches with their emphasis on God's deliverance of his people. King was speaking to fellow ministers when he lamented in the often-taught "Letter from Birmingham Jail" that white Christian moderates were the greatest hindrance to the advancement of Black citizenship.[1] Why did so many religious white southerners see King as an agitator, aiming to disrupt their way of life? Why did their political leaders argue against national civil rights legislation based on states' rights? Again, religion sheds some light. Most white southerners followed a segregationist theology, which argued that scripture supported segregation and that Christians should not be involved in "political issues" such as civil rights, and their faith emphasized individualism, personal responsibility, and relationships.[2] Even if they agreed that African Americans should have full citizenship rights, top-down laws challenged the very frameworks and patterns structuring white southern evangelicals' lives. Southern states' massive resistance, then, can be more fully understood when we consider how white southern evangelicalism worked.

When students study religious changes, not only will their understanding of US history improve, but so will their historical thinking skills. Studying religious history invites them to inhabit the past as a foreign country, a place that is both familiar and radically different from the present.[3] For students with or without religious affiliations, the strangeness of the religious past, taught well, can foster, as Sam Wineburg says, "those virtues once reserved for theology—humility in the face of our limited ability to know, and awe in the face of the expanse of human history."[4] These characteristics are necessary for democratic society. Yet, religion can be difficult to include within surveys of US history at the high school and college levels. Why is that?

Religion often represents charged subject matter and occupies a complicated place in public schools. It is the sort of thing people say not to talk about at the dinner table or in polite company. People often have strong opinions, and for some people religious belief (or lack of it) is central to their identities. Some educators in public schools may not know how to talk about religion in academic terms that foster a strong citizenry committed to the common good amid a culture that values the separation of church and state.

We want to state up front that helping students explore how religion functioned in US history does not break down the separation of church and state. Controversy over how to teach history in American society has ebbed and flowed, and history teachers and curriculum in public schools are often under scrutiny. Teaching religion academically does not mean proselytizing (which one of this book's chapters addresses). Instead, addressing religion in US history means doing history well. To ignore religion would be akin to ignoring politics in American history—both were influential in shaping American life. Further, to teach fairly what happened in the past and to equip our students to live wisely in a pluralistic, democratic society in the present, we need to help students become conversant with religion in the past. As teachers, we must help students engage in these difficult conversations.

But even if we want to help students understand how religions have shaped US history, we have relatively few resources for the task. Despite the good work done by historians of American religion, after the Civil War, religion appears almost nowhere in the general historiography, emerging mostly in the civil rights movement (focusing on Black southern supporters of the movement) and the rise of the Religious Right.[5] High school and college-level books, too, treat religion episodically at best.

Besides the ahistorical lack of coverage, a second issue remains for those teaching US history survey courses: these courses are packed already, and every passing year brings new content that we feel pressure to "cover." How can one add religion into a course already bursting at the seams with material?

Solutions *Understanding and Teaching Religion in US History* Offers

So, what's a teacher to do? There are only so many books a teacher can read over the summer to catch up on different aspects of US history, and it is impossible to keep up with scholarly developments across the entire span of a nation's history. This book provides a realistic solution for teachers. While we cannot cover all the religious groups and significant religious moments in American history in a short volume, we have gathered excellent scholars who lay out the significant issues in their areas of expertise and provide concrete teaching suggestions you could incorporate tomorrow in your classes. Each chapter concludes with additional resources for understanding and teaching that subject that the author did not mention in the prose or footnotes. There are many excellent materials, including other books in this series like *Understanding and Teaching Native American History*, that can help you learn more about different religious people, periods, and themes. We chose this approach, rather than offering encyclopedic coverage of more topics, because more in-depth but accessible chapters provide ample resources and ideas that teachers can adapt to their individual classrooms. History teachers teach students, first and foremost, and you know best how to use the primary sources, historical context, and teaching ideas we have offered with your particular students.

You should imagine using the chapters in this book to facilitate the kind of discussions teachers love to have about how best to convey content, cultivate skills, and foster historical habits of mind. One of our main goals in this book was to foster a sort of watercooler conversation, in which the pedagogical approaches of the teachers writing was clear. The diversity of voices in this collection is a strength, as some readers will connect more with one approach than another. Each chapter provides an orientation to the key conversations about how religion played an important part in shaping commonly taught periods and themes in US history. But perhaps more importantly, each author also describes how they teach that material, offering sources that have worked in their classrooms, questions they use, and specific activities to try. As master teachers, they address the assumptions and frameworks their students often bring to the classroom, and how they challenge, complicate, and enhance their students' knowledge. The authors have also included sources that are available online and in printed texts, and at the end of each chapter they have provided a short list of recommended readings so that teachers can further explore that particular topic. The chapters within this book can work as quick period and thematic primers, or as a more substantial course guide, offering ideas about how to weave religion into subjects you already teach. Overall, this book will assist teachers in bridging the gap between scholarly expertise and the US survey classroom and will help teachers prepare to teach specialized courses in religious history at the secondary or college level.

Historians craft overarching narratives of US religious history differently. Some, for instance, emphasize religious pluralism throughout US history, while others craft narratives that show the nation's mostly Protestant origins becoming more pluralistic in periods such as the late nineteenth-century immigration, the rise of Americans' perceptions of themselves as a Judeo-Christian (rather than Protestant) nation in the 1930s, and the expansion of Eastern religions in the United States after the 1965 Immigration and Nationality Act. Our approach falls more in the latter category. Because Christianity dominated the American landscape, from the founding of the nation's first colonies to the middle of the twentieth century, a large proportion of the chapters in this volume grapple with the effects that Christianity (and particularly Protestantism) had on the United States. But despite the dominance of variations of Protestantism in the colonial period, and looking ahead to the influx of Roman Catholics in the nineteenth century and the more pluralistic environment of the late twentieth and early twenty-first centuries, this book importantly includes chapters on the Native American religious experience, Islam in America, Judaism, and Asian religious influences in American life. Furthermore, the book's structure also suggests two other keys to our approach. First, considerations of race, class, and gender necessarily shape how we understand religion in American history. Second, while Christianity was a significant religion in the United States, from the beginning it was one of several religions influencing life on the continent, and there was never a guarantee that it would become or remain the dominant religious expression.

The book's first section offers frameworks for teaching religion in US history classrooms. It addresses key general issues in teaching American religious history and focuses on the religious, racial, and gendered diversity of religious experiences, highlighting how these themes can complicate and contextualize subjects in the US history survey. In the first chapter, Thomas S. Kidd lays out his philosophy of how to teach religion in history, recommending a model that does not proselytize but that also does not pretend that the teacher is strictly objective. Next, Kevin M. Schultz presents a solution to the fundamental problem of how to incorporate religion into an already full curriculum by illustrating how diverse religious identities have been persistent parts of American identity. In the third chapter, Karen J. Johnson addresses the inherent difficulty of talking about religion and race in the classroom, a convergence of subjects one cannot avoid when teaching about religion in US history. She provides teachers with ways to think through their students' differing experiences and encourage students to learn — as whole people, with emotions, bodies, and as intellects.

The next six chapters in the frameworks section of the book explore different groups' experiences that should be integrated, rather than side-barred, in US history narratives. Chapters in this section on African Americans, women, Native Americans, Muslims, Judaism, and Asian religions both lay out key overarching themes and dive into specific moments to integrate these groups' narratives into US history. Paul Harvey highlights key moments in African American religious history to show how teaching this history requires modifying the common narrative of American religious history as one of freedom to help students reframe their understanding of the United States. Andrea L. Turpin shows how religious beliefs shaped key moments in women's history to help students grapple with the reality that religious motivations often underlay both conservative and liberal approaches to women's place in American society. Prioritizing Native Americans' voices, Melissa Franklin Harkrider helps teachers challenge prevailing narratives of early American history that distort the realities of Native American religious experience and contribute to the continued marginalization of Native communities in contemporary American society. Jaclyn A. Michael offers three moments in US history—the slave trade, the civil rights movement, and 9/11—that teachers can use to incorporate the experiences of American Muslims into their classrooms, dismantling stereotypes that Muslims do not belong in the United States. Elijah Siegler challenges the common assumption that non-Western religions are not American by exploring the influence of Asian religions (principally Hinduism, Buddhism, and Daoism) in America. Jonathan Krasner explains the fluidity of Judaism in its American context, and how Jewish self-perceptions have changed over time amidst persistent antisemitism.

The book's second section helps teachers incorporate religion into specific periods of US history using sources that give voice to many people—Native American, white, Latinx, African American, Protestant, Catholic, and Jewish. In the lead chapter, Adrian Weimer demonstrates the importance that religion played on the political and devotional cultures of early Puritans. John Howard Smith follows up this chapter by challenging the typical static storyline of the Great Awakening that many historians have written about for decades, instead positing that the series of revivals in America during the eighteenth century were much more radical and ecstatic in nature than previously thought. John Fea then explores whether America was founded as a Christian nation, showing the complexity of answering this question from a historical perspective. Daniel L. Dreisbach continues this discussion of America's religious founding by looking at the constitutional role that religion played in public life during the Early Republic, citing specific state legislation passed, the US Constitution, and public speeches made by the founders as a guide for understanding this period in United States history. John G. Turner offers ways to use Mormons' role in westward expansion to illuminate the political dynamics of US expansion. Mark Noll then brings us to the start of the Civil War and the heated debates among Americans and their use of the Bible to argue for or against the institution of slavery.

Even as religion became more fractured after the Civil War, it continued to play significant roles in the shaping of American life. In her chapter on religion and American imperialism, Kimberly Hill suggests how teachers can use key concepts such as civilization to understand western migration, missions, and Europeans' colonizing efforts. Heath Carter challenges historians' long focus on churches' lethargic response to the late nineteenth century's industrial crises by showing how white and Black working-class believers helped galvanize the labor movement, and how middle-class women, unwilling to wait on the clergy to take the initiative, became activists in slum and tenement districts. Phillip Luke Sinitiere argues that the prosperity gospel, the belief in divinely sanctioned material accumulation and the spiritualizing of material conditions, is the most quintessential of American religions, and he helps teachers complicate this often-simplified faith by connecting it to key moments of change in US history. George Marsden takes up a more well-known aspect of US history, explaining how, in the early twentieth century, just as Protestantism seemed to be successfully holding on to its influences (as in Prohibition and immigration restriction), it suffered its most serious divide—between fundamentalists and modernists.

Alison Collis Greene explores religious leaders' conflicted relationship with the New Deal as Americans found in the state a more reliable set of social supports than they had ever before experienced. Matthew Avery Sutton observes how President Roosevelt drew on the idea of "religious freedom" as a justification for intervention in World War II and how various American groups responded to that idea, and he traces how American policymakers and religious activists used the concept of religious freedom to shape the Cold War, especially in the crusade against "godless communism." J. Russell Hawkins turns to the civil rights movement, highlighting the contingency of the struggle by studying the movement's religious conflicts revealed in the stark disagreement between sincere Christians regarding God's view of racial integration. Darren Dochuk closes the book's chronological portion by using the parallel biographies of Phyllis Schlafly and Beverly LaHaye, two leading female activists in their generation of conservative movement politics, to track forces of religious, cultural, socioeconomic, and political change that explain the rise of the Religious Right.

Ultimately, *Teaching and Understanding Religion in US History* will help teachers guide students through crucial issues relating to religion in the American past using a historical lens. As teachers, we care about our students, our subjects, and the common good. Our hope is that this book will help you, the teacher, meet the goals you already have for your classes, goals fundamental to the discipline of history such as teaching students to consider context, marvel at contingency, track change over time, debate causality, and understand complexity.[6] In line with best practices of teaching history and social studies, each chapter will help you understand the content *and* think about how to use the content to help students adopt these historical habits of mind, habits that not only make them better historians as they think critically about the past, but also help us all create a better future.

NOTES

1. Martin Luther King, "Letter from Birmingham Jail," The King Center, May 1, 1963, https://www.africa.upenn.edu/Articles_Gen/Letter_Birmingham .html. The letter is available widely online.

2. Jane Dailey, "Sex, Segregation, and the Sacred," *Journal of American History* 91, no. 1 (June 2004): 119–44; David L. Chappell, *A Stone of Hope: Prophetic Religion and the Death of Jim Crow* (Chapel Hill: University of North Carolina Press, 2004); Rusty Hawkins, "Religion, Race, and Resistance: White Evangelicals and the Dilemma of Integration in South Carolina, 1950–1975" (PhD diss., Rice University, 2010); Carolyn Renee Dupont, *Mississippi Praying: Southern White Evangelicals and the Civil Rights Movement* (New York: New York University Press, 2013); Charles Marsh, *God's Long Summer: Stories of Faith and Civil Rights* (Princeton, NJ: Princeton University Press, 1997).

3. John H. Arnold, *History: A Very Short Introduction* (Oxford: Oxford University Press, 2000), 6–7.

4. Sam Wineburg, *Historical Thinking and Other Unnatural Acts: Charting the Future of Teaching the Past* (Philadelphia: Temple University Press, 2001), 24.

5. Kevin M. Schultz and Paul Harvey, "Everywhere and Nowhere: Recent Trends in American Religious History and Historiography," *Journal of the American Academy of Religion* 78, no. 1 (March 1, 2010): 129–62, https://doi.org/10.1093/jaarel/lfp087; Jon Butler, "Jack-in-the-Box Faith: The Religion Problem in Modern American History," *The Journal of American History* 90, no. 4 (March 2004): 1357–78.

6. Bruce VanSledright, *The Challenge of Rethinking History Education: On Practices, Theory and Policy* (New York: Routledge, 2011), chap. 3; Thomas Andrews and Flannery Burke, "What Does It Mean to Think Historically?," AHA, *Perspectives on History*, January 1, 2007, https://www.historians.org/publications-and-directories/perspectives-on-history/january-2007/what-does-it-mean-to-think-historically.

PART ONE

Frameworks for Teaching Religion in American History

Teaching American Religious History Academically

THOMAS S. KIDD

Religious topics can raise some of the most unique pedagogical challenges a teacher will ever face. Religion
implicitly (or explicitly) raises questions of belief, or nonbelief, in ways
that are different from teaching about this-worldly issues. I routinely
teach the first half of the American history survey, and issues of religion and faith come up constantly, from the founding of the colonies
in America to sectional conflict over slavery. The topic of faith can also
take unexpected personal turns. For example, once when I was teaching the First Great Awakening in my American history survey course, a
student came to my office and wanted to discuss what it meant to be
"born again," because he was concerned that he was, in fact, not born
again. This is a bit different challenge for a history teacher than explaining the invention of the steamboat or analyzing *Marbury v. Madison*!

In this essay I want to recommend practices for teaching religious
history academically, by which I mean teaching it in a way that is appropriate to the classroom, as opposed to a pulpit on Sunday morning, or
on an atheist blog. Believers, agnostics, and nonbelievers all have their
own challenges in teaching religion academically, but there is also a lot
of overlap in how they all can and should tackle the subject profession-
ally. Among the key issues teachers of religious topics need to consider
are the *setting* in which we teach, *self-awareness* of our own religious commitments, and *empathy* for the religious convictions of people in the past.

In my journey from BA degree to a college teaching position, I covered a pretty wide range of institutions. I went to a public university in
the South (Clemson University) for the BA and MA, a private Catholic

15

university in the Midwest (Notre Dame) for my PhD, and I have spent all my teaching career thus far at a private Baptist university (Baylor) in Texas. (To cap it off, in 2022 I moved to Kansas City to teach full-time at Midwestern Baptist Theological Seminary.) Admittedly, Clemson had a more visible Christian presence (albeit an informal one) than public/ secular schools in other regions of the country presumably have, but still the role of believing professors at a school such as Clemson is different than it is at Notre Dame or Baylor. A professor's stance vis-à-vis spiritual matters would be different yet again at religious schools that are smaller, more overtly pietistic, or more doctrinally uniform than Notre Dame or Baylor. The way you teach religion academically depends to some extent on the setting in which you teach and the students with whom you work.

If you teach at a public or secular private school, there will be no expectation that you are accountable to an institutional religious perspective, save perhaps for a commitment to secularism itself (i.e., a separation of the spheres of religion and "scientific" knowledge). First Amendment requirements mandate that a public university and its employees cannot give preference to one denomination or religion. Does that mean that teachers must set aside their own religious convictions at a public or secular school? Not necessarily. Devout people will of course keep practicing their faith when employed in such settings. Some devout professors certainly self-disclose their convictions at public or secular institutions and are protected in doing so by the principles of academic freedom and free speech. Yet professors who wear their faith on their sleeve in public school settings do so with mixed results. One foreign language professor I had at Clemson gave his "testimony" as a believer on the first day of class. Even to me as a person of Christian faith, it didn't seem to be quite the right time or occasion to do it. But another professor of mine in political science sometimes spoke about his religious and cultural convictions when course topics warranted it, and he was enormously popular as a teacher, even among some nonbelieving students (though I am sure he turned off a few others).

A religious or denominational setting for a school will often necessitate a different approach, especially when religious topics come up naturally as part of a course. Religiously informed teaching generally falls into two categories: *content-driven* and *pietistic*. Pietistic religious teaching is not my focus in this essay, but in some confessional contexts teachers may be welcome to or be expected to pray with their students, talk about their own commitment to God and congregation, or otherwise model a life of devotion. Here we are thinking about teaching religious history academically, however, which lends itself to a *content-driven* focus.[1] In my American history class, I certainly devote entire class periods to subjects that have little or nothing to do with religion. Since I am teaching at a Baptist and (more generally) Christian university, however, and since my own research specialty is religious history, I look for opportunities to infuse the class with religious themes more than history professors would do in some other institutional contexts, especially those teachers who do not have religious history research specializations. Although most college American history survey courses would at least mention the First Great Awakening, I have the students do one of the two main paper assignments on that topic, using a book of documents I edited on the Great Awakening. (The other main paper assignment is currently on the US War with Mexico in the 1840s. This is a topic with religious significance, but not a religious topic per se.)[2]

Similarly, I introduce occasional content related to Baptist history, in recognition of our institutional setting. These topics include Rhode Island founder Roger Williams's (brief) tenure as a Baptist or the founding of Baylor in 1845 at the end of the long Second Great Awakening, the massive, decades-long era of Baptist and other evangelical churches' growth in the early nineteenth century. I observed similar content decisions at Notre Dame. For example, as a teaching assistant there I led discussion sections on the Know-Nothing movement of the 1850s, focusing especially on the Know-Nothings' accusations that Catholics were incompatible with the American democratic project because of their ostensible allegiance to a foreign power (the papacy). Again, the Know-Nothings are a common topic in the American history survey, but the issue of anti-Catholicism has special relevance at Notre Dame.[3]

Public or secular school teachers certainly should feel free to inject religious content, too, although some history teachers especially at the secondary level may be wary about the risk of parents' complaints or (in extreme cases) lawsuits over religious instruction. If public school teachers are careful not to shift into proselytizing, then instruction about religion should not only be legal but also an essential, healthy part of an American history curriculum. Students at public schools or colleges may need more guidance about why religious content is relevant to a history course. A teacher in such a context can likely make fewer assumptions about students' positions relative to religion content (i.e., sympathy vs. hostility, familiarity vs. ignorance). Students at public schools will normally represent a wide range of perspectives and experience with any given religious topic. They could range from traditionalist believers to staunch skeptics, and anything in between. This is also true of students at many religious colleges, but in those settings most students will at least not be surprised to have a history professor give substantial coverage to religion.

A second and related major issue in teaching religion academically is self-awareness about one's own religious commitments (or lack thereof), and what difference those commitments make in one's teaching on religion.[4] Historians who came of age before postmodern thought became widely accepted might once have suggested that one's spiritual beliefs should not make any difference in one's writing or teaching, even on religion. In this older modernist view, one must remain "objective" and set one's personal convictions aside. In some cases, this strain of modernist historiography could lead to some truly implausible claims. I once heard about a believing Baptist scholar who wrote on Baptist history in America, but who insisted that his faith made no difference in his writing. He was just laying out facts, he said. Since we tend to be familiar with postmodern theory and paradigms of knowledge in today's academy, we might shake our heads at this type of perspectival naivete. Yet many teachers in the contemporary academy still give little thought to how their own beliefs about religion might shape the content, or especially the *tone*, of their teaching about spiritual content. Good academic teaching about religion cannot allow fawning admiration for our subjects, but neither can it allow sneering contempt.

Whether the subject is politics, culture, or religion, professional historians today generally doubt that anyone can approach historical topics with pristine "objectivity." Some scholars have suggested that the concept of objectivity itself is fatally flawed, and that it usually masks some kind of agenda for power. Others have argued that objectivity is salvageable, as long as we acknowledge that it does not mean an impartial "neutrality," through which one supposedly approaches history with no preexisting commitments, inclinations, or cultural baggage. Location matters, and perspective matters. If you are a feminist teaching women's or gender history, it makes a difference; if you are a libertarian teaching political history, it makes a difference. Surely, then, if you are a traditional believer or a committed atheist (or something in between), it makes a difference when you teach religious history.[5]

What difference our belief actually makes can vary widely, however. Coming at history with a perspective on religion (which we all do) does not always lead naturally to special pleading for one's "team." The traditional believer, for example, might be bitterly critical of the charlatans and exploiters who have given faith a bad reputation. The atheist might find religious experience intriguing and might admire people of faith who have acted in accord with their convictions. This disposition was part of the genius of the mid-twentieth-century historian Perry Miller, the greatest scholar of the American Puritans. Miller was an atheist, but he wrote with immense sophistication and empathy about the Puritans, a group that most historians before Miller's time had dismissed as unprogressive and depressing.[6]

Arguably the most serious errors in teaching on religion come when a lack of self-awareness leads the teacher wittingly or unwittingly to dismiss, belittle, and condemn people of different convictions from them. Or they might unconsciously shape evidence to suit their own convictions. In such biased cases, the traditional believer can tend to find traditional-believing "good guys" everywhere in the past, whereas the atheist always finds heroic skeptics wearing the "white hat" in their preferred history narrative. Again, pristine objectivity is not a realistic goal. Intellectual virtues such as fairness, honesty, self-awareness, and scholarly detachment are achievable standards, however, and they will mark the best teaching on religion. Self-awareness will help us steer clear of our teaching pitfalls and the temptation to foist simplistic religious stories on our students.

A by-product of healthy self-awareness is empathy for one's historical subjects. Whatever faith convictions we have, all of us will encounter people of faith in the past whom we find wrongheaded and maybe even despicable. We need not hide the evidence from students that could lead them to the same conclusions. However, we want to present past actors in portraits that those figures would recognize themselves. Even if we dislike them, we should present their beliefs in a manner that seems explicable and even plausible, if you assumed what those past actors assumed.

The need for empathy is especially acute when the historic believers in question espouse tenets that may seem irrational or distasteful today. More to the point, if many of your students are likely to regard the beliefs of a group in the past as ridiculous or "stupid," it puts an even greater premium on your ability as the teacher to make those beliefs explicable. For example, many of my students have no patience for the classic Puritan belief in predestination, or the idea that God "elects" believers to salvation and leaves others on their path to hell. Even though many of my students are professing Christians, they often find the doctrine of predestination to be unfair and abhorrent. Thus, I try to explain the concept in as comprehensible way as I can. Some of this comprehensibility begins with making connections to beliefs they *do* affirm. The Puritans, I note, believed that God was incomprehensibly powerful, and that he was sovereign over all of humanity. (So far so good, to my believing students.) So why would that God leave open to chance, or to human decision, an issue of such great import as people's salvation, especially when the Puritans assumed that all people naturally reject God because of original sin? Students probably don't walk away from that class meeting believing in predestination (which is not my goal), but my hope is that they will no longer find it stupid. Helping students understand that smart people in the past have thought differently about God than they do is one of our primary goals in teaching the history of religion.

A few students might come into my class believing in a controversial doctrine such as predestination already. If they do, however, they are in the minority. It is exceedingly important for the teacher to extend empathy on topics where only a minority of students might find the belief plausible. This is the case in my teaching on the origins of Mormonism, or the Church of Jesus Christ of Latter-day Saints. Many of my students are largely unfamiliar with Mormonism, or if they are familiar with it, they have grown up believing it is a "cult" (in the pejorative sense, not the sociological sense). It is also likely that I may have one or two believing Mormon students in my survey course in any given semester, which sets up a teaching scenario in which I need to be especially aware of how students in a minority group, whether a religious, ethnic, or other minority, might feel vulnerable during class discussion. Mormonism is not my faith tradition, and as a matter of theological conviction I do not believe that Joseph Smith's revelations were true. Empathy certainly does not require us to affirm all beliefs as equally valid, or to assert that sincere conviction alone makes your religious belief "true for you." In a history class, especially in public school contexts, the truth or falsity of a particular faith claim is not the primary concern anyway.

In spite of my theological and institutional position, I want to convey to my Baylor students that I take Mormons and Mormon beliefs seriously, in addition to helping them understand the historic context in which it emerged (the Second Great Awakening and the "Burned-Over District" of upstate New York). One of the points that I make to the students, then, is what an impressive and elaborate production that the Book of Mormon is, especially given Joseph Smith's limited education. I note that Mormons would attribute this unusual sophistication of the text to its divine origins. My hope is that any Mormon students would feel that I present Mormon history in a way that conveys respect for their tradition and shows why intellectually serious people might be Mormons. The last thing empathetic teachers would want to do is to confirm students' preexisting biases and to further marginalize students who are in a minority. Teachers at a confessionally Mormon school such as Brigham Young, conversely, would need to be sensitive to the views of students who are not Mormons. Setting makes a huge difference as to which students may be in a minority, and which subjects require the most pedagogical care.

One of the greatest difficulties with regard to empathy in teaching is how to present beliefs that you regard as patently immoral. For example, in my American history course we deal with slaveholders who were professing Christians. One document that I assign raises this problem: the secret diary of Virginia planter William Byrd, from the early 1700s. Byrd considered himself a Christian, and his diary regularly records him reading the Bible (in the original languages) alongside brutal episodes of slave whippings and other lurid punishments. The toxic combination of religion, class, race, and unchecked power in the diary makes Byrd one of the most unappealing characters in our course. Yet there is still a level at which we, as teachers and students of history, are required to enter Byrd's mental world and to understand how his actions made sense to him. This raises questions—hard ones to consider, for some Christian students—about what the Bible actually teaches regarding slavery (it tends to accept its existence, at least in ancient forms). Empathy does not require us, however, to endorse a radical form of relativism that would regard Byrd as having a historically different but morally valid way of life.[7]

Ironically, one of the most pressing dilemmas facing teachers of religious subjects is how to deal with past actors with whom they *sympathize*, meaning that they share many or all of a person's religious convictions. How do you treat someone's beliefs fairly when you think that they are true, and that the person's life is worthy of emulation? Being willing to admit a person's faults and inconsistencies is, of course, an important place to start for the teacher seeking fairness. For example, I have a positive view of the late evangelist Billy Graham, and so would many of my students (though fewer and fewer will have heard of him). Thus, when discussing Graham, it is important for me to concede that (as he admitted) Graham made serious errors of judgment in politics, especially in his close alliance with President Richard Nixon. Popular, pietistic biographies of such figures often downplay or excuse failings in heroes of faith, but hagiography (pietistic biography of saints) is not the proper mode for academic teaching or writing. Messianic or prophetic figures in history, such as Jesus of Nazareth, present special challenges in this vein, because their followers often proclaim that these figures *were* in fact morally perfect. There are thus no faults in them to concede. Occasional sectarian figures in American history could raise such dilemmas for a few teachers or students, but American history teachers can (happily) leave most such problems to those who cover survey courses such as World History to 1500 and topics such as the origins of major world religions.

I once had a conversation with a scholar who works on the history of Reformed and evangelical piety. He wrote with such warmth and understanding about the topic that I supposed he must be out of a similar faith background. To my surprise, when I asked him, he told me that he was an atheist. This, to me, is a great model of historical empathy about religion. As a Christian myself, I saw in his writing such a level of empathy for evangelical spirituality that I assumed incorrectly that he might embrace the same sort of piety. It turned out that he just had a great capacity for empathizing with people of spiritual commitments that he did not share. Such empathetic capacity is a worthy goal for any of us who seek to teach religion in history academically.

ADDITIONAL RESOURCES

Glanzer, Perry L., and Nathan F. Alleman. *The Outrageous Idea of Christian Teaching*. New York: Oxford University Press, 2019.

Haskell, Thomas L. "Objectivity Is Not Neutrality: Rhetoric vs. Practice in Peter Novick's *That Noble Dream.*" *History and Theory* 29, no. 2 (May 1990): 129–57.

Novick, Peter. *That Noble Dream: The "Objectivity Question" and the American Historical Profession*. New York: Cambridge University Press, 1988.

Retz, Tyson. *Empathy and History: Historical Understanding in Re-enactment, Hermeneutics and Education*. New York: Berghahn Books, 2018.

Tinklenberg, Jessica L. ed. *Empathy and the Religious Studies Classroom: Spotlight on Teaching. Religious Studies News*, January, 2020. American Academy of Religion, 2020. https://rsn.aarweb.org/sites/default/files/PDFs/Spotlight%20on%20Teaching/ Empathy_and_the_Religious_Studies_Classroom_Spotlight_on_Teaching_Jan_2020.pdf.

Notes

1. Perry L. Glanzer and Nathan F. Alleman, *The Outrageous Idea of Christian Teaching* (New York: Oxford University Press, 2019), 100.

2. Thomas S. Kidd, *The Great Awakening: A Brief History with Documents* (Boston: Bedford/St. Martin's, 2007).

3. For example, "Basic Principles of the American Party of Virginia" (1856), Digital Public Library of America, https://dp.la/exhibitions/outsiders-president -elections/anti-outsider-platforms/know-nothing-party-1856.

4. For an introduction to a Christian approach to history, see David Bebbington, *Patterns in History: A Christian Perspective on Historical Thought,* 4th ed. (Waco, TX: Baylor University Press, 2018). Views on historical approaches in other monotheistic traditions include Moshe Rosman, *How Jewish Is Jewish History?* (Oxford: Littman Library of Jewish Civilization, 2007); David N. Myers and David B. Ruderman, eds., *The Jewish Past Revisited: Reflections on Modern Jewish Historians* (New Haven, CT: Yale University Press, 1998); and Aziz Al-Azmeh, *The Times of History: Universal Topics in Islamic Historiography* (Budapest: Central European University Press, 2007).

5. Thomas L. Haskell, "Objectivity Is Not Neutrality: Rhetoric vs. Practice in Peter Novick's *That Noble Dream*," *History and Theory*, 29, no. 2 (May 1990): 129–57.

6. See, for example, Perry Miller, *Errand into the Wilderness,* new ed. (Cambridge, MA: Belknap Press, 1956).

7. Louis B. Wright and Marion Tinling, eds., *The Secret Diary of William Byrd of Westover, 1709–1712* (Richmond, VA.: Dietz Press, 1941).

Adding Religion to Themes You Already Teach

Religion as a Component of Diversity in America

Kevin M. Schultz

In 2004, Yale historian Jon Butler wrote a seminal article in the *Journal of American History* describing what he called "the religion problem in Modern American History." The problem, he argued, was that the vast majority of US history courses only bring up religion in a few set pieces, such as the Second Great Awakening, the Scopes "Monkey" Trial, the Black Freedom Struggle, perhaps JFK, and the Religious Right, and then largely skip over it for the rest of the semester. Butler playfully called religion a "Jack-in-the-Box." It pops up to dominate the story for a minute, then goes away. The problem with this, he argued, is that Americans' faith has been consistently present throughout the nation's history, even if the shape and character of that faith has changed constantly. Why does religion seem to disappear from the US history survey?[1]

It turns out there are good reasons for it. For one, because of the history of litigating religious issues in the United States, Americans are fearful of discussing religion in the public square, and the schoolhouse is as public as it gets. For another, there are so many faiths to consider it is hard to think of oneself as an expert in any but a handful. But the most important reason religion drops in and out of the survey like a jack-in-the-box is perhaps the simplest: we teachers have to make choices

24

about what to include and what to leave out. We cannot cover all of any single topic. Unless you are teaching a course on labor history, one cannot simply focus on workers' movements at the expense of everything else. Talking about just politics leaves out far more than it includes. My lectures on the New Deal or World War II could easily be expanded into semester-long courses, but I have to make choices about what to leave out. To slightly alter Butler's question: what does not appear as a jack-in-the-box in our surveys?

But there is a fix. If we look at Butler's point from another angle, we might pause to wonder if religion should be included not just as a series of "set pieces" but instead as a persistent part of Americans' identities. What if we introduce religion in unexpected places in order to demonstrate its continued importance? What if we see religion as just another marker of identity in the pluralistic place we call America? It is no longer acceptable to sequester African American history to just the month of February or just to the units on slavery and civil rights. Why should we marginalize faith to the standard set pieces and then leave it out the rest of the time?

Looking at faith throughout American history is especially important when we consider that one of the most persistent themes of American religious history—the diversity of its people and the variety of faiths they practice—echoes one of the central themes of the rest of American history—American diversity and the subsequent contestations for power and recognition. What if we tied these two strands together? What if we included religion every time we discussed American diversity? If pluralism is one feature of our surveys (and how can it not be?), there is no reason religion cannot function as a constant piece of that puzzle. The effect of thinking of it that way is that religion becomes a steady strum in American history, just as it is in American life in general.

～

There are various ways I emphasize religious diversity as a key theme in my survey class. From the beginning, I employ open-ended questions that (I hope) seem pertinent to students. For instance, early in the unit on American independence I pose the question of how religious the United States was when the country was founded. Pondering this question, we not so much as move past the Boston Tea Party and the Intolerable Acts, but we put a slight religious bend on the analysis and demonstrate the religious pluralism that was at play from the very beginning.

We explore some of the various Native American faiths that occupied the land before the first European settlers arrived. We examine the importance of the First Great Awakening as a possibly unifying event before the chain of events that led to the Revolution even began. But mostly we look at the intense religious diversity that existed throughout the British colonies before the Revolution.

One of my favorite primary sources in revealing this early diversity is a series of maps of colonial New York. The earliest map I employ is of New Amsterdam (New York) harbor in 1664. Etched the year the Dutch sold New York to England, the map shows no steeples nor houses of worship. Surely they were there, but they were not prevalent.[2] The second map is *A View of Fort George with the City of New York from the SW*, from the 1730s. It shows the southern tip of Manhattan, revealing a small scattering of religious buildings.[3] The third image is the most dramatic, showcasing the dramatic growth of religiosity in the colonies. The *Prospect of the City of New York* from 1771 is an encyclopedic look at the religious diversity of New York City just before the Revolution.[4] Showing civic buildings and other prominent landmarks, the map also shows the houses of worship for the Quakers, the Anabaptists, the Moravians, the Lutherans, Methodists, Old Dutch Church, Jews, Catholics, the North Dutch Calvinist Church, the North Dutch Church, and the Presbyterians. They are all there, and more. However else you want to imagine the nation at the time of its political founding, it was not religiously unified.

Recognizing this amazing diversity helps explain the institutions of religious freedom that exist in the United States today. To understand that, I frequently turn to the question of how the original states dealt with pluralism in their founding constitutions, and especially religious pluralism. Virginia had the most magnificent debate, between Patrick Henry, who wanted state-endorsed religion, and James Madison and Thomas Jefferson, who wanted the state to remain out of the business of religious advocacy because they feared Baptists outnumbered Episcopalians. The result was Thomas Jefferson's memorable Virginia Statute for Religious Freedom, an amazing teaching document, which resolved "that no man shall be compelled to frequent or support any religious worship, place, or ministry, whatsoever, nor shall be enforced, restrained, molested, or burthened in his body or goods, nor shall otherwise suffer on account of his religious opinions or belief; but that *all men shall be free to profess, and by argument to maintain, their opinion in matters*

26

of religion, that the same shall in no wise diminish, enlarge, or affect their civil capacities."[5]

As other essays in this volume indicate (most notably those by John Fea and Daniel L. Dreisbach), the Virginia Statute for Religious Freedom is a remarkable tool for teaching, but Virginia did not immediately set the long-term example for other states. Many of the other early state constitutions limited officeholding or voting to "Christians only" or some other designation, but they all gave it up in the early years of the Republic. In any case, each state was so different in what it prohibited or allowed that there was no consensus. Massachusetts had mandatory religious taxes for religious groups, though they could be distributed however a taxpayer wished. Vermont only tolerated Protestants. Pennsylvania mandated that its legislators believe in a God of rewards. South Carolina said, "Christian Protestant religion shall be deemed, and is hereby constituted . . . the established religion of this state." New York forbade Catholics from holding public office for the first twenty-five years of its existence.[6] Fascinatingly, it was the often the long-term failures of these discriminatory constitutions that served as the lodestar for the federal government. Nonetheless, it is important to balance pursuit of religious freedom by many Americans with the equally powerful attempt to maintain a stable faith (whatever it might be) as the moral bedrock of the nation.

It is often said that the state constitutions were testing grounds for what became the US Constitution, and as we have seen, when it came to religion, the lesson was clear: there were just too many faiths to prioritize any one of them. When the Constitutional Convention met in 1787, the conveners more or less left out religion. As Benjamin Franklin said, "The Convention, except for three or four persons, thought Prayers unnecessary." Not wanting to have religious controversy cause potential dissent in the new government, the US Constitution only mentions faith or religion twice, once when it refers to its time as the "Year of our Lord," and the second, in Article VI, where it disallows religious tests as a qualification for serving in any federal office. The First Amendment was added at the insistence of the anti-Federalists, and its language clearly deals with the question of religious pluralism by disallowing the federal government from establishing a single national faith, nor preventing worshipers of any faith from freely exercising the demands of their religion. Even more than the Virginia Statute for Religious Freedom, the First Amendment is something I pore over with students, because it became the foundation for all the legal disputes regarding religious pluralism that were to follow.[7]

The Founders' compromises on faith—to allow free exercise, to keep the federal government from endorsing one religion over any other, the rejection of religious prejudice in office holding—prompted a reaction of sorts, and when I teach the Second Great Awakening I always be sure to introduce students to a powerful concept that then sticks with us through the remainder of the course: the Protestant moral establishment. The concept comes from historian David Sehat's indispensable *The Myth of American Religious Freedom*.[8] Taking the lead from the wild diversity of state constitutions, Sehat argues that despite (or perhaps because of) the inability of Protestants to proclaim their superiority in the United States via political means (because Protestants themselves were so disparate), they turned to social and cultural means. The result was that a baseline Protestant establishment dominated American cultural affairs for a long time, eventually being upheld by the courts as "common law." Sehat's book is filled with numerous examples and stories, but I always start with the one about a man named Ruggles, a New Yorker, who, in 1811, while probably drunk, shouted in a public venue, "Jesus Christ was a bastard and his mother must be a whore." Ruggles was arrested and charged with blasphemy, a charge he claimed lacked merit because New York did not have a blasphemy law and, even more to the point, the state's constitution by then guaranteed general religious freedom.

The court did not care. It found Ruggles guilty, somewhat remarkably citing the common law of the state. Because Protestant Christianity was a part of the Anglo-American way of life, the court held, blasphemy was a punishable crime. To contend otherwise would be "to corrupt the morals of the people, and to destroy good order."[9]

The *Ruggles* case had a domino effect, creating a precedent for other decisions, which, once the US Supreme Court signed on in 1844, codified outside the confines of legislative statute a "moral establishment" of Protestantism that existed throughout the remainder of the nineteenth century and well into the twentieth. From *Ruggles* forward, the United States lived with what Sehat has called a "proxy religious establishment" that ruled from the courts and bled into society at large. As the American jurist James Kent put it, this coercive Protestant moral establishment came into being "not because christianity was established by law, but because christianity was . . . the basis of public morals."[10]

We historians all knew this Protestant construct existed in American life at least throughout the nineteenth and early twentieth centuries, but we did not have a name for it until Sehat provided one. I ask my students why no mail gets delivered on Sundays. Their once vacant faces are now filled with an answer: the Protestant moral establishment dictated it so. Why were individual rights for women so hard to win? The Protestant moral establishment sanctified women's role in the family and largely forbade their entrance into the public sphere. How could Protestant teaching materials be common in American public schools but Catholic ones be disallowed? Catholics promoted the wrong kind of morals. Upholding moral order was even one argument the courts deployed in the *Plessy v. Ferguson* decision. By naming a broad, flexible concept in my "set piece" about the Second Great Awakening, I get to use the concept throughout the remainder of the course. Thus religion does not disappear like a jack-in-the-box; it just gets remade as a form of social control, designed, of course, to control pluralism.

~

The Protestant moral establishment is a key concept especially as we turn to the massive waves of immigrants coming to the United States from 1881 to 1924. The religious diversity brought by these immigrants becomes a third way I infuse religion, like a marinade, in my survey course. We recall the vast diversity of the nation at the country's outset and the way the Founding Fathers dealt with it; we discuss the Protestant response by building the long-standing moral establishment; and then we discuss the wide variety of faiths that made the question of religion even more pressing throughout the twentieth century. The vast majority of migrants who came to the United States at the turn of the twentieth century were Roman Catholics and Jews, and these ethnoreligious groups changed the nature of the United States. For one thing, they came in such number and grew in such stature that they were some of the first to directly challenge the Protestant moral establishment at its weakest spot, which was, ironically enough, its most religious aspects. Beginning in the 1910s and 1920s, Catholic and Jewish challenges to Protestant codes began to poke holes in the concept of the Protestant establishment itself. Sabbath laws and Catholic schools prompted some of the first legal challenges, with advocates of pluralism almost always falling back on the language codified in the First Amendment. The fight was on, and it was eventually largely won by advocates of religious pluralism. Their goal, generally speaking, was to ensure there were no religious restrictions on full access to American life, and that the United States lived up to its ideological definition of itself as a beacon of freedom as enshrined in the Constitution. Their vision was helped by the simultaneous fragmenting of the Protestant moral establishment, as from the 1910s onward evangelicals separated from fundamentalists, and both drifted from liberal Protestants (see George Marsden's chapter in this book). The backlash nature of the Scopes trial makes more sense to students when we understand the modernists as defending the pluralistic nature of the country and William Jennings Bryan and the Fundamentalists as trying to conserve what was numerically slipping away. By World War II, the modernists' vision of an ideological nation that allowed the free practice of wildly different religious faiths became the nation's standard operating procedure.

One story I rely on when teaching the ideological Americanism that emerged in this period is the Four Chaplains. In February 1943, right in the middle of World War II, a German U-boat torpedoed the USS *Dorchester* late at night. It was a troop transport ship, filled with more than nine hundred young men. Upon hearing the explosions and the captain's call to abandon ship, the four chaplains aboard—a Catholic, a Jew, and two Protestants—performed their military duty admirably, distributing life jackets to the dozens of young soldiers who had run to the upper decks without grabbing their own vests. They then encouraged the young soldiers to take the plunge into the icy Atlantic. Quickly, though, all the extra life jackets were gone, and several soldiers remained unprotected. The four chaplains then did something heroic. They looked at one another knowingly, and then each unbuckled his own life vest and handed it to four young soldiers, all without giving a second thought to the faith of the recipient. Survivors of the wreck last saw the four chaplains praying arm in arm as the ship descended to the bottom of the Atlantic. Alexander Goode, the Brooklyn-born rabbi, was reciting the Sh'ma—the affirmation of the unity of God—just as the icy waters engulfed the ship forever. In a nation struggling to identify itself by ideas, not race or religion, the story came to symbolize wartime sacrifice and interfaith tolerance between Protestants, Catholics, and Jews. It also became a perfect symbol of a new kind of America, one defined by democracy, freedom, liberty, and selfless giving to the greater cause. This was the ideological Americanism that propelled the nation through the Second World War and the Cold War, and religious groups, especially Catholics and Jews, were key to crafting it. I often show my students the postage stamp the US Postal Service crafted as a display of the Four Chaplains' heroism.[11]

~

By paying attention to the pluralistic faiths of these early twentieth-century migrants, it becomes easier to explore and understand the journeys of those who came after the Immigration Act of 1965, which opened immigration to the United States again. It was only after 1965, for example, that Hindus, Sikhs, and Muslims came to the United States in significant numbers (see Elijah Seigler's chapter for more on Asian religious influences in America and Jaclyn Hall's chapter for more on Islam in America). Interestingly, those numbers are still incredibly small: Muslims, Sikhs, Hindus, and all the other minority faith members together constitute barely 2 percent of the US population (Jews, meanwhile, also constitute something below 2 percent of the American population, and the total of non-Christian religious peoples is still less than 6 percent all together).[12]

These statistics tie in to a question we explore toward the end of the course. In the final week I ask my students, "Is the United States today more or less religious than it was in the past?" This question forces students to challenge orthodox and often religious assumptions that the United States has fallen from some religious holy land. Declension narratives typically only make sense as political statements or stories about rock 'n' roll bands. In this final section, though, I share with students polling data and historical recapitulations about religious commitments. I give them the latest polling data from both the Pew Research Center and the historical data from the American Religious Identity Survey (ARIS).[13] We go over it (the web pages are amazing teaching tools). Students are surprised to see the fastest growing religious group in the United States by far is not Muslims or Mormons, but "nones"—those Americans who profess no religious faith commitments at all. These people might be spiritual, or they might not be. But they certainly do not claim to belong to any faith group. Students are shocked to see that their generation is the one leading more and more Americans to claim they have no faith commitments. Students recognize that, for the first time in recorded history, fewer than half of Americans are Protestants, and that the percentage of Catholics is at or just below 20 percent of the population for the first time since the late nineteenth century.

Again, students engage in fundamental sourcing questions as we go over the data: What does modern polling data tell us anyway? How reliable is it? But mostly students are fascinated by great varieties of faith in the United States, and by the fact that, by compelling no one to believe in anything, religion in American history has taken a curious course that reflects the compromises imposed by trying to respect diversity. Eventually we ponder the reasons why their generation is leading the charge toward secularity. The answer I hear most often reflects the one put forward by Robert Putnam and David Campbell in their 2011 book, *American Grace: How Religion Divides and Unites Us*: the actions done by the Religious Right in the name of religion have turned the younger generation away from faith. If that is what religion looks like, says this younger generation, then I do not want anything to do with it.[14]

The striking thing, as I am now used to pointing out, is that it is the harsh attempts at imposing one's faith on another that most troubles them about the Religious Right. Perhaps this younger generation is learning the lesson that the Founding Fathers bequeathed to the nation, and that the nation has struggled to live up to ever since: in a nation founded on ideals of democracy, equality, and freedom, where pluralism and diversity are to be respected and recognized, compelling one to act on the beliefs of others is morally wrong, and that any attempts to do so will be fought against mightily.

ADDITIONAL RESOURCES

Frederic, Harold. *The Damnation of Theron Ware, or Illumination*. New York: Duffield & Company, 1915.

Johnson, Paul E., and Sean Wilentz. *The Kingdom of Matthias*. New York: Oxford University Press, 1994.

Moore, R. Laurence. *Religious Outsiders and the Making of Americans*. New York: Oxford University Press, 1986.

Putnam, Robert D., and David E. Campbell. *American Grace: How Religion Divides and Unites Us*. With the assistance of Shaylyn Romney Garrett. New York: Simon & Schuster, 2011.

Schultz, Kevin M. *Tri-Faith America: How Catholics and Jews Held Postwar America to Its Protestant Promise*. New York: Oxford University Press, 2011.

Sehat, David. *The Myth of American Religious Freedom*. New York: Oxford University Press, 2011.

NOTES

1. Jon Butler, "Jack-in-the-Box Faith: The Religion Problem in Modern American History," *Journal of American History* 90, no. 4 (March 2004), 1357–78.

2. Johannes Vingboons, "Nieuw Amsterdam ofte nue Nieuw Iorx opt' teylant Man," 1664, colored print, Geheugen van Nederland (Memory of The Netherlands), Selections from the Map Collections, National Archives, The Hague, The Netherlands, available at Global Gateway, Library of Congress, accessed November 22, 2019, http://international.loc.gov/cgi-bin/query/r?intldl/awkbbib :@field(DOCID+@lit(awkb012367)).

3. Possibly Burgis William (artist) and John Carwitham (engraver), *A View of Fort George with the City of New York from the SW*, ca. 1764, hand-colored engraving, Albany Institute of History & Art, accessed November 1, 2019, https:// www.albanyinstitute.org/collections/collections-database-results/yearrange/ to/perpage/48/keywords/View--of--Fort--George.

4. Hugh Gaine, *Prospect of the City of New York*, 1771, woodcut, copyprint, New York Almanac, the American Antiquarian Society, Worcester, Massachusetts, available at JHCB Archive of Early American Images, John Carter Brown Library, Brown University, accessed November 1, 2019, https://jcb.lunaimaging .com/luna/servlet/detail/JCB~1~1~4151~6510005:Prospect-of-the-City-of-New -York.

5. Thomas Jefferson, "A Bill for establishing Religious Freedom, printed for the consideration of the People," 1779. A nice link to the statute, with a short historical explanation, is from the Virginia Museum of History and Culture, accessed November 3, 2019, https://www.virginiahistory.org/collections-and -resources/virginia-history-explorer/thomas-jefferson. Another useful teaching essay (with a PDF of the document) is found in the Virginia Encyclopedia founded by the Virginia Humanities Center, accessed November 22, 2019, https:// www.encyclopediavirginia.org/virginia_statute_for_establishing_religious_free dom_1786.

6. The best source is John Fea, *Was America Founded as a Christian Nation? A Historical Introduction (Louisville, KY: Westminster/John Know Press, 2011)*.

7. Ibid.

8. David Sehat, *The Myth of American Religious Freedom* (New York: Oxford University Press, 2011).

9. Ibid., 61.

10. Ibid., 64.

11. Bureau of Engraving and Printing, U.S. #956 3c, Four Chaplains stamp, 1948, Rotary Press, Washington, DC. Much of the story comes from my book, Kevin M. Schultz, *Tri-Faith America: How Catholics and Jews Held Postwar America to Its Protestant Promise* (New York: Oxford University Press, 2011), 3–7. The US postage stamp can be found several places, including: https://postalmuseum.si

.edu/exhibition/about-us-stamps-modern-period-1940-present-commemora tive-issues-1940-1949-1948-1949-3, accessed October 27, 2023.

12. "The American Religious Landscape in 2020," *PRRI* (July 8, 2021). https:// www.prri.org/research/2020-census-of-american-religion/, accessed October 27, 2023.

13. See especially the Pew Religious Landscape Study, accessed November 5, 2019, https://www.pewforum.org/religious-landscape-study/; ARIS (American Religious Identification Survey), accessed November 5, 2019, https://commons .trincoll.edu/aris/about-aris/.

14. Robert D. Putnam and David E. Campbell, *American Grace: How Religion Divides and Unites Us,* with the assistance of Shaylyn Romney Garrett (New York: Simon & Schuster, 2011).

Talking about Religion and Race in the Classroom

KAREN J. JOHNSON

While the professional scholarship on the intersection of religion and race in US history is flourishing, the subject does not often appear in secondary and college classrooms in sustained and rigorous ways. The many essays addressing this intersection are a magnificent resource. Like religion and gender, religion and sexuality, or religion and class, the combination of religion and race can make for difficult conversations because of the lack of consensus on *how* to talk about race, especially within polarized contexts. Wading into these troubled waters can help students develop historical thinking skills, begin to understand the history behind our contemporary racial dynamics, look for the common good, and cultivate the habit of listening well to others, thus fostering a stronger civic fabric. Here I suggest general principles for fostering good historical inquiry into these subjects. Since I am a white woman, and since society would see most of my students as white, I recognize that most of my racialized white students' sheltering from conversations about race does not match the experiences of teachers and students of color. The ideas I discuss should be matched, amended, and added to depending on teachers' and students' perspectives.

First, we must develop working definitions of our terms, which is rather difficult given their fluidity and the lack of consensus in the academy and popularly. I understand religion to be how people, institutions, and cultures orient themselves to the divine, to one another, and to the world. Religion as a category is expansive, but it cannot be understood in American history without considering race, and vice versa. Because they shape one another, religion and race are "co-constituted categories." As other essays in this volume demonstrate, the meanings of religion and race have changed over time. Neither are stable or monolithic, and they operate in personal and systemic ways.

Sociologists use specific definitions for words such as "racism," "prejudice," and "discrimination." Sociologists argue that any individual person can (and we all do) harbor prejudice toward other people. We make decisions about others based on assumptions. Generally, sociologists argue that racism is not the same as prejudice. Racism is a specific form of oppression that requires one group to hold power over another group, limiting the other group's access to resources. In this academic framework, racism is not what many people commonly think it is: an individual's view of another person. Racism is, rather, a group form of oppression.

But in practice, sociologists do not all mean the same thing when they talk about "racism." There are at least three different definitional emphases in the sociological literature.[1] Some conflate racism and prejudice, understanding racism to be an attitude, the conscious evaluations or unconscious dispositions one group of people holds toward another. Others emphasize racism as a cultural phenomenon in which racial meanings are extended to relationships that were not previously understood as racial. For instance, people of Asian descent may understand the persistence of racial inequality through a set of frameworks (i.e., Black people do not work as hard as Asians, so Asians do better economically) that they then substantiate with stories. Still other sociologists think about racism as structural, arguing, for instance, that the housing market, health services, and criminal justice system are racist because of the extent of racial inequality in those fields. These sociologists emphasize how these inequalities developed in the past or consider how they are being maintained and reproduced currently. As with the cultural category, structural racism can exist without people intentionally being racist, because the systems we have inherited perpetuate inequality.

I find that many students have a hard time moving beyond the individualistic definition of racism with which they have come to class. Racism historically was not just a problem of people, however, but of systems, and helping students see the systemic aspects of racism is crucial to understanding religion's and race's intersections.[2] White students, especially, can feel like the teacher or other students are attacking them by talking about racism, which can shut down learning. I find that students' presentist use of "racism"—mapping their assumptions about how racism works in the present onto the past—can inhibit my teaching goals of helping them consider how race and religion functioned on personal and systemic levels. While students of color may see the systemic aspects of racism more clearly, they too can fall into presentist uses of "racism" and "racist" and can fail to see the strangeness of the past. For instance, when thinking about the changing meanings of race, servitude, and slavery in the colonies, students must understand that, initially, the category of religion mattered more to determine if a person could be enslaved than their race.[3]

While it could work to lead with definitions, I do not. Instead, I have students study the sources, asking how race and racial assumptions functioned in different settings. This helps students see race's malleable nature and how racialized structures and cultures changed over time. It also helps students practice charity toward their historical subjects and reduces anxiety among those who feel like they need to prove they are not racist. In short, I try to help students avoid presentism, setting aside our current assumptions to understand those in the past. Then students can discuss change over time considering, for instance, how the essentialist attitudes of the nineteenth-century phrenologists who studied the shapes of human skulls to determine the inherent traits of the different races were similar to and different from white ethnic Catholics resisting housing integration in the early to mid-twentieth century.[4]

The nineteenth-century scientists (and I emphasize that contemporaries considered this real science) conducted their studies in a slave society that had come to depend on assumptions about white people's inherent superiority, assumptions that were being challenged by Christian abolitionists. Even most abolitionists, however, assumed it was Americans' manifest destiny to populate the entire continent, partly because they believed they were inherently superior to Indians. In this context, scientific advancements supported white people's dominance. By the late nineteenth century, the science of racial hierarchies was common knowledge and on display on the midway outside the 1893 World's Fair, where white visitors could see various stages of "savagery" and "civilization." As one white observer noted, "viewing man in his primitive state, black, half-clad, it occurs to me why you are the only race not on exhibition. The exhibit is for you, and you are the crowning glory of it all."[5] These racial frameworks were the context for President McKinley's conviction that after praying to "Almighty God for light and guidance," he concluded that the United States must annex the Philippines "to educate the Filipinos, and uplift and civilize and Christianize them, and by God's grace do the very best we could by them, as our fellow-men for whom Christ also died" (see Kimberly Hill's chapter for more context).[6]

In the twentieth century, while cultural racism was at play, structural racism played a significant role in shaping white ethnics' responses to potential Black neighbors. When Martin Luther King Jr. joined open housing marches in Chicago, he stated that he had never seen racism this virulent in the South. The white Catholics who cursed him may have held individually prejudiced attitudes, but they were also caught in a web not of their making. Their faith revolved around geographical parishes, and they had invested their savings into the bricks and mortar of their homes. Because of redlining and other housing discrimination, integrated neighborhoods were a near impossibility. To these white Catholics, Black neighbors meant they would have no choice but to move and break up their parish (for more on religion in the civil rights movement see J. Russell Hawkins's chapter).[7] These two examples illustrate the complexity of the interactions between race and religion, available when we help our students explore past actors and their contexts, rather than starting with the label "racist."

I tell my students up front that we are going to be very careful in our use of the words "racism" and "racist," and that we will focus more on how race functioned. This prompts healthy discussion, raising issues of the ethics and importance of labels. I find these limits helpful, however, for a second reason in addition to the problem of presentism. If we use "racism" and "racist" without care, too easily our discussions of race can devolve into judgment of "racist" historical actors, flattening them into caricatures and thus avoiding complexity and context, which are key to historical thinking. For instance, if we start by labeling the Ku Klux Klan as racist, we neither recognize them as fellow members of the human race because we have othered them, nor do we practice historical empathy. If we contextualize them, however, we discover that they were not a fringe group in America (and so not dismissible as "irrational" or "senseless") and that their moderate Protestant faith was central to their beliefs.[8] In part because of the fundamentalist/modernist divide (see George Marsden's chapter), they resisted social justice efforts as a modernist social gospel and instead understood their acts of racial terror to be sacrifices, akin to Jesus's suffering on the cross, to defend the poor and the helpless. Understanding these ideas prevents us from dismissing the KKK as irrational, as many of my students want to do initially, and instead provokes wonder at the strangeness of the past, reveals the sometimes deadly intersections of religion and race, and can lead to pondering how our own contexts can blind us to evil.

Who Is in the Classroom? Knowing Your Students

Teachers do not just teach a subject. We also teach our subject's habits of mind, and (ideally) we teach specific students. As teachers, we need to think about our students' blind spots and understand their context and views on religion and race.

Few students will come to a class able to account for religion's or race's change over time; they will likely see both as timeless. Many students may find contextualizing religious belief threatening at a deep level because, for instance, the process can make their faith seem less divine or true. I emphasize that historical actors' actions and beliefs, especially if they are different from what students know as normal, do not disparage a faith or its practitioners. People in the past lived in contexts and, like us, could not see some things clearly. Other students may have familiarity with massive changes in their own lives or people they know, such as friends or family choosing one religion over another or rejecting religion all together. It may be helpful, too, to remind students (many of whom will be committed in theory to equality) that people in the past have used religion to both promote racial hierarchies and to tear them down.

Students from different racial and ethnic backgrounds will have different approaches to race in the present and past. Some students of color may have experienced personal racism and may have parents or family members who have prepared them well for the intricacies of race, but others may not have the tools to see the complexity of systems of racial oppression. Some white students, too, may lack the tools to see the complexity of racialization inherent in society. Many students may not want to talk about race in the present or the past. Students of color may feel fatigued, especially if they operate in a mostly white setting or because they want to be known as individuals, not as representatives of a racial group. Many may think that racial issues will go away if we just stop talking about and naming race.

Lumping "students of color" (or white students) into one category masks their diverse experiences of contemporary racial dynamics. For instance, because of the hierarchies of race in America, students of Asian descent, whom whites often deem a model minority that other races should emulate, will experience race differently than African Americans. Even "Asian" as a category is incomplete. "Asian," like "Italian" was at the turn of the twentieth century, is a made-up category that matters in the United States. As people became "Italian" rather than Sicilian when they moved to the United States, an "Asian" student today may identify more with her Korean (or Chinese or Filipino) background or just consider herself "American" despite questions she fields about where she is *really* from. While we attend to the diversity, broad categories can be helpful. Many students of color may find that studying race in the past, which dismantles mostly positive narratives about American history, makes historical study more engaging because it aligns more with their experiences (see Paul Harvey's chapter for further discussion on how studying Black religious history complicates freedom narratives of US history).[9] And students from mixed racial backgrounds—an increasing number of young women and men—beautifully complicate these already complex dynamics.

Highlighting race and religion's contribution to racialization may seem strange to many white students. This position may be magnified if, like most white people in America, they live in segregated places where race *appears* not to be an issue, despite the reality that all-white settings are, in fact, racialized. Research shows that many white people think a "colorblind" approach to race is best. They do not want to see a person's color, but rather judge others as individuals with specific merits. They will likely see racism as an individual bad act and be blind to how racialized systems have limited people of color's access to resources historically (not just during slavery) and in current contexts. They will likely give more weight to a person's intent, rather than the results of the person's actions. Teachers, and especially white teachers who constitute most secondary and postsecondary educators, need to be clear with themselves about their assumptions about race and religion too, and work to account for them in the classroom.[10]

Most students will have simple content frameworks. Many will assume that race mattered in American history during slavery and the civil rights movement. White students, especially, may assume that race in America is a Black/white binary, given the prevalence of this framework and the significance of the history. Depending on their relationship to faith communities, they may think of religion as something that operates only for good (especially if it is the one they practice), or only for bad. This history, then, has the potential to help students see complexity, as they engage the past with humility.

Students' racial identities, religious positions, and content assumptions intersect with their epistemological positions on what history is. Some may be naive realists, thinking that the textbook's narrative is true. Many will likely be naive relativists, thinking that history is based on opinions, and will be unable to deal with conflicting accounts of the past because they think that everyone is entitled to their opinions. I joke that they may be entitled to their opinions, but not to their facts. Yet even if we are using the same facts, students need to learn how to deal with conflicting arguments. They need to become critical pragmatists, able to sift through and contextualize evidence, capable of weighing the strengths of competing accounts because they know that historical evidence and accounts will differ.[11] Helping students become critical pragmatists can move them toward a strong civic life because they develop the habit of trying to understand why other people believe what they do, rather than dismissing others with whom they disagree.

Ground Rules for Talking about the History of Religion and Race

The classroom is a place where students can practice seeking the common good with respect for other people. Studying religion and race requires engaging topics many people would prefer to avoid, despite their salience in the present and the past. Even though we are studying the past, students and teachers alike are bound to offend one another. Making our classrooms safe, then, is crucial. By safe, I do not mean comfortable, or a place where no one will feel affronted, or where we will not explore difficult issues. School should be a place to engage tough questions, where teachers who care about their students as whole people foster creative tension. History as a discipline requires tension; we straddle between the present and the past, we sit with the past's strangeness and familiarity.[12]

By safe I mean that the classroom must be a place where people listen with empathy, forgive one another, give one another the benefit of the doubt, seek to understand others' interpretations, and, at times, agree to disagree as they approach the wicked problems of religion and race in history. In the classroom, students should be willing to learn and grow. Historical study of religion and race requires that we set aside fears of being politically correct and, instead, ask questions and engage the issues respectfully. There may be moments when students want to withdraw, upset by the teacher's or a classmate's position. In those moments, if the students are able, they must choose to engage. How can teachers foster this sort of environment?

One of my goals with my students is to create a culture of "we" instead of "us versus them." I emphasize that we need each other to do history well; we will bring different questions to the table and see different things in the sources based on our contemporary positions in society. Students in my classes do not always know one another, so I invest time early on doing getting-to-know-you exercises so they can build trust and see each other as individual people, not as representatives of some particular group. The internet is full of icebreaker ideas; I suggest you adopt ones that fit your teaching style and course design.[13]

I also ask that students not leave the class and talk with a peer (particularly from the same racial, religious, or political background) about what another classmate said. Instead, they must be willing to work through arguments with a classmate with whom they disagree. If someone says that another student has offended them, the one committing the offense should not immediately defend their position but ask for clarification. The one offended should also clarify the other's arguments. At times, I need to step in and help facilitate this process. This "we" can also be fostered by deliberative discussion, instead of debate. When students debate, they can too easily assume that there is a right and a wrong perspective. Debate's sometimes pugnacious structure can inhibit students from really benefiting from others' arguments. Deliberative discussion, by contrast, is akin to barn raising, with people working together to build something—in this case weighing arguments and counterarguments carefully together.[14]

I find it helpful to state that these subjects are charged and that everyone will feel uncomfortable or offended at some point. If you, the teacher, are uncomfortable talking about race or religion, you may want to name your discomfort. This move requires a posture of humility and a willingness to continue to learn; I state up front that I am still learning academically and practically about the subject matter. You may also help students feel more comfortable with their discomfort. You all are wading into difficult territory, but territory that matters tremendously in US history, and to not account for these issues is to not do that history well. These subjects also relate profoundly to what it means to be human. While it may be difficult, the payoff in terms of helping your students grow individually and corporately can be great.

To foster this growth, create space in your classroom for multiple perspectives. Whether or not you name your perspectives, teach in a way that creates space for multiple perspectives. Teachers have incredible power to silence some voices and promote others, and if you are not careful, you can create a culture of students wanting to please you by agreeing with you. I counter this, for instance, by using secondary sources that offer different interpretations for students to consider. Doing so can model respectful disagreement. Do not lead students toward what you think is the right conclusion but help them make evidence-based arguments. Even small word choices can be meaningful. Should, for example, people owned legally in the past be referred to as "slaves," or as "people owned by other people," or in another way? Part of the discipline of history's great power is that it teaches us to listen well to others. Neither we nor our students must adopt the positions of those in the past, but we do need to be willing to understand them and possibly be changed by them, as we would in an authentic encounter with another person in the present.

Because of the power of race and religion in the present, do not assume that your students should or will offer diverse perspectives. As a way to help those who may feel marginalized (whether it's a Black student in a mostly white class, a conservative student in a mostly liberal class, or a nonbelieving student in a mostly religious class), the teacher should offer different perspectives, presenting them empathetically. Do not ask a student to speak for all the people of his or her race, political party, religion, and so forth (as in, "Michael, what's the Black perspective on this issue?" or "Sophie, what do Catholics think about this?").

I also remind students of perspectives they might want to dismiss. If talking about the civil rights movement to conservative students, you might help them ponder the Black Power critique of the government's support for civil rights as coopting the movement, removing the potential for real revolution.[15] If talking about the rise of the Religious Right to mostly Democratic students, you might remind them how America's rising multiculturalism could also be read as a withdrawal from "traditional" moral values in light of, say *Engle v. Vitale* (1962), which forbade school-sponsored prayer in public schools (see Darren Dochuk's chapter for more on the subject). As I introduce multiple perspectives, I try to be explicit about how I am practicing empathy, because I want my students to adopt this habit of mind.

Be aware, too, of how your students use the language of inclusion and exclusion regarding the past, as well as agency. White students, especially, can unintentionally assume that whiteness is normative, saying, for instance, that "Americans" gave "African Americans" full citizenship during Reconstruction or with the Civil Rights Act of 1964 and the Voting Rights Act of 1965. As a white person, I ask, were "we" giving power to Black people during Reconstruction, letting them become American? Or were they already American? Historical study offers great resources to contextualize the contested religious and racialized meanings of "American."

Exploring the history of religion and race and fostering a safe space means not only offering grace between the historians in the room, but also offering grace to the dead. We, the living, face a great temptation to use our knowledge as power (and, indeed, many would argue that we cannot escape from knowledge as power). But to further historical inquiry and to foster charity in the present, we must use our knowledge to practice charity toward others. Students must learn to treat the dead with a "pastoral imagination," understanding them in their context.[16] Seeing the past as strange, as different, is the bread and butter of historical thinking. As the research demonstrates, however, it is one of the hardest cognitive moves for students to make.[17] It requires suspending judgment and not holding the dead and their contexts to our contemporary standards. It requires seeing people as complex, just as we are complex, and not dismissing them as evil by twenty-first-century standards. To be fair historically, we must help our students do the hard work of understanding the past before we evaluate the dead's actions from a moral perspective.

Teaching All Our Students

We teachers see our students as people, not just as minds on a stick. At all levels of education, teaching students to think historically, which means attending to change over time, complexity, contingency, context, and causality, is a crucial aspect of caring for our students as people.[18] Thinking historically also means asking good questions, making connections, and humbly recognizing the limits to our knowledge.[19] When students develop these habits toward the dead, they can extend them to the living, to the parent whose standards they dislike, to the political party whose reasoning disgusts them, and to themselves when they try to understand why they act in certain ways.

But we cannot understand the knotty problems of religion and race in US history on an intellectual level alone. We do our students a disservice if we try to keep our study of the past solely on an intellectual plane. After all, we are discussing humans, people who had profound worth and who, like us, did not only think but loved, laughed, and cried. As Parker Palmer argues in his classic *The Courage to Teach*, good teaching requires teachers to bring all of ourselves, not just our minds, to the table.[20] While *we* can choose to build the emotionally difficult material into our lesson plans, our students have less choice about encountering it. Therefore, it is essential to provide not only the historical thinking skills but also other resources to help them engage the often painful past as whole people.

I find it helpful to grieve the suffering and the oppression in America's past. This process should happen *after* doing the work of history. The spiritual discipline of lament, so prominent in the Hebrew scriptures in books such as Lamentations (*Eicha* in Hebrew), can be a helpful model to adapt for the classroom. Lament requires identifying suffering and oppression and grieving over it. Because lament names oppression as wrong, it is a political act. Through lament, we can express "crippling pain in the face of an almost unspeakable reality," while asking (although not answering) "how can this be?"[21] People approach lament from various positions. The prophet Jeremiah, who wrote the book of Lamentations, had been faithful while his people had not. Following him, those who lament identify with both those who are unjustly hurt *and* those who have done great evil.[22] So in the classroom, we name evil as we grieve the profound losses that the late nineteenth-century white missionary schools inflicted on Native Americans through their cultural genocide (for more complexity see Melissa Harkrider's chapter). Characterized by humility, we do not condone the missionaries' actions, but we realize that were we missionaries who merged Americanization and Christianity, we too would have assumed it righteous to "kill the Indian and save the man."

While laments are common in many religious traditions, teachers can adapt this impulse in public school and secular classrooms. Students could write poetry or draw pictures conveying lament, or sit quietly and reflect. I find that lament helps students move between the past and the present with humility, provides an outlet for anger, and, for white students especially, prevents white guilt from paralyzing them. The point is to provide space for students to acknowledge emotions that arise as they encounter the past, particularly for those whose ancestors (they could be defined religiously, racially, politically, etc.) were either the recipients of injustice or acted in a way that they in the present see as wrong. Lament is fundamentally paradoxical; it grieves death but still hopes. The Hebrew prophets who lamented hoped in God, and though they were surrounded by death, they—and we—still had the breath of life and so could act. Our breath, too, requires some response to what we have learned. Most crucially, we must not see lament as catharsis because this prophetic tradition does not absolve its practitioners from shaping the present. Lament begins in mourning and, at the same time, moves toward a requirement of some form of action, justice, and restoration.

Celebration can also be helpful in the classroom, as the history of religion and race has moments, people, and events whose virtues are heroic and inspiring—even timeless. Leading students to fix their minds on those subjects can bring life to the classroom. As with lament, celebration should come only after doing history, offering our students flawed people and moments to emulate in the present.

Lament and celebration can lead to moral reflection, inspiring us to consider what we can learn *from*, not just *about*, the past. The National Council for Social Studies standards, applicable to the secondary classroom, support moral reflection, given the standards' emphases on teachers leading their students in ethical reasoning and informed action.[23] Many historians, on the other hand, would eschew moral reflection, arguing that it can muddy our ability to interpret the past as objectively as possible. My response is that moral reflection is appropriate only after one understands what happened. It should never be full of mere condemnation (as in, look at how awful those white southern segregationists were) but should drive its practitioners to humbly look inward to their own failings and see more clearly how the pain of the past continues to be reflected—powerfully—in our present society. Moral reflection, moreover, can help students avoid educated despair, or becoming overwhelmed by society's problems and unable to see any solutions.[24]

Moral reflection—coupled with history's emphasis on how people and structures change over time, and how that change is often contingent on people choosing to act—can help our students from across the political spectrum shape our world in kind, creative ways. As I tell my students, stories about "our" past are stories about who "we" are.[25] And together, not with self-righteousness, but with the humility that historical thinking requires, we can work toward the common good.

ADDITIONAL RESOURCES

Harvey, Paul. *Bounds of Their Habitation: Race and Religion in American History.* Lanham, MD: Rowman & Littlefield, 2016.

Hawkins, J. Russell, and Phillip Luke Sinitiere, eds. *Christians and the Color Line: Race and Religion after Divided by Faith.* New York: Oxford University Press, 2013.

Jennings, Willie James. *The Christian Imagination: Theology and the Origins of Race.* New Haven, CT: Yale University Press, 2010.

Noll, Mark A. *God and Race in American Politics.* Princeton, NJ: Princeton University Press, 2009.

Tisby, Jemar. *The Color of Compromise: The Truth about the American Church's Complicity in Racism.* Grand Rapids, MI: Zondervan, 2019.

NOTES

1. Jiannbin Shiao and Ashley Woody, "The Meaning of 'Racism,'" *Sociological Perspectives* 64, no. 4 (2021): 495–517.

2. Seeing racism as systemic and enacting solutions at the policy level is a key argument in much contemporary antiracist literature such as Ibram X. Kendi, *How to Be an Antiracist* (New York: One World, 2019).

3. See, for instance, John Wood Sweet, *Bodies Politic: Negotiating Race in the American North, 1730–1830* (Baltimore: Johns Hopkins University Press, 2003).

4. For white ethnic Catholics, see John T. McGreevy, *Parish Boundaries: The Catholic Encounter with Race in the Twentieth-Century Urban North* (Chicago: University of Chicago Press, 1996); Karen J. Johnson, *One in Christ: Chicago Catholics and the Quest for Interracial Justice* (New York: Oxford University Press, 2018); Timothy Neary, *Crossing Parish Boundaries: Race, Sports, and Catholic Youth in Chicago, 1914–1954* (Chicago: University of Chicago Press, 2016). For race in the nineteenth century, see James Poskett, "Phrenology, Correspondence, and the Global Politics of Reform, 1815–1848," *Historical Journal* 60, no. 2 (June 2017): 409–42; Bruce R. Dain, *A Hideous Monster of the Mind: American Race Theory in the Early Republic* (Cambridge, MA: Harvard University Press, 2002).

5. Quoted in *Savage Acts: Wars, Fairs, and Empire, 1898–1904* (American Social History Project, 2006). The film *Savage Acts* is teachable with care and is available at ASHP, https://ashp.cuny.edu/savage-acts-wars-fairs-and-empire-1898 -1904.

6. General James Rusling, "Interview with President William McKinley," *The Christian Advocate*, January 22, 1903, http://historymatters.gmu.edu/d/5575/.

7. McGreevy, *Parish Boundaries*.

8. Kelly Baker, *Gospel According to the Klan: The KKK's Appeal to Protestant America, 1915–1930* (Lawrence: University Press of Kansas, 2011).

9. Bruce VanSledright, *The Challenge of Rethinking History Education: On Practices, Theory and Policy* (New York: Routledge, 2011), chap. 2.

10. A classic starting point is Peggy McIntosh, "White Privilege: Unpacking the Invisible Knapsack" (1989), in *On Privilege, Fraudulence, and Teaching As Learning: Selected Essays, 1981–2019*, 29–34 (New York: Routledge, 2019). See also Robin DiAngelo, *What Does It Mean to Be White? Developing White Racial Literacy* (New York: Peter Lang, 2017).

11. VanSledright, *The Challenge of Rethinking History Education*, chap. 4.

12. Sam Wineburg, *Historical Thinking and Other Unnatural Acts: Charting the Future of Teaching the Past* (Philadelphia: Temple University Press, 2001), chap. 1.

13. I usually have students talk, answering questions ranging from Would you rather eat a stick of butter or a gallon of ice cream? to What is the best piece of advice you have received? Spending time on social and emotional growth pays huge dividends for classroom inquiry and growth.

14. Don McCormick and Michael Kahn, "Barn Raising: Collaborative Group Process in Seminars," *Exchange: The Organizational Behavior Teaching Journal* 7, no. 4 (1982): 16–20.

15. A useful resource for teaching the civil rights movement is Steven F. Lawson, Charles Payne, and James T. Patterson, *Debating the Civil Rights Movement, 1945–1968*, 2nd ed. (Lanham, MD: Rowman and Littlefield, 2006).

16. Beth Barton Schweiger, "Seeing Things: Knowledge and Love in History," in *Confessing History: Explorations in Christian Faith and the Historian's Vocation*, ed. John Fea (Notre Dame, IN: University of Notre Dame Press, 2012), 60–82.

17. Wineburg, *Historical Thinking and Other Unnatural Acts*; Sam Wineburg,, *Why Learn History (When It's Already on Your Phone)* (Chicago: University of Chicago Press, 2018); Bruce A. Lesh, *Why Won't You Just Tell Us the Answer? Teaching Historical Thinking in Grades 7–12* (Portland, ME: Stenhouse, 2011).

18. Thomas Andrews and Flannery Burke, "What Does It Mean to Think Historically?," AHA, *Perspectives on History*, January 1, 2007, https://www.historians.org/publications-and-directories/perspectives-on-history/january-2007/what-does-it-mean-to-think-historically.

19. Lendol Calder, "Uncoverage: Toward a Signature Pedagogy for the History Survey," *Journal of American History*, March 2006.

20. Parker Palmer, *The Courage to Teach: Exploring the Inner Landscape of a Teacher's Life* (San Francisco: John Wiley & Sons, 2007).

21. Leora Batnitzky, Preface to *Lament in Jewish Thought: Philosophical, Theological, and Literary Perspectives*, ed. Ilit Ferber and Paula Schwebel, (Berlin: De Gruyter, 2014), xiii.

22. Soong-Chan Rah, *Prophetic Lament: A Call for Justice in Troubled Times* (Downers Grove, IL: InterVarsity Press, 2015).

23. "The College, Career, and Civic Life (C3) Framework for Social Studies State Standards: Guidance for Enhancing the Rigor of K-12 Civics, Economics, Geography, and History" (Silver Spring, MD: National Council for the Social Studies, 2013), https://www.socialstudies.org/sites/default/files/c3/c3-framework -for-social-studies-rev0617.pdf.

24. Nel Noddings and Laurie Brooks, *Teaching Controversial Issues* (New York: Teachers College Press, 2017).

25. Lendol Calder, "The Stories We Tell," *OAH Magazine of History* 27, no. 3 (2013): 5–8.

African American Religious Experiences and Narratives of American History

PAUL HARVEY

American religious history and American history are often told as stories of freedom. Historians have emphasized, for example, the democratization of Christianity in the nineteenth century and the pluralization of religions more recently. Looking at African American religious history compels us to change that narrative. For example, the "democratization of American Christianity" was part of the same process by which slavery exploded through the Deep South. Likewise, African Americans after the Civil War had to forge religious institutions within the hostile environment of a white South determined to maintain white supremacist control of the region. In the twentieth century, the growth of groups such as the Moorish Science Temple and the Nation of Islam compelled attention to the very terms on which the state defined "race" and "religion." What did it mean, when asked by census takers to fill in their race, that some African Americans in northern cities refused to check "white" or "Negro," but instead wrote in "Moorish." More recently, the rise of a resurgent white supremacist movement compels a reexamination of the narrative of progress that frames the major stories of American religion.

This essay will focus on suggesting more complex narratives for teaching that African Americans' historical experiences compel teachers to employ. Students will benefit by paying attention to Black religious experiences precisely because this history complicates the narrative of freedom. Two themes in African American religious history that many teachers may employ to complicate students' narratives are, first, that of the Black church's centuries-long quest for justice and, second, stories of how religion, especially Christianity, has both created and dismantled race and racial hierarchies.

Understanding African American Religious History

"Among our people generally the church is the Alpha and Omega of all things," the Black intellectual, abolitionist, and nationalist Martin Delany wrote in 1849. "It is their only source of information—their only acknowledged public body—their state legislature—their only acknowledged advisor." As a founder (along with Frederick Douglass) of the seminal antebellum Black newspaper the *North Star* (1847–51) and later a proponent of emigration to Africa, Delany was a keen observer of the role of the Black church in providing a public forum for a people generally enslaved, ignored, or scorned by white Americans. If hyperbolic, his description of the role of the church is a common one in many assessments of African American religious life. "The Negro church of to-day is the social centre of Negro life in the United States, and the most characteristic expression of African character," the great black intellectual W. E. B. Du Bois wrote in his 1903 classic *Souls of Black Folk*.[1]

Were Delany and Du Bois alive today, they would be shocked to read a blog post from a prominent scholar in the field asserting, "The Black Church, as we've known it or imagined it, is dead." African Americans still go to church in large numbers, he admitted, and identified with religious institutions in higher proportions than virtually any other group in American society. Nonetheless, as this scholar concluded, "the idea of this venerable institution as central to black life and as a repository for the social and moral conscience of the nation has all but disappeared."[2] Through all periods of American history, Black churches were expected to answer to all social needs—to be the "Alpha and the Omega of all things"—ignoring the socially repressive conditions in which African Americans have lived their lives and practiced their faiths. "The burden of black religion" is that it has been weighed down with too heavy a load.[3]

That burden became evident during the 2008 election. "God bless America? No! God damn America," the Rev. Jeremiah Wright, former pastor to Barack Obama during his years in Chicago, thundered from the pulpit, shocking whites who watched the same clip endlessly replayed on cable television and the internet during the 2008 election. But Wright's jeremiads, in fact, arose from a prophetic tradition dating back over two centuries. Moreover, Black religious institutions of all types, Christian and non-Christian, continue to thrive, and Black ministers and church people exercise a disproportionate influence in their communities. Democratic presidential candidates know this; it's why they routinely put African American churches on the docket of their campaign stops, particularly when hitting the trail in the South.

No study of American history could suffice without a close accounting for Black American religious thought and practice. Yet, despite the occasional prominence of Black churches and church people in significant American historical events—most recently, the civil rights movement—most Americans have little sense of their rich and complex history; and few students will as well. African American religion was once called the "invisible institution." Fortunately, there are readily available resources now to make it visible and prominent in the teaching of American history.

Intersections between African American Religious History and American History

One place to start in teaching the subject is using the idea of religious "myths," that is to say, stories from religious traditions that explain how the world came to be as it is. In the case of African Americans, Christian myths about the origins of human races played an important role in the formation, revision, and reconstruction of racial categories in the modern world. For example, one single verse from the book of Acts, "And hath made of one blood all nations of men for to dwell on all the face of the earth, and hath determined the times before appointed, and the bounds of their habitation," proved useful both for proponents of racial separation and segregation (since God gave races the "bounds of their habitation") and for proponents of racial equality ("of one blood"). In short, *religion* played a significant part in creating and revising ideas about *race*.

More specifically, Christianity necessarily was central to the process of *racializing* peoples—that is, to imposing categories of racial hierarchies upon groups of humanity or other societies. Students could consider, for example, texts from earlier American history debating whether African Americans who had been baptized necessarily should be freed, given that slavery was a status supposedly relegated for "heathens." One good text for this is Morgan Godwyn's *The Negro's and Indians Advocate*, available freely online.[4]

If Christianity fostered racialization, it also undermined it. Biblical passages were powerful but ambiguous, and arguments about God's Providence in colonization, the slave trade, and the proselytization of slaves were contentious. For example, the Old Testament abounded with passages about slavery as an accepted institution, and the Apostle Paul advised slaves to obey masters, but the New Testament also noted that there would be neither slave nor free, for all were equal under Christ. Christian myths and stories were central to the project of creating racial categories in the modern world. But the central text of Christianity, the Bible, was also amenable to more universalist visions, as nineteenth-century Black abolitionists made abundantly clear. Students could read portions of (for example) David Walker's *Appeal* from 1829, in which the African Methodist challenged the hypocrisies of proslavery American Christianity (available online).[5]

For much of the eighteenth and even more so nineteenth centuries, race and religion were joined in the project of civilization. Christianizing others involved civilizing them. At other times, the joining of Christianization and civilization underwrote idealistic crusades of bringing formerly enslaved peoples into American citizenship. In other instances, the intertwining of Christianity, civilization, and whiteness justified the complete exclusion of peoples from the American Republic. The first American citizenship law of 1790, for example, defined membership in the Republic as a privilege of white men, just as early African Methodist Episcopal leaders were petitioning Congress for their rights; and the Dred Scott Supreme Court decision of 1857 infamously insisted that Black men had no rights that white men were bound to respect, even as Black church people organized into conventions to pressure for respect of those rights.

In short, the connections between religion and race have been complicated. Idealism and imperialism often joined in projects both inspiring and ignoble. For example, the enslavement of African American people, the explosion of Protestant evangelicalism, and the gradual spread of antislavery ideas in nineteenth-century America occurred virtually simultaneously.

In the twentieth century, Christian thought helped undermine the racial system that it had been instrumental in creating. In the 1950s and 1960s, Black civil rights activists in the Congress of Racial Equality, the Southern Christian Leadership Conference, and the Student Nonviolent Coordinating Committee emerged from Black churches and finally penetrated the walls of segregation (for more on the civil rights movement, see J. Russell Hawkins's chapter). The civil rights revolution in American history was, to a considerable degree, a religious revolution, one whose social and spiritual impact inspired numerous other movements around the world. The website of the Bay Area Veterans of the Civil Rights Movement (https://www.crmvet.org/) provides ample examples of this.[6] Protestors in places as diverse as Czechoslovakia in 1968, Soweto in the 1980s, and Tiananmen Square in 1989 drew inspiration from the American civil rights movement.

Historically, African American Christianity has faced a number of paradoxes that have arisen from the ambiguous status of Black people as Africans and Americans. The first fundamental paradox is this: white Americans spread Christianity among Black Americans intending not only to evangelize people of color but also to make them more secure and contented in their enslavement. The result was precisely the opposite: ultimately, African American Christianity provided the language and the spirit of African American survival under slavery and of African American freedom movements toward the destruction of apartheid. America once was called the nation with the soul of a church; riffing on that, one scholar has referred to the Black church as the "church with the soul of a nation." Black Christian parishioners, for example, empowered the civil rights movement, the most important social movement of twentieth-century American history. During the civil rights era, they seemed to be the most powerful body of Christians in America in terms of being able to move a nation socially and politically.

The second paradox is that, on the one hand, the very popularity and singularity of the term "the Black church" suggests a unified force formed out of the Christianization of Black Americans during the Great Awakenings, the creation of Black denominations and other religious structures, and the effective political movements that arose in part out of those institutions during the civil rights era. Historically, Black Christians in America overwhelmingly have been identified with Protestant denominations, a legacy of the simultaneous rise of slavery and Protestant evangelicalism in the Deep South. Black Protestants, moreover, historically have been overwhelmingly Baptist and Methodist. African Americans have been one of the most Protestant ethnic groups in the country per capita.

On the other hand, "the Black church" and its leaders have been the target of relentless criticism. Black religious institutions have been as beleaguered as they have been powerful. Their most eloquent and elegiac defenders and its fiercest critics have come from within the Black community. In short, the church with the soul of a nation has been, for much of its history, a symbol of frustrated longings.

And a final paradox: Black Christians provided many of the shock troops for the social revolution of the civil rights movement. Moreover, African Americans from about the New Deal (1930s) forward have become associated with a powerful and solid voting bloc for liberal-left candidates in politics, *even though* the theology of many Black churches historically has been conservative and devoutly evangelical. The Black evangelical understanding of sin as both personal and social, and the historic Black evangelical emphasis on the coming Kingdom of God expressed through measures for racial equality, provide evidence for this. In the civil rights years, by rejecting the fundamental premises of mid-twentieth-century optimism and returning instead to the prophetic tradition of biblical texts, Black churches empowered a movement that cleansed the soul of a nation.

Primarily because of the star power of Malcolm X (and of celebrities and sports stars such as Muhammad Ali and Kareem Abdul-Jabbar), students are often interested in digging into "the Black Muslims" (more properly referred to as African American Islam). Teachers can take advantage of this to introduce students to a variety of traditions outside Christianity that have formed an important part of the African American religious experience. African American religion today operates within a society that is religiously pluralist in a way that, ironically, reflects the early American world, when peoples and religions from around the world met on this continent (obviously with the Africans being an unwilling and coerced part of that "encounter"). Since the 1965 Hart-Celler Act, which remade American immigration law, the American religious landscape has incorporated Muslims, Buddhists, Hindus, Sikhs, and practitioners of African-based religions coming from the Caribbean such as Haitian Vodun and Cuban Santería.

Since the 1990s, congregations largely composed of recent African immigrations have sprung up through urban America. The growth of

African Pentecostal churches in American cities has been especially notable. So has the significant migration of Ethiopians, both Muslims and those from the historic Eastern Orthodox tradition of the home country. And the recruitment of Afro-Latins into Pentecostal and Black American Catholic congregations continues to diversify African American religious expressions. Something as simple as sending students to the "internet yellow pages" of a local community (particularly in larger urban areas) will open up the eyes of many to the diversity contained even just within the African American religious tradition.

An institution defined by the very struggle for civil rights faces both opportunities and dilemmas in a post–civil rights era. On the one hand, the church has been one of the relatively few Black institutions to survive and thrive in the post–civil rights era. This is because African American religious institutions came about not simply because of the imposition of Jim Crow but because Black Americans from the late eighteenth century forward nurtured their churches as their own institutions. In recent years, the historic contrast between the often conservative theology and the liberal politics of Black churches has been narrowing and even closing to some degree. Activists on the religious-political right have exploited ideological affinities (especially in the areas of abortion and gay rights) to forge interracial alliances especially around issues of gender and sexuality. Nonetheless, Black churches also remained aligned with the civil rights agenda, and Black voters still reliably turn out for Democratic and liberal candidates.

In recent years, Black parishioners increasingly have responded to the "megachurch" phenomenon and to the charismatic call of televangelists and prosperity gospel proponents. In African American Christianity, this is most evident in the star preacher Thomas Dexter (T. D.) Jakes, born to a working-class family in West Virginia and now a preacher in Dallas who pushes "prosperity theology" to an integrated crowd of enthusiastic listeners. A generation ago, Martin Luther King was certainly the best-known Black minister; twenty years ago, it was Jesse Jackson. Now, it could be one of several figures, but T. D. Jakes (and other neo-Pentecostal Black ministers) would certainly be in the running.

Pedagogy and Sources

Few students will know of the long and complex relationship of Christianity, slavery, and freedom among African Americans.

Most who do know a little will try to put it in a convenient category of Christianity being "forced" on slaves without their consent, or of Christianity solely as a liberating religion. Others, knowing of Martin Luther King, assume that "the Black church" was always behind the civil rights movement, or they may simply accept criticisms of Black Christianity as always subservient.

A wealth of information and sources, formerly hidden or hard to access, is now available for teachers. One of the most important lies in the riches contained within the digitized collections of the University of North Carolina's Documenting the American South (https://docsouth .unc.edu/index.html). The site contains a wealth of primary sources, from slave narratives to reflections from nineteenth-century free people of color to twentieth-century narratives of life and religion in the segregated South. The narrative of Daniel Alexander Payne, for example, shows the powerful push for respectability that animated many educated nineteenth-century Black religious leaders, while excerpts from the Spirituals give aural evidence of the power of African American folk traditions.

Surveying some key documents of African American religious history can quickly lead students into different and more interesting paths. Consider this document: In 1723, a plaintive plea from an anonymous group of mixed-race slaves arrived in the letter file of a newly installed bishop who oversaw Anglican affairs in the American colonies. Brought up in the Church of England, they wrote to complain about the law "which keeps and makes them and there seed Slaves forever." Their letter concluded with an explanation of why they did not sign their names, "for freare of our masters for if they knew that wee have Sent home to your honour wee Should goo neare to Swing upon the Gallass tree." These slaves insisted that their religious status gave them rights to freedom and respect. They were willing to fight for those—in imploring pleas to imperial officials, and sometimes in rebellions against governing authorities. Such eighteenth-century documents give some flavor to the long and complex story of African Americans and the dominant religious traditions of North America.[7]

Or consider, from the nineteenth century, the part of Frederick Douglass's first autobiography, *Narrative of the Life of Frederick Douglass, an American Slave* (available online) where he makes a plea that his criticism of white slave masters' Christianity not be confused with his endorsement of Christianity as a whole, considered in its true self. Or from the twentieth century, consider a classic source such as "Letter from Birmingham Jail," a document that rises to the level of one of the great classics of American history (also available online). In it, Martin Luther King points out that the greatest enemy to Black freedom is not the racist Klansman, but the white moderate (including the nine ministers addressed in the letter). King also quotes the famous theologian Reinhold Niebuhr in pointing out that "groups are more immoral than individuals." King's letter provides an excellent jumping-off point for considering how it was that the Bible Belt produced a society of the greatest racial repression in American history. Scenes from the documentary series *Eyes on the Prize* (available online) can foster exploration of this paradox. For example, the third segment of the first series of *Eyes on the Prize*, entitled "Ain't Afraid of Your Jails," culminates with a stirring set of documentary images of the Freedom Rides of 1961, a moment when students pushed the movement forward, beyond where movement elders originally had wanted it to go.

The connection between religion, civil rights, and social justice in everyday life found an especially powerful connection in the "local people" who did much of the actual work of the civil rights movement. In Montgomery, the churches played a central role, and the success there led to the formation of the Southern Christian Leadership Conference (SCLC), King's organization for the remainder of his life. In the 1960s, following an unsuccessful campaign in Albany, Georgia, where organizing efforts were stalemated by a clever local sheriff, a longtime Baptist pastor in Birmingham, the Reverend Fred Shuttlesworth, persuaded King to stage a major campaign in that brutally racist working-class town. Civil rights activists such as Shuttlesworth mixed the language of evangelicalism with the tenets of American civil religion. An encyclopedia entry from Shuttlesworth's biographer, available online, provides a plethora of links and sources to explore his remarkable career.[8]

Religion and social justice were also inseparable in the mind of Fannie Lou Hamer. Daughter of a sharecropper in Ruleville, Mississippi, she experienced sexual abuse and later sadistic torture at the hands of local policemen. Hamer rose to prominence in the 1960s as a liaison between "local people" and national civil rights leaders. With her wicked sense of humor, spirited singing voice, and uncompromising stance on justice, Hamer articulated a liberation theology that sustained her through years of struggle and turmoil. She quoted the Bible expertly and led congregational song, qualities that served her admirably in the 1960s.

In 1962, at a Student Nonviolent Coordinating Committee (SNCC) meeting in a rural church, Hamer and a few others volunteered to register for voting. This serious act of political defiance against the state regime earned them a beating in the county jail. Hamer eventually won a seat in the Mississippi Freedom Democratic Party's delegation—originally sent as a protest against the all-white official state delegation—to the Democratic national convention of 1964. Hamer incited Lyndon Baines Johnson's special ire as she delivered an impromptu national address explaining why the Freedom Democratic Party would not settle for the compromise of taking two seats on the official state delegation (that address is readily available on YouTube).

During the civil rights era, cultural tools deeply rooted in the community made the mass democratic movement and a revolution in religion and race powerful. The sacred music of the movement—the freedom songs—harnessed that spirit and empowered local people. Movement activists converted widely known spirituals, hymns, church anthems, and popular songs into versions of civil rights manifestos. Participants propelled the music forward with enthusiastic singing, bodily movement, and the rhythmic accompaniment of spirited hand clapping and foot stomping, products of two centuries of communal musical rituals in African American religious communities. As protestors filled penitentiaries throughout the South, they sang to each other and to the lawmen arresting them. Dozens of new verses of familiar songs—drawing from Black hymnody and gospel music, labor movement songs, and popular ditties—spontaneously arose in jail cells, picket lines, and boycott lines. Freedom songs inspired a level of active and sacrificial resistance that overcame the efforts of the southern white establishment to persuade, coerce, or terrify Blacks into continued subordination to the Jim Crow order. Excerpts from part 3 of the first series of *Eyes on the Prize*, focusing on the movement in Albany, Georgia, provide particularly effective examples of the origin and role of freedom songs in the depths of the civil rights struggle.

In looking at more contemporary issues, students often bring questions about the relevance of church institutions or leaders in contemporary life, even if they acknowledge or understand something about their importance in the past. White students, in particular, typically would have no experience in attending services of a black congregation. But an excellent way to introduce students to the richness of the African American religious tradition is through music, because in many senses that's what they have been hearing for their whole lives, through the venue of American popular music.

In the post–civil rights era, some suggested that America had moved into a "post-racial" era, despite the overwhelming statistics documenting racial inequality in American society. Social justice and civil rights today centrally involve issues of economic justice, a theme taken up most recently by the de facto successor to the Martin Luther King tradition, the Reverend William Barber, leader of the "Moral Mondays" movement in North Carolina. Having students look at his addresses, readily available on YouTube, will provide them exposure to the contemporary relevance of the civil rights tradition. Thus, activists who have mined the connection between religion, civil rights, and social justice will have plenty of work to do in the future. The struggle continues, and Frederick Douglass's words remain true today: "without the struggle, there is no progress." Religion will remain central to that struggle, even though religious institutions are not always well adapted to carrying on the struggle.

ADDITIONAL RESOURCES

Bay Area Veterans of the Civil Rights Movement. Civil Rights Movement Archive. Duke University Libraries. https://www.crmvet.org/.

Blum, Edward. *W. E. B. Du Bois: American Prophet*. Philadelphia: University of Pennsylvania Press, 2007.

Emerson, Michael, and Christian Smith. *Divided by Faith: Evangelical Religion and the Problem of Race in America*. New York: Oxford University Press, 2001.

Evans, Curtis. *The Burden of Black Religion*. New York: Oxford University Press, 2008.

Gin Lum, Kathryn, and Paul Harvey, eds. *The Oxford Handbook of Religion and Race in American History*. New York: Oxford University Press, 2018.

Harvey, Paul. *Through the Storm, Through the Night: A History of African American Christianity*. Lanham, MD: Rowman & Littlefield, 2011.

NOTES

1. *North Star*, 16 February 1849, quoted in Paul Harvey, *Through the Storm, Through the Night: A History of African American Christianity* (Lanham, MD: Rowman and Littlefield, 2011); W. E. B. Du Bois, *Souls of Black Folk*, chap. 10, Project Gutenberg eBook, http://www.gutenberg.org/files/408/408-h/408-h.htm.

2. Eddie Glaude, "The Black Church Is Dead," HuffPost, February 24, 2010, accessed July 22, 2010, http://www.huffingtonpost.com/eddie-glaude-jr-phd/the-black-church-is-dead_b_473815.html.

3. Curtis Evans, *The Burden of Black Religion* (New York: Oxford University Press, 2008), 280.

4. Morgan Godwyn, *The Negro's & Indians Advocate, Suing for their Admission into the Church; or, Persuasive to the Instructing and Baptizing of the Negro's and Indians in our Plantations* (London, 1680), https://babel.hathitrust.org/cgi/pt?id =uc1.co46017615;view=1up;seq=15.

5. David Walker's *Appeal*, 1829, Resource Bank, Judgment Day, Part 4: 1831–1865, https://www.pbs.org/wgbh/aia/part4/4h2931.html.

6. See Paul Harvey, "Civil Rights Movements and Religion in America," *Oxford Research Encyclopedia*, http://oxfordre.com/religion/view/10.1093/acre fore/9780199340378.001.0001/acrefore-9780199340378-e-492. This article contains an extensive set of primary sources, many available freely online, in its concluding section.

7. "Releese us out of this Cruell Bondegg": An Appeal from Virginia in 1723, Thomas N. Ingersoll, *The William and Mary Quarterly* 51, no. 4 (October 1994): 777–82. See also the primary source appendix to Harvey, *Through the Storm, Through the Night*.

8. Andrew Manis, "Fred Lee Shuttlesworth," *Encyclopedia of Alabama*, accessed November 14, 2019, http://www.encyclopediaofalabama.org/article/h-1093.

Religion in American Women's History

A N D R E A   L .   T U R P I N

For the past ten years I have taught both a US history survey and a two-part course sequence in American women's history at Baylor, a Christian university that admits students of all faiths and none. Because of the institution's identity, my students consistently have a strong interest in religion. Many of my students think of women's history as only the history of feminism and assume feminism and religion are incompatible. Both beliefs are false. This combination skews their understanding of women's diverse contributions to American history. Religion comes in both conservative and liberal varieties, and both have empowered women in some ways and restricted them in others. Perhaps most importantly, many American women have historically made their religious convictions, practices, and communities a significant component of their identities.

Although perhaps magnified at Baylor, these same interests and assumptions characterize a large percentage of college students throughout the nation. Given students' perspectives, I work to relate religious history to women's history throughout my courses both to connect with students' interests and to challenge their assumptions. My passion as a teacher is to help break down students' mental boxes of what sorts of ideas, identities, and practices "automatically" go together by giving them historical examples that break the mold. I then have them wrestle with why different people in the past may have believed and acted in ways that were distinct both from each other and from us.

When introducing the topic of religion and women in the classroom, I recommend a very simple and very informative classroom exercise.

Ask students to share their answers to the question: "When you hear the word 'feminist,' what does that term mean to you?" Ask follow-up questions: "Can someone be both religious and feminist?" "Does it matter what type of religion?" "Why might some women not want to be called feminist?" These types of questions help tease out students' assumptions, allowing us to lead them into better understanding of how views on religion and views on gender have historically intersected in a wide variety of ways.

In the last decade, scholarship on American women's religious history has grown considerably but has not always made its way into textbooks. This essay will therefore offer some simple ways to incorporate religion into discussions of women in American history, without trying to be exhaustive.

Colonial America: Puritans

Students and teachers alike often do associate religion with colonial women—thanks in part to cultural references such as the fictional New England Puritan women in Nathaniel Hawthorne's *The Scarlet Letter* and the real ones in the Salem Witch Trials. Using students' passing familiarity with these stories is a great way to draw them in before complicating their understanding. The approach to Bible interpretation dominant during the colonial era—as well as in many Christian traditions today—reserved the role of minister for men and pronounced husbands the heads of households. Yet Puritans also taught that women and men had equal spiritual value, and they granted both sexes equal access to church membership (reserved for those who could give reliable testimony of their Christian conversion).[1]

A good exercise in both historical thinking and gender analysis is to introduce Puritan beliefs and gender roles and then ask students whether they think more men or more women were church members at that time and why. Then tell students that, starting with the second generation of Puritans, about two-thirds of church members were women. Ask if students can think of potential reasons. (Historians cannot prove the answer, but possibilities include greater equality in the church than in other aspects of colonial society, more frequent brushes with death through childbirth, or particular concern with passing on faith to children.) Then tell students that the same proportion of men and women are church members today, and ask if that information changes their answers.[2]

The American Revolution: Phillis Wheatley

Phillis Wheatley is a great person to introduce to students to enrich the class's understanding of gender, race, and religion in the American Revolutionary Era. Phillis Wheatley was born a free woman in West Africa but sold into slavery at the age of seven or eight. She was purchased by a wealthy evangelical tailor in Boston, John Wheatley, to be a personal slave for his wife Susannah. The Wheatleys recognized Phillis's exceptional intelligence and gave her an education closely matching the best available to white men of her age—which was far more than that available to almost any other slave or any other woman, Black or white. Phillis wrote her first of many poems at age fourteen. The Wheatleys sponsored the publication of a book of her poems in 1773 but did not free her until shortly thereafter.[3]

Phillis Wheatley challenges students' understanding of the Revolutionary Era because she and her poetry did not fit in boxes. An enslaved Black, female, evangelical, patriot writer, Phillis wrote poetry that connected race, religion, and revolution, often in ways that cut across the sensibilities of both her time and ours. She adopted the evangelical Christianity of her owners and their patriot political convictions—but opposed their practice of enslaving Africans. Contrary to modern expectations, her poems did not explicitly analyze the difference in female or male experience or the ethics of gender roles.

Many of Wheatley's poems are brief, all are available online, and they can easily be analyzed with students in the classroom. Compare, for example, the short poems "On Being Brought from Africa to America" and "On the Death of General Wooster." In the first, Wheatley in one sense argues that her enslavement was positive because it introduced her to Christ. But then she turns around and argues that both Black and white people can experience conversion, implying an equality between the races. In the second poem, Wheatley champions the American cause in the Revolutionary War against the British—but warns that God may not bless that just cause so long as Americans continue to practice the unjust act of slavery. By contrast, Wheatley never explicitly addresses her status as a woman within her poetry. Rather, she makes the implicit claim of equality to men in both intellect and moral authority by writing in genres dominated by men and making clear claims about right and wrong on controversial issues.

Ask students what they think might account for this difference (historians do not know for sure): Was it because antislavery activism was much more prominent than feminism at the time? Perhaps Wheatley simply thought antislavery activism more important? Or might Wheatley have interpreted the Bible to teach at least some meaningful distinctions between the sexes but none between the races? Return to this question when teaching about why some women linked feminism and antislavery activism in the next century (discussed below).

The Nineteenth and Early Twentieth Centuries: Women and Reform

Religion plays a central role in the drama of three interconnected aspects of nineteenth-century American history that relate to women: expanding educational and vocational opportunities for women, their participation in reform movements such as abolitionism, and first-wave feminism and suffrage activism. Theologically conservative and liberal Black and white women combined gender ideals and religious beliefs in different ways as they sought to reform American society during this era. Multiple primary sources, discussed below, are available online to help students grapple with the way that religious identities and beliefs both constrained women in the past and served as creative inspiration for pursuing a good life and contributing to social reform.

Education

Educational opportunities for women exploded after the American Revolution. Historians have articulated several causes for the change. Notably, "Republican motherhood," the idea that women needed education to teach voting sons (and brothers and husbands) both virtue and civics demanded that women in turn receive a better education. Similarly, the expansion of common (public) schools to further train new citizens was more cheaply staffed by women—who could legally be paid less than men until 1963—and whose teaching was seen as an extension of mothering. Finally, many Protestant women experienced evangelical conversion to faith in Christ in the revivals known as the Second Great

Awakening. In most of their denominations, they could not pastor or preach, so these women sought the training that would enable them instead to serve as missionary-minded teachers of children and youth in their hometowns, in the American West, and abroad.[4]

Nuns likewise founded schools to spread the Catholic faith. Catholic immigration, particularly from Ireland, grew steadily in the first half of the nineteenth century, and many parts of what would become the American West were already dominated by Catholics of Spanish or Mexican descent. The Catholic church made formal space in female religious orders for single women to share in the church's ministry in a way with no Protestant equivalent. Catholic "women religious" saw as part of their mission the founding and instructing of schools. Many Protestants worried that if they did not likewise train women to be teachers, they would lose the race to establish educational institutions. Unsuspecting Protestants might then send their children to Catholic schools and lose them to what they believed to be heresy.[5]

A helpful exercise is to have students read one or more online documents related to the 1837 founding of the first permanent institution of women's higher education in the United States: Mount Holyoke Female Seminary, in South Hadley, Massachusetts.[6] Ask students to analyze how its Protestant founder Mary Lyon tied together ideas about gender, class, and religion.

Lyon was an "evangelical pragmatist."[7] She believed a conversion experience was necessary to make someone right with God, and that it was accordingly important to train as many people as possible—female and male, poor and rich—to communicate that message to lead people to salvation. She therefore designed Mount Holyoke both to be affordable to poor women and to provide them the top-quality education that men received, so more people would have the best intellectual resources to commend the Christian gospel. (Although it was not her main emphasis, Lyon also argued the importance of outcompeting Catholic women in establishing schools.) Her own school would not quite reach collegiate level during Lyon's lifetime, but eventually grew into Mount Holyoke College. In service to the main goal of spreading the gospel, Lyon ignored gender norms she believed to be less important. For example, to fundraise for the institution, she traveled unaccompanied and spoke freely with strangers during the journey. But when gender ideals helped her goals, she embraced them; Lyon had students do all the domestic work of the school to drive down costs.[8]

Lyon's evangelical pragmatism did not extend to educating Black women—indeed she forbid abolitionist debates within the school to unify students and donors behind an evangelistic message on which they could agree. But it was not predetermined that her logic would produce this result. Another evangelical school, Oberlin Collegiate Institute (later College) in Ohio, carried evangelical pragmatism to this alternative logical end when it became the first coeducational college in the world the same year Mount Holyoke opened—while simultaneously admitting Black and white students. By training every type of student under the same roof to conserve funds, Oberlin hoped to supply as many missionary teachers and pastors as possible. Fears of miscegenation (sex between the races) dominated this era, so Oberlin was an extraordinary example of the power of religious belief to change social practice.[9]

Reform Movements

Different complicated dynamics occurred within other reform movements. The widespread nineteenth-century belief that women were more naturally religious and moral than men—as long as they remained relatively unsullied by the commercial world outside the home—actually led many women to create new voluntary benevolent societies that sought to extend the moral influences of the home into wider society. Some religious women believed their moral authority constituted an imperative to push against what they saw as artificial constraints against its exercise. These women violated accepted gender norms by speaking to mixed audiences that included men and women, getting more directly involved in politics by petitioning Congress, and speaking out against more controversial issues such as alcohol, prostitution, and slavery. Other religious women thought that the imperative to spread women's moral influence should never contradict accepted gender norms, which they believed to be grounded in scripture. These women organized noncontroversial benevolent societies that focused on aiding poor women and children.[10]

There are some excellent primary sources available for exploring the logic of these different approaches. Have students compare selections from the letters between Catharine Beecher and the Grimké sisters on abolitionism, religion, and women's roles, available online.[11] Liberal Protestant educator Catharine Beecher's gender essentialism meant that she did not believe women ought to advocate publicly for political issues such as abolitionism—although it also meant that she believed mothers and female teachers should be given more religious influence over children than male ministers. Meanwhile, famous southern white Quaker abolitionist sisters Sarah and Angelina Grimké believed that doing everything one could to advance the common good was a requirement God placed on all moral creatures—women as well as men. Any gender ideals that cut against this larger good were therefore by definition unchristian. Students can then consider a third option: Catharine's Episcopalian sister Harriet Beecher Stowe's masterpiece *Uncle Tom's Cabin* (1852) publicly advocated for abolition in a way widely considered feminine: through a novel. Chapter 9, "In Which It Appears That a Senator Is But a Man," available on Google Books, features a wife who influences her politician husband to support abolition through her less learned but nevertheless superior piety.

Feminism and Suffrage

Religion intersected women's suffrage efforts in similarly unpredictable ways. Religious beliefs of the major players cover a wide range. Some suffragists were motivated by their faith, while others lost or altered their religious beliefs as they wrestled with suffrage. Students would benefit by thinking through the cause and effect between religious belief of various sorts and suffrage advocacy.

The most clear-cut case involves the Quakers. Adherents of this religious group often took the lead in midcentury feminist activism. The Grimké sisters were ardent suffragists as well as abolitionists. The Quaker Lucretia Mott partnered with Elizabeth Cady Stanton, raised Presbyterian, to hold the 1848 Seneca Falls Convention for women's rights. Stanton in turn would later partner with the Quaker Susan B. Anthony.

Historians tend to agree that the Quakers' distinctive theology was a root cause of their overrepresentation in the suffrage movement. Unique among Protestants, Quakers asserted the existence of an "inward light," a pointer God placed within all people to lead them to spiritual truth if they chose to listen. Some Quakers believed the inward light would always confirm the Bible, while others believed it could lead beyond it. But all believed both women and men possessed the light. Quakers did not have formal pastors, but rather "ministers" who were recognized by the community as hearing the inward light particularly well (Quaker meetings consisted of everyone sitting in silence until someone was moved by the light to speak). Local meetings recognized women as ministers on par with men and often commissioned women to serve as traveling preachers. Throughout American religious history, traditions that placed more emphasis on this sort of direct communication with the divine have also tended to embrace less rigid gender roles. Several Native American tribes affirmed a belief in what would later be known as "two-spirit" people, who often received an opposite-sex identity during a vision quest. Spiritualist mediums were often female, and Pentecostals often supported female ministers.[12]

The suffrage coalition split after the Civil War as a result of disagreement on whether to back the Fourteenth and Fifteenth Amendments to the US Constitution that granted Black men citizenship and the right to vote without extending the vote to women. The American Woman Suffrage Association (AWSA), led by Lucy Stone and Frederick Douglass, advocated endorsing the Black vote first and then later seeking to persuade each state to add women's suffrage. Stone shifted from evangelical Congregationalism to Unitarianism over the course of her life, whereas Douglass was a licensed preacher in the African Methodist Episcopal Zion Church.

The National Woman Suffrage Association (NWSA), led by Elizabeth Cady Stanton and Susan B. Anthony, opposed the amendments because they excluded women. After the Fifteenth Amendment passed in 1870, they fought to further amend the Constitution to guarantee women's right to vote rather than try to change each state's laws. Stanton, although raised Presbyterian, later became a "freethinker" who questioned traditional religion because of the suffrage opposition she encountered from many mainstream Protestant ministers. Anthony, raised Quaker, later became Unitarian like Stone and ultimately agnostic. Yet the single most effective suffrage organizer of the later nineteenth century was a pious Methodist: Frances Willard, president (1879–98) of the Women's Christian Temperance Union (WCTU). In addition to temperance advocacy, Willard encouraged WCTU members to "Do Everything," which prominently included advocating for woman suffrage so their moral voice would shape government.

In the late nineteenth century, the AWSA and the NWSA combined into NAWSA (National American Woman's Suffrage Association), which would spearhead the fight until the Nineteenth Amendment guaranteeing suffrage to all American women passed in 1920. Suffrage advocacy during these years reflected some of the increasing religious diversity that resulted from wide-scale immigration, particularly by Catholic and Jewish Europeans, in the decades around 1900.[13]

NAWSA was for most of its existence led by one of the first ordained female Methodist ministers, Anna Howard Shaw, and a freethinker, Carrie Chapman Catt. Its more radical spinoff, the National Woman's Party (1916), was co-led by a Quaker, Alice Paul, and a Catholic, Lucy Burns. Burns was unusual among educated Catholic women for her suffrage advocacy; most argued instead that the women's movement, dominated by Protestants, would create social chaos. More liberating to women in the long run would be to gradually apply the principles of the ancient faith to the new situation. Of course, many Protestant women opposed suffrage too. Larger suffrage organizations tended to marginalize women of color, but these advocates for suffrage also ran the religious gamut. Anti-lynching and suffrage campaigner Ida B. Wells-Barnett taught a men's Bible class at a Presbyterian church, and Chinese American suffragist Mabel Ping-Hua Lee took over her late father's position as director (functionally, minister) of the First Chinese Baptist Church of New York City. Meanwhile, suffragist Lillian Wald, a nurse and settlement house founder, was Jewish. Many of the women and children she served through her social work were immigrant Jews living in poverty, but she also reached across the color line to help found the National Association for the Advancement of Colored People (NAACP).[14]

Ask students what they make of all this. If both suffragists and anti-suffragists often appealed to the Bible to justify their respective positions, was their faith really what determined their political stance? Or, since many different faith communities appealed to the Bible, perhaps it was a matter of which religious group one identified with? Yet most Catholics did not side with Lucy Burns. Nonetheless, we cannot throw out the significance of specific theological traditions entirely: Quaker theology, for instance, clearly made a difference. Elizabeth Cady Stanton concluded that the Protestant faith was wrong because so many of its ministers opposed suffrage. By contrast, Frances Willard believed Christian faith required suffrage advocacy and concluded instead that those ministers did not properly understand the implications of their faith. Did underlying beliefs or just personality determine this difference? Use this discussion to help students wrestle with the bigger questions of history: the ways historians struggle to balance the relative power of ideas, social factors, and contingency when explaining past events.[15]

The Twentieth Century: Rights Movements and Culture Wars

Coverage of religion in women's history is often stronger for the colonial and nineteenth centuries than the twentieth. Reading backward from the culture wars and rise of the Religious Right (see Darren Dochuk's chapter), many historians either assume religious Americans—especially women—played little role in the rights movements of the mid-twentieth century, or that their role was solely oppositional.

An exception to historians' assumption of religion's irrelevancy to midcentury social reform is the civil rights movement. Women's role in the movement, however, can sometimes get abbreviated, especially in survey courses with a lot of material to cover. Yet women of faith were central to its success. Women outnumbered men in Black (and white) churches, and the Black church often formed the core of the Black community and the civil rights movement specifically. Men received more fame, but women used their relational networks to hold together local coalitions of activists and were better at recruiting.[16] Arguably, the most prominent woman of faith to highlight in the civil rights movement is Fannie Lou Hamer (see Paul Harvey's chapter). She often motivated discouraged crowds of volunteers by singing hymns (examples of her singing are available on YouTube).

Contrary to stereotype, second-wave feminism also included religious alongside secular women. As historian Ann Braude has noted, an early photograph of seven of the founders of the National Organization for Women (NOW) reveals a mix of religious and secular women, including a nun dressed in habit (Sister Joel Reed), an African American Methodist lay leader (Anna Arnold Hedgeman), and a secular Jew (Betty Friedan).[17] Not pictured was Pauli Murray, who would go on to become the first African American female Episcopal priest.[18]

At the same time, it is true that many religious women did not find their interests represented within the feminist movement. Some Black women, for example, joined the explicitly patriarchal Nation of Islam Black nationalist religious movement (see Jaclyn Michael's chapter for more on NOI). They embraced the conservative dress required of

Nation women as a sign of their dignity and worth: they were not on display for white men. Also, although the earliest leaders of the pro-life movement were men—because they were Catholic priests—religious women soon came to assume leadership in this cause. Notably, the proposed Equal Rights Amendment (ERA) to the Constitution that would forbid gender distinctions in laws was defeated by a coalition of religious women in the organization STOP (Stop Taking Our Privileges) ERA, under the direction of pious Catholic Phyllis Schlafly (see Darren Dochuk's chapter for more on the ERA and Schlafly). These women valued aspects of "traditional" femininity as central to their God-given identity.[19]

Church attendance was the chief distinction between women who opposed the ERA (98 percent) and women who supported it (31–48 percent).[20] Yet up to half of ERA supporters were religious, and several religious women's groups, such as the Women's League for Conservative Judaism, engaged in pro-choice activism.[21] And sometimes religious convictions produced effects that defied liberal-conservative binaries. In the 1970s, progressive evangelical women opposed abortion while embracing the ERA. The Catholic Estela Ruiz paradoxically claimed power as a lay leader in a male-run church through her devotion to the Virgin Mary, often understood as the model submissive woman. Ruiz established Mary's Ministries in the mid-1990s after the Virgin instructed her to lead other women to Christ's mother for practical spiritual guidance.[22] Clearly religion of various types sometimes restricted and sometimes empowered American women, but it consistently provided significant—and too often historically overlooked—context for their contributions to American history.

ADDITIONAL RESOURCES

Brekus, Catherine A., ed. *The Religious History of American Women: Reimagining the Past*. Chapel Hill: University of North Carolina Press, 2007.

Butler, Anthea D. *Women in the Church of God in Christ: Making a Sanctified World*. Chapel Hill: University of North Carolina Press, 2007.

Johnson, Emily Suzanne. *This Is Our Message: Women's Leadership in the New Christian Right*. New York: Oxford University Press, 2019.

Koester, Nancy. *We Will Be Free: The Life and Faith of Sojourner Truth*. Grand Rapids, MI: William B. Eerdmans, 2023.

O'Donnell, Catherine. *Elizabeth Seton: American Saint*. Ithaca, NY: Cornell University Press, 2018.

Westerkamp, Marilyn J. *The Passion of Anne Hutchinson: An Extraordinary Woman, the Puritan Patriarchs, and the World They Made and Lost.* New York: Oxford University Press, 2021.

NOTES

1. A teachable overview of Puritan women's lives is Laurel Thatcher Ulrich, *Good Wives: Image and Reality in the Lives of Women in Northern New England, 1650–1750* (New York: Vintage Books, 1991).

2. On the numerical dominance of women within American religious traditions, see Ann Braude, "Women's History *Is* American Religious History," in *Retelling American Religious History,* ed. Thomas A. Tweed (Berkeley: University of California Press, 1996), 87–107.

3. For more information, see Vincent Carretta, *Phillis Wheatley: Biography of a Genius in Bondage* (Athens: University of Georgia Press, 2011).

4. Andrea L. Turpin, *A New Moral Vision: Gender, Religion, and the Changing Purposes of American Higher Education, 1837–1917* (Ithaca, NY: Cornell University Press, 2016), 1–62.

5. A collection of contextualized primary source documents on the experience of Catholic women religious during these years can be found in Rosemary Radford Ruether and Rosemary Skinner Keller, eds., *Women & Religion in America: A Documentary History, vol. 1, The Nineteenth Century* (San Francisco: Harper & Row, 1981), 101–49. For the Protestant reaction, see Amanda Porterfield, *Mary Lyon and the Mount Holyoke Missionaries* (New York: Oxford University Press, 1997), 39–41.

6. Several circulars and letters Mary Lyon wrote explaining her vision for Mount Holyoke are included in Edward Hitchcock, ed., *The Power of Christian Benevolence Illustrated in the Life and Labors of Mary Lyon* (Northampton, MA: Hopkins, Bridgman, 1851), available on Google Books. See especially the brief version, 212–13, and fuller versions, 232–38 (esp. 234–36), 295–98, and 298–308.

7. Turpin, *New Moral Vision,* 24.

8. For more background on Lyon accessible on JSTOR, see Andrea L. Turpin, "Ideological Origins of the Women's College: Religion, Class and Curriculum in the Educational Visions of Catharine Beecher and Mary Lyon," *History of Education Quarterly* 50, no. 2 (2010): 133–58.

9. Turpin, *New Moral Vision,* 63–87.

10. Anne M. Boylan, *The Origins of Women's Activism: New York and Boston, 1797–1840* (Chapel Hill: University of North Carolina Press, 2002).

11. "The Grimke-Beecher Exchange," Uncle Tom's Cabin & American Culture: A Multi-Media Archive, University of Virginia, http://utc.iath.virginia.edu/abolitn/grimkehp.html.

12. Thomas D. Hamm, *The Quakers in America* (New York: Columbia University Press, 2003); Will Roscoe, *The Zuni Man-Woman* (Albuquerque: University

of New Mexico Press, 1991); Ann Braude, *Radical Spirits: Spiritualism and Women's Rights in Nineteenth-Century America*, 2nd ed. (Bloomington: Indiana University Press, 2001); Grant Wacker, *Heaven Below: Early Pentecostals and American Culture* (Cambridge, MA: Harvard University Press, 2001).

13. Wonderful charts of the growth of various religious groups in US history are available in Edwin Scott Gaustad and Philip L. Barlow, *New Historical Atlas of Religion in America* (New York: Oxford University Press, 2001).

14. Multiple biographies of all these women are easily accessible online. A good discussion of the differences between religious and freethinking suffragists can be found in Kathi Kern, *Mrs. Stanton's Bible* (Ithaca, NY: Cornell University Press, 2001). Details on Mabel Lee are available in chapters 2 and 11 of Cathleen D. Cahill, *Recasting the Vote: How Women of Color Transformed the Suffrage Movement* (Chapel Hill: University of North Carolina Press, 2020). On Catholic women's attitudes, see Kathleen Sprows Cummings, *New Women of the Old Faith: Gender and American Catholicism in the Progressive Era* (Chapel Hill: University of North Carolina Press, 2009).

15. A version of this section first appeared as Andrea L. Turpin, "Can Suffragists Teach Us about Religion's Relationship to Politics?" *The Anxious Bench*, September 18, 2019, https://www.patheos.com/blogs/anxiousbench/2019/09/can-suffragists-teach-us-about-the-relationship-between-religion-and-politics/.

16. Kathryn L. Nasstrom, "Down to Now: Memory, Narrative, and Women's Leadership in the Civil Rights Movement in Atlanta, Georgia," *Gender and History* 11, no. 1 (1999): 113–44; Charles M. Payne, *I've Got the Light of Freedom: The Organizing Tradition and the Mississippi Freedom Struggle* (Berkeley: University of California Press, 1995).

17. It is the first photograph shown in this video: Harvard University, "Betty Friedan and the National Organization for Women | Radcliffe Institute," November 13, 2013, video, 1:22, https://www.youtube.com/watch?v=fI6VU5drptk.

18. Ann Braude, "Faith, Feminism, and History," in *Religious History of American Women: Reimaging the Past*, ed. Catherine A. Brekus (Chapel Hill: University of North Carolina Press, 2007), 232–52.

19. Ula Yvette Taylor, *The Promise of Patriarchy: Women and the Nation of Islam* (Chapel Hill: University of North Carolina Press, 2017); Daniel K. Williams, *Defenders of the Unborn: The Pro-Life Movement before* Roe v. Wade (New York: Oxford University Press, 2016); Donald T. Critchlow, *Phyllis Schlafly and Grassroots Conservatism: A Woman's Crusade* (Princeton, NJ: Princeton University Press, 2005).

20. Critchlow, *Phyllis Schlafly*, 221.

21. "Conservative" Jews are the moderates on the spectrum between "Orthodox" and "Reform."

22. Rachel Kranson, "From Women's Rights to Religious Freedom: The Women's League for Conservative Judaism and the Politics of Abortion, 1970–1982,"

in *Devotions and Desires: Histories of Sexuality and Religion in the Twentieth-Century United States*, ed. Gillian Frank, Bethany Moreton, and Heather R. White (Chapel Hill: University of North Carolina Press, 2018), 170–92; Brantley W. Gasaway, *Progressive Evangelicals and the Pursuit of Social Justice* (Chapel Hill: University of North Carolina Press, 2014); Kristy Nabhan-Warren, "Little Slices of Heaven and Mary's Candy Kisses: Mexican American Women Redefining Feminism and Catholicism," in Brekus, *Religious History of American Women*, 294–317.

Teaching Native American Religious Experiences and Narratives in the Classroom

MELISSA FRANKLIN HARKRIDER

R ecent scholarship in American religious history and Native American studies has examined the complexity and nuance of Native religious beliefs and practices in United States history. Notably these studies have emphasized the importance of shifting the focus in the study of American Indian spirituality from the motivations and intentions of missionaries to the experiences of Indigenous women and men. Vine Deloria Jr. (Standing Rock Sioux), Clara Sue Kidwell (Choctaw and White Earth Chippewa), George Tinker (Osage), and Homer Noley (Choctaw), for example, have demonstrated the strength and intricacy of Native religious traditions and the influence of these beliefs and rituals in shaping Indians' diverse responses to Christianity.[1] Recently Native scholars have also assessed the problematic ways in which non-Native scholars have studied Indigenous religious traditions to serve their own agendas or career ambitions. Their research has resulted in greater accountability between non-Native scholars and Native communities.[2] Well-researched case studies and monographs by non-Native scholars have also enriched the study of Indigenous religions in the United States.[3] These dynamics have led to an increasing tendency to address questions such as "What do Native people want to convey about their religious experiences to others?" and "How can their narratives deepen everyone's understanding of religion in the United States?"

Incorporating these lessons into the history curriculum in secondary schools and college classrooms, however, presents several challenges.

Native American spirituality is often neglected in most surveys of religion in the United States. Traditional Indigenous religious beliefs and Native responses to Christianity are relegated to a few sections on cross-cultural contact and missions and draw heavily from missionary records. Most accounts of Indigenous religions focus predominately on the eighteenth and nineteenth centuries, with little attention to Native American communities or their religious practices in the twentieth century.[4]

The scholarship in American religious history and Native American studies offers guiding principles for studying Native American religious experience. Below I offer suggestions for how to teach historical thinking while also engaging students with the complexity of Native spirituality in American history. These observations are offered with gratitude for the work of Native men and women whose narratives and expertise have provided the richly nuanced understanding of Native American religious beliefs and practices from which this chapter draws its recommendations. The scholarship of Dr. Brady DeSanti (Lac Courte Oreilles Ojibwe) on "Teaching Native American Religions and Philosophies in the Classroom," for example, is an invaluable resource for those seeking guidance on how to help their students understand Native American religions.[5]

Guidelines for Teaching about American Indian Religious Experiences

I suggest beginning a study of Native American spirituality by examining three issues: the prevalence of stereotypes about American Indians, the importance of place in Native experience, and the complexity of Native religious expression. One way to help students engage with these points is to present them as a framing device at the outset of a lesson or unit and then ask students to examine these themes in greater depth through a specific case study.

Stereotypes and Realities in Native American Religious Experience

Many students understand Native Americans primarily in terms of the images and descriptions about American Indians in mainstream media. These stereotypes must be acknowledged and analyzed in comparison with the realities of Native experience. In children's literature and in US history texts, Native Americans are variously depicted as "uncivilized," "innocent children of the forest," and "vanishing relics" of a distant past.[6] In American religious history, Native spirituality is often studied through the lens of missionary accounts in which Indians are portrayed as either willing converts or staunch opponents of the gospel. One way to help students identify flawed depictions of Native Americans and move beyond unhelpful dichotomies is to have them compare examples of non-Native depictions of Indian religious practices and Native accounts of religious experience (see below for more ideas).

The Importance of Place in Native American Religion

In their stories of origin and identity, Native peoples stress the importance of place. Their religious experiences are rooted in the lands their communities called home for centuries before the arrival of European settlers and the spread of Christianity. Unfortunately, many non-Native accounts ignore these distinctive traditions for a more generalized view of Indigenous religion as simply a love of nature and living things (think of Disney's *Pocahontas*). Such abstractions, however, obscure the diversity and complexity of Native religious traditions. As Devon Abbott Mihesuah (Choctaw) explains, "Each tribe has its own religious traditions, with ceremonies to mark the seasons, to give thanks, to ask for prosperous hunting and growing, in addition to specific ways to sing, dance, and to bury their dead."[7] Natives understand spirituality in terms of a person's embodied existence in a particular place and time. For Indian people, everyday actions such as eating, working, learning, and playing are all imbued with religious significance. Worship is a part of one's daily activities rather than compartmentalized into a daily or weekly regimen.

The Complexity and Diversity of Native Religious Experience

Missionary accounts that describe interactions between white evangelists and Indians often focus on the individual in their accounts of religious conversion. These narratives can provide a rich description of the challenges and obstacles to the spread of Christianity in the United States. The correspondence of white and Native believers also conveys the sincerity of religious expression and the development of the faith of both missionaries and Indians. Yet, the focus on the individual creates obstacles to understanding the breadth and depth of Indigenous religious experience. Indian people existed within a world shaped by distinctive religious traditions and complex kinship networks. Their responses to Christianity, whether acceptance, accommodation, or opposition, were shaped by their culture and relationships with other Indigenous peoples. A recognition of the importance of culture and community to Natives helps students develop a more nuanced understanding of Indigenous religious beliefs and practices.

Teaching Native Spirituality in United States History

The three themes I describe can provide a central focus for the examination of Indigenous religion in different periods in United States history. To examine these themes, a history teacher can organize the study of Native spirituality around key historical concepts, such as change over time, context, and complexity. In this way, studying Native spirituality also becomes a way to teach historical thinking.[8]

A chronological approach encourages students to understand Native religious experiences in terms of development over time and in light of particular historical contexts and could work as a single unit or be incorporated into a US history or US religious history survey. One challenge with studying Native spirituality chronologically is that the prevailing narratives of the development of the United States often emphasize the expansion of white civilization across North America (see Kim Hill's chapter for further discussion of the notion of "civilization").[9] Too often in these stories Indians become obstacles to the development of progress and democracy. The tendency to select certain Native communities to represent key historical moments can also have the limiting effect of presenting Indians as artifacts of the past. Thus, the Taino become an example of first encounters between Europeans and Indians in the fifteenth-century Caribbean. The Cherokee are utilized as the case study for Christianization and Indian removal. The Lakota represent Indian resistance with the Ghost Dance Movement. A chronological approach that discusses different historical developments in the same region is a helpful way to avoid this challenge because it enables students to see the diversity of tribal communities in one region and study how Native peoples responded differently to key changes in American history from the precontact period to the twentieth century. This strategy works especially well if the instructor and students study the region in which they currently reside because students are able to see Indians as "still here" and as people who are resilient and thriving rather than as relics from another place or time.

Case studies of Indian experience in the Great Lakes region from their earliest settlement to contemporary realities work well to illustrate these points. In the classroom, my students read narratives that emphasize Native voices and perspectives in primary and secondary sources.

Origins and Homelands

Accounts of Native American spirituality in North America must begin with Native understandings of their sacred histories and stories. A diverse range of tribal communities, including the Ojibwe, Menominee, Ho-Chunk, and Potawatomi called the Great Lakes region home long before the arrival of European settlers. Their oral traditions provide rich details about their tribes' origin in this place and their stories about relations between Indian people, the land, and its inhabitants.

Instructors can help students engage with the study of Native oral tradition by beginning with an exercise that encourages students to compare non-Native stereotypes about American Indians with Native depictions of their beliefs and practices. For example, short film clips, if taught with sensitivity and thoughtfulness, can often work well to facilitate a conversation about non-Native perceptions of Native people and their spirituality. For high school audiences, songs such as "What Makes the Red Man Red" from Disney's *Peter Pan* (1953) or "Colors of the Wind" from Disney's *Pocahontas* (1995) could be used in conjunction with narratives from Menominee, Ojibwe, or Potawatomi traditions to discuss Native American identity and values. For college students, selections from the documentary *Reel Injun* (2009) by Cree filmmaker Neil Diamond is a useful source, particularly for late twentieth-century stereotypes about American Indians. After showing the digital media, I ask students to provide concrete responses to questions such as "How do these videos depict the appearance, dress, speech, and beliefs of Native men and women?" "What do these examples reveal about non-Native assumptions about Indigenous people?"[10] Students then view short film presentations about Native spirituality from Native perspectives and discuss these questions: "How do Native men and women describe their beliefs and practices?" "How do the specific language and culture of Natives shape their religious experience?" "In what ways do these narratives challenge non-Native assumptions about Indian spirituality and culture?" For the Great Lakes region, I use two video segments from the *Tribal Histories* series produced by PBS Wisconsin: "St. Croix Ojibwe History" by elders Mitchell La Sarge and Wanda McFaggen and "Potawatomi History" by elders Jim Thunder and Mike Alloway Sr.[11] The pairing of these video resources with non-Native stereotypes about Indigenous peoples often encourages students to think more critically about their own assumptions of Native peoples and prepares them to engage in a more nuanced discussion of Native spirituality.

I also assign Native accounts of creation and tribal origins to help students understand the importance of place and historical context in Native religious experience. Two useful texts for the Great Lakes region are Simon Pokagon's account of the creation of humanity from the *Pottawatomie Book of Genesis* (1901) and Eddie Benton Banai's Ojibwe narrative of the Great Flood from the *Mishomis Book* (1988).[12] Both accounts include characters and vocabulary unfamiliar to most students, so I often provide a handout that describes key figures, including Waynaboozhoo and Wazhushk, as well as concepts such as *mino-bimaddiziwin*, "to live a good life."[13]

As students develop a more nuanced understanding of Native spirituality, they also develop historical thinking skills such as the importance of understanding the centrality of place and the complexity of Indigenous accounts of their origins. One way to begin the discussion of Pokagon and Banai's texts is to have students consider the context in which each narrative was created and then evaluate the opportunities and challenges of using oral tradition in the study of religious experience. Students can then be encouraged to contemplate questions that focus directly on the texts: "How do these stories convey Indians' view of their place in the world and the relationships among humans and the earth's other inhabitants?" "How do these texts challenge prevailing views of Native spirituality?" "How do these narratives link Indigenous identity to a particular people or place?" To facilitate student understanding of the complexity of Native religious experience, an instructor can also ask questions that analyze religious beliefs and practices in further depth, such as "In these tales, what constitutes right behavior and what are the consequences of wrongdoing?" "How do these accounts reveal agreement and disagreement with historical accounts of tribal migrations from different places to their current homelands?"[14] The latter question can be particularly valuable in helping students wrestle with issues of change and continuity over time as well as the contested nature of historical knowledge.

Cross-Cultural Contact (1603–1850)

Studying Native American spirituality in the period of cross-cultural contact entails the careful consideration of the claims and perspectives of Indians and European settlers. To encourage thoughtful engagement with Native and non-Native religious experiences, I often ask students to consider the underlying political and theological principles that shaped Native and Euro-American claims to Indigenous lands. Native American historians, for example, emphasize the ways in which Native communities in the Great Lakes created complex societies founded upon reciprocity and interdependence. Native experience recognized the important, but often different, contributions of men and women. Both were needed to survive and balanced one another in many Indian communities. Gender shaped language, identity, and governance in Indian communities—men and women might speak distinct dialects of the same language, matrilineal and patrilineal societies might determine kinship differently, and in some communities groups of women selected which men would serve as tribal leaders. Kin-based social groups also helped define Native understandings of order and harmony. Later, they shaped Native relations with Europeans whom they perceived as outsiders who could bring disorder, but who could also be incorporated into reciprocal relationships through kinship arrangements.[15]

One primary source that illustrates the importance of reciprocity and interdependence in tribal relations is the Haudenosaunee account of the creation of the Great League of Peace and the *Laws of the Confederacy* (1900). In 1900, the Six Nations Council of Grand River in Ontario appointed ten tribal chiefs to describe the formation of the Haudenosaunee league and compile a record of their system of government. After reading a short selection from this document, I divide students into small groups to analyze the duties and responsibilities delegated to one of the five nations mentioned in the document: Mohawk, Oneida, Cayuga, Seneca, and Onondaga. Students consider questions such as "How is leadership within the confederacy determined?" "How does this agreement balance the obligations and responsibilities of different nations within the confederacy?" "What rights and duties are delegated to tribal chiefs and clan mothers?" "How does the agreement address potential sources of disorder and conflict?[16]

To understand the political and religious claims that undergirded European colonization, legal scholars and historians who study European colonization in the Atlantic world use the term "Doctrine of Discovery." This concept describes the legal principles used by different European nations to justify their claims over Indigenous peoples and their homelands. This doctrine rested upon the assumption that "civilized" and "Christian" nations immediately acquired political, economic, and religious authority over Indigenous lands by virtue of claiming that land upon discovery by a representative of that nation. This ideology would later be incorporated in the legal principles of the United States and helped shape federal and state relations with Indian nations within its borders.[17]

Instructors can help students understand the aims and assumptions underlying colonization by assigning short excerpts from texts such as the papal bull "Inter Caetera" (1493), the *Treaty of Tordesillas* (1494), a report from Giovanni da Verrazzano to Francis I (1524), Sir Walter Raleigh's text "Of the Voyage for Guiana," (1596), and Samuel de Champlain's "Map of New France for the Literate Public" (1612). Instructors can pose a range of discussion questions that ask students to consider how historical developments shaped papal, Spanish, French, and English perceptions of power and possession at different periods and geographical locations. Students can investigate these texts for similarities and differences and evaluate the reasons for agreement and disagreement among these documents.[18]

Native responses can be more difficult to find, but Native speeches were occasionally incorporated in the records of European observers, such as Recollect missionary Chrestien LeClerq. LeClerq lived and worked among the Mi'kmaq tribe in eastern Canada and recorded a Mi'kmaq elder's reflections on civilization and the assumptions of French settlers.[19] This text provides students with the opportunity to assess a range of key issues such as "What does the Mi'kmaq elder's speech reveal about Indigenous views of political power, social relations, and religious practices among Native and French settlers?" "How does the text challenge French claims about religion and civilization?" "What are the limitations of using records, such as LeClerq's text, which transcribes a Mi'kmaq speech, to study Indigenous perspectives?"

Indian Resistance and Removal (1775–1890)

For many Native communities, the eighteenth and nineteenth centuries were a period of heightened conflict with European settlers characterized by outbreaks of war, rounds of diplomacy, and the dispossession of Native land and resources, as well as the loss of Native lives.[20] I often assign a variety of readings that encourage students to investigate Native and non-Native responses to the process of treaty making, land encroachment, and Indian removal. Ojibwe accounts, for example, show the complexity and diversity of responses among Native peoples to white settlement, land dispossession, and their forced removal from their homelands.

I typically ask students to read selections from the following texts: the Treaties of Prairie du Chien (1825–30), the autobiography of John Tanner (c. 1780–1846), and two Ojibwe narratives—the *History of the Ojibway People* by William Whipple Warren (1825–53) and *Night Flying Woman* by Ignatia Broker.[21] John Tanner, a white fur trader raised among the Ottawa and Ojibwe, provides a rich description of settler expansion and Indian removal from the perspective of a man who worked as an interpreter and trader in white and Native communities. William Whipple Warren, the son of an Ojibwe woman from the La Pointe Band in Wisconsin and an American fur trader, also worked as a trader and interpreter, but his account reflects his perspective as a mediator between Ojibwe and white cultures in this period of conflict. Broker's account of her ancestor Oona, also known as Night Flying Woman, recounts Oona's experiences among different Ojibwe communities in Minnesota and her role in helping these communities navigate the changes wrought among Indians in the late nineteenth century. These narratives also encourage students to consider how their religious beliefs and practices shaped the ways Protestants, Catholics, and traditionalists responded to the developments of this period. I ask students questions such as "How do these texts convey the motivations and claims of different Native communities, settler groups, and state and federal authorities in the contest over territories and resources in this period?" "How did religious ideology shape how white settlers and Natives responded to the settlement of Euro-Americans and the forced dispossession and migration of tribal communities?" "How do different Indigenous peoples describe their experiences of removal and remember these events today?"

Allotment and the Boarding School Era (1870–1934)

In the late nineteenth and early twentieth centuries, tribal communities worked assiduously to maintain aspects of their culture as they sought to preserve their claim to their homelands or settled in new territories. As the military conflicts of the mid-nineteenth century ended, Indigenous people faced new pressures by federal and state officials to assimilate to mainstream life in the United States. New policies were designed to deal with Indian resistance on reservations and encourage assimilation. Federal acts such as the Dawes Allotment Act (1887) sought to force Natives to adhere to American ideas of individual property rights, agricultural cultivation, and social customs. In the same period, Indian boarding schools, many run by Protestant and Catholic missionaries, sought to provide an education for Indian children that would encourage their assimilation. Federal law mandated attendance at these schools, and children were often removed from their families and communities for years during their education. At boarding school, Native children faced multifaceted attacks on their culture and identity. They were given new "English" names, forced to cut their hair and dress in uniforms, and punished for speaking their Native languages or practicing tribal customs.[22]

Native accounts of the process of this period for the Great Lakes Region include several autobiographies that describe how Native children and their parents responded to the development of boarding schools and the pressures of acculturation. One useful exercise for this period is to ask students to evaluate how white and Native accounts describe the aims and impact of Indian education on Native communities. Reading these texts can help students develop an awareness of the historical context that shaped government policies toward Indians while also emphasizing the complexity of Native responses to such initiatives. Reports of white administrators such as Merrill E. Gates, college president and educational reformer, and Captain Richard Pratt, superintendent of the Carlisle Indian School, provide students with the opportunity to examine the context that shaped white activists' critique of the federal government's Indian policies and their reasons for advocating the dismantling of reservations and the establishment of education institutions that would encourage assimilation among Indian youth.[23]

Selections from the narratives of Night Flying Woman (White Earth Ojibwe), Mountain Wolf Woman (Winnebago), Ohiyesa, also called

Charles Eastman (Santee Sioux), and Zitkala-Ša (Yankton Dakota Sioux) show the diverse responses of Native communities to Indian education and how their cultural and religious beliefs and practices shaped and in turn were impacted by these developments.[24] Some communities, such as groups of Ojibwe, relocated to be nearer to government schools so their children could still live with their families and learn tribal ways. Others, such as the families of Mountain Wolf Woman and Zitkala-Ša, were pressured to send their children away to institutions run by missionaries or the federal government. Zitkala-Ša's narrative, for example, describes in poignant detail the ways such institutions sought to strip Indian children of their languages, cultures, and identities. In some cases, as in Ohiyesa's experience, Native Christians such as his father wanted their children to take advantage of educational opportunities and supported their attendance at preparatory schools such as Kimball Union Academy and universities such as Dartmouth College.

Teachers might ask students, "How did Native religious traditions and cultural practices shape the diverse range of responses—acceptance, accommodation, and resistance—to allotment and boarding schools?" "How do Native accounts describe continuity and change in their religious experiences in the nineteenth and early twentieth centuries?" "How did contact with other tribal communities, through Native experiences at boarding schools and with organizations such as the Society for American Indians, influence Native men and women's understanding of their identities and religious traditions?"

Self-Determination and Sovereignty in the Twentieth Century

In the twentieth century, tribal communities increasingly asserted their claims to Native territories, their sovereignty as nations, and the importance of their cultural and religious practices. In the second half of the twentieth century, developments such as the federal government's policy of termination and its relocation programs brought dislocation and economic hardship to many Native individuals and their communities. Yet, many Indians also drew upon their relationships within their tribal communities and their religious traditions to oppose termination and advocate for greater political autonomy. Native Americans in urban environments formed organizations such as the Native Indian Youth Council (NIYC) and the American Indian Movement (AIM). Native activism prompted legislation such as the Indian Self-Determination and

Educational Assistance Act (1975), the Indian Child Welfare Act (1978), the American Indian Religious Freedom Act (1978), and the Native American Grave Protection and Repatriation Act (1990).[25]

Primary sources that discuss Native spirituality in this period range from autobiographies, edited collections of oral histories, and multimedia resources.[26] To discuss Native activism in the Great Lakes region, I often use short documentaries that highlight how the beliefs and practices of Native communities have shaped their responses to contemporary challenges.

The documentary *Wounded Warriors* was produced in partnership between PBS Wisconsin and the Menominee tribe in 2011. It incorporates interviews with Menominee elders and veterans to discuss warrior traditions among the Menominee, the high rate of Native enlistment in the armed forces, and their role in the Vietnam, Iraq, and Afghanistan conflicts. It chronicles efforts among Menominee veterans to use traditional practices to heal the emotional, mental, and physical wounds that often impact Native veterans and their families.[27]

To help students understand the importance of treaty rights to Native communities and their preservation of natural resources, I often ask students to view *Manoomin: Food That Grows on the Water* (2019) and read excerpts from Thomas Pecore Weso's *Good Seeds: A Menominee Indian Food Memoir*. These resources incorporate interviews with elders from the Sokaogon Chippewa (Mole Lake Ojibwe) and Menominee communities to discuss the centrality of wild rice to tribal culture and their efforts to preserve this resource for future generations.[28]

Another useful account is the story of Arlene Blackdeer, an educator and language apprentice for the Hoocak Waaziija Haci Language program created by the Ho-Chunk Nation of Wisconsin. Blackdeer describes the program's efforts to connect Ho-Chunk youth with elder Native speakers to strengthen their language skills. These youth apprentices become teachers to other students in Ho-Chunk language classes in the tribal community. The documentary vividly demonstrates the connection between language, culture, and spirituality for many Native communities and the vital role of elders in conveying cultural knowledge to multiple generations.[29]

For discussions of how Native spirituality shapes contemporary Indian life, I often ask students to reflect individually and in small groups on these questions: "How do Native traditions inform how Indians define and respond to the challenges confronting Indigenous people in contemporary society?" "What developments have shaped Native religious expression in different communities in the late twentieth and early twenty-first centuries?" "How do Indians convey a sense of change and continuity in their religious beliefs in their narratives?"

Conclusion

The inclusion of the study of Native American spirituality enriches our understanding of the diverse forms of religious expression in United States history. Emphasis on the voices and perspectives of Indian men and women, in comparison with non-Native accounts, provides teachers and students with a more complete and nuanced understanding of the beliefs and practices of different tribal communities. Consideration of key principles such as the prevalence of stereotypes in the depictions of Native peoples, the importance of place in Indian spirituality, and the diversity of religious expression within tribal communities can helpfully frame the examination of Native American religious traditions. Studies that include texts that span the breadth of American history from early accounts of tribal origins to twentieth-century reflections on Indian life offer a useful corrective to the tendency to depict Natives and their religious traditions as relics of a distant past. Native women and men demonstrate in these accounts the resilience of Indigenous societies and the flourishing of Native beliefs and practices throughout North American history.

ADDITIONAL RESOURCES

DeSanti, Brady, and Kristofer Ray, eds. *Understanding and Teaching Native American History.* Madison: University of Wisconsin Press, 2022.

Martin, Joel. *The Land Looks After Us: A History of Native American Religion.* New York: Oxford University Press, 2001.

Pesantubbee, Michelene. *Choctaw Women in a Chaotic World: The Clash of Cultures in the Colonial Southeast.* Albuquerque: University of New Mexico Press, 2005.

Smoak, Gregory E. *Ghost Dances and Identity: Prophetic Religion and American Indian Ethnogenesis in the Nineteenth Century.* Berkeley: University of California Press, 2006.

Tedlock, Dennis, and Barbara Tedlock, eds. *Teachings from the American Earth: Indian Religion and Philosophy.* New York: Liveright, 1975.

Treat, James. *Around the Sacred Fire: Native Religious Activism in the Red Power Era.* New York: Palgrave Macmillan, 2003.

NOTES

1. See Vine Deloria Jr., *God Is Red: A Native View of Religion* (New York: Putnam, 2003); James Treat, ed., *Native and Christian* (New York: Routledge, 1995); Clara Sue Kidwell, Homer Noley, and George Tinker, eds., *A Native American Theology* (Maryknoll, NY: Orbis, 2001).

2. Devon Mihesuah, ed., *Natives and Academics: Researching and Writing about American Indians* (Lincoln: University of Nebraska Press, 1998); Linda Tuhiwai Smith, *Decolonizing Methodologies: Research and Indigenous Peoples* (London: Zed Books, 2012); Waziyatawin Angela Wilson, "Indigenous Knowledge Recovery Is Indigenous Empowerment," *American Indian Quarterly* (2004) 28, no. 3–4 (2004): 359–72; Susan Miller and James Riding In, eds., *Native Historians Write Back: Decolonizing American Indian History* (Lubbock: Texas Tech University, 2011); Christopher Vecsey, *The Paths of Kateri's Kin* (Notre Dame, IN: University of Notre Dame Press, 1997); Michael McNally, *Honoring Elders: Aging, Authority, and Ojibwe Religion* (New York: Columbia University Press, 2009); Julie Cruikshank, Angela Sidney, Kitty Smith, and Annie Ned, *Life Lived Like a Story: Life Stories of Three Yukon Native Elders* (Lincoln: University of Nebraska Press, 1992).

3. Michael D. McNally, "The Practices of Native American Christianities," in *American Christianities: A History of Dominance and Diversity*, ed. Catherine Brekus and W. Clark Gilpin (Chapel Hill: University of North Carolina, 2011), 59–75; Joel Martin, *The Land Looks After Us: A History of Native American Religion* (New York: Oxford University Press, 2007). For a summary of Native American religion for secondary students and teachers, see Joel Martin, *Native American Religion* (New York: Oxford University Press, 1999). See also Joel Martin and Mark Nicholas, eds., *Native Americans, Christianity, and the Reshaping of the American Religious Landscape* (Chapel Hill University of North Carolina Press, 2010); Richard Pointer, *Encounters of the Spirit: Native Americans and European Colonial Religions* (Bloomington: Indiana University Press, 2007); Sergei Kan, *Memory Eternal: Tlingit Culture and Russian Orthodox Christianity through Two Centuries* (Seattle: University of Washington Press, 2015); Nancy Shoemaker, "Kateri Tekawitha's Tortuous Path to Sainthood," in *Negotiators of Change: Historical Perspectives on Native American Women*, ed. Nancy Shoemaker (New York: Routledge, 1995), 49–71.

4. For a substantive text that incorporates discussion of Native American spirituality, see Jon Butler, Grant Wacker, and Randall Balmer, eds. *Religion in American Life: A Short History* (New York: Oxford University Press, 2011).

5. Brady De Santi, "Teaching Native American Religions and Philosophies in the Classroom," in *Understanding and Teaching Native American History*, eds. Kristopher Ray and Brady DeSanti (Madison, WI: University of Wisconsin Press, 2022), 198–213.

6. Native writers have produced several invaluable resources that discuss the problem of Native American stereotypes in American literature and US history. For elementary and secondary students, a useful resource is the National Museum of the American Indian text *Do All Indians Live in Tipis?* (New York: HarperCollins, 2007). For college classrooms, several recent monographs analyze the prevailing stereotypes and realities of Native communities. See Devon A. Mihesuah, *American Indians: Stereotypes and Realities* (Atlanta, GA: Clarity Press, 1996); Anton Treuer, *Everything You Wanted to Know about Indians but Were Afraid to Ask* (St. Paul: Minnesota Historical Society, 2012); Philip J. Deloria, *Playing Indian* (New Haven, CT: Yale University Press, 1998); Deloria, *Indians in Unexpected Places* (Lawrence: University Press of Kansas, 2004).

7. Mihesuah, *American Indians Stereotypes and Realities*, 71.

8. Thomas Andrews and Flannery Burke, "What Does It Mean to Think Historically?," AHA Perspectives on History, January 2007, https://www.histo rians.org/Perspectives/issues/2007/0701/0701tea2.cfm.

9. Waziyatawin Angela Wilson, "American Indian History or Non-Indian Perceptions of American Indian History?," *American Indian Quarterly* 20, no. 1 (1996): 3–5; Donald Fixico, ed. *Rethinking American Indian History* (Albuquerque: University of New Mexico Press, 1997); Susan Sleeper-Smith, Juliana Barr, Jean M. O-Brien, Nancy Shoemaker, and Scott Manning Stevens, eds., *Why You Can't Teach United States History without American Indians* (Chapel Hill: University of North Carolina Press, 2015).

10. See "What Makes the Red Man Red," from *Peter Pan*, Walt Disney Productions (Burbank, CA: Walt Disney Home Video, 2007); "Colors of the Wind," from *Pocahontas*, Walt Disney Productions (Burbank, CA: Walt Disney Home Video, 2005); Neil Diamond et al., *Reel Injun* (New York: Lorber HT Digital 2009).

11. *Tribal Histories of Wisconsin*, PBS Wisconsin (2015–17), https://pbswis consin.org/watch/tribal-histories/.

12. Eddie Benton Banai, "The Great Flood," excerpt from *The Mishomis Book*, Keweenaw Bay Indian Community. Natural Resources Department, accessed August 13, 2020, http://nrd.kbic-nsn.gov/sites/default/files/The-Great-Flood .pdf. See also Edward Benton-Banai, *The Mishomis Book: The Voice of the Ojibway* (St. Paul, MN: Indian Country Press, 1988); Simon Pokagon, *Pottawattamie Book of Genesis: Legend of the Creation of Man* (Hartford, MI: C. H. Engle, 1901), Newberry Library, https://archive.org/details/ayer_319_p65_p7_1901/mode/2up. See also John Low, "Transcript of the Pottawattamie Book of Genesis: Legend of the Creation of Man," in *Imprints: The Pokagon Band of the Potawatomi Indians and the City of Chicago* (East Lansing: Michigan State University Press, 2016), 197–99.

13. For a discussion of Ojibwe and Potawatomi spirituality, see Basil Johnston, *Ojibway Heritage* (New York: Columbia University Press, 1976); Thomas

Peacock and Marlene Wisuri, *Ojibwe Waasa Inaabidaa: We Look in All Directions* (St. Paul: Minnesota Historical Society Press, 2002); James A. Clifton, George L. Cornell, and James M. McClurken, *People of the Three Fires: The Ottawa, Potawatomi, and Ojibway of Michigan* (Grand Rapids: Michigan Indian Press, 1986).

14. See also Karen Tigerman, ed., *Wisconsin Indian Literature: Anthology of Native Voices* (Madison: University of Wisconsin Press, 2006). For broad surveys that include early Native narratives from different regions, see Colin Calloway, ed., *The World Turned Upside Down: Indian Voices in Early America* (New York: Bedford/St. Martin's Press, 2016), 1–39; Peter Nabokov, *Native American Testimony* (New York: Penguin, 1999), 3–20.

15. Theda Perdue and Michael Green, *North American Indians: A Very Short Introduction* (New York: Oxford University Press, 2010), 9–17.

16. Arthur C. Parker, *The Constitution of the Five Nations of the Iroquois Book of the Great Law* (Albany: New York State Museum Bulletin, no. 184 (1916): 97–113. The Oneida Nation of Wisconsin is one of the Haudenosaunee tribal communities that emphasize the Great Law of Peace and formation of the Haudenosaunee Confederacy in their tribal history. See Oneida Nation of Wisconsin, "Kayanala? Kówa—Great Law of Peace," https://oneida-nsn.gov/our-ways/our-story/great-law-of-peace/.

17. For a concise discussion of the Doctrine of Discovery, see Robert Miller, "The Doctrine of Discovery, Manifest Destiny, and American Indians," in *Why You Can't Teach United States History without American Indians*, ed. Susan Sleeper-Smith, Juliana Barr, Jean M. O'Brien, Nancy Shoemaker, and Scott Manning Stevens, eds. (Chapel Hill: University of North Carolina, 2015), 87–100; Lindsay Robertson, *Conquest by Law: How the Discovery of America Dispossessed Indigenous Peoples of the Land* (Oxford: Oxford University Press, 2005). For Native scholarship on the Doctrine of Discovery, see Susan Miller, "Native Historians Write Back," *Wicaso Sa Review: A Journal of Native American Studies* 24, no. 1 (2009): 25–45; Mark Charles and Soong-Chan Rah, *Unsettling Truths: The Ongoing Dehumanizing Legacy of the Doctrine of Discovery* (Downers Grove, IL: InterVarsity Press, 2019).

18. "Inter Caetera" in The Doctrine of Discovery (1493), the Gilder Lehrman Institute of American History, https://www.gilderlehrman.org/history-resources/spotlight-primary-source/doctrine-discovery-1493; "The Treaty of Tordesillas (1494)," The Avalon Project: Documents in Law, History, and Diplomacy, Lillian Goldman Law Library, Yale Law School, Yale University, https://avalon.law.yale.edu/15th_century/mod001.asp; "Letter from Giovanni da Verrazzano to Francis I (1524)," American Beginnings, 1492–1690, the National Humanities Center, https://nationalhumanitiescenter.org/pds/amerbegin/contact/text4/verrazzano.pdf; Sir Walter Raleigh, "Of the Voyage for Guiana (ca. 1596)," in *The Discovery of Guiana by Sr. Walter Raleigh*, ed. Benjamin Schmidt

(New York: Bedford/St. Martin's, 2008), 136–40; Samuel de Champlain, "A Map of New France for the Literate Public," in *Samuel de Champlain: Founder of New France*, ed. Gayle K. Brunelle (New York: Bedford/St. Martin's, 2012), 52–53.

19. Chrestien LeClerq, *New Relation of Gaspesia, with the Customs and Religion of the Gaspesian Indians*, trans. and ed. William F. Ganong (Toronto: Champlain Society, 1910), 104–6.

20. Calloway, *The World Turned Upside Down*, 78–79, 139–42, 150–52, 165–66, 187–90; Timothy J. Shannon, ed., *The Seven Years' War in North America: A Brief History with Documents* (New York: Bedford/St. Martin's, 2014); Amy S. Greenberg, *Manifest Destiny and American Territorial Expansion: A Brief History with Documents* (New York: Bedford/St. Martin's 2012). In the Great Lakes region, Native accounts of resistance and removal include Daniel McDonald, *Removal of the Pottawattomie Indians from Northern Indiana* (Plymouth, IN: D. McDonald, 1898); Gary Clayton Anderson and Alan Woolworth, eds., *Through Dakota Eyes: Narrative Accounts of the Minnesota Indian War of 1862* (St. Paul: Minnesota Historical Society, 2010).

21. Many treaties associated with Native land are available online at the following sites: "Why Treaties Matter — Self Government in Dakota and Ojibwe Nations," Minnesota Indian Affairs Council, the Minnesota Humanities Center, Smithsonian Museum of the American Indian, https://www.mnhum.org/program/why-treaties-matter/; "Documents Relating to Indian Affairs," Digital Collections of the University of Wisconsin–Madison Libraries, University of Wisconsin Madison, https://uwdc.library.wisc.edu/collections/History/Indian TreatiesMicro/. See also John Tanner, *The Falcon* (New York: Penguin, 1994); William Warren, *History of the Ojibway People*, ed. Theresa Schenck (St. Paul Minnesota Historical Society Press, 2009); Ignatia Broker, *Night Flying Woman: An Ojibway Narrative* (St. Paul: Minnesota Historical Society Press, 1983). John Tanner and William Warren's texts are also available through Google Books: John Tanner, *A Narrative of the Captivity and Adventures of John Tanner* (London, 1830); William Warren, *History of the Ojibways (St. Paul, MN: Minnesota Historical Society, 1885)*.

22. See Frederick Hoxie, *The Final Promise: The Campaign to Assimilate the Indians, 1888–1920* (Lincoln: University of Nebraska Press, 1984); David Adams, *Education for Extinction: American Indians and the Boarding School Experience, 1875–1928* (Lawrence: University Press of Kansas, 1995); Brenda Child, *Boarding School Seasons: American Indian Families, 1900–1940* (Lincoln: University of Nebraska Press, 1998); K. Tsianina Lomawaima, *The Called It Prairie Light: The Story of the Chilocco Indian School* (Lincoln: University of Nebraska Press, 1994).

23. Merrill E. Gates, "Land and Law as Agents in Educating Indians," *Seventeenth Annual Report of the Board of Indian Commissioners* (1885), 763–84. See also H.R. Exec. Doc. no. 1, 49th Cong., 1st Sess. (1885), available at the University of Oklahoma College of Law Digital Commons in the Indian and Aboriginal Law

Collection, https://digitalcommons.law.ou.edu/cgi/viewcontent.cgi?article=6768 &context=indianserialset; Captain Richard Pratt, "Kill the Indian, and Save the Man" (1892), at History Matters: The U.S. Survey Course on the Web, http://historymatters.gmu.edu/d/4929.

24. See Broker, *Night Flying Woman*, 63–101; Nancy Oestreich Lurie, ed., *Mountain Wolf Woman, Sister of Crashing Thunder: The Autobiography of a Winnebago Indian* (Ann Arbor: University of Michigan Press, 1961), 18–28; Charles Eastman, *From Deep Woods to Civilization: Chapters in the Autobiography of an Indian* (Boston: Little, Brown, 1916), 16–35, 59–88; Zitkala-Ša, *American Indian Stories, Legends, and Other Writings* (New York: Penguin, 2003), 87–114.

25. Vine Deloria, *The Nations Within: The Past and Future of American Indian Sovereignty* (New York, Pantheon, 1984); Donald Fixico, *Indian Resilience and Rebuilding: Indigenous Nations in the Modern American West* (Tucson: University of Arizona Press, 2013); Kathleen Fine-Dare, *Grave Injustice: The American Indian Repatriation Movement and NAGPRA* (Lincoln: University of Nebraska Press, 2002); Paul Chaat Smith and Robert Allen Warrior, *Like a Hurricane: The Indian Movement from Alcatraz to Wounded Knee* (New York: New Press, 1996); David Wilkins and K. Tsianina Lomawaima, *Uneven Ground: American Indian Sovereignty and Federal Law* (Norman: University of Oklahoma Press, 2001); Brian Hosmer and Colleen O'Neill, eds., *Native Pathways: American Indian Culture and Economic Development in the Twentieth Century* (Boulder: University of Colorado Press, 2004).

26. See Ada Deer, *My Fight for Native Rights and Social Justice* (Norman: University of Oklahoma Press, 2019); Dennis Banks, *Ojibwa Warrior: Dennis Banks and the Rise of the American Indian Movement*, with Richard Erdoes (Norman: University of Oklahoma Press, 2011); Louise Erdrich, *Books and Islands in Ojibwe Country* (Washington, DC: National Geographic Books, 2003). See also Anton Treuer, ed., *Living Our Language: Ojibwe Tales and Oral Histories*; L. Gordon McLester III and Laurence Hauptman, eds,. *A Nation within a Nation: Voices of the Oneidas in Wisconsin* (Madison: Wisconsin Historical Society Press, 2014); Terry Straus, ed., *Native Chicago* (Chicago: Albatross Press, 2002).

27. *Wounded Warriors*, PBS Wisconsin, 2011. https://wisconsinfirstnations.org/wounded-warriors/.

28. *Manoomin: Food That Grows on the Water*, The Ways, PBS Wisconsin Education, https://wisconsinfirstnations.org/ways-manoomin-food-grows-water/; Thomas Pecore Weso, *Good Seeds: A Menominee Indian Food Memoir* (Madison: Wisconsin Historical Society Press, 2016).

29. *Language Apprentice: Bringing Back the Ho-Chunk Language*, The Ways, PBS Wisconsin Education, https://wisconsinfirstnations.org/ways-language-apprentice-bringing-back-ho-chunk-language/.

Teaching American Islam in the American History Classroom

JACLYN A. MICHAEL

The historian of religion J. Z. Smith asserted that the crucial task in the academic study of religion is to make the familiar strange, and the strange familiar.[1] There is perhaps no other topic in American history for which this undertaking is more relevant than teaching about American Islam. Students come to the classroom today with more information—and disinformation—about Islam and Muslims than ever before. They have ideas about what they think America is, and about what Islam is, and they often assume these two are separate categories of experience.[2]

In my teaching on American Islam, I put the voices and diverse experiences of American Muslims at the center of our learning. In this essay I discuss three themes of that formative past, focusing on strategies and primary sources that have proved effective in the classroom. The origins of American Islam in the Atlantic slave trade, Black American Muslim activism in the twentieth-century civil rights era, and American Muslim responses to 9/11 are key units in a course in which I bring attention to American Muslim voices through the use of primary source materials and varieties of media. My emphasis on diverse Muslim voices and experiences serves as a primary method for dismantling stereotypes and Islamophobic arguments against Muslims belonging in an American context. Highlighting the contributions and diversity of the American Muslim community as voiced and experienced by Muslims themselves ultimately challenges how Islam and Muslims are constructed as the monolithic, unfamiliar, illiberal other.

Builders of a Nation: The Origins of American Islam in the Atlantic Slave Trade

I introduce the history of American Islam with stories of Muslims who were forcefully brought to North America through the Atlantic slave trade. Scholars of this historical period estimate that up to 10 percent of slaves taken from the African continent were Muslim.[3] Much of what we know about these African Muslims is based on their diaries and artifacts, such as amulets and objects decorated with written verses of the Qur'an. Oral histories gathered in the 1930s by members of the Georgia Writers Project include memories of African Muslim women living on the Georgia coast who prayed five times a day, engaged in meditative *dhikr* rituals, and wore hijabs.[4] These histories document the earliest Muslim contributions to the very building of America in their labor as slaves and suggest new ways for students to understand American slavery.

Other useful sources to illustrate the roles of African Muslims in early American history include the writings and works of Omar ibn Sayyid. A well-known Muslim slave due in large part to his 1831 autobiography, Sayyid's account is the only known slave memoir to exist that was written in Arabic.[5] Sayyid was born in 1770 and lived in the Fulani community in what today is Senegal. He received an education in the recitation and interpretation of the Qur'an, as well as the *hadith* literature (accounts of what the Prophet Muhammad said and did compiled by his close companions). In 1807 he was captured in West Africa and enslaved in Charleston, South Carolina. After severe mistreatment from his first master, Omar escaped, was caught, and was subsequently jailed. While imprisoned, Omar used dirt from the floor to write verses of the Qur'an in Arabic on the jail walls. This gained the attention of prominent leaders and, later, abolitionists. Upon his release sixteen days later, Omar was sent to work in a North Carolina household, where he remained for the rest of his life.

Letters written by Omar ibn Sayyid were translated into English and circulated within abolitionist networks. Sayyid became known in elite circles for being a literate slave as well as a Muslim. While it is said that he converted to Christianity later in life, there is doubt that Omar would have fully abandoned his Muslim identity.[6] In his narration of his life, Omar offers an important clue. After calling on the name of Allah, the compassionate and the merciful (a standard Muslim invocation), Omar provided a commentary on verses from the sixty-seventh chapter of the Qur'an, "Surat al-Mulk" ("The Sovereignty"). Themes in Omar's discussion, and this particular chapter, include the idea that only Allah has sovereignty over humanity and all creation. Allah's power and authority over all things is central to Islamic discourse and practice and serves as a provocative reminder in a situation of enslavement. Omar ibn Sayyid's reference to this belief as he recounts his life serves a dual purpose as both a testimony to his Muslim identity and a critique of the ideology of slavery in colonial America.

There are many materials on enslaved Muslims easily accessible in print and on the internet.[7] Memoirs from the life of Auyba Suleyman Diallo, a slave educated in the Qur'an and Arabic, are available as an online resource on the National Humanities Center's website.[8] The autobiography of Omar ibn Sayyid is available in an English translation that includes several essays that provide historical context.[9] The Library of Congress has made available online the Omar Ibn Said Collection, a set of nearly forty original documents available in digital format, in English and Arabic.[10] The College of Charleston's Lowcountry Digital History Initiative includes information about the lives of less-famous African Muslims who lived on the Georgia Sea Islands, mentioned earlier in this chapter.[11] A helpful classroom exercise is to compare images of the first page of the Arabic and English language versions of Omar's biography. Without translating the Arabic, I ask students who they think Omar's intended audience was, and who would have been interested in the English version translated by Henry Cotheal. We consider how the Arabic version suggests a reader who was also literate in Arabic and that Omar wanted to limit his autobiography's audience to that readership. I also ask students how the experiences and writings of Muslim slaves change their assumptions about literacy and religiosity in the African slave community. The experiences of these earliest American Muslims should prompt students to reflect on how they illustrate the diverse religious character of this era of American life. Literate and educated Muslim slaves such as Omar ibn Sayyid also contradict the narrative that slaves lacked knowledge of reading, writing, and culture.

The Inspiration of Islam: American Muslims and the Civil Rights Era

In the 1950s and 1960s, Muslims were among the leading voices of Black American activism. They often converted to Islam early in their adult lives and drew on Islamic resources to construct identities for Blacks that were Islamic and American. Islam has long been a resource for Black American religious protest and for expressions of Black cultural power. In context of the Great Migration (roughly 1910 to 1970) of Blacks fleeing the Jim Crow South seeking new opportunities in the urban North and West, Black American Muslim leaders articulated a new, empowering identity for Black Americans that was also authentically Islamic.[12] These Muslims drew from Islamic values and authoritative texts to develop programs of liberation from racial and gendered oppression. One such Black American Muslim leader was Malcolm X. Born Malcolm Little in 1925 in Nebraska, he converted to Islam while imprisoned for larceny in Boston. His connections to Elijah Muhammad and the Nation of Islam began as a series of letters between himself and Muhammad. The Nation of Islam combines core Islamic practices such as ritual prayer, fasting, and pilgrimage to Mecca with a political program of Black activism and uplift. Theologically, the Nation teaches that Blacks are inherently divine and superior to whites, which is controversial for many Muslims because it leads to the divinization of figures other than God.[13]

After his release from jail in 1952, Malcolm became a formal leader in the Nation and was designated the head of two of the Nation's organizational temples, one in Boston and the other in Harlem. Malcolm's contributions to the Nation's development were significant; under his leadership, the community grew to nearly forty thousand members by 1960. Malcolm ended his association with the Nation in 1964 due to fundamental differences with Elijah Muhammad. Later that year, he went on his first *hajj* pilgrimage to Mecca. Now named Al-Hajj Malik Al-Shabazz, he actively worked in the Black American Sunni community until his assassination in 1965. Malcolm's trajectory from a convert to a leader in the Nation of Islam to his later break with that community is well-known to students today in part due to the popularity of his autobiography. However, the ways in which Islam influenced his life and his activism are often not as well known.

In order to show students how being Muslim informed Malcolm's American identity, I assign the portions of his autobiography in which he describes his experience of going on the *hajj* pilgrimage.[14] Recounting the words of a letter he wrote to his wife while on the journey, Malcolm described his amazement at the unity of Muslims in Mecca, in spite of their diverse races and ethnicities. He testified that this literal demonstration of religious and racial solidarity challenged the seemingly inherent nature of racial disunity shaped by his American experience:

> America needs to understand Islam, because this is the one religion that erases from its society the race problem. Throughout my travels in the Muslim world, I have met, talked to, and even eaten with people in America who would have been considered "white" —but the "white" attitude was removed from their minds by the religion of Islam. I have never before seen *sincere* and *true* brotherhood practiced by all colors together, irrespective of their color.[15] (Emphasis in original)

He concluded with the assertion that if more Americans affirmed the oneness of a monotheistic God, it would lead them also to recognize the fundamental oneness of humanity, irrespective of race. Recalling how American social life was dominated by the civil rights movement when Malcolm wrote these words in 1964, I discuss with students how going on the pilgrimage and literally experiencing the unity of the Muslim community in the holy city of Mecca allowed Malcolm to reframe how he understood racial strife in America. I conclude by offering a rejoinder to how Malcolm's description of Muslim unity irrespective of color depicts a diverse religious community in idealized language. As with any social group, marginalization and discrimination based on race and other identity categories also exist within the Muslim community.

My emphasis on the histories of Black American Muslims who participated in the civil rights movement places Muslims at the center of our learning and discussion. This shift in framing reveals how Black American Muslims created American institutions such as religious schools and newspapers, thus participating in the continued building of the nation. They also further developed America's unique religious fabric as their communities and institutions grew. American Muslims such as Malcolm X were convinced that Americans had something to learn from Islam, because its emphasis on unity could provide a new way forward toward greater racial equity. The idea that Islamic values could inform American discourse is provocative and generates reflection on how conceptions of America and Islam are often constructed as two separate categories of experience.

American Muslim Reactions to 9/11:
Turning Fear into Funny

Like all Americans, Muslims also had strong and emotional reactions to the events of September 11, 2001 (9/11). Yet in my teaching and public outreach, I find that many have not considered how American Muslims themselves felt about and reacted to the terror attacks. Putting American Muslim voices at the center of our learning reveals that they were just as fearful and outraged as other Americans. Documentaries and films are some of the more effective ways to allow American Muslim perspectives on the events of 9/11 to be at the center of that discussion. A useful series is PBS's *America at a Crossroads*, which is a collection of twenty documentaries on the impact of 9/11 around the world and in America. In one episode, several American Muslims are interviewed about how they felt on that day.[16] These Americans described the fear they experienced going to a public mosque, feeling afraid to wear a headscarf in public, and told their stories of being profiled and interrogated at American airports. I use sources such as these to give students the opportunity to discover Muslim voices often overlooked in teaching and learning about that event. This practice can serve to humanize a community that is often dehumanized in the media and in political discourse.

One of the most engaging topics in this unit is Muslim American stand-up humor. These men and women participate in the discourse of Muslim belonging by turning fearmongering into an opportunity to laugh at the absurdities behind these attitudes.[17] Minorities participating in publicly performed humor is part of a long American tradition of comedy that documents cultural critique, assimilation, and social anxieties.[18] While Muslim humor certainly existed prior to 9/11, that event threw American Muslims into the cultural spotlight and focused new, and generally suspicious, public attention on them.[19] Muslim stand-up comics are taking advantage of this attention and humorously debate the stereotypes and realities of American life and the Muslim place in American society.

In his performances, comedian Azhar Usman tells a joke that addresses the elephant in the room: negative associations with being Muslim. "I'm going to do something you've never seen a Muslim do before!" Usman exclaims. He pauses, grins broadly, and continues: "Smile!"[20] Sociologist Mucahit Bilici has described the post-9/11 situation of American Muslims as one that is defined by "negative charisma," and it is precisely this relevance that comedians such as Usman seize upon and invert in order to produce laughs and new understandings about Islam and Muslims.[21] Comic Maysoon Zayid points out the incongruities used to define her in jokes about the supposed threat she presents to public safety at the airport. Zayid has cerebral palsy, and she jokes about how this condition serves to deepen others' suspicions that she is up to something:

> So I walk in and they see an Arab trying to board a plane. But as I mentioned before I have cerebral palsy, which means I shake all the time. So they don't see just an Arab, they see a shaky Arab, and they're like, that bitch is nervous! And I'm usually crying also, because I'm terrified of flying. And the reason I'm terrified of flying is because I know that if God forbid, the plane I'm on crashes *they will blame me*.[22]

In this joke, Zayid reverses the dread behind the assumption that an Arab in an airport is a terrorist by emphasizing her anxieties about flying. Through sharing her palsy and her own unease, Zayid cultivates empathy from an audience that might be more inclined to fear someone who looks like her. Muslims at the airport is a common theme in the joking repertoire of comics who embody the racialized idea of a Muslim threat to security.[23] They use the comedic strategy of inversion to reveal the absurdities that inform how Americans come to understand Muslims and their relationships to public life within public spaces of surveillance.

The subjects of 9/11, terrorism, and Islamophobia can be difficult topics in the American classroom today. Humor and jokes offer a relief from the heaviness of these topics and are very engaging for students. Performances of Muslim American comics are often easily found on YouTube, Netflix, and other social media. The "Allah Made Me Funny" troupe is featured in a 2008 documentary that is widely available in university and local libraries.[24] These comics and others are featured in the episode on Muslim American comedy that is part of the *America at a*

Crossroads series.[25] Instructors may need to guide students in dissecting the details and contexts of this humor. Students are eager to discuss the role that stand-up humor plays in American social life beyond just being something that makes us laugh. I ask if students feel that stand-up humor can also make us think, and what the many takeaways might be for audiences. We also compare the fear of American Muslim responses to 9/11 with the funny assertiveness of this public humor. There is perhaps no other field of cultural production that is more American than stand-up comedy. The popularity of Muslims in this performance genre provides engaging primary sources for helpful reflection on the question of how Muslims belong in America today.

Centering Muslims in an American History Course

Teaching the Muslim history of the United States is essential in the American classroom, especially in light of continuing Islamophobia even at the highest levels of national politics.[26] The claim that Muslims are not American informs many anti-Muslim attitudes, yet the historical sources directly contradict assertions such as this. In this essay, I advocate for a course on American history that centers the voices and experiences of American Muslims in order to respond to the contexts that shape how and what our students know about Islam and Muslims. Important takeaways include the long history of American Islam, which began with the labor of African Muslim slaves before America was a nation. Islamic concepts inspired Black American activism during the civil rights era, and Muslims were some of the leading voices of movements against oppression. Muslim Americans have not been silent in the years following 9/11, when they are often the targets of public humiliation, racial profiling, disproportionate policing and surveillance, and hate crimes.

A survey of American history from this minority perspective reveals Muslim contributions to the very foundations of what America is today. The Islamic history of America shows that Muslims helped to build America, that Muslim leaders shaped American civic discourses and institutions, and that Muslims are prominent advocates for social justice in America today. This course perspective from "below" restores humanity to communities stripped of their personhood by ideological arguments that challenge their place in American social life.

ADDITIONAL RESOURCES

Bilici, Mucahit. *Finding Mecca in America: How Islam Is Becoming an American Religion*. Chicago: University of Chicago Press, 2012.

Chan-Malik, Sylvia. *Being Muslim: A Cultural History of Women of Color in American Islam*. New York: New York University Press, 2018.

Curtis, Edward E., IV., Ed. *The Columbia Sourcebook of Muslims in the United States*. New York: Columbia University Press, 2008.

Curtis, Edward E., IV. *Muslims in America: A Short History*. New York: Oxford University Press, 2009.

GhaneaBassiri, Kambiz. *A History of Islam in America: From the New World to the New World Order*. New York: Cambridge University Press, 2010.

Khabeer, Su'ad Abdul. *Muslim Cool: Race, Religion, and Hip Hop in the United States*. New York: New York University Press, 2016.

"Islam." Pluralism Project. Harvard University. https://pluralism.org/islam.

NOTES

1. J. Z. Smith, *Relating Religion: Essays in the Study of Religion* (Chicago: University of Chicago Press, 2004), 389.

2. On teaching Islam in the post-9/11 classroom, see Brannon Wheeler, ed., *Teaching Islam* (New York: Oxford University Press, 2003); Courtney M. Dorroll, ed., *Teaching Islamic Studies in the Age of ISIS, Islamophobia, and the Internet* (Bloomington: Indiana University Press, 2019).

3. See the discussion of the problem of estimates in Sylviane A. Diouf, *Servants of Allah: African Muslims Enslaved in the Americas* (New York: New York University Press, 1998), 46–48.

4. Quoted in Edward E. Curtis IV, *Muslims in America: A Short History* (New York: Oxford University Press, 2009), 16–18. The *dhikr* ritual is meant to remember the qualities and attributes of Allah by repetition of Allah's names, short phrases, or verses from the Qur'an.

5. Curtis, *Muslims in America*, 11–14.

6. Ibid., 13. Curtis states that this autobiography is "full of dissimulation," and given the circumstances of enslavement, surely many Muslims had to conceal aspects of their religious lives.

7. The website of the National Museum of African American History & Culture's collection "African Muslims in Early America: Religion, Literacy, and Liberty" provides historical context and primary source images of diaries, Muslim prayer beads, and African Muslim portraits for use in the classroom. See "African Muslims in Early America," National Museum of African American History and Culture, July 5, 2019, https://nmaahc.si.edu/explore/stories/collection/african-muslims-early-america.

8. The sources on Diallo are available at the National Humanities Center Resource Toolbox, Becoming American: The British Atlantic Colonies, 1690–1763, "a Slave About Two Years in Maryland," accessed September 10, 2019, http://nationalhumanitiescenter.org/pds/becomingamer/growth/text5/diallo.pdf.

9. Omar Ibn Said, *A Muslim American Slave: The Life of Omar Ibn Said*, trans. Ala Alryyes (Madison: University of Wisconsin Press, 2011).

10. The archives are on the Library of Congress website of the collection, as Image 1 (first page of the English translation) and Image 16 (page of the Arabic original). See "Omar Ibn Said Collection," n.d., The Library of Congress, accessed October 30, 2019. https://www.loc.gov/collections/omar-ibn-said-collection/.

11. The Lowcountry Digital History Initiative is available at http://ldhi.library.cofc.edu. Accessed October 31, 2023.

12. On Islam as a resource, see Sylvia Chan-Malik, *Being Muslim: A Cultural History of Women of Color in American Islam* (New York: New York University Press, 2018), 4, 17. On Muslim leaders' influence, see Kambiz GhaneaBassiri, *A History of Islam in America* (New York: Cambridge University Press, 2010), 219.

13. For more on the history and theology of the Nation of Islam, see Edward E. Curtis IV, *Islam in Black America: Identity, Liberation, and Difference in African-American Islamic Thought* (Albany: State University of New York Press, 2002).

14. Malcolm X and Alex Haley, *The Autobiography of Malcolm X* (New York: Ballantine Books, 2015), 366–93.

15. Ibid., 391.

16. Ricki Green et al., "The Muslim Americans," *America at a Crossroads*, Public Broadcasting Service and WETA-TV, 2007.

17. I analyze this phenomenon and the work of several American Muslim comics in my article "American Muslims Stand Up and Speak Out: Trajectories of Humor in Muslim American Stand-up Comedy," *Contemporary Islam* 7, no. 2 (2013), 129–53.

18. For a social history of American humor see Joseph Boskin, *Rebellious Laughter: People's Humor in American Culture* (Syracuse, NY: Syracuse University Press, 1997). Glenda Carpio's *Laughing Fit to Kill: Black Humor in the Fictions of Slavery* (New York: Oxford University Press, 2008) examines the historical and contemporary role of humor in Black American culture.

19. For more on the history of humor in Muslim discourse see my article "Contemporary Muslim Comedy," in *Handbook of Contemporary Islam and Muslim Lives*, ed. Marc Woodward and Ronald Lukens-Bull, eds. (New York: Springer Reference, 2018, 1–13).

20. Azhar Usman, "Allah Made Me Funny—Azhar Usman 2/2." YouTube, accessed September 10, 2019, https://www.youtube.com/watch?v=HeHPijoJZIA.

21. Mucahit Bilici, "Muslim Ethnic Comedy: Inversions of Islamophobia," in *Islamophobia/Islamophilia: Beyond the Politics of Enemy and Friend*, ed. Andrew Shryock (Bloomington: Indiana University Press, 2010), 195–208; 197.

22. Maysoon Zaid, comedian. "Stand Up For Democracy" live performance. New York City. November 5, 2005.

23. For more examples of this type of joke, see Mucahit Bilici, *Finding Mecca in America: How Islam Is Becoming an American Religion* (Chicago: University of Chicago Press, 2012), 171–97.

24. Andrea Kalin, director, *Allah Made Me Funny* (Potomac Valls, VA: Unity Productions Foundation, 2008).

25. Glenn Baker, director and producer, *"Stand Up: Muslim American Comics Come of Age," America at a Crossroads*, WGBH Boston, Public Broadcasting Service, 2008.

26. For a historical and contemporary analysis of Islamophobia that includes discussion of successive late twentieth and early twenty-first century American presidential administrations, see Deepa Kumar, *Islamophobia and the Politics of Empire: 20 Years after 9/11* (New York: Verso Books, 2021).

Asian Religious Influences in American Life

ELIJAH SIEGLER

The theme of Asian religions in America is broad enough to be a whole volume. This chapter concentrates on the traditions of Buddhism, Hinduism, and Chinese traditional religions. There are many benefits to incorporating Asian religions in America (ARA from now on) in any US history or religion in American history survey course. ARA illuminates many key themes: Identity, immigration, race, Americanization, representation, transnationalism, and more. This chapter begins with an orienting thematic overview of the rich tapestry of Asian religious influences, followed by five "threads" of that tapestry and finally a section on resources including texts, websites, and field trips. This chapter does not focus much on the religions of Asian Americans (the majority of whom are Christian), but there are several very accessible resources to gain a quick overview.[1]

Orientations

It is important for students to understand that the US has long been involved with Asian cultures and religions. Most students will be able to name examples of Asian fashion, food, culture, and philosophy that have impacted the United States in recent years, from K-Pop to anime to pho. This fascination with the East proceeds on a venerable cycle that is often forgotten so that each Asian fad seems like an original discovery. So it is too with religious and spiritual ideas from the East. Meditation classes or yoga retreats may seem to be a recent trend, but historians have shown they held interest for small groups of Americans since the middle of the nineteenth century.

Asking your students to discuss the continuing appeal of ARA should make for a fruitful discussion. For the last few centuries, a steady coterie of Western seekers (of truth, enlightenment, escape) has found *something* in the wisdom of the East. For many, Asian religions' paths to self-knowledge and self-realization act as a corrective to Western scientific materialism on the one hand and Western religious dogma on the other. Most importantly, it is crucial that students understand that a key factor accounting for the presence of Asian religions in America is the active participation of Asian religious propagators. In other words, ARA are not just a matter of demand, but also of supply.

Although the total number of practitioners of Asian religions (primarily Buddhism and Hinduism) has been growing steadily, the percentage is small, only about 2 percent of the US population. But ARA have an importance beyond their numbers, as this chapter shows.

First Thread: Nineteenth-Century Immigration

In the nineteenth century, the dominance of Protestantism in America was threatened because of immigration, and Protestants fought back. The story of Catholic and Jewish immigration from Europe—and the images of Ellis Island and tenements in New York City—are well known. It is a shame that the story of Asian immigration to the US West Coast is less well known. It is a double shame that telling this story through the lens of religion is rarely done in high school and college courses because this material can generate discussion on not only immigration and racism, but the very definition of religion.

Although nineteenth-century America saw Buddhists arriving from Japan, and Sikhs and Hindus from India, I focus here on Chinese immigration, for which we have more documentary evidence and interpretive analysis. The first recorded migration of Chinese people to the United States mainland came in 1848, the year gold was discovered at Sutter's Creek in California. By 1880, there were over one hundred thousand Chinese residents. Most Chinese lived in California, but as a proportion to the general state population, Chinese were more prevalent in Idaho and Montana.

The Chinese brought their religion with them, but not in the same way as other immigrants to North America did. Unlike Italian Catholics, the Chinese were not accompanied by clergy, nor were they supported by ecclesiastical structures that created branch churches in the new land. Different from Jews in America, the Chinese did not set up independent temples as centers of learning. Rather, for the Chinese in America, organized religion remained in the hands of associations representing the interests of immigrants from particular clan villages (who supposedly shared a common ancestor, or lineage) or geographical areas in China. In San Francisco, for example, the six main lineage associations, known as the "Six Families," were in charge of funeral arrangements, financial security, and protection against outsider malefactors. They were also quick to build temples enshrining a patron deity of a certain region.[2] What is generally considered to be the oldest temple in San Francisco's Chinatown, the Tian Hou Temple, was built by the Sze Yap Company in 1852 and was located on the fourth floor of a narrow building on a one-block street. It is still around, and images are available online, though the common spelling now is Tin How.[3]

Tian Hou (transliterated as Tien Hau in Cantonese), which literally translates as the "Empress of Heaven," is the name of a semi-historical, virtuous maiden who was said to have lived from 960 to 987 on an island off the coast of southeastern China, and who was divinized into a patron goddess of fishermen and sea voyagers. People credit Tian Hou for safely bringing the first group of Chinese immigrants across the ocean. Thus the construction of a shrine in her honor was both recognition of her presence in the New World and a gesture of thanks for her protective influence.

By the 1880s, there were uncounted Chinese temples in small towns across the western United States, probably numbering in the hundreds. Besides Tian Hou (known as Mazu in Taiwan), other preeminent gods of Chinese America included Beidi (the God of the North), the red-faced guardian Guan Gong, and Guanyin, the Chinese version of Avalokitesvara, the Bodhisattva of Compassion. The temples were known as "Joss Houses," and the fragrant incense burning there were known as "Joss Sticks" (the word "Joss" being a corruption of the Portuguese word for God).

However, second-generation Chinese Americans, under pressure to Americanize, seemed less interested in traditional Chinese religious heritage. Hundreds of Chinatown temples throughout the American West were abandoned one by one. A few temples reopened in the 1970s as tourist attractions, selling the idea of "exotic Oriental religions," and a few more saw new life thanks to the post-1965 wave of Chinese immigration.

Teaching about nineteenth-century Chinese temples in the United States is a great way to demonstrate the continuity of Chinese religious traditions: common religious practices in these Chinese American temples include fortune telling, making sacrifices to a variety of deities, and venerating the ancestors, and we have evidence that these same practices occurred during the Shang Dynasty (1600–1046 BCE). Behind these practices, students can learn about the continuity of religious values: the respect for family lineage, the mutual dependency of the living and dead, the importance of fate. And most obviously, students will understand just how long ARA have been present.

Second Thread: The 1893 Columbian Exposition and the World's Parliament of Religions

Taking place under the auspices of the Columbian Exposition in Chicago, the 1893 World's Parliament of Religion was called by its president "an event of race-wide and perpetual significance," because it featured, for the first time, representatives of many religious traditions speaking on a more or less equal footing with their Anglo-American hosts.[4] The "ten great religions" were symbolized by the ringing of ten bells to open the Parliament. (Indigenous traditions were not among the "ten great religions.")

The Parliament brought Asian religious spokesmen for Hinduism, various branches of Buddhism, Confucianism, and Jainism to the West to present their religious beliefs on a platform shared with liberal Protestants, Catholics, and Jews. The most popular Asian delegate was a young Hindu swami named Vivekenanda (1863–1902). He presented Hinduism as a religion that was both progressively ecumenical and intensely heartfelt. After the Parliament, Vivekananda, who spoke English with fluency and eloquence, went on a lecture tour of the United States and founded the Vedanta Society, which could be considered the oldest Asian religious group in the United States that appealed to non-Asians. Today the Vedanta Society has a few thousand members in the US and around twenty centers.[5]

Notable Asian Buddhist leaders were also invited to the Parliament, including Dharmapala (1864–1933), a Theravada Sri Lankan monk, and Soyen Shaku (1859–1919), a Japanese Zen abbot. Several of Shaku's disciples immigrated to American and formed the root of most Zen lineages in the country. In the wake of the Parliament, Buddhism came to be seen by a small number of open-minded Euro-Americans as a viable life path, not just an exotic philosophy. By the turn of the twentieth century, the United States was home to perhaps two to three thousand Buddhist converts and tens of thousands more Buddhist sympathizers.

One hundred years after the original Parliament, a second was convened in Chicago, and now Parliaments of the World's Religions meet every few years in cities around the world.[6] Productive discussions can center around how the Parliament ties into ideas about American imperialism, exceptionalism, and internationalism, as well as how Asian religions were represented at the original Parliament. It is clear from their speeches the delegates emphasized the rational aspect of their tradition at the expense of the devotional. And, of course, representatives of Indigenous Asian religions were not invited at all—but their cultures were represented as part of the Exposition, at Midway Plaisance, not far from the building where the Parliament was held. Here, amid carnival rides and games of chance, visitors could gawk at living ethnographic displays—human zoos, really—with Natives of the islands of Java, Samoa, Hawaii, and many others.[7]

Third Thread: Influences of Asian Religions on American Cultural and Intellectual History

American history courses that teach important cultural and intellectual movements such as the Enlightenment, rationalism of the Founding Fathers, Transcendentalism, and the various counterculture movements of the twentieth century would deepen their students' interest by showing how Asian religions were an essential part of these movements. Also, students enjoy learning about lesser-known movements—such as the metaphysical boom of the late nineteenth century, unthinkable without the impact of ARA—because they bring out the unconventionality embedded in US history.

Students may be surprised to know that several of America's Founding Fathers had a serious intellectual interest in Asian religions. Perhaps this was because their religious and philosophical orientations were not conventionally Christian. They seemed particularly interested in Confucianism, which they took to be a religious system based on social ethics, not the worship of transcendent beings. In 1738, Benjamin

Franklin's newspaper published twenty pages of a British translation of Confucius. And in the 1810s, Thomas Jefferson and John Adams, by then former presidents, exchanged detailed letters about Hindu doctrine.[8]

European scholars translated early Buddhist and Hindu texts from Sanskrit and Pali, showed that they were more ancient than Jewish and Christian scriptures, and touted them as the very source of human religiousness. These translations made their way to America and deeply influenced the emerging Transcendentalist philosophy, which proposed a spiritual reality that could be known through intuition, as developed by Henry David Thoreau, Ralph Waldo Emerson, and others. Transcendentalists helped found the American Orientalist Society in 1842. And we know that Thoreau and Emerson read the Upanishads and the Bhagavad Gita, two important Hindu scriptures, in translation.[9]

The Transcendentalist periodical *The Dial* printed the Lotus Sutra and other Buddhist and Hindu texts. In 1878, the Transcendentalist Bronson Alcott published an American edition of *The Light of Asia*, a best-selling biography of the Buddha. It should be noted that neither Emerson, Thoreau, nor Alcott ever met a practicing Buddhist or Hindu from Asia. For them, Asian religions were purely textual phenomena.

It is far more likely students will have heard of Thoreau and Emerson than Madame Helena Blavatsky, but that makes the task of introducing her to them all the more enjoyable. Madame Blavatsky represents an exemplary American life: an immigrant who reinvented herself in America. Blavatsky cofounded the Theosophical Society in 1875, which was largely responsible for introducing popular Asian religious ideas into American culture (such as karma, nirvana, and chakra). Scholars have argued that the New Age movement of the 1970s and 1980s was a Theosophical revival movement.

Theosophists received their otherworldly wisdom from the Ascended Masters, a hierarchically organized assemblage of spiritually advanced beings devoted to the betterment of humanity. Significantly, the masters were mostly of "Oriental" origin and were sometimes seen to congregate in Tibet. Thus the Theosophical Society was seminal in popularizing the idea of Tibet as a repository for spiritual wisdom. As they introduced Buddhist and Hindu terms into the American spiritual lexicon, Theosophists were at the same time giving Asians (Indian Brahmins and Ceylonese Buddhists, mainly) new pride in their own traditions. The main institutional form of Theosophy today is the Theosophical Society of America.[10]

Colonel Henry Olcott, who cofounded the Theosophical Society with Blavatsky, later went to Ceylon (modern-day Sri Lanka), where the Buddhist monk Dharmapala became his protégé. Dharmapala went on to be an influential delegate to the 1893 Parliament in Chicago, of which another leading Theosophist, William Q. Judge, was a vice-president. Theosophy aside, the Parliament's Asian delegates were models for generations of Asian religious teachers coming to America. Other Indian masters followed the path blazed by Vivekananda. For example, Paramhansa Yogananda (1893–1952) came to the United States in 1920, founded the Self-Realization Fellowship (SRF), and published a best-selling spiritual memoir, *Autobiography of a Yogi* (1946).[11] By 1937, some 150,000 people had taken the Self-Realization Fellowship's initial correspondence course.

Meanwhile, students of Soyen Shaku went on to the found Zen Centers in New York, San Francisco, and Los Angeles in the 1920s and 1930s. A new generation of non-Asian Zen leaders studied in Japan in the 1950s, setting the scene for the "Zen boom." Indeed, in American intellectual, cultural, artistic, and history fields, Zen has exercised outsize influence, profoundly shaping the counterculture.

In the 1950s, Beat writers, such as Allen Ginsburg, Gary Snyder, and Jack Kerouac, attracted by the Zen spirit of spontaneity, its language about authenticity and of finding enlightenment inside yourself instead of outside, and its distrust of language, incorporated Buddhist themes into their poetry and novels.[12] By the late 1960s, Westerners on the whole were familiar enough with Asian ideas to create a natural market for ARA. This familiarity was due to the availability of mass-market paperback editions of Asian "spiritual classics," including the Bhagavad-Gita and the Daodejing. Other influential books included popularized explanations of Buddhism by D. T. Suzuki, a Japanese émigré who was trained in both Buddhist and Western philosophy and who, as a young man, served as Soyen Shaku's translator at the 1893 Parliament, and by Alan Watts, a British ex-Episcopalian priest. Finally, college-level courses in Buddhism and Asian religions in general became more common.

This rise of interest is often attributed to the "spiritual hunger" of the hippie/boomer generation. Both mainstream religion and consumer capitalism were seen as empty promises. Disenchanted with Western values, a noticeable minority of Westerners sought an immediate experience of ecstasy or transcendence. Gurus or masters from the East could provide these experiences through techniques of yoga, through meditation or chanting, or through direct transmission.

After the Zen boon of the 1950s and 1960s, yoga experienced yet another renaissance in the 1970s, and then another in the early 2000s. More recently, the word "mindfulness," taken from a form of Theravada Buddhist meditation, became a ubiquitous term applied to eating, parenting, and so on. Are yoga and mindfulness pure distillations of ancient Asian religious teachings, adapted for the modern world? Or are they commercialized venues that use a thin veneer of "Oriental" trappings to exploit gullible Americans? These are important questions that, in recent years, high school and college students have become more than willing to answer. Indeed, they are exhaustingly attuned to the nuances of appropriation and authenticity, and broaching these subjects is a surefire way to generate animated discussion. There are wonderful monographs, suitable for teaching more advanced students, on the Americanization of yoga and of mindfulness.[13]

Fourth Thread: Japanese Internment Camps and Other Occurrences of Prejudice against Asian Religions in America

Many Asian religious leaders felt the brunt of the anti-Asian sentiment that was running high at the turn of the twentieth century, which drew little distinction between East and South Asia. In 1882, in response to nativist pressure, Congress passed the Chinese Exclusion Act, suspending all Chinese immigration; it was the first law to prohibit the arrival of a specific ethnic group. This racist law was justified in part because Chinese were classified as "pagan." In the wake of that and other various racist laws and statutes, the Chinese American population began to drop. In 1924 the National Origins Act assigned an annual quota of zero for Chinese immigrants. In the classroom, simply mentioning Chinese people when speaking about immigration restrictions and the scientific racism of the early twentieth century will complicate the narrative.

The racist term "Yellow Peril" was coined in an editorial cartoon of 1895 depicting a terrifying Buddha menacing the Christian West.[14] It referred to the supposed dangers of Japanese and Chinese immigrants, who were seen as unable to assimilate into American culture. It saw its anti-Hindu equivalent in the common terms "The Turban Tide" and

"The Hindoo Invasion." Indeed, Vivekenanda and his successors evoked powerful antipathy from Christian missionaries, who were worried about the spreading of "Hindu Heathenism." Popular prejudice held that the swamis mostly attracted rich and gullible women.

But the most prominent example of prejudice against ARA began when, two months after the attack on Pearl Harbor, President Franklin Roosevelt signed Executive Order 9066, ordering all Japanese Americans sent to internment camps. There were ten different camps in six states, mostly in remote desert areas. Some 120,000 Americans were interned altogether, in what is widely seen as one of the most shameful episodes in US history.

All Japanese Americans were interned, regardless of their religious background (which included Catholic and Protestant), but 60 percent of Japanese Americans practiced Buddhism. Most of them belonged to the Jodo Shinshu denomination, part of Pure Land Buddhism, a mainstream school that emphasized prayers to be reborn in the pure land. Buddhist Japanese Americans were hit particularly hard by the internment. Even before Executive Order 9066 was signed, the FBI investigated Buddhist temples in America and often detained Buddhist priests for questioning. Was that calligraphic scroll really sacred scripture? It could be a secret code.[15]

Anti-Japanese sentiment increased the interest of young Japanese Americans (many of whom could not read Japanese) in Buddhism. In 1944, the American wing of the Jodo Shinshu denomination, organized in 1899 in San Francisco as the Buddhist Mission of North America, changed its name to the Buddhist Churches of America.[16] Its wartime liturgy was created by the only Jodo Shinshu priest not imprisoned in the camps: a former Jew named Julius Goldwater. The liturgy included a call-and-response, hymns, and an exhortation, all in language that echoes an American Christian church service.[17] This is a wonderful teaching moment about how Japanese Buddhists, in an effort to prove their "Americanness," made their organizational and ritual something resembling Protestantism. Many ARAs and other non-Christian religions underwent similar processes. And, of course, the internment has echoes in current political debate.[18]

While official government-sanctioned bias against ARA would never be as explicit again, prejudice continued. From the 1960s to the 1980s, much of the cultural panic about "cults" that "brainwash" American youth was based in fear and hatred of religions from Asia, whether

Hare Krishna from India or the Unification Church (better known as the Moonies) from Korea. Students might be encouraged to do web searches for recent news stories about Buddhist, Hindu, or Sikh houses of worship being vandalized. Finally, students might reflect on how classifying popular Chinese religions and Hinduism as "polytheist" puts them in tension with American missionary activities. Evangelicals continue to use words such as "idol worship," "superstition," "heathenism," and "satanism" to describe them.[19]

Fifth Thread: Post-1965 Immigration

The increase of Asian religions post-1965 was not only because of a growing interest in Asian religions, as outlined in the third thread. A decisive factor was a change in immigration law in the West. The US Immigration Act of 1965 ended the national origins quota system that had severely restricted Asian immigration since 1924. Similar immigration reforms took place around the same time in Western Europe and Canada. These changes removed race-based restrictions on immigration and allowed a substantial number of Asians, including spiritual leaders, into the West for the first time.

Tibetan Buddhist teachers first came to the West via India when they were forced out of Tibet by the 1959 Chinese Communist invasion. Post-1965 saw immigration from Theravada Buddhist countries; these immigrants were generally more traditionalist than Chinese and Japanese Buddhist immigrants from the nineteenth century, and their religious life focused on the monastery. Many of these Theravadin immigrants were refugees (from Laos, Cambodia, and Vietnam) and represented a range of ethnicities, including Sinhalese (Buddhist Sri Lankans) and Thai. These immigrant communities established temples called Wats or Viharas with monks in residence as centers for community and cultural preservation.

The well-known post-1965 ARA Hare Krishna, more formally the International Society for Krishna Consciousness (ISKCON), provides a rich case study because students can learn about how Asian religions grow and change in the American context, as well how prejudice against ARA manifests itself. The movement was founded in India by Swami Prabhupada (1896–1977). Prabhupada was an Indian businessman until he was initiated by a guru in 1933 and told to bring to the West the "Krishna Consciousness," which can be traced to a sixteenth-century

Bengali revival of a devotional form of Hinduism to Krishna, an avatar of Vishnu. Prabhupada arrived in 1965 in New York City and a year later founded the organization known as Hare Krishna.

Prabhupada quickly gathered a coterie of young Euro-Americans whom he taught to practice *sankirtana*, public singing and dancing in praise of Lord Krishna. To sing and dance in this manner was to practice *bhakti*, a Hindu term for following a path of loving devotion. This unconventional behavior, along with the male converts' shaved heads with one long lock remaining, gave the group some notoriety. By the mid-1970s, fifty ISKCON temples had been established throughout the United States, many with public vegetarian restaurants.

The late 1970s was the beginning of troubled times for ISKCON. Swami Prabhupada died without leaving a clear successor, and even before his death ISCKON's membership was in decline and its public image was tarnished. By the 1990s, leadership passed to a collective with the late Prabhupada chosen as the sole guru. Membership picked up as more and more South Asian immigrants to the West began to join, which has produced the unique situation of Euro-American gurus teaching South Asian immigrants.[20]

Although there are some easy online resources, the one indispensable text when teaching Asian religions in America is *Asian Religions in America: A Documentary History* edited by Thomas Tweed and Stephen Prothero.[21] Nothing has surpassed it since its 1999 publication. Every topic mentioned in this chapter has primary source documentation in this volume. Its range of primary documents stretch from a short "Oriental Tale" written by Benjamin Franklin in 1788 to a 1997 official pamphlet from Hsi Lai Temple in suburban Los Angeles, one of the largest Buddhist temples outside Asia. In between are newspaper and magazine articles, bills of law, letters from converts and missionaries, excerpts from the works of notable authors including Mark Twain, Walt Whitman, T. S. Eliot, and teachings of masters and gurus from ARA. The editors have written helpful introductions to each reading, as well as for each of the four parts of the chronological division. The introduction includes a ten-page overview of Asian religions, although there are better sources for such an overview.[22] One reference work, *Asian American Religious Cultures*, is also recommended for library purchase.[23]

The Pluralism Project, founded by Diana Eck, has been tracking and teaching about Asian religions in America since the early 1990s. It has a website, a textbook, and a related film.[24] Its approach is ethnographic—

an approach that works well for students, who like to learn about ARA in practice, not just in theory. Visiting websites of various denominations (see notes throughout for some examples) is an easy place to start, but if possible, field trips to local temples or meditation centers are highly recommended. These can be transformative experiences for students.

ADDITIONAL RESOURCES

Eck, Diana L. *A New Religious America: How a Christian Country Has Become the World's Most Religiously Diverse Nation.* San Francisco: Harper, 2002.

Lum, Kathryn Gin. *Heathen: Religion and Race in American History.* Cambridge, MA: Harvard University Press, 2022.

Tweed, Thomas, and Stephen Prothero, eds. *Asian Religions in America: A Documentary History.* New York: Oxford University Press, 1999.

"What Is Pluralism?" The Pluralism Project. Harvard University. Accessed March 17, 2020. http://pluralism.org/.

NOTES

1. See, for example, "Asian American Religions," Oxford Research Encyclopedia of Religion, accessed April 25, 2020, https://oxfordre.com/religion/view/10.1093/acrefore/9780199340378.001.0001/acrefore-9780199340378-e-502; "Asian Americans: A Mosaic of Faiths—Pew Research Center," accessed April 25, 2020, https://www.pewforum.org/2012/07/19/asian-americans-a-mosaic-of-faiths-overview/; "Teaching Asian American Religions and Religiosities: Guest Editor's Introduction," accessed April 25, 2020, http://rsn.aarweb.org/spotlight-on/teaching/asian-american-religions/guest-editor's-introduction.

2. Richard Madsen and Elijah Siegler, "The Globalization of Chinese Religions and Traditions," in *Chinese Religious Life*, ed. David A. Palmer, Glenn Shive, and Phillip L. Wickeri (New York: Oxford University Press, 2011), 228.

3. The best selection of images I have found is actually on Trip Advisor: "Tin How Temple," San Francisco, accessed March 17, 2020, https://www.tripadvisor.com/Attraction_Review-g60713-d557323-Reviews-Tin_How_Temple-San_Francisco_California.html.

4. John Henry Barrows, "Words of Welcome," quoted in Thomas A. Tweed and Stephen Prothero, *Asian Religions in America: A Documentary History* (New York: Oxford University Press, 1999), 128. Speeches from Soyen Shaku, Dharmapala, and Vivekenanda are also included, 130–40.

5. USA Centers, Vedanta Society of Northern California, accessed March 17, 2020, https://sfvedanta.org/resources/usa-centers/.

6. Parliament of the World's Religions, accessed March 17, 2020, https://parliamentofreligions.org/.

7. See images at The Midway Plaisance, accessed November 20, 2023, https://smarthistory.org/worlds-columbian-exposition-midway/.

8. These letters are published in Tweed and Prothero, *Asian Religions in America*, 48–51.

9. See Tweed and Prothero, *Asian Religions in America*, 92–98.

10. "Some Frequently Asked Questions about Theosophy," Theosophical Society in America, accessed March 17, 2020, https://www.theosophical.org/about/faq.

11. Yogananda's *Autobiography of a Yogi* is excerpted in Tweed and Prothero, *Asian Religions in America*, 181–84. A well-illustrated, albeit hagiographic, account of Yogananda's life can be found online at "Parahamsa Yoganda," Self-Realization Fellowship, accessed April 24, 2020, https://yogananda.org/paramahansa-yogananda.

12. Good primary sources include Kerouac's novel *Dharma Bums (1958; New York: Penguin, 2006)*, and Ginsberg and Snyder's widely-anthologized poems "Wichita Vortex Sutra" and "Smokey the Bear Sutra," respectively.

13. Andrea Jain, *Selling Yoga: From Counterculture to Pop Culture* (Oxford: Oxford University Press, 2014); and Jeff Wilson, *Mindful America: The Mutual Transformation of Buddhist Meditation and American Culture* (Oxford: Oxford University Press, 2014). See also the highly teachable documentary film *Kumaré* (directed by Vikram Gandhi, Future Bliss Films, 2011).

14. The cartoon is available at Yellow Peril-Wikipedia, accessed March 17, 2020, https://en.wikipedia.org/wiki/Yellow_Peril#/media/File:Voelker_Europas .jpg.

15. For primary sources, see Tweed and Prothero, *Asian Religions in America*, 163–72.

16. "A Buddhist Community of Friends and Families," Buddhist Churches of America, accessed March 17, 2020, https://www.buddhistchurchesofamerica.org/.

17. See Tweed and Prothero, *Asian Religions in America*, 172–77.

18. See "Advice for Modern America, from When Buddhism Was Seen as a National Threat," Lion's Roar: Buddhist Wisdom for Our Time, accessed March 17, 2020, https://www.lionsroar.com/advice-for-modern-america-from-the-painful-history-of-american-buddhism/. The classic article on religion in the internment camps is Gary Y. Okihiro, "Religion and Resistance in America's Concentration Camps," *Phylon* 45, no. 3 (1984): 220–33, accessed February 24, 2020, doi:10.2307/274406. Also highly recommended is Duncan Ryūken Williams's *American Sutra: A Story of Faith and Freedom in the Second World War* (Cambridge, MA: Harvard University Press, 2019).

19. "Using TV, Christian Pat Robertson Denounces Hinduism as 'Demonic,'" *Hinduism Today*, July 1995, accessed March 17, 2020, https://www.hinduismtoday.com/modules/smartsection/item.php?itemid=3502.

20. Edwin Bryant and Maria Ekstrand, eds., *The Hare Krishna Movement: The Postcharismatic Fate of a Religious Transplant* (New York: Columbia University Press, 2004); and ISKCON, https://www.iskcon.org/.

21. For Buddhism in America, see Peter Feuerherd, "How American Buddhism Is Like an Elephant," *JSTOR Daily*, April 10, 2018, accessed March 17, 2020, https://daily.jstor.org/american-buddhism/; Livia Gershon, "When Buddhism Came to America," *JSTOR Daily*, January 7, 2019, accessed March 17, 2020, https://daily.jstor.org/when-buddhism-came-to-america/. For Hinduism in America, see Amanda Lucia, "Hinduism in America," *Oxford Research Encyclopedia of Religion*, accessed March 17, 2020, https://oxfordre.com/religion/view/10.1093/acrefore/9780199340378.001.0001/acrefore-9780199340378-e-436.

22. See, for example, the Oxford University Press series "Very Short Introductions" or an introductory textbook on Asian religions, such as Randall Nadeau, *Asian Religions: A Cultural Perspective* (Malden, MA: Wiley-Blackwell 2014).

23. Jonathan H. X. Lee et al., *Asian American Religious Cultures* (Santa Barbara, CA: ABC-CLIO 2015).

24. The Pluralism Project, accessed March 17, 2020, http://pluralism.org/; Diana L. Eck, *A New Religious America: How a Christian Country Has Become the World's Most Religiously Diverse Nation* (San Francisco: Harper, 2002.; the film is *Becoming the Buddha in LA*, available at https://vimeo.com/173501793.

Teaching the Jewish Experience in the American History Classroom

Themes and Sources

JONATHAN B. KRASNER

Introduction

When the board members of Shaare Tefila Congregation, in Silver Spring, Maryland, exited their synagogue at the conclusion of a board meeting on Monday evening, November 1, 1982, they were horrified to find Nazi and Ku Klux Klan symbols and epithets spray-painted in red and black on the building walls, playground equipment, and a parked car. Among the most horrifying images was a picture of a gas chamber door upon which was scrawled "Dead Jew" and "In, Take a Shower Jew." The culprits, a group of inebriated young men who also defaced a nearby pharmacy, were quickly apprehended. Legal proceedings revealed that the men were affirmed white supremacists who were familiar with Nazi ideology; two sported white nationalist tattoos, including a Nazi eagle and a burning cross.[1]

What distinguished this incident from the 828 other cases of anti-Semitic vandalism, arson, and bombing reported to the Anti-Defamation League of B'nai Brith, in 1982, was that the congregation's leaders responded, not only by filing criminal charges in state court, but also a civil suit in federal district court charging the perpetrators with civil rights violations under the Civil Rights Act of 1866.[2] A United States

Supreme Court ruling, in a 1976 case, paved the way for white people to seek redress under this act for incidents of racial discrimination. But since the Holocaust, Jewish Americans typically bridled at any efforts to classify Jews as a race, because it evoked discredited eugenics and Nazi race science. Indeed, it was precisely on that basis that lower courts dismissed the congregation's suit, asserting that it wasn't sufficient that the vandals believed that the Jews were a race, if those beliefs were factually inaccurate. But in a 1987 unanimous ruling, the Supreme Court reversed the earlier decisions. The crux of the court's reasoning focused on the evolving meaning of the term "race," which in the nineteenth century connoted not merely supposed biophysical population differences, but national origin. When Congress passed the Civil Rights Act of 1866, it "intended to protect from discrimination identifiable classes of persons who are subjected to intentional discrimination solely because of their ancestry or ethnic characteristics," Justice Byron White's majority opinion concluded.[3]

It may seem odd to open a discussion about the teaching of American Judaism in the context of the American history classroom with an anecdote about a somewhat obscure late twentieth-century legal case. But *Shaare Tefila v. Cobb* underscores three important features of Jewish life in the United States that are critical to an appreciation of how Jewish Americans are embedded into but remain somewhat dissonant from America's social fabric. The first involves the matters of categorization and historical experience. Like any social category, Jewish American is historically contingent and necessarily fluid. While many students in our classes, Jews included, relate to Jewish Americans as a religious community, Jewish Americans' self-perception has shifted over time, as have the attitudes of their Christian neighbors and the ways in which Jews have been classified within America's governmental apparatus.

Second, the incident underscores the endurance of antisemitism as a feature of American life. While the pervasiveness of antisemitism has waxed and waned in various eras of American history, it never disappeared and has grown in recent years. The persistence of antisemitism provides insight into the Jewish American psyche, helping explain why Jews continue to view themselves as a minority despite the economic and social advances they have made since the mid-twentieth century.

Finally, *Shaare Tefila v. Cobb* sheds light on the relationship between Jewish Americans and the American polity. Jewish Americans have historically navigated an ongoing tension between the desire to fit in, which sometimes involved minimizing the dissonances between Jewish interests and those of the Christian majority, and a need to stand out, by asserting their rights as a minority group. At various times in American history, Jews have sought coalitions with other victims of religious and racial discrimination. Their efforts to promote American pluralism and the separation of church and state, while often contested, have nevertheless profoundly influenced American culture and even its mythos.

Due to space constraints, this essay focuses primarily on the theme of what constitutes Judaism and Jewish people's historical experiences, while more briefly touching on antisemitism and the relationship between Jewish Americans and American government. Throughout, I offer examples of how I use primary sources to teach historical thinking skills. As education scholar Sam Wineburg explains, historical thinking skills are important for students to master, not because we hope that they will all become professional historians, but because these skills "prepare students to tolerate complexity, to adapt to new situations, and to resist the first answer that comes to mind."[4]

Defining American Judaism

Many students come into our classes with the assumption that religion is a "timeless category," synonymous with personal faith and belief, not recognizing that it is a modern Protestant creation. Teaching about Judaism's encounter with the Americas offers an opportunity for students to explore how the privatization of religion was historically contingent process. When considering how to integrate the Jewish experience into the American history classroom, one generative organizing question is "What constitutes Judaism?" As religious studies professor Leora Batnitzky argues in her book, *How Judaism Became a Modern Religion*, a central preoccupation in the Jewish encounter with modernity has been the question of how a totalizing system of cultural practices, values, beliefs, and allegiances could be transformed so as to fit into the modern, Protestant category of religion.[5] As we will see, Jews who employed the strategy of conformity to American (=Protestant) understandings of religion in order to gain social acceptance and legal protection emphasized what they saw as the religious components of Judaism while downplaying or discarding the cultural and legal aspects. (This project began in Germany but was eagerly adopted by Jewish reformers in the United States.) Other Jews, however, resisted the impulse toward reconstruction, arguing that the cultural and legal aspects were integral to Judaism.

The evolving nature of Jewish Americans as a social category is bound up with the development of the modern nation-state. In medieval Europe, Jews were accorded corporate status, meaning that they were recognized, not as individuals, but as members of a distinct entity with its own internal organization and legal footing. Not only did corporate status impact Jewish relations with the governing power, but it played a constitutive role in how Jews self-identified and were perceived by others: as a separate ethno-religious group.

The events of 1654–55 that led to the establishment of the first Jewish community in North America illustrates the corporate status of Jews in the colonial period. While individual Jews appear to have traded in the colonies prior to the mid-seventeenth century, the successful petition of twenty-three Jewish refugees, fleeing Portuguese-occupied Recife, Brazil, to establish a permanent presence in Dutch New Amsterdam, was a notable milestone. The Dutch colonial governor, Peter Stuyvesant (1612–72) was opposed to granting the Jews' request but was overruled by the directors of the Dutch West India Company. The right to settle and trade was granted to Jews as a group, rather than as individuals. The correspondence between Stuyvesant and the company, as well as the Dutch Jewish petition to overrule Stuyvesant's decision, make for edifying reading with students. They are available in Gary Zola and Marc Dollinger's *American Jewish History: A Primary Source Reader*, an indispensable aid to anyone seeking relevant primary source materials on the Jewish American experience.[6]

Stuyvesant, the son of a clergyman and a devoted elder in the Dutch Reformed Church, refers to the Jews as a "deceitful race" and "hateful enemies and blasphemers of the name of Christ," suggesting that he viewed them both as a distinctive ethnic group and as a religious group, while the Jews self-identify as "merchants of the Portuguese nation," "Portuguese Jews," and "the Jewish nation," which also connotes national and religious associations. Their identification as Portuguese Jews would have been understood to mean that they practiced according to the rites and customs of Spanish and Portuguese (i.e., Sephardic) Jewry.[7] It was also a reminder that they were descendants of the Jews who were persecuted and expelled from Spain and Portugal under the Inquisition. Indeed, it was Spain and Portugal's importation of the Inquisition to their American colonies that compelled the Jews in Recife to flee after the Portuguese conquest of that city from the Dutch. As an aside, it is equally interesting that the company's directors ultimately relent and order Stuyvesant to allow the Jews to "travel and trade to and in New Netherland and live and remain there," not primarily out of sympathy for the Jews—indeed, they claimed to share Stuyvesant's prejudices—but because Jews are among the company's principal shareholders.[8]

Initially, Jewish Americans functioned as part of a Spanish and Portuguese Jewish diaspora. They settled primarily in port cities, including Charleston, Newport, New York, Philadelphia, Richmond, and Savannah, allowing them to maintain close social, cultural, and economic relations with kinsfolk in other communities on the eastern seaboard, Amsterdam, Bordeaux, London, and the Caribbean. The Jews in each city were organized around a single congregation, which provided for their religious, educational, and communal needs, and was recognized by others as the Jewish community's representative body.

This system changed in the wake of the American Revolution. Protestant religious dissenters lobbied for liberty of conscience for all Protestants and religious disestablishment in the states, while leading political figures, including Benjamin Franklin (1705–90), Thomas Jefferson (1743–1826), and James Madison (1751–1836), under the influence of Enlightenment ideas, went even further and advocated for the abolition of religious oaths for officeholders and extending religious freedom to all native-born free people, regardless of religion. These principles were enshrined in the federal Constitution and were gradually adopted by most state legislatures.

Influenced by the zeitgeist, Jews revised their synagogue constitutions, democratizing their governance structure and making membership optional rather than obligatory. Synagogues that tried to buck this trend found that they lacked the power to enforce membership and respect for their legal and taxing authority.[9] Beginning in 1795, but especially after 1820, larger communities, including Philadelphia, New York, and Charleston, witnessed the establishment of multiple synagogues, many following the rites and traditions of the increasing number of Jewish immigrants from Central and Eastern Europe (i.e., Ashkenazi Jews). The Revolution ushered in a new "diverse and pluralistic" era that ended the "intimate coupling of synagogue and community."[10]

Thus, the bond between the religious and cultural aspects of Jewishness was significantly weakened as Jewish worship became privatized and the role of the congregation circumscribed.

In the German states, where the Jewish emancipation process was more fraught and prolonged, Jewish thinkers in the late eighteenth century consciously adapted Judaism to better conform to the Protestant notion that "religion denotes a sphere of life separate and distinct from all others, and that this sphere is largely private, not public, voluntary and not compulsory."[11] If Judaism lacked political aspirations seemingly at variance with loyalty to the state in which they resided, supporters of Jewish emancipation reasoned, Jews could be integrated into the body politic. Hence, Judaism as a religion was created so that it complemented and harmonized with the modern nation-state.[12]

German-speaking Jews from Central Europe, who began arriving in large numbers in the United States in the 1840s, imported German Reform Judaism to a receptive public that had already begun experimenting with reforms to Jewish worship primarily designed to bring the synagogue into alignment with the aesthetic sensibilities of neighboring Protestant and Unitarian churches. Students can explore the evolution, over the course of the nineteenth century, from more external forms of acculturation to a sweeping theological realignment that stripped away manifestations of Jewish particularism in favor of a universalizing, confessional faith. One might begin by asking students to compare the portrait of America's first native-born clergyman, Gershom Mendes Seixas (1745–1816), which is available online in the Loeb Database of Early American Jewish Portraits, and the roughly contemporaneous portrait of Unitarian minister, Joseph Stevens Buckminster (1784–1812), on the website of the Boston Athenaeum.[13] Note that both leaders don the Geneva gown and clergy preaching bands characteristic of Protestant and Unitarian clergy. Next, students might analyze an 1824 letter to the leadership of Charleston's Congregation Beth Elohim, from forty-seven members, mostly in their twenties and thirties, advocating reforms to worship, including greater use of the vernacular and the abridgement of the Sabbath prayer service.[14] While neither of these aesthetic reforms would violate Jewish law, they represented significant changes to long-standing custom. Take care to point out that like many religious innovators, the reformers made the case that the proposed actions were meant to safeguard Judaism. "We wish not to overthrow, but to rebuild; we wish not to destroy, but to reform and revise the evils complained of," they pleaded. But their perception of what constitutes a dignified service derived from the wider Protestant context within which they were situated. The rejection of the petition by synagogue elders precipitated a congregational schism, and the creation of a Reformed Society of Israelites.

Finally, the Pittsburgh Platform, which was adopted at an ecclesiastical convening of nineteen rabbinic reformers, in November 1885, constitutes a mature expression of Judaism as a rational, universal faith.[15] An analysis of the statement's planks underscores the rabbis' systematic effort to expunge from Judaism any impulse that conflicted with this vision, including expressions of national belonging, the belief in a messianic return to Palestine, and the establishment of a sovereign Jewish state. They also rejected the authority of Jewish law, which they recognized as subject to change over time, and any particularistic ceremonies and rituals that did not derive from moral principles. Two years earlier, Hebrew Union College, a new Jewish seminary in Cincinnati, Ohio, scandalized traditionalists when it violated kosher laws by serving four biblically prohibited foods (clams, crabs, shrimp, and frogs' legs) and mixing dairy and meat at a banquet in honor of its first class of rabbinic ordinees. The original banquet menu is available as part of an online exhibit that includes many other visual and textual sources.[16] What became known as the "Trefa [Non-Kosher] Banquet" possibly began as a caterer's error, but it was seized upon by the college's president, Isaac M. Wise (1819–1900), as an opportunity to throw down the gauntlet. Once a voice of moderation and Jewish unity, Wise derided the "kitchen Judaism" of his opponents, signaling his unreserved embrace of the project of Jewish reformation.[17]

Students should understand that despite the growth of American Reform Judaism in the mid- to late nineteenth century, Judaism's contours remained contested, even among Jews of Central European extraction. Many persisted in relating to their Jewishness in social and communal terms, rather than in its religious aspects, by joining fraternal organizations, reading Jewish newspapers, and advocating on behalf of oppressed and indigent Jews in other countries. The oldest and largest Jewish fraternal organization, the International Order of B'nai B'rith, was founded in 1843. An 1876 membership certificate, created by lithographic artist Louis Kurz (1834–1921), can be effectively used in the classroom as a visual representation of B'nai Brith's fusing of religious and social concerns. Readily available on the web through the Library of Congress, a rich online repository of visual sources, the iconography includes religious, domestic and patriotic symbols, as well as biblical scenes and images of fraternal benevolence, such as visiting the sick, caring for the orphaned, and consoling the bereaved.[18]

To be sure, many Jews avoided the term "nation" out of sensitivity to accusations that they harbored dual political loyalties. But they had no compunction about using the term "race," which carried many of the same connotations while being devoid of the obvious baggage.[19] One conspicuous example is the popular English lyrics to the Hanukkah hymn "Rock of Ages," which included the lines "Children of the martyred race/Whether free or fettered/Wake the echoes of the songs/ Where ye may be scattered."[20] The late nineteenth-century translation of the medieval Hebrew hymn, which was frequently sung at Hanukkah candle-lighting ceremonies in the United States, coincided with the revival of Hanukkah in reaction to the growing popularity of Christmas and its establishment as a national holiday in 1870. Students can compare the popular version with a more literal translation and see how the authors substituted an emphasis on bloodshed, vengeance, and deliverance, with themes such as God's salvation, universal brotherhood, and freedom from tyrants, which could be more easily reconciled with American values and the spirit of the Christmas season.

The turn-of-the-century influx of Jewish immigrants from Eastern Europe—most fleeing poverty, antisemitism, and forced conscription in Imperial Russia—further undermined efforts to reach consensus on the nature of American Judaism. The newcomers' Jewish self-understanding was shaped by an entirely different political and social context than their Central European counterparts. The czarist regime treated Jews warily as one of many distinct nationalities within its supranational empire, vacillating between policies promoting segregation and Russification. Jewish aspirations for emancipation in Russia went unrealized until 1917, fueling a nascent Jewish cultural nationalism grounded in cultural, linguistic, and political distinctiveness. While many of these immigrants were eager to assimilate into American society, the prospect of discarding Judaism's ethnic and cultural manifestations and remaking Judaism as an religious faith held little appeal. Students can get the flavor of secular Jewish thought by reading an excerpt from Chaim Zhitlowsky's (1865–1943) "Our Future in the Land."[21] This Russian-born intellectual was a prominent architect of secular Jewish culture who believed that a viable American Jewish identity could be "built on the foundation of the Yiddish language," cultural production, and education. Indeed, he considered the privatization of religion as a threat to Jewish unity and continuity. Even Eastern European proponents of a religiously centered American Judaism rejected the Reform movement. Rabbi Mordecai M. Kaplan (1881–1983), the leading Jewish religious thinker of the first half of the twentieth century, championed the idea that Judaism was a civilization, not merely a faith tradition.[22]

Some Eastern European Jewish immigrants made a religion out of their commitment to radical politics, while others rallied behind the nascent Zionist movement. Zionist advocacy for the establishment of a Jewish national home in Palestine, the historic Land of Israel, as a response to the persistence of antisemitism in Europe, received a chilly reception from those who sought to root out expressions of Jewish national allegiance in an effort to reconceive Judaism as a religion, including many Reform Jews. It was also opposed by religious traditionalists who believed that mass Jewish immigration to Palestine should occur only in connection with a divinely initiated epoch of messianic redemption. But Zionism attracted the support of prominent lawyer and future Supreme Court justice Louis D. Brandeis (1856–1941), himself a Boston Jewish brahmin of Central European extraction. In 1915, Brandeis published an article entitled "The Jewish Problem: How to Solve It," in which he attacked the allegation that American Jewish support for the upbuilding of a Jewish national home in Palestine was inconsistent with American patriotism.[23] Reading an excerpt of this remarkable apologia will help students appreciate the pressure that American Zionists felt, from Reform Jews as well as non-Jewish opponents, to refute the charge of dual loyalties. Students should recall that as fairly recent immigrants disproportionately involved in socialist politics and trade unionism, Eastern European Jews were politically vulnerable, particularly to charges of disloyalty.

By the 1930s, even the Reform movement was compelled to backtrack on its rejection of Zionism due to the rise of Nazism and genocidal antisemitism in Europe, coupled with America's enforcement of strict immigration restrictions. The optimism that fueled bold expressions of religious universalism gave way to isolation and concern for Jewish survival. An effective classroom discussion can be built around the comparison of the Pittsburgh Platform with the Reform movement's 1937

Columbus Platform, which advocated for the reclamation of some particularistic rituals and ceremonies and beheld in "the rehabilitation of Palestine . . . [a] promise of renewed life for many of our brethren."[24]

Jew Hatred

While antisemitism in the United States was never as pervasive as the systematic oppression, discrimination, and marginalization of Black people, neither was it a marginal phenomenon.[25] We have already seen that anti-Jewish prejudice colored the reception of the early Jewish colonists.

Confronted with Gentile ambivalence and hostility, colonial Jewry adopted a low profile. There are few better expressions of this impulse than the architecture of the Newport, Rhode Island, synagogue, Jeshuat Israel, photographs of which are readily available on the internet.[26] The oldest surviving synagogue building in North America, it was designed by Rhode Island resident Peter Harrison and dedicated in 1763. The Georgian style brick box exterior, with its hipped roof unadorned arched windows was purposely conceived to be unobtrusive, while the interior, with its two story ark, ionic colonnades, and ornate furnishings was a lavish blending of high-style Georgian design and an imagining of the biblical tabernacle.[27]

Even after the Jews were granted legal equality, social and economic discrimination persisted, as did anti-Jewish stereotyping. In the nineteenth century, much of the ambivalence was a function of the disconnect in the American mind between received and perceived wisdom about Jews, between "the mythic Jew" and "the Jew next door."[28] Jews were subjected to aggressive Protestant missionizing, which became an impetus for the organization of the first Jewish Sunday schools and the publication of the earliest known Jewish American newspaper.

Anti-Jewish sentiment spiked during times of economic and political uncertainty when the public was inclined to scapegoating and conspiracy mongering. Agrarian populists, the urban poor, and northeast patrician intellectuals—the most vocally antisemitic elements of American society during the Gilded Age—felt victimized by rapid industrialization and frequent up-and-down swings of the business cycle and used Jews as a foil to express their fears about the excesses of industrial capitalism. As one historian observed about the rhetoric of this era, "older religiously based talk about Jews as the bearers of a defective religion, deniers of the truth of Christianity, melded effortlessly with 'the Jew' as the beneficiary of the new economic order, and indeed according to some . . . as its agent."[29] A rich visual text that can be used to explore this phenomenon is illustrator Leon Barritt's (1852–1938) 1898 editorial cartoon, "The Commercial Vampire," in which a bloodthirsty bat with stereotypically Jewish features, representing the department store, is perched over the skulls of devoured small businesses.[30] The cartoon mixes age-old religiously grounded canards, such as the blood libel, with a more modern racially grounded antisemitism that deployed grotesque images of Jewish racial characteristics to argue for the inherent inferiority of Jews.

Stereotypes and fabrications provided an impetus for the erection of social and institutional barriers to Jewish integration and advancement that amplified during the Progressive Era. It also influenced American immigration policy, most notably the Emergency Quota Act (1921) and the Johnson-Reed Act (1924), which effectively reduced Jewish immigration to a trickle. Antisemitism in the United States reached its peak between 1920 and 1944.

Two of the most notorious and influential purveyors of Jew hatred during the interwar years were industrialist Henry Ford (1863–1947) and populist Catholic preacher Father Charles Coughlin (1891–1979). Each was viewed as a voice of authority: Ford as an entrepreneurial automobile manufacturer, the man who introduced America to the Model T, and Coughlin as a charismatic radio preacher—a forerunner of the contemporary televangelists and demagogic media personalities—who effectively channeled the economic, political, and cultural grievances of his audience in the midst of the Depression. Both trucked in a noxious mélange of religious calumnies, political conspiracy theories, and pseudo-race science. Their influence stemmed from their ability to reach millions of individuals, the former through his newspaper, the *Dearborn Independent*, which was distributed at Ford automobile dealerships, and the latter over the radio, where his program reached as many as forty-five million listeners.

One of the most challenging but potentially impactful experiences I have had teaching with primary sources is reading and analyzing Coghlin's November 20, 1938, radio address, "Persecution—Jewish and Christian," with my students.[31] The address, which was delivered shortly after Kristallnacht, the Night of the Broken Glass, in Germany, requires careful parsing and should be contextualized with reference to the strongly isolationist currents of the day. Coughlin offers a master class in demagoguery; he repeatedly claims to be sympathetic to the Jewish victims, while explaining away the Nazis' actions as a response to Jewish-inspired communism and claiming that Christian suffering at the hands of communists, internationalists and those who were "anti-Christ" far exceeded that of the Jews.[32] Ask students to analyze Coughlin's use of rhetoric, consider how his message might have been received by Jewish and non-Jewish listeners, and consider who might have been his target audience. They might also reflect on parallels between Coughlin and contemporary radio and television personalities.

Jews and the State

Jewish support for the Roosevelt administration and the New Deal was overwhelming and cemented an alignment with the Democratic Party that endured into the twenty-first century, despite their increased prosperity. Jews served in Franklin D. Roosevelt's (1882–1945) administration in greater numbers than any previous governments. Nevertheless, as in the past, there were limits to Jewish political power. In the late 1930s and early 1940s, Jews were mostly powerless to assist their brethren in Europe in the face of State Department resistance to greasing the wheels of immigration. Even after word of Hitler's "final solution" was leaked to the outside world, in 1942, the American government took no action to rescue Jews until January 1944, when Roosevelt's Jewish secretary of the treasury, Henry Morgenthau Jr. (1891–1967), prevailed upon the president to establish the War Refugee Board.

Indeed, throughout most of American history, Jewish access to political power was limited even while their legal status and religious rights were secure. As a miniscule minority of about two thousand individuals in the 1790s, Jews mostly watched debates about the establishment and free exercise of religion from the sidelines. They received their rights on the federal level and in most states, along with everyone else and not as was often the case in Europe, as a special privilege. While the synagogue communities of the colonial era maintained social control without resort to government intervention, the "severing of the bonds between religion and citizenship hastened the fracturing of Jewish communities and the privatization of Judaism."[33] They placed great meaning in a letter from George Washington (1732–99) to the Jews of Newport, in which he affirmed that all citizens, regardless of their religious persuasion, were afforded "liberty of conscience and [the] immunities of citizenship."

Washington's letter, which is a marvelous teaching tool, was extolled by subsequent generations and even cited in Supreme Court decisions.[34] It is remembered in part for its assertion that "the Government of the United States, which gives to bigotry no sanction, to persecution no assistance, requir[ing] only that they who live under its protection should demean themselves as good citizens in giving it on all occasions their effectual support." Washington paraphrased this statement from the letter of welcome that the Newport congregation's leader sent to the president on the occasion of his visit to Rhode Island in August, 1790. But all his own was his arguably more significant assertion in the letter: "It is no more that toleration is spoken of as if it were the indulgence of one class of people that another enjoyed the exercise of their inherent natural rights." The letter amounts to an affirmation of American religious pluralism, a promise that America would be not merely a haven where religious minorities would be granted toleration but a home.

Historically speaking, this is not to say that the government and entrenched power elites have always made good on that promise. Nevertheless, after the Second World War, America became more open to Jews (and Catholics) of European descent, allowing them to more fully take advantage of their conditional whiteness. As social and economic barriers fell, Jews rapidly assimilated into the American middle class. By 1955, sociologist Will Herberg (1901–77) could describe America as "a triple melting pot" of Protestants, Catholics, and Jews.[35] As Jews moved to the suburbs, they participated in the 1950s religious revival, building synagogue centers that combined religious, educational, and social functions, and demonstrating increased interest in theology and Bible study. Concurrently, Jewish secularism, robustly on display during the early twentieth century, went into eclipse, partially in reaction to McCarthyism.

Arguably, Jewish Americans' greatest religious fervor was reserved for postwar liberalism, and they played an active role in shaping its contours. As Jews began feeling less vulnerable, they assumed a more visible role in safeguarding their religious and civil rights. Their disproportionate support for organized labor and the Black civil rights movement and their strict separationist interpretation of the First Amendment were driven in part by empathy with the downtrodden and a commitment to religious liberty and social justice. But their political stance also stemmed from a belief that forging liberal consensus and coalitions with minorities and other interest groups would safeguard their own status in American society.[36]

In the legal realm, prior to the Second World War, Jews were often reticent about assuming a leading role in promoting religious equality and church-state separation. For example, despite the existence of a substantial Jewish community in Cincinnati with a vested interest in public education policy, Jews declined to actively abet the legal challenge to the practice of Bible reading in the city's public schools, which fomented the so-called Bible War of 1869–73. Jonathan Sarna and David Dalin's useful source reader, *Religion and State in the American Jewish Experience,* includes excerpts from a 1922 letter in which Louis Marshall, a prominent lawyer and president of a major Jewish defense organization, suggests that the problem of Bible reading could be diffused if Protestants, Catholics, and Jews could compose an agreed upon list of readings that are "free from theological bias." Instructors might encourage students to consider Marshall's recommendation to avoid discussing Bible reading "in any public meetings that are apt to become acrimonious" in light of recent contentious school board meetings across the country related to culture war issues. On the occasions when they did object to perceived violations of state and federal guarantees of religious equality, Jews were often reminded of their minority status and the widespread perception that America was a Christian country.[37]

By the time Marshall wrote his letter, Jews were increasingly advocating for a strict separationist position. Another document in Sarna and Dalin's reader, a 1906 policy statement by a conference of Reform rabbis, argued that "religion is the concern of the individual alone" and has no place in schools or other state-funded institutions. Students should take notice of the rabbis' rhetorical strategy of liberally utilizing quotations from the nation's founders, including Thomas Jefferson and James Madison, to support their argument. After the Second World War, Jewish defense organizations, particularly the American Jewish Congress (AJC) and its legal counsel, Leo Pfeffer (1910–93), advocated zealously for strict separationism through the courts, routinely submitting amicus briefs and even litigating landmark cases, including *McCollum v. Board of Education* (1948), which challenged religious instruction in public schools, and *Engel v. Vitale* (1962), which outlawed state-composed prayers. In a demonstration of the Jewish community's growing sense of security, the AJC and like-minded Jewish organizations willingly cooperated in these cases with religious dissenters and nonbelievers, as well as mainline Protestants. Pfeffer's autobiographical reflections, also available in the Sarna-Dalin reader, can be used to demonstrate how his absolutist position on church-state separation was shaped by a childhood experience in public school, where he endured mandatory Bible reading and the threat of released-time religious instruction.[38]

By the late 1960s, however, the Jewish consensus on church-state separation was fraying, as religiously traditional Orthodox Jews made common cause with traditionalist Catholics and evangelical Protestants on issues such as government aid to parochial schools. In contrast to religious and politically liberal Jews, who have watched in horror, since the mid-1980s, as the Renquist and Roberts courts dismantled pieces of the wall of separation, Orthodox Jews gravitated to an interpretation of the First Amendment that emphasized religious equality over separationism, allowing religion a greater role in the public square. As early as 1965, a group of Orthodox Jewish professionals, mostly lawyers, created the National Jewish Commission on Law and Public Affairs to serve as a counterweight to Pfeffer and the mainstream defense organizations and to defend the legal interests of the Orthodox Jewish community. Political scientist and communal activist Marvin Schick described the organization's approach to church-state relations in a 1967 report, which is accessible to the general reader.[39] Students should note that Schick describes the Jewish community's support of strict separationism as "robot-like" and "idol worship" and calls for Jews to follow the approach of Catholic and many Protestant organizations that approach decisions about whether to support legislation such as the Elementary and Secondary Education Act, which provided some government support for parochial schools, from a "practical" as opposed to an "ideological" perspective.

Even in the twenty-first century, the three themes discussed in this chapter remain relevant. Judaism in America continues to evolve in response to new challenges, such as increased interfaith marriage, that invite a reevaluation of the relationship between belief, tradition, culture, and ethnicity.[40] At the same time, the rise of white nationalism and extremist ideologies on the right, the blurring of the line between anti-Zionism and antisemitism by elements on the progressive left, and the upward trend of anti-Jewish hate crimes since the mid-2010s point to the persistence of antisemitism in American life. Finally, the Jewish community continues to negotiate its relationship to the state regarding issues ranging from religious liberty in the workplace and government aid to parochial schools to reproductive freedom and religious exemptions from nondiscrimination laws.

ADDITIONAL RESOURCES

Ben-Ur, Aviva. *Sephardic Jews in America: A Diasporic History*. New York: New York University Press, 2012.

Dinnerstein, Leonard. *Antisemitism in America*. Rev. ed. New York: Oxford University Press, 1995.

Leibman, Laura Arnold. *Messianism, Secrecy and Mysticism: A New Interpretation of Early American Jewish Life*. London: Vallentine Mitchell, 2013.

Meyer, Michael, *Response to Modernity: A History of the Reform Movement in Judaism*. Detroit: Wayne State University Press, 1995.

Raider, Mark A. *The Emergence of American Zionism*. New York: New York University Press, 1998.

NOTES

1. Naomi W. Cohen, *"Shaare Tefila Congregation v. Cobb*: A New Departure in American Jewish Defense? *Jewish History* 3, no. 1 (Spring 1988): 96–97; Annalise E. Glauz-Todrank, "Judging and Protecting Jewish Identity in *Shaare Tefila Congregation v. Cobb*," in *Who Is a Jew? Reflections on History, Religion, and Culture*, ed. Leonard Greenspoon (West Lafayette, IN: Purdue University Press, 2014), 43–44.

2. "ADL Reports That Anti-Semitic Vandalism in U.S. Declined in 1982," *Jewish Telegraphic Agency*, January 11, 1983, accessed April 13, 2023, https://www.jta.org/archive/adl-reports-that-anti-semitic-vandalism-in-u-s-declined-in-1982.

3. Cohen, *"Shaare Tefila Congregation v. Cobb*," 104; *Shaare Tefila Congregation v. Cobb*, 481 U.S. 615 (1987).

4. Sam Wineburg, "Thinking Like a Historian," *Teaching with Primary Sources Quarterly* 3, no. 1 (Winter 2010), accessed May 15, 2023, https://www.loc.gov/static/programs/teachers/about-this-program/teaching-with-primary-sources-partner-program/documents/historical_thinking.pdf.

5. Leora Batnitzky, *How Judaism Became a Religion* (Princeton, NJ: Princeton University Press, 2011), 1-28.

6. Gary Zola and Marc Dollinger, eds., *American Jewish History: A Primary Source Reader* (Waltham, MA: Brandeis University Press, 2014), 10–12.

7. The Jewish people are diverse and comprise various cultural groups, including Sephardic Jews, who have their roots in the Iberian peninsula; Ashkenazi

Jews, who trace their heritage to Eastern and Central Europe; and Mizrahi Jews, who represent the communities of the Middle East, Central Asia, and North Africa; each are shaped by distinct historical, economic, and geographic forces.

8. For background on the Jewish arrival in New Amsterdam and the Inquisition, see Jonathan Sarna, *American Judaism: A History*, 2nd ed. (New Haven, CT: Yale University Press, 2019), 1–8.

9. Jonathan D. Sarna, "The Impact of the American Revolution on American Jews," *Modern Judaism* 1 (1981), 149–60.

10. Jonathan D. Sarna, "American Judaism," in *From Haven to Home: 350 Years of Jewish Life in America*, ed. Michael W. Grunberger (Washington, DC: Library of Congress, 2004), 135.

11. Batnitzky, *How Judaism Became a Religion*, 13.

12. Ibid., 13–40.

13. "Gershom Mendes Seixas," John L. Loeb, Jr., Database of Early American Jewish Portraits, accessed May 15, 2023, https://loebjewishportraits.com/biography/gershom-mendes-seixas/; *Reverend Joseph Stevens Buckminster* by Gilbert Stuart, Boston Athenaeum, accessed May 15, 2023, https://bostonathenaeum.org/explore-learn/special-collections/paintings-sculpture-online/reverend-joseph-stevens-buckminster/.

14. See "Memorial to the President and Members of the Adjunta of Kahal Kadosh Beth Elohim of Charleston, South Carolina, Demanding Religious Reform, December 23, 1824," in Zola and Dollinger, *American Jewish History*, 79–80.

15. The Pittsburgh Platform is widely available online, including on the American Jewish Archives website, accessed May 15, 2023, https://www.americanjewisharchives.org/snapshots/the-pittsburgh-platform-defining-american-reform-judaism-1885/. It can also be found in Jacob R. Marcus, ed., *The Jew in the American World: A Source Book* (Detroit: Wayne State University Press, 1996), 241–43.

16. The banquet menu is available on the Library of Congress "From Haven to Home" online exhibit, accessed ay 15, 2023, https://www.loc.gov/exhibits/haventohome/haven-home.html.

17. On the "Trefa Banquet" see Lance J. Sussman, "The Myth of the Trefa Banquet: American Culinary Culture and the Radicalization of Food Policy in American Reform Judaism," *American Jewish Archives Journal* 57 (2005): 29–52. Sarna has an accessible treatment of American Reform Judaism in *American Judaism*.

18. Louis Kutz, *Independent Order of B'nai B'rith Membership Certificate* (Milwaukee: American Oleograph, 1876). The item is downloadable from the Library of Congress website, accessed May 15, 2023, https://www.loc.gov/item/89711885/.

19. On Jews, race, and whiteness, see Eric Goldstein, "'Different Blood Runs through Our Veins': Race and Jewish Self-Definition in Late Nineteenth Century America," *American Jewish History* 85 (1997), 29–55; and Goldstein, *The Price of Whiteness: Jews, Race, and American Identity* (Princeton, NJ: Princeton University Press, 2006). "Rock of Ages" as an example of the popular discourse is suggested by Hasia Diner in *How America Met the Jews* (Providence, RI: Brown Judaic Studies, 2017), 49.

20. Both the popular translation of "Rock of Ages" (*Maoz Tzur*) by Gustav Gottheil (1827–1903) and Marcus Jastrow (1829–1903) and a more literal translation are available at *Jewish Heritage Online Magazine*, accessed May 15, 2023, https://www.jhom.com/calendar/kislev/maoz_tsur.htm.

21. A section of Zhitlowsky's essay, translated to English from the original Yiddish, appears as "Yiddish and the Future of American Jewry (1915)" in *The Jew in the Modern World: A Documentary History*, ed. Paul Mendes-Flohr and Jehuda Reinharz (New York: Oxford University Press, 2011), 551–52.

22. On Jewish radicalism in the United States, see Tony Michels, *A Fire in Their Hearts: Yiddish Socialists in New York* (Cambridge, MA: Harvard University Press, 2005). On American Judaism in the early twentieth century and Mordecai Kaplan's thought, see Sarna, *American Judaism*; Batnitzky, *How Judaism Became a Religion*; Mel Scult, *The Radical American Judaism of Mordecai M. Kaplan* (Bloomington, IN: Indiana University Press, 2015).

23. An excerpt of "The Jewish Problem: How to Solve It," can be found in Zola and Dollinger, *American Jewish History*, 168–69. A slightly different excerpt of the same text is also available under the title "Zionism Is Consistent with American Patriotism," in *The Jew in the Modern World*, 555–56.

24. The Columbus Platform is widely available on the internet. See, for example, "Article the Guiding Principles of Reform Judaism," accessed May 15, 2023, https://www.ccarnet.org/rabbinic-voice/platforms/article-guiding-principles -reform-judaism/.

25. See Jonathan Sarna, "Antisemitism in America: 1654–2020," in *The Cambridge Companion to Antisemitism*, ed. Steven Katz (Cambridge: Cambridge University Press, 2022).

26. Photographs of the exterior and interior of the synagogue are available on the website of the National Trust for Historic Preservation, https://saving places.org/places/touro-synagogue, and the Touro Synagogue National Historic Site, https://www.nps.gov/tosy/index.htm, which also includes background about the synagogue's construction and history. A virtual tour of the Newport synagogue interior is available at JewishHistory.com, http://jewishhistory.com/ TOURO/. (All websites accessed on May 15, 2023.)

27. My description of the inspiration for the interior design is based on Laura Leibman, "Sephardic Sacred Space in Colonial America," *Jewish History* 25 (2011): 13–31.

28. Sarna, "Antisemitism in America," 396.

29. David Koffman, Hasia Diner, Eric Goldstein, Jonathan Sarna, and Beth Wenger, "Roundtable on Antisemitism in the Gilded Age and Progressive Era," *Journal of the Gilded Age and the Progressive Era* 19 (2020): 3.

30. Barritt's cartoon is available on the Library of Congress website, accessed May 15, 2023, https://www.loc.gov/item/95522881/. The cartoon was drawn two years after the publication of Bram Stoker's *Dracula*, when America was in the midst of a vampire craze. On the long association of vampires with Jews see, Jack Halberstam, "Technologies of Monstrosity: Bram Stoker's *Dracula*," reprinted in Halberstam, *Skin Shows: Gothic Horror and the Technology of Monsters* (Durham, NC: Duke University Press, 1999), 86–106.

31. A transcript of Coughlin's speech is downloadable on the American Catholic History Classroom website, accessed May 15, 2023, https://cuomeka.wrlc.org/files/original/50b004fa185e86c9079c4ad288f49ac1.pdf. Students can also listen to an excerpt of the speech to get a sense of Coughlin's power as an orator at Great Jewish Books Teacher Resources, Yiddish Book Center, accessed May 15, 2023, https://teachgreatjewishbooks.org/3-radio-transcript-excerpt-speech-father-charles-coughlin-1938-and-audio-broadcast.

32. Understandably, some educators are reluctant to share racist and antisemitic writings with their students out of concern for their emotional well-being or a desire to promote an inclusive learning environment. But, assuming that students are sufficiently mature to engage in analysis and critical thinking, reading such documents with our students forces them to confront uncomfortable truths about the past, while teaching them to read discerningly, and may even empower them to become change agents in the present.

33. Jonathan Sarna, "American Jews and Church-State Relations: The Search for 'Equal Footing,'" in *Religion and State in the American Jewish Experience*, ed. Jonathan Sarna and David Dalin (Notre Dame, IN: Notre Dame Press, 1997), 3; Hasia Diner, *The Jews of the United States, 1654 to 2000* (Berkeley: University of California Press, 2004), 42.

34. The original letter from the Hebrew Congregation of Newport and Washington's reply can be viewed and downloaded from the website of the Loeb Visitor's Center at the Touro Synagogue National Historic Site, accessed May 15, 2023, https://www.loebvisitors.org/george-washingtons-letter/. The website also includes historical background.

35. On the invention of tri-faith America, see Kevin Schultz, *Tri-Faith America: How Catholics and Jews Held Postwar America to Its Protestant Promise* (New York: Oxford University Press, 2013).

36. On Jews, civil liberties, and liberalism, see Stuart Svonkin, *Jews against Prejudice: American Jews and the Fight for Civil Liberties* (New York: Columbia University Press, 1997); Marc Dollinger, *Quest for Inclusion: Jews and Liberalism in Modern America* (Princeton, NJ: Princeton University Press, 2000).

37. Sarna and Dalin, *Religion and State*, 191–97. The reader also includes a helpful introductory essay on Jews and church-state issues, as well as a panoply of other documents related to church-state issues, ranging from Sunday "Blue" laws to Hanukkah menorah lighting in the public square. For further background on Jews and church-state litigation in the mid-late twentieth century, see Gregg Ivers, *To Build a Wall: American Jews and the Separation of Church and State* (Charlottesville, VA: University Press of Virginia, 1995).

38. Pfeffer's autobiographical reflections are excerpted in Sarna and Dalin, *Religion and State*, 234–36.

39. An excerpt of the report is available in Sarna and Dalin, *Religion and State*, 262–64.

40. For a demographic snapshot of Jewish Americans today, see Pew Research Center, "Jewish Americans in 2020," May 11, 2021, accessed May 15, 2023, https://www.pewresearch.org/religion/2021/05/11/jewish-americans-in-2020/.

PART TWO

Teaching Religion in American History in Specific Periods

Political Reform and Devotional Culture in Early New England

A D R I A N   C H A S T A I N   W E I M E R

Accurate portrayals of the Puritan movement continue to elude teachers, in part because historians remain divided on whether the culture was oligarchical or proto-democratic, stifling or creative, and in part because instructors focus on moments of crisis such as the Salem witch trials, rather than more routine or long-standing elements. There is no one way to approach Puritanism, but two often misunderstood aspects of the movement are worth exploring: their political reforms and devotional culture—specifically their responses to suffering and prosperity. Both aspects are nearly impossible to understand without knowledge of the broader early modern Anglophone world. This chapter attempts to provide a relevant background for understanding colonial Puritans within their own seventeenth-century context. It assumes complementary material on traditional Native American religions, not covered here. Spending time on Puritans creates a bridge between the Protestant Reformation, English constitutional traditions, and early America; it can also help students gain confidence in approaching intellectually challenging and long-influential texts.

Puritan Political Culture

One of colonial Puritans' most distinctive contributions was political reform, a reform that drew strongly but not exclusively on religious convictions. Whatever else we might say about the Puritan-led colonies—Plymouth, Massachusetts Bay, Connecticut, and New Haven —in few places did ordinary people have as much say in their government. It is true that Massachusetts Bay failed to incorporate Quakers such as William Robinson or radicals such as Samuel Gorton. Yet, compared with England or other colonial regions, a high percentage of people in New England contributed to political decision-making. Towns annually elected their own representatives, called deputies, who made up the lower house of the General Court, the governing institution. Women and enslaved people did not vote, as was true elsewhere in the English Atlantic. Middling-class women, however, had more legal access and credibility in New England than in England at the time, where legal privileges tended to correlate with class or status. The freemen (voters) in each colony annually elected the governor, deputy governor, and magistrates, who constituted the upper house. New Englanders deeply prized the liberty enshrined in colony charters of electing their own leaders.[1] Levels of participation, along with literacy—prioritized for Bible-reading—were unusually high. All this is not to say that New England colonies were democracies. Colonists lived in a highly stratified society and tended to repeatedly elect the same elite representatives. Liberty for them meant liberty from arbitrary or unbounded rule, and liberty to choose godly leaders who would help them fulfill what they saw as biblical obligations to God and to the community.

What did Puritans do with their political privileges? Their efforts at reform grew from the belief that Christ was king of the civil realm as well as of the church, and so civil institutions should reflect biblical ideals. Inspired by Hebraic traditions of equity, they set about reforming the legal system in ways that people in England had been trying to accomplish for centuries but were blocked by landed interests. Colonists simplified the law code and eliminated many of the fees that had kept poor people from fully benefiting from legal services. In Massachusetts Bay they made these services widely available through the *Body of Liberties*, the 1648 edition of which would be "the first printed code of laws in the Western world."[2] They guaranteed due process, trial by jury, and the right of appeal. In practice they eliminated torture. Still, the courts carefully regulated disorderly speech and behavior. Those who disrespected magistrates, interrupted church services, or amassed great fortunes without giving back were called to account, often by fines, sometimes by whipping, banishment, or, in the case of four Quakers who returned after banishment, death. Native Americans and Africans— free or enslaved—had only partial access to the system, if that.

Legal reform was possible because the system of patronage by which many judges and clerks in England acquired their posts did not exist in these colonies. Neither did a professional class of lawyers. Paired with comprehensive aid from both congregations and local government for the elderly, orphans, and the mentally or physically challenged, these reforms meant that there was surprisingly little poverty among the Anglo-American population in the seventeenth century. If a town accepted a family, which generally meant the head of household agreed with its vision of a common life, then most likely that family would not find itself homeless or hungry. These practices, based in biblical notions of the community as the "body of Christ," as well as English common law and an older Christian humanist tradition, comprise a significant part of the region's history.

But, students often ask, wasn't the franchise (voting rights) severely limited in Massachusetts? The answer is yes and no. Whereas in England voting would have been based on hereditary privilege, guild membership, or wealth, early Massachusetts Bay and New Haven linked voting rights to church membership. For Puritan leaders, the logic went something like this: broad-based governments such the Roman Republic had historically failed because people voted in corrupt leaders who sought selfish gain rather than choosing virtuous men who promoted the common good. Limiting the franchise to church membership increased the chances that people would elect leaders who cared about the community's welfare. Those joining Puritan churches agreed to a covenant that essentially tasked the congregation with helping individuals live a godly life—one characterized by honesty, charity, and humility. People in these kinds of accountable relationships seemed less likely to vote in a demagogue who would betray the people's liberties. Therefore, in 1631 the Massachusetts General Court linked the franchise for colony-wide elections to church membership. Those who had full membership in a local church could vote for the upper house—the assistants, deputy governor, and governor. On the town level, inhabitants who were not full church members could vote in local elections after 1647 and often took on substantial leadership roles. Furthermore, the *Body of Liberties* gave non-freemen (non-voters) and even non-inhabitants the right to petition the government if they had experienced an injustice.

The question then follows: how high was the bar to full church membership, and thus to full political rights? In a spiritual sense, it was high. Closer to late-medieval mystics than modern Protestants, Puritans understood the Christian life to be both rational and intensely experiential. Although practice varied among churches, most agreed a true Christian could articulate, in biblical and personal terms, their spiritual journey—not that they had arrived at a mountaintop, but that they were, in fits and stumbles, on the path. Becoming a full church member meant offering the congregation either a convincing profession of faith or narrative about God's work in one's life. These professions or narratives made joining the church much more difficult than it would have been in most places in England. On a practical level, however, almost everyone who attempted to become a full church member was accepted by local congregations. Someone whose profession or narrative came across as prideful, shallow, or overly self-assured might receive encouragement from the minister to try again the following year (along with a commitment to spiritual shepherding). But there is almost no evidence that those who kept trying were denied full church membership. Some full church members declined the franchise to which they were entitled, probably because they did not want to take on the heavy civic responsibilities, such as jury duty, that the franchise entailed. In short, the spiritual bar was high, and many did not attempt it, but very few who undertook the journey were turned away.

As far as we can tell, the standard for church membership was not lowered for women or Native Americans, who were also expected to demonstrate high theological literacy and depth of experience. Native American church membership forms a distinct case. In Natick, Massachusetts, when Nipmuc and Massachusett Christians first offered relations in front of neighboring Anglo-American clergy, the clergy did not initially approve them, so these churches took much longer to form. Even after approval, Anglo-Americans were slow to offer the Native churches reciprocity in sacraments. Native American Christians did not simply reproduce English Protestantism but rather adapted it in line with their own goals of family, community, and cultural survival. These innovative forms of Christian practice were especially notable on Martha's Vineyard, where the Wampanoag preacher Hiacoomes allowed Native mourning rites to continue and expanded deacons' duties to include traditional Wampanoag modes of distributing charity.[3]

Excluded from membership in Puritan churches, Quakers, Gortonists, and other Protestant sects, as well as Portuguese Jews, tended to settle in Rhode Island. In this smaller colony, founded in 1636 by Roger Williams after his banishment from Massachusetts Bay, the franchise and public office had no religious test. The colony was troubled, however, by near-constant internal political disagreements, so that its legal and judicial institutions took longer to stabilize. Newport, Rhode Island, would become a major port in the transatlantic slave trade. Enslaved Africans most likely brought with them Catholic, Muslim, or other religious traditions, although archival records for these practices in the early period are difficult to find. With the exception of French outposts in Maine, few European Catholics migrated to early New England, where an anti-Catholic culture that associated "popery" with absolutism in church and state held sway.

The link between church membership and the franchise has led some historians to mistakenly characterize the Massachusetts Bay Colony as a theocracy, and students, used to modern norms of church-state separation, will often assume that is the case. Puritans sometimes used the term "theocracy," but what they meant was Christ's ultimate kingship over the civil realm as well as the spiritual realm, not rule of the state by religious leaders. Members of the Calvinist tradition, Puritans observed clear lines between the "spiritual" and "temporal" kingdoms. As the French reformer John Calvin had said, Christ delegates powers to political leaders over the temporal realm and religious leaders over the spiritual realm; neither should reach over into the other's sphere, though they should cooperate.[4]

New England colonies generally barred ministers from holding political office. Among the most learned and respected men in the colonies, clergy had a strong influence on laypeople's views. They often advised the General Courts (at the magistrates' request) on ethical matters such as the conditions for just war or constitutional issues such as the relationship between the colonies and England. But magistrates were free to reject ministers' advice, and even a magistrate who was excommunicated by the church would not lose his political office. There was no theocracy in Puritan New England in the sense that religious leaders controlled the state. At the same time, the Bible informed their efforts to create a different kind of society, one that—while far from perfect—prioritized the interests of middling townspeople rather than aristocratic elites.

Sample Lesson on the *Body of Liberties*

A closer look at the 1641 *Body of Liberties* (https://www .mass.gov/info-details/massachusetts-body-of-liberties) can help students understand the kinds of legal reforms prized by colonists. A rich document, it can intimidate students because of the older, sometimes technical language.[5] Assigning a few short sections, however, can work well in the classroom. Instructors might note that the ideas are based in English common law as well as the Bible, that spelling was not yet standardized in the seventeenth century, and that the capital laws were not always enforced. The General Court periodically revised the laws and distributed them so people across the colony had access—itself a major reform. The following questions, based on specific sections in the *Body of Liberties*, may encourage deeper discussion regarding legal reform and its limits.

1. The 1641 *Body of Liberties* begins by grounding liberties in "humanitie, Civilitie, and Christianitie" and claiming that these liberties "hath ever bene and ever will be the tranquillitie and Stabilitie of Churches and Commonwealths." Why might the text begin with these categories, and what basis for law do the categories imply?

2. The right to petition is found in Section 12, which says, "Every man whether Inhabitant or Forreiner, free or not free shall have libertie to come to any publique Court, Councel, or Towne meeting, and . . . present any . . . petition . . . so it be done in convenient time, due order, and respective manner." Why was the right to petition so important? Who might have had more or less access to the English norms of convenience, order, and respect specified in the last clause?

3. Section 60 says, "No church censure shall degrade or depose any man from any Civill dignitie, office, or Authoritie he shall have in the Commonwealth." What does this prohibition tell us about the relationship between church and state in early Massachusetts Bay?

Puritans on Suffering and Prosperity

Another aspect of Puritan culture that deserves rethinking is their approach to devotional life, and especially the relationship between suffering, prosperity, and providence (God's work in the world). The over-teaching of Jonathan Edwards's "Sinners in the Hands of an Angry God" means that students often associate Puritan sermons with fire-and-brimstone preaching. Further, nonspecialists sometimes take the word "puritanical"—coined by the movement's detractors and today synonymous with "self-righteously overscrupulous" or "emotionally repressed"—as an accurate reflection of Puritan culture. It is true Puritans discouraged dancing, attending the theater, profanity, and idle jesting. They wore bright colors, however, and held ideals similar to most English people regarding companionate marriage, warm family life, and deep friendship. Most of their sermons advocated practical piety: orienting the heart toward love for God and neighbor, even when life was difficult. Understanding Puritan devotional ideals helps students think more accurately about Puritan attitudes toward sin, suffering, work, leisure, and community.

In class I sometimes ask students: In modern America, if a person's house burns down, or the stock market collapses, or a marriage proposal is rejected, what resources are available to cope with loss? Early modern devotional rituals included extensive resources to help people deal with suffering or "affliction." For Puritans, the first stage in the ritual usually involved self-examination. If life is hard, Puritan devotional manuals advised, Christians should search their hearts by the scriptures to see if they have sinned or wronged someone. If they can take any responsibility for harming themselves or someone else, then they should do it—apologize to God and neighbor and make necessary reparations. This interior housecleaning enabled a clearer vision of self, others, and circumstances. Critics of the movement have (mistakenly) labeled these practices of self-examination and thorough repentance as forms of self-flagellation or even self-hatred. It is true that intense sorrow over sin could spiral downward into despair. In general, however, the rituals were designed to rightly order the affections—loving God first—and to prepare the heart for divine comfort. Rather than stifling emotions, the devotional steps channeled them in ways Puritans saw as bringing ultimate satisfaction. So the Ipswich matron Sarah Goodhue, in the midst of a difficult pregnancy with twins and worrying she would not survive the delivery, engaged in these devotional rituals, then wrote, "I hope I can by experience truly say, that Christ is the best, most precious, most durable portion, that all or any of you can set your hearts' delight upon."[6]

One academic theory, long refuted but still circulating, posited that Puritans' insecurity about their relationship with God—their inability to feel assurance of their salvation—fed a "Calvinist work ethic" that ultimately fueled capitalism. The theory, pioneered by the nineteenth-century German sociologist Max Weber, assumed that Puritans were perennially anxious; that they saw financial success as a sign of divine approval; and that therefore Puritans worked very hard at becoming prosperous as an affirmation of their chosenness by God. The problem with this theory is that Puritans said repeatedly that affliction was as likely to be a sign of divine favor as prosperity. Suffering, if rightly improved, could initiate a transformation of the heart. In this framework, God might send affliction as a punishment for sin but could also send it as a test or preparation for great spiritual service. Prosperity, however, could easily be a divine chastisement—it could numb the soul and lead to spiritual weakness. Puritan ministers often sought to relieve anxiety about salvation by counseling that if individuals were concerned about spiritual things and seeking God, then they were probably on the right path. One of their favorite verses, appearing in many sermons, was Jesus's words: "Come unto me, all ye that labour and are heavy laden, and I will give you rest" (KJV).[7]

If colonists valued industry and shunned idleness—which they did—it was not because they saw wealth as a sign of salvation, or poverty as spiritually disqualifying. Like most Calvinists, they generally understood all Christians—farmers and midwives, as well as ministers—to have a vocation, or divine calling to a form of work. Overwork—laboring to the neglect of spiritual practice or family—could be as dangerous as idleness. Even so, Puritans generally considered industriousness, along with humility and generosity, as marks of spiritual maturity, and held in disdain those who did not work diligently to care for their children and community. These convictions could lead to cultural misapprehensions. Anglo-Americans often condescendingly accused Native people—even Native churchmembers—of idleness, and scorned their seasonal patterns of work and leisure.

Stockpiling wealth drew scrutiny. An obligation for people to give excess resources to the poor in "ordinary" times, and to give even painfully in "extraordinary" times (drought, war, etc.) in fact formed the main point of John Winthrop's *Model of Christian Charity*, a lay sermon. Often called the "City on a Hill" sermon, this work is frequently cited out of context, assuming early New Englanders saw themselves as a pristine, shining model for others to emulate. Winthrop's themes center instead on heartfelt generosity and sacrifice for the common welfare. To display true charity, according to the *Model*, is to recognize oneself, through Christ, in the needy person and so to give with affection and joy. Winthrop believed that if colonists "entertain each other in brotherly Affeccion" and were "willing to abridge our selves of our superfluities [extra things], for the supply of others necessities," then God would dwell in New England. If they did not—if they acted cold-heartedly toward each other and oppressed the poor—then God's spirit would depart. Winthrop concluded, "for wee must Consider that wee shall be as a City upon a Hill, the eies of all peple are uppon us; so that if wee shall deale falsely with our god in this worke wee have undertaken and soe cause him to withdrawe his present help from us, we shall be made a story and a by-word [laughingstock, cautionary tale] through the world"—bringing shame on the church and on Christianity itself.[8] The sense of the passage is more of a warning than a celebration. Winthrop's *Model* urged colonists—like all Christians—toward humility and generosity. They failed to live up to these high ideals, of course. More often than not, they were among the first to acknowledge their own failures.

Sample Lesson on John Winthrop and Michael Wigglesworth

John Winthrop, *A Modell of Christian Charity,* https://history.hanover
.edu/texts/winthmod.html
Michael Wigglesworth, *Meat out of the Eater*[9]
    Part I, Meditation VII, The worldly man's Prosperity Is onely gilded Misery, https://quod.lib.umich.edu/e/evans/N00104.0001.001/1:2.7?rgn
=div2;view=fulltext.
    Part 2, RIDDLES Unriddled OR Christian Paradoxes, Joy in Sorrow, Song I, https://quod.lib.umich.edu/e/evans/N00104.0001.001/1:10.1?rgn
=div2;view=fulltext.

The devout Puritan John Winthrop served as a longtime governor of the Massachusetts Bay Colony. While Winthrop's *Modell of Christian Charity* is lengthy, the second-to-last paragraph works well for teaching. It begins, "Now the onely way to avoyde this shipwracke, and to provide for our posterity, is to followe the counsell of Micah, *to doe justly, to love mercy, to walk humbly with our God.*" This paragraph contains the famous "citty upon a hill" passage; it also summarizes Winthrop's social ethic regarding affectionate generosity and the common good. The following questions may generate student discussion:

1. According to John Winthrop, what does it mean for colonists to "entertaine each other in brotherly affection"?
2. What will happen if they do? What might happen if they do not?

One of the most widely read poets in early New England, Michael Wigglesworth made the Puritan devotional tradition available to laypeople in easily memorized verse. When teachers assign Wigglesworth's poetry they most often choose his *Day of Doom,* a ballad about Judgment Day. Almost as popular at the time, however, was Wigglesworth's devotional poem *Meat out of the Eater.* The title references the riddle in Judges 14, where bees make their home inside a lion's carcass (the honey is the "meat," the lion the "eater"). Rather than reading the poem straight through, colonial readers would have turned to the section that most spoke to their current situation—loneliness, sickness, and so on. It served as a manual for devotional practice, the aim of which was not to suppress emotion but rather to harness natural affection for spiritual use—to turn "worldly sorrow" into "godly sorrow"—with the ultimate goal of divine comfort and power. A pastor in Malden, Massachusetts, Wigglesworth was frequently ill and sometimes depressed. He states in the poem that his guidance is born of experience: "I have not told thee Tales,/ Of things unseen, unfelt,/ But speak them from Experience:/ Believe it how thou wilt." These devotional practices helped him find personal consolation, and so he wrote them down for laypeople's use. Discussion questions that might help students explore Puritan devotional culture include the following:

1. According to Wigglesworth's Meditation VII, why can worldly prosperity, or a life where people "live and lie at ease,/While others are in pain," lead to spiritual danger?
2. Wigglesworth writes in Joy in Sorrow, Song I: "If then thou art a Saint/ That languishest in Grief:/ God hath provided Cordials/ To yield thy Soul relief." What are these "cordials" (comforting medicines or drinks) and why are they supposed to bring "relief"?

ADDITIONAL RESOURCES

Bremer, Francis J. *Lay Empowerment and the Development of Puritanism.* New York: Palgrave Macmillan, 2015.

Hall, David D. *Reforming People: Puritanism and the Transformation of Public Life in New England.* New York: Knopf, 2011.

Hambrick-Stowe, Charles. *The Practice of Piety: Puritan Devotional Disciplines in Seventeenth-Century New England.* Chapel Hill: University of North Carolina Press for the Institute of Early American History and Culture, 1982.

Peterson, Mark. *The City-State of Boston: The Rise and Fall of an Atlantic Power, 1630–1865*. Princeton, NJ: Princeton University Press, 2019.

Valeri, Mark. *Heavenly Merchandize: How Religion Shaped Commerce in Puritan America*. Princeton, NJ: Princeton University Press, 2010.

Van Engen, Abram. *Sympathetic Puritans: Calvinist Fellow Feeling in Early New England*. New York: Oxford University Press, 2015.

Weimer, Adrian Chastain. *A Constitutional Culture: New England and the Struggle against Arbitrary Rule in the Restoration Empire*. Philadelphia: University of Pennsylvania Press, 2023.

NOTES

1. This and the following paragraphs draw on Cornelia H. Dayton, *Women before the Bar: Gender, Law and Society in Connecticut, 1639–1789* (Chapel Hill: University of North Carolina Press for the Institute for Early American History and Culture, 1995); David D. Hall, *Reforming People: Puritanism and the Transformation of Public Life in New England* (New York: Knopf, 2011); George Lee Haskins, *Law and Authority in Early Massachusetts: A Study in Tradition and Design* (New York: Macmillan, 1960); Michael Winship, *Godly Republicanism: Puritans, Pilgrims, and a City on a Hill* (Cambridge, MA: Harvard University Press, 2012); Barry Levy, *Town Born: The Political Economy of New England from Its Founding to the Revolution* (Philadelphia: University of Pennsylvania Press, 2009); David Konig, *Law and Society in Puritan Massachusetts: Essex County, 1629–1692* (Chapel Hill: University of North Carolina Press, 1979).

2. Hall, *Reforming People*, 148; see also Haskins, *Law and Authority*, 117–21.

3. Francis Bremer, *Lay Empowerment and the Development of Puritanism* (New York: Palgrave Macmillan, 2015); Richard Cogley, *John Eliot's Mission to the Indians before King Philip's War* (Cambridge, MA: Harvard University Press, 2009); James Ronda, "Generations of Faith: The Christian Indians of Martha's Vineyard," *William and Mary Quarterly* 38, no. 3 (July 1981): 371–79.

4. John Calvin, *Institutes of the Christian Religion*, ed. John McNeill (Louisville: Westminster John Knox Press, 1960), Book 4, chap. 20.

5. "The Massachusetts Body of Liberties" (1641) in *Old South Leaflets* (Boston: Directors of the Old South Work, n.d. [ca. 1900]), 7: 261–80, digitized by the Hanover Historical Texts Project, https://history.hanover.edu/texts/masslib.html.

6. Sarah Goodhue, "Monitory," in *Puritans in the New World: A Critical Anthology*, ed. David D. Hall (Princeton, NJ: Princeton University Press, 2004), 183. The following paragraphs also draw on Adrian Chastain Weimer, "From Human Suffering to Divine Friendship: *Meat out of the Eater* and Devotional Reading in Early New England," *Early American Literature* 51, no. 1 (2016): 3–39; Weimer, "Affliction and the Stony Heart in Early New England," in *Puritanism and Emotion in the Early Modern World*, ed. Alec Ryrie and Tom Schwanda (New York:

Palgrave Macmillan, 2016): 121–43; Charles Hambrick-Stowe, *The Practice of Piety: Puritan Devotional Disciplines in Seventeenth-Century New England* (Chapel Hill: University of North Carolina Press for the Institute of Early American History and Culture, 1982); Jeffrey A. Hammond, *Sinful Self, Saintly Self: The Puritan Experience of Poetry* (Athens: University of Georgia Press, 1993; N. H. Keeble, *The Literary Culture of Nonconformity in Later Seventeenth-Century England* (Leicester, UK: Leicester University Press, 1987); David D. Hall, *Ways of Writing: The Practice and Politics of Text-Making in Seventeenth-Century New England* (Philadelphia: University of Pennsylvania Press, 2008); Matthew Brown, *The Pilgrim and the Bee: Reading Rituals and Book Culture in Early New England* (Philadelphia: University of Pennsylvania Press, 2007); Andrew Cambers, *Godly Reading: Print, Manuscript and Puritanism in England, 1580–1720* (New York: Cambridge University Press, 2011); Charles Cohen, *God's Caress: The Psychology of Puritan Religious Experience* (New York: Oxford University Press, 1986); Martha Finch, *Dissenting Bodies: Corporealities in Early New England* (New York: Columbia University Press, 2010).

7. On Puritans and economic life see Mark Valeri, *Heavenly Merchandize: How Religion Shaped Commerce in Puritan America* (Princeton, NJ: Princeton University Press, 2010); Mark Peterson, *The Price of Redemption: The Spiritual Economy of Puritan New England* (Stanford, CA: Stanford University Press, 1997); Philip Benedict, *Christ's Churches Purely Reformed: A Social History of Calvinism* (New Haven, CT: Yale University Press, 2002).

8. John Winthrop, *A Modell of Christian Charity* (1630) in *Collections of the Massachusetts Historical Society* (Boston, 1838), 3rd series 7:31–48, digitized by the Hanover Historical Texts Project, https://history.hanover.edu/texts/winth mod.html; for the longer history of this sermon, which was not well known in its own time, see Abram Van Engen, *City on a Hill: A History of American Exceptionalism* (New Haven, CT: Yale University Press, 2020).

9. Michael Wigglesworth, *Meat out of the eater: or, Meditations concerning the necessity, end, and usefulness of afflictions unto Gods children. All tending to prepare them, for, and comfort them under the crosse* (Cambridge [Mass.], 1670), 25–31, digitized by the Early English Books Online Text Creation Partnership, https://quod .lib.umich.edu/e/evans/N00104.0001.001/1:2.7?rgn=div2;view=fulltext; 162–65, https://quod.lib.umich.edu/e/evans/N00104.0001.001/1:10.1?rgn=div2;view= fulltext.

Teaching the First Great Awakening

JOHN HOWARD SMITH

Sarah Prentice of Grafton, Massachusetts, often underwent episodes of intense spiritual ecstasy that, according to her husband, Solomon, "Much Effected her Body to that Degree
that She was Scarce able to Stirr hand or foot for some few Minuits."
In 1742, at the height of the revivals known as the First Great Awakening, Grafton was a nexus of tumultuous evangelical energy, and in that
year one of Sarah's episodes was unprecedented in its intensity. Her
astonished neighbors and frightened husband, himself a minister and
fervent supporter of the revivals, realized that this incident was far different from earlier ones. What she had presumed to have been her conversion ten years before, she now realized, was but a shadow of what
she now experienced. Others claimed that conversion conferred spiritual perfection and even physical immortality. In Ipswich, Massachusetts, Lydia Halliday declared before her neighbors in the 1750s that the
spirit of Christ permeated her body and raised her "above All Saints
and Angels."[1]

Beginning in the 1730s, colonial Americans experienced an unprecedented period of evangelical Christian revivalism known as the First
Great Awakening. Some among a rising generation of clergymen pushed
for a deeper personal commitment to Christ emphasizing heightened
emotionalism in public and private worship. Some of the more radical
"New Lights" even encouraged their audiences to question the qualifications of their ministers and abandon those whose commitment to the
true faith was absent or feeble. These more radical New Lights took these
ideas to theological and behavioral extremes that threatened established

153

societal norms and church organizational order. This more zealous religious group was opposed by the elder, firmly established clergy who deprecated New Light antiauthoritarianism and religious individualism. Called "Old Lights," these more conservative ministers deplored what they perceived to be anarchic and indecorous tendencies in the revivals. The majority of New Lights, more moderate in their approach to revivalism, also criticized excessive "enthusiasm" in religious belief and practice, but the responses of ordinary people to evangelicalism and radical theologies speaks to a general preference for New Light extremism.[2]

The First Great Awakening is traditionally presented to students as a response to the rapid pace of demographic and economic expansion in early eighteenth-century British America. Commonly taught alongside the Enlightenment, as though the revivals were part of the intellectual ferment, revivalism is considered by some textbook authors to be an experience that, along with the advent of consumerism, unified the colonies in preparation for the American Revolution. Most histories of the Awakening tend to confine it to a ten-year period ending on or about 1745, as well as emphasizing it as an event taking place mainly in New England and, to a lesser extent, the middle colonies of Pennsylvania and New Jersey. Recent scholarship has managed to widen the scope of the Awakening to include the southern colonies, a broader chronology, and focus upon demographic groups previously underrepresented or ignored: women, African Americans, Indians, and lower-class Americans, who rarely show up in classroom discussions of the revivals. Teachers can enrich students' understanding of the Awakening by addressing its more complicated nature, particularly its radicalism, by raising the voices of those who have been for too long ignored.[3]

Understanding and Teaching the Radical Revivals

Students must first understand the strange perspective of the religious experiences of the revivals. As Ezra Stiles of Connecticut, a major critic of the revivals, reflected, "Multitudes were seriously, soberly and solemnly out of their wits" in the 1740s and 1750s. Like-minded men such as Boston's Charles Chauncy, whom the revivalists called Old Light, repeatedly drew attention to the most baffling and outrageous incidents of revivalist excesses to discredit the Awakening as nothing more than temporary mass insanity. Moderate New Lights defended the revivals but excoriated radicals in their ranks for "indecent" behaviors both behind and in front of the pulpit. They averred that these were the exception rather than the rule. Historians and textbook authors have generally followed suit, minimizing New Light radicalism in favor of emphasizing the relatively sober evangelicalism of Jonathan Edwards as defining the Awakening. Nevertheless, these excesses are fundamental aspects of the First Great Awakening. The dynamics of the First Great Awakening diverged sharply from earlier instances of "covenant renewals" that were merely reaffirmations of a congregation's commitment to theological principles and church doctrine. Examples abound of religious radicalism associated with the Awakening that eventually became integral parts of Protestant Christianity in America. Men, women, and even children had incredible visions, prophetic dreams, or near-death experiences, or they fell into trances to speak in unknown languages or proclaim their rebirth as transformed people.[4]

One way to help students understand the varying degrees of otherworldly religious experiences is to start with someone students will likely have heard of: Jonathan Edwards. Those who listened to his preaching encountered the supernatural in surprising ways. Radical revivalist Rev. Stephen Williams noted in his journal in May 1741, "I hear of strange & unusuall things at Suffield & Elsewhere," later writing to the reverend Eleazar Wheelock of Connecticut about "strange . . . Extasies" reported by converts throughout southern New England. Williams meticulously chronicled many incidents of extremism throughout New England. During a visit to Suffield, Edwards oversaw the conversion of more than ninety people, three of them African American slaves. An unnamed traveling companion noted that on the next day, after an extraordinarily passionate sermon delivered by Edwards on the necessity of repentance and conversion, spiritually moved parishioners carried the energy from the meetinghouse to a nearby house. According to the account, a roaring sound could be heard from a great distance away from the house that became almost deafening when they arrived. Inside, a "Confus'd" mixture of "Sobs," and "Groans & Screeches" evocative of "women in the Pains of Childbirth" mingled with "Houlings and Yellings, which to Even a Carnal Man might point out Hell" that went on for over two hours. Eventually people came to their senses, with most returning to their homes with feelings "of Peace & Joy," others seeming still to be in the throes of "Rapture."[5]

Historians normally depict Jonathan Edwards as a moderate revivalist who conferred legitimacy to the Awakening, but he nevertheless sanctioned some radical evangelical behaviors decried by Old Light critics. Edwards was initially dismayed by radical evangelicalism and the theatricality of New Light ministers and troubled by people claiming extraordinary experiences, but after observing the highly theatrical Anglican revivalist, George Whitefield, Edwards gradually incorporated much of Whitefield's performative rhetorical style. Edwards's most famous sermon, one that is usually the only one associated with him in most textbooks, is *Sinners in the Hands of an Angry God* (1741), which remains a prime example of this transition, though by no means the only one. Students who read the sermon, or have excerpts read to them in class, can get a strong sense of the emotional impact of New Light preaching upon audiences. The first nine paragraphs of the "Application" are the most evocative, and contains the sections most often quoted in works about the Awakening and Edwards's role in it. While *Sinners* is not representative of Edwards's entire body of sermonic works, it does capture the spirit of radical revivalism at that time. I often read excerpts to students, seeking to channel Edwards in an almost matter-of-fact style, rather than in the "hellfire and brimstone" fashion that typifies much evangelical preaching today. Students often respond in interesting ways to a reading of the more vivid passages from *Sinners*, and this can be the launching point for insightful discussions. Some may recall hearing such "hellfire and brimstone" sermons in their own churches or hearing such things when seeing televangelists on TV or the internet. Teachers can then explain how the First Great Awakening was the beginning of popular American evangelicalism.[6]

Another powerful sermon by a Delaware Valley Presbyterian evangelical, Gilbert Tennent, titled *The Danger of an Unconverted Ministry* (1740), lays out in stark contrast the dire predicament of believers who may be led by an unconverted or spiritually deadened minister. Students gain additional insight into the import of Tennent's argument when asked what they would do if, hypothetically speaking, the classroom were a church where the instructor is the minister, and a significant portion of the class believed that he is not converted. Students thus learn about the waves of church divisions leading to outright denominational schisms and the splitting of churches within communities known as separatism. Sometimes a church would break into factions, not necessarily over a minister's qualifications or level of religious zeal, but over the degrees to which the word of God should affect people emotionally. Although Edwards's *Sinners* is best read or recited in an even tone, *The*

Danger of an Unconverted Ministry does bear a more vigorous delivery, which drives home the critical point to students of the gravity of the revivals. I normally assign excerpts from *Sinners* and *Danger*, as well as accounts penned by ordinary people who had extraordinary reactions to evangelical preaching, but the best effects are to be had when these primary sources are—in a sense—acted out by the instructor and even the students themselves.[7]

Teaching about the Awakening's Periphery

Too often the First Great Awakening is presented to students as an event driven by white Euro-American men dealing almost exclusively with white audiences who together bring out a significant change to Protestant religious culture in pre-Revolutionary America. However, as the experiences of women, African Americans, and the continent's Indigenous peoples prove, the redefining of religion engendered by the Awakening makes it much more than a mere prelude to the American Revolution or an opportunity to comment upon the democratic character of late colonial American society.

One of the most compelling written accounts of visionary evangelicalism is that of Hannah Heaton of North Haven, Connecticut, who composed an autobiographical "spiritual history" for the benefit of her children. Originally from rural Southampton, Long Island, Heaton was powerfully affected at the age of twenty when she heard George Whitefield and Gilbert Tennent during a joint preaching tour in Connecticut in early 1741. She began attending a revivalist Separate church, and before long she began to feel a stirring in her soul, and then she heard the voice of Christ instruct her to "seek and you shall find[,] come to me all you that are weary and heauiladen[,] and I will give you rest." She then saw "a louely go[o]d man with his arm open[,] ready to receiue me[,] his face was full of smiles[,] he lookt white and ruddy and was just such a sauiour as my soul wanted." She believed that this incredible man was Jesus Christ himself, and her heart swelled with gratitude and an overwhelming feeling of love. But late one night she had a terrifying nightmare of the "devil in the shape of a great snake all on a flame with his sting out" who violently set upon a hapless sinner, and for the rest of her life Heaton feared demonic attack to such a degree that she often dreaded lying down in her own bed to sleep "for fear of the deuil that he would distress me" in her dreams. She went on to have other encounters with Satan in the 1750s, her faith sorely tested even as she felt the reassuring hand of Christ on her shoulder.[8]

Some women, such as Bathsheba Kingsley of Westfield, Massachusetts, believed that their experiences qualified them to assume for themselves the mantle of the ministry, while others, such as Sarah Osborne (described below), simply reported incredible spiritual experiences. Students introduced to selected passages from both women's accounts learn not just about female religious sensibilities at this time, but also how ordinary people responded to evangelicalism. The white female presence in the First Great Awakening is far greater and more significant than is traditionally understood, as evidenced by firsthand accounts of revival audiences becoming emotionally overwhelmed in response to revival sermons. Exposing students to women's voices in the Awakening not only solidifies the fact of their presence in students' minds but also stimulates discussion about feminine influence upon evangelicalism as it grew to define Christianity in America after the Revolution.[9]

While many of the "transported" were white middle-class people, they also included illiterate white and African American common people and youngsters, which inspired radical New Lights to remind their audiences that all are equal in God's eyes. Old Light critics saw in this individual lay empowerment a dangerous attempt to undermine the established social and spiritual order. This seemingly democratic aspect of the Awakening has been thought erroneously to have influenced a liberalizing trend in colonial politics that led to the American Revolution, but for radical New Lights it presaged a restoration of the spirit of first-century Christianity. Episodes of converts taking celestial journeys or assuming spiritual power so permeated revivalism by 1742 that it was assumed by radical New Lights that no conversion was real unless "a person must be in a sort of trance and . . . see wonders." This was believed to be corrosive to spiritual decorum and clerical authority, even by some New Lights. Evangelical conversion narratives, replete with references to the climbing of holy mountains, encounters with rampaging bulls, and glimpses at the "Book of Life," the names inscribed in blood on its luminous pages, exhibit unbroken threads of continuity to medieval European religious folklore, mixed with literalist apocalypticism. The most common motif found in these visions is that of seeing either God or Christ sitting on celestial thrones, surrounded by choirs of angels straight out of the twentieth chapter of the Book of Revelation. Old Lights repeatedly focused upon this aspect of the revivals to deprecate evangelicalism's undermining of spiritual and doctrinal order, and moderate New Lights were similarly uncomfortable with such excesses of "enthusiasm."[10]

Edwards's wife, Sarah, experienced several ecstatic "transports" of her own in 1741–42, at which Jonathan privately rejoiced but declined to discuss publicly apart from describing them as happening to an anonymous male parishioner in *Some Thoughts Concerning the Present Revival of Religion* (1742). In Sarah Edwards, Jonathan had an exemplar of the "complete" Christian and incontrovertible evidence that charismata was a positive development in true Christianity and not a delusion of rank "enthusiasm" or spiritual naivete. "Now if such things are enthusiasm," he declared, "and the fruits of a distempered brain, let my brain be evermore possessed of that happy distemper!" However, students who read the relevant passage about her will notice that he changes her into an unnamed man, and this can become a lively topic of classroom discussion concerning Edwards's reasons for obscuring his wife's identity. Sarah Osborn (1714–96) of Newport, Rhode Island, is yet another case in point. Her account of her spiritual travails not only reveals an astonishing self-awareness and candor, but also how she earned the admiration and respect of her male counterparts, who lauded her Calvinist orthodoxy and carefully endorsed her lay authority. Another remarkable aspect of Osborn's career is in her cultivation of African American evangelization.[11]

Teaching students about African Americans' revival experiences can complicate their assumptions that enslaved people had little agency. Some enslaved people, previously indifferent to Christianity but now freshly converted, began to look for a contemporary Moses to lead them out of bondage and to their own promised land, or for a Messiah to lead them in an apocalyptic war of liberation against the whites. Instructors should begin by explaining how some West African religious beliefs and practices survived the Middle Passage to become incorporated into African American Christianity, which refused to be a faith emphasizing docility and obedience to slaveowners, as well as denying the conventional wisdom of white supremacy. Albert J. Raboteau, in *Slave Religion: The "Invisible Institution" in the Antebellum South*, offers many excerpts from African and African American primary sources that give students an understanding of how evangelical Protestantism appealed to slaves in particular. The best examples are found in chapter 3, "Cathechesis and Conversion."[12]

Old Light critics and nervous slaveholders alleged that the revivals inspired the potential for slave revolts, leading to a forceful campaign to establish a strict program of slave Christianization designed to preclude any African American notions of liberation in this life. The Awakening was never as strong in the South as it had been in the northern colonies before the French and Indian War because of its apparent effect upon the enslaved population, whose hopes for collective liberation awakened in the years just before the American Revolution. Before 1740, the majority of clergymen rarely considered African Americans, particularly slaves, as fit subjects for conversion. As a result, most slaves practiced some hybrid form of native West African religions or mixed a form of Christianity with West African components, while some adhered to Islam. However, in the wake of Whitefield's first two tours of the colonies, beams of the New Light shone upon scattered slave populations throughout the Eastern Seaboard. The result was a concerted effort to convert slaves to Christianity in the 1750s and 1760s that constitutes the First Great Awakening's greatest legacy. While white clergymen tried to exert control over slaves with a faith emphasizing humility and docility, African Americans crafted a faith of their own through the synthesis of traditional West African religions and European Christianity. Although beyond the timeline of the Awakening, a reading from Nat Turner's *Confession* about his visionary experiences can be powerful. A similar dynamic animated a transformation of the religious landscape in Indian Country.[13]

Although some American Indians participated in the Protestant Awakening, the nativist Indian Awakening was not fundamentally Christian (for more on Native American religion, see Melissa Franklin Harkrider's chapter). Nonetheless, exposing students to this material can help them see how religion could be a unifying force throughout North America. The best way to do this is to ensure that American Indians are a recurrent presence in teaching early America, which gives students a context for understanding the origins of these nativist movements. Some historians would not include these nativist Indian revivals in their definition of the Great Awakening, but teaching students about Indians' experiences and fostering students' deliberation over whether or not to include these revivals in their definition of the Great Awakening can help them see how historians construct categories and narratives. Some Indians' experiences were clearly Christian, and while white evangelical missionaries enjoyed some success proselytizing to Indian communities, resistance to a religion that justified land theft and annihilationist warfare remained strong. Indian conversion was complicated; many refused to commit fully, abandoned their newfound faith, or pretended conversion as a tactic to curry favor with traders and colonial authorities, but some genuinely basked in the New Light.[14]

Many Indians' religious experiences led them to distance themselves from European Americans. Indian peoples living along the middle-colony frontier experienced their own religious awakening in the 1740s and 1750s, as self-proclaimed "prophets" and religious reformers traveled all over the backcountry preaching spiritual and tribal—sometimes racial—unity. All railed against rampant alcoholism, dependence upon white people's tools and technology, and the consuming ignorance of the old ways, most pointedly the old religion, which, as nativist Indian revivalists said, the Master of Life punished with death, warfare, and loss—both of land and of power. The only remedy, they insisted, was the reinvigoration of the old faith, which took the form of a blended reinvention of traditional tribal religions. The best example of this was Neolin, a Delaware "prophet" whose experience meeting the Master of Life resulted in his producing a kind of map showing how whites had blocked the traditional Indian path to the afterlife and redirected them to the Christian hell. Misunderstood by missionaries as a "bible," Neolin's map was meant to show Indians how to reclaim their spiritual destiny through religious renewal. Showing this map to students and encouraging them to analyze it allows them to see what Neolin was talking about in almost the same way that his audiences did.[15] The map is digitized online.[16]

The First Great Awakening is not commonly understood to have gripped Indian Country, but with the inclusion of non-Christian religions and Indian cultural revivalism, the Awakening becomes a much larger and even more significant event. As with the Protestant revivals, the Indian Great Awakening was just as unifying as it was a contentious and divisive experience. That the latter was motivated by Native, mainly Delaware, religion and not by Christianity does not alter the fact that there was a spiritual revival in Indian Country that ran parallel to the one coursing through Anglo-America. Subsequent historians of the eighteenth century have variously ignored this or argued that the Indian Awakening was exclusively a Christian one upon which New Lights such as David Brainerd and Jonathan Edwards congratulated themselves. Omitting Native religious and spiritual renewal from the study and teaching of the Awakening propagates a colonialist denial of the legitimacy of non-Christian religions and further obscures the Indian presence in early America. Indeed, the omission of peoples residing on the periphery of colonial British America not only does a disservice to them but also distorts the Awakening in a way that unfairly narrows the scale and significance of the event.[17]

Conclusion

Historians and instructors have generally deemphasized the more overtly charismatic elements of the First Great Awakening, most likely due to a contemporary discomfort with the intensity of religious feelings. Although some historians have argued that the 1700s were a period of steadily declining Christian belief and practice, and that the First Great Awakening was a nonevent, the eighteenth century was a period of steadily increasing public and private religiosity. The seeming decline in religiosity before the Awakening had more to do with dissatisfaction with the institutional nature of Christianity and frustration with doctrinal and theological disputes between and within denominations. The throngs of people who flocked to see George Whitefield preach and swooned in their seats at the vivid descriptions of hell in Jonathan Edwards's *Sinners in the Hands of an Angry God*, speak not to decline and growing secularism, but to popular spiritual hunger that evangelicalism sated. The active participation of laypeople, especially women and African Americans, and the reinvention of traditional American Indian religions all make this Awakening popular.[18]

ADDITIONAL RESOURCES

Lambert, Frank. *Inventing the "Great Awakening"*. Princeton, NJ: Princeton University Press, 1999.

Lambert, Frank. "'I Saw the Book Talk': Slave Readings of the First Great Awakening." *Journal of African American History* 87 (Winter 2002), 12–25.

Smith, John Howard. *The First Great Awakening: Redefining Religion in British America, 1725–1775*. Madison, NJ: Fairleigh Dickinson University Press, 2015.

Stout, Harry S. *The Divine Dramatist: George Whitefield and the Rise of Modern Evangelicalism*. Grand Rapids, MI: William. B. Eerdmans, 1991.

Winiarski, Douglas. "Souls Filled with Ravishing Transport: Heavenly Visions and the Radical Awakening in New England, 1742." *William and Mary Quarterly*, 3d Ser., 61 (January 2004), 3–46.

Winiarski, Douglas L. *Darkness Falls on the Land of Light: Experiencing Religious Awakenings in Eighteenth-Century New England*. Chapel Hill: University of North Carolina Press, 2017.

NOTES

1. Daniel Rogers, diary, January 29, 1742, Rogers Family Papers, 1614–1950, Ser. II, box 5B, New York Historical Society, New York; William G. Mcloughlin, ed., *The Diary of Isaac Backus*, 3 vols. (Providence, RI: Brown University Press, 1979), 1:293–94; Rogers, diary, 27 March 1742; J. M. Bumsted, "Presbyterianism in 18th Century Massachusetts: The Formation of a Church at Easton, 1752," *Journal of Presbyterian History* 46, no. 4 (1968): 243–53; Ross W. Beales Jr., ed., "Solomon Prentice's Narrative of the Great Awakening," *Proceedings of the Massachusetts Historical Society* 83 (1971): 135.

2. See John Howard Smith, *The First Great Awakening: Redefining Religion in British America, 1725–1775* (Madison, NJ: Fairleigh Dickinson University Press, 2015), 137–40, 149–69.

3. A typical example of the way textbooks characterize the Awakening is found in James L. Roark, Michael P. Johnson, Patricia Cline Cohen, Sarah Stage, and Susan M. Hartman, *The American Promise: A History of the United States*, 7th value ed. (Boston: Bedford/St. Martin's, 2017): "Colonial revivals expressed in religious terms many of the same democratic and egalitarian values expressed in economic terms by colonists' patterns of consumption. . . . Like consumption, revivals contributed to a set of common experiences that bridged colonial divides of faith, region, class, and status" (117). For a detailed historiographic survey of the Awakening, see Smith, *The First Great Awakening*, 3–7. Major correctives to faulty chronologies and interpretations of the Awakening include Smith, *The First Great Awakening;* and Douglas L. Winiarski, *Darkness Falls on the Land of Light: Experiencing Religious Awakenings in Eighteenth-Century New England* (Chapel Hill: University of North Carolina Press, 2017).

4. Jonathan Edwards to George Whitefield, February 12, 1739/40, in *The Works of Jonathan Edwards*, Jonathan Edwards Center, Yale University, http://edwards .yale.edu/archive?path=aHRocDovL2Vkd2FyZHMueWFsZS5lZHUvY2dpL dpL WJpbi9uZXdwaGlsby9nZXRvYmplY3Qw/Yy4xNT01OjIyLndqZXW8=; Ezra Stiles, *Discourse on the Christian Union* (Boston, 1761), 50. On covenant renewals, see Michael J. Crawford, *Seasons of Grace: New England's Revival Tradition in Its British Context* (New York: Oxford University Press, 1991), 43–45.

5. "Diary of the Reverend Stephen Williams," 1715–82, 10 vols., typescript, Storrs Public Library, Longmeadow, MA, 3:368–71; Stephen Williams to Eleazar Wheelock, March 16, 1741, April 15, 1741; Winiarski, "Jonathan Edwards," 697, 738–39.

6. Jonathan Edwards, *Sinners in the Hands of an Angry God* (1741), in *The Works of Jonathan Edwards* Online, http://edwards.yale.edu/archive?path=aH

RocDovL2Vkd2FyZHMueWFsZS55lZHUvY2dpLWJpbi9uZXdwaGguaZXdwaGh9nZX
RvYmplY3QucGw/Yy4yYMTooNy53amVu.

7. Gilbert Tennent, *The Danger of an Unconverted Ministry* (1740), Cengage, http://college.cengage.com/history/ayers_primary_sources/danger_unconver ted_ministry.htm.

8. Barbara E. Lacey, "The World of Hannah Heaton: The Autobiography of an Eighteenth-Century Connecticut Farm Woman," *William and Mary Quarterly*, 3rd ser., 45 (April 1988): 282–89.

9. Catherine L. Brekus, *Strangers and Pilgrims: Female Preaching in America, 1740–1845* (Chapel Hill: University of North Carolina Press, 1998), 23–26.

10. Douglas L. Winiarski, "Souls Filled with Ravishing Transport: Heavenly Visions and the Radical Awakening in New England," *William and Mary Quarterly*, 3rd ser., 61, no. 1 (January 2004): 8–9, 11–12, 14–17, 36–37, 40–41.

11. Jonathan Edwards to Joseph Bellamy, January 21, 1741/42, in *Works of Jonathan Edwards Online*, 16:99; Sarah Pierpont Edwards, "Narrative" (1742), reprinted in Sereno Edwards Dwight, *The Life of President Edwards* (New York: G. & C. & H. Carvill, 1830), 181; Edwards, *Some Thoughts Concerning the Present Revival, Works of Jonathan Edwards*, 4:340, 331; George M. Marsden, *Jonathan Edwards: A Life* (New Haven: Yale University Press, 2004), 239–42; Charles E. Hambrick-Stowe, "The Spiritual Pilgrimage of Sarah Osborn (1714–1796)," *Church History* 61 (December 1992): 408–21; Catherine A. Brekus, *Sarah Osborn's World: The Rise of Evangelical Christianity in Early America* (New Haven, CT: Yale University Press, 2013), chaps. 4, 8, 9.

12. Albert J. Raboteau, *Slave Religion: The "Invisible Institution" in the Antebellum South*, rev. ed. (New York: Oxford University Press, 2004), chaps. 1–2.

13. Raboteau, *Slave Religion*, ix, 128–31.

14. Most works on the Great Awakening only lightly cover Indian communities. Exceptions include Jane T. Merritt, "Dreaming of the Savior's Blood: Moravians and the Indian Great Awakening in Pennsylvania," *The William and Mary Quarterly*, 3rd ser., 54 (October 1997), 723–46; and Linford D. Fisher, *The Indian Great Awakening: Religion and the Shaping of Native Cultures in Early America* (New York: Oxford University Press, 2012).

15. Thomas Prince Sr., ed., The Christian History, Containing Accounts of the Revival and Propagation of Religion in Great-Britain and America, 2 vols. (Boston, 1744, 1745), 2:21; Merritt, "Dreaming of the Savior's Blood."

16. "'Mah-tan'-tooh, or the Devil, standing in a flame of fire, with open arms to receive the wicked." In Archibald Loudon, A selection, of some of the most interesting narratives, of outrages, committed by the Indians, in their wars, with the white people . . . (Carlisle [Pa]: A. Loudon, 1808–11), Monroe Wakeman and Holman Loan Collection of the Pequot Library Association, on deposit in the Beinecke Rare Book and Manuscript Library, Pequot L92, accessed June 14, 2023, https://collections.library.yale.edu/catalog/2021568,

17. David Zeisberger, "1769 Diary," quoted in Gregory Evans Dowd, *A Spirited Resistance: The North American Indian Struggle for Unity, 1745-1815* (Baltimore: Johns Hopkins University Press, 1992), 32–33; Charles E. Hunter, "The Delaware Nativist Revival of the Mid-Eighteenth Century," *Ethnohistory* 18 (Winter 1971), 42–43; Winiarski, "Souls Filled with Ravishing Transport," 11–12; Jonathan Edwards, *Life of David Brainerd* in *The Works of Jonathan Edwards*, Vol. 7, ed. Norman Pettit (New Haven: Yale University Press, 1985), 326–27; Thomas S. Kidd, *The Great Awakening: A Brief History with Documents* (Boston: Bedford/St. Martin's, 2007), 117–73, 198–99. See also Fisher, *The Indian Great Awakening*.

18. Butler, *Awash in a Sea of Faith: Christianizing the American People* (Cambridge, MA: Harvard University Press, 1990), 165–74. Butler was partly trying to refute an argument made by Patricia U. Bonomi in *Under the Cope of Heaven: Religion, Society, and Politics in Colonial America* (New York: Oxford University Press, 1986), chaps. 4–5.

Was America Founded as a Christian Nation?

JOHN FEA

"Was America Founded as a Christian Nation?" Culture warriors, evangelical Christians, academics,
school boards, and those responsible for state K-12 curriculum standards
are deeply invested in this question. Those who argue that America *was*
founded as a Christian nation often believe that the United States has
been held hostage by secularists trying to change the Christian identity of their country. These evangelicals, many of whom affiliate with
the political movement known as the Christian Right, want to restore,
renew, and reclaim the supposedly Christian origins of the nation and
use their understanding of the American founding to justify policy on
a host of moral and cultural issues that will accomplish this task. Of
course, those who do *not* believe that America was founded as a Christian nation use the history of the founding to defend the idea that the
United States is a secular nation that should always champion the separation of church and state and resist efforts to promote religion.

Neither of these political approaches are very helpful for getting
our students to grasp the relationship between religion and politics
at the time of the founding. American history teachers concerned with
teaching students something about eighteenth-century America should
be wary of politicizing the question "Was America founded as a Christian nation?" In fact, I would argue that this is a bad historic question.
Why? Because the debate over this question did not reach any degree
of intensity until very recently. In other words, no one was asking it
in 1776 or 1787. We must be careful not to superimpose this question,
which entered public discourse with the rise of the Christian Right in

the 1970s, on the eighteenth-century world of the people who built the American republic.

History teachers are always looking for continuity between the past and the present. But it is also important that they educate students in what historian Gordon Wood has called the "pastness of the past." Or as the British novelist L. P. Hartley once said, "the past is a foreign country; they do things differently there."[1] The American Founding Fathers lived in a world that was fundamentally different from our own. It was a world in which there was largely only one religious game in town—Christianity. Yes, there were some tiny Jewish communities located in seaport towns, and it is likely that a form of Islam was practiced among African slaves, but much of the culture was defined by the powerful influence of Christianity, especially Protestant Christianity.

The founders had very divergent views about the relationship between Christianity and the nation they were forging. As I tell my students, we need to stop treating the founders as a monolithic whole. Thomas Jefferson and James Madison, for example, were strong advocates for the complete separation of church and state. These Virginians led the successful movement for the disestablishment of the Church of England in the immediate aftermath of the American Revolution. In 1777, Jefferson came to the defense of religious dissenters in Virginia—especially evangelical Baptists and Presbyterians—who had long chafed under religious Anglican persecution. He composed a "Bill for Establishing Religious Freedom in Virginia," which protected all individuals from government coercion in matters of religion. In 1786, the heart of this bill was passed by the Virginia Assembly as the "Virginia Statute for Religious Freedom."[2] The statute rejects wholeheartedly the colonial practice of paying taxes to support an established state church, calling this tradition both "sinful and tyrannical." Jefferson argued that religious belief should have no bearing whatsoever on whether a person is qualified to hold public office, and government should never impede on the free practice of religion.[3]

The Virginia Statute for Religious Freedom remains one of the most important statements on religious liberty ever written, and teachers should rush to share it with their students. As a historian, I am particularly interested in how the statute received broad support from both religious skeptics such as Jefferson and rural Virginia evangelicals. One helpful way of teaching the document is to assign it alongside Baptist accounts of persecution at the hands of Anglicans. For example, Lewis

Peyton Little's 1938 volume *Imprisoned Preachers and Religious Liberty in Virginia* provides court records and other primary sources of Baptist preachers pelted with apples and stones, drowned in rivers, physically abused, and beaten with whips for challenging the authority of Virginia's established church. Students familiar with twenty-first-century conservative evangelical arguments that America was founded as a Christian nation are often surprised to learn that eighteenth-century evangelicals were willing to cooperate with an unbeliever such as Jefferson in order to secure religious liberty.

Other founders, such as George Washington and John Adams, stressed that religion was essential to the cultivation of a virtuous citizenry, an essential trait of any successful republic. Washington's belief that the United States needed to be a religious republic is evident most clearly in his so-called Farewell Address of 1796, published shortly before he left the presidency. "Of all the dispositions and habits which lead to political prosperity," Washington wrote, "religion and morality are indispensable supports." Adams was convinced that religion was the only true foundation of moral happiness in the American republic. "There is no such thing [morality]," Adams wrote, "without a supposition of a God. There is no right or wrong in the universe without the supposition of a moral government and an intellectual and moral governor." While serving as president he told the officers of a Massachusetts militia brigade, "Our constitution was made only for a moral and religious people. It is wholly inadequate to the government of any other." Washington and Adams never wavered in their convictions that government was responsible for promoting religion. Both presidents regularly called for days of fasting and prayer and believed that churches should play a vital role in the moral improvement of the nation.[4]

Declarations of fasting and prayer are easily accessible online.[5] I like to use John Adams's 1798 proclamation calling for a day of fasting, humiliation, and prayer written on the eve of war with France, which allows students to see both continuity and change in history. Many students will connect Adams's proclamation with modern events such as the National Day of Prayer or the National Prayer Breakfast. But they will also notice Adams's call for prayer was overtly Christian. It includes references to "Redeemer of the World" and the "Holy Spirit" that one does not normally see in presidential calls for prayer made in today's more pluralistic society. Finally, have students read Adams's declaration alongside Thomas Jefferson's well-known 1808 letter to Reverend

Samuel Miller. In this letter, the third president is skeptical about such presidential proclamations. Jefferson was willing to *recommend*, but not *prescribe* national days of fasting and prayer.[6] Explore with your students why this might be the case.

It is true that the founders, by signing the Declaration of Independence, probably believed certain things about God and religion. Though the declaration was not meant to be an official statement of American religious values, it *does* make appeals and references to God. I regularly distribute a copy of the declaration to students and ask them to work in groups to find all these references. After the students complete this exercise, we come back together as a group and try to make sense of what these references to God mean in their eighteenth-century context. A close examination of that God-language sheds light on the religious worldview of its writers and its endorsers. These men affirmed what Thomas Jefferson, the primary author of the declaration, described as "Nature's God." This phrase was often used by eighteenth-century deists who believed that God created the world, instilled it with natural laws of science, morality, and politics, and allowed it to function based on those laws without any further divine interference. In addition, Jefferson wrote that the "Creator" endows his creation with certain unalienable rights, including "Life, Liberty, and the Pursuit of Happiness." Deists, freethinkers, and Enlightenment liberals such as Jefferson would have no problem affirming the idea that natural rights came from God. Though they might prefer this reference to God to be more explicit, Christians could also affirm this belief.

In the final paragraph of the Declaration of Independence, Jefferson appeals to the "Supreme Judge of the World for the Rectitude of our Intentions ... That these United Colonies are, and of Right ought to be, FREE AND INDEPENDENT STATES." Unlike the references to "Nature's God" and the "Creator," the phrase "Supreme Judge of the world" suggests that the God to whom Congress is appealing will one day judge humankind. While we normally think of God judging his creation as part of Christian theology, it was indeed possible for one to reject some of the central tenets of Christianity, such as the Trinity or the resurrection of Jesus Christ, and still believe that human beings would be judged in the next life for their moral conduct in this one. Indeed, all the major Founding Fathers believed in a God who judges the good and the bad. While the Continental Congress's use of the phrase "Supreme Judge of the world" certainly tells us a bit more about the attributes of the God of the declaration, it does not definitively identify this God as uniquely Christian. The same might be said for the last reference to God in the declaration: "And for the support of this Declaration, with a firm reliance on the protection of divine Providence, we mutually pledge to each other our Lives, our Fortunes and our sacred Honor." The term "providence," as it was used in the eighteenth century, implies an active God who is sustaining the world through his sovereign power. This is not the distant God of the deists, but a God who is ordering his creation. By mentioning providence, Congress was affirming its belief that God would watch over America and protect it in this revolutionary time of uncertainty, trial, and war. It reflects a view of God held by most of the representatives seated in the room during the summer of 1776.[7] If done well, this close reading of the Declaration of Independence will complicate the narratives that some students will bring with them to class. Jefferson's God was not distant, remote, or uninvolved in his creation. But neither was this the God of Christianity—the God who revealed himself in the form of a man and died for the sins of the world. I will usually conclude this class period by warning students not to neglect historical context in their search for a useable past.

While the Declaration of Independence references God four times, the Constitution never mentions God (except for the phrase "The Year of Our Lord, 1787"—a common eighteenth-century way of dating a document that was probably added to the document well after the members of the Constitution Convention left Philadelphia). The Constitution makes one reference to religion. Article VI affirms that "no religious Test shall ever be required as a Qualification to any Office or public trust under the United States." The framers of the Constitution made clear that a person could not be excluded from serving their country in a new national government based solely upon their religious convictions. The voters of the United States were given the liberty to vote for candidates to federal office who were Protestants, Catholics, Muslims, or atheists.

The writers of the *Federalist Papers* generally did not appeal to God as a means of convincing the states to ratify the Constitution. They extolled the benefits of Article VI and spoke glowingly about their decision to champion religious freedom for officeholders. James Iredell of North Carolina, a future Supreme Court justice, went so far as to argue that he had no problem with Americans choosing political officials who were "pagans" were "Mahometans," or had "no religion at all."[8]

This was not the case, however, for the Anti-Federalists, the men who openly opposed the ratification of the Constitution. Most students will be unfamiliar with the writing of the Anti-Federalists, and many will be surprised to learn that these opponents of the Constitution were deeply religious and strong advocates for a Christian nation. While Anti-Federalist opposition was always more political than it was religious, many Anti-Federalists rejected the Constitution because it did not make any explicit appeals to God. Since the religious language of the Anti-Federalist writers is often deeply embedded in the midst of their political arguments, I have developed a document that includes excerpts some authors who had the most to say about religious themes. One of the most scathing critiques of the godlessness of the Constitution came from William Petrikin, an Anti-Federalist from Carlisle, Pennsylvania. Writing under the pseudonym "Aristocrotis," Petrikin attacked the framers of the Constitution as elitists who preferred a refined religion of "nature" over a religion of "supernatural divine order." He chided that members of the Constitutional Convention for denying a belief in God, the "immortality of the soul," the "resurrection of the body," and a "future state of rewards and punishments." Anti-Federalists especially attacked Article VI because it placed no Christian qualifications on officeholders. Samuel," an Anti-Federalist from Massachusetts, worried that the lack of a religious test for office would mean that "a Pagan" or a "Moheometan" might serve the country in the "most important trusts." "A Watchman," writing from western Massachusetts, feared that the Constitution opened the door for "the Jews, Turks, and Heathen to enter into publick office, and be seated at the head of the government of the United States."[9] By reading these excerpts, students will inevitably raise questions about present-day political alignments. Today, most defenders of the idea that the United States was founded as a Christian nation are also some of the strongest defenders of an originalist reading of the Constitution. Any discussion of the Anti-Federalists will challenge students to think historically about the Constitution and come to grips with the fact that it was the strongest opponents of this founding document who were the strongest adherents to a Christian America.

Yet anyone who wants to use the Declaration of Independence and the Constitution to argue against the importance of religion in the American founding must reckon with all those state constitutions that require officeholders to affirm the inspiration of the Old and New Testaments, obey the Christian Sabbath, or contribute tax money to support a state church. Students of religion and politics in the eighteenth-century must always read the US Constitution alongside these local documents. As noted above, the new commonwealth of Virginia rejected both a religious establishment and a religious test for office. But the Virginia state constitution was the exception to the rule. For example, the Massachusetts Constitution of 1780 affirmed that all members of society had the "right as well as the duty" to "worship the SUPREME BEING, the great Creator and Preserver of the university." The framers of this state constitution (John Adams was the primary drafter) had a limited understanding of what constituted the religious rights of its citizens. The document implies that religious rights were not afforded to those who did not worship God. While the Massachusetts government affirmed liberty of conscience in matters of religion, the Congregational Church remained the state's established church. Adams and the other framers made sure that anyone serving in the Massachusetts state government was a Christian. The governor of the state was required to "declare himself to be of the Christian religion," and anyone else elected to "State office or to the Legislature" needed to "believe the Christian religion, and have firm persuasion of its truth." The framers of the 1780 Massachusetts Constitution were concerned with promoting Protestant religion as a means of maintaining moral and public order in the state.[10]

The rest of the New England and state constitutions, with the exception of Rhode Island, adhered closely to the Massachusetts model of religious liberty. In the period between the American Revolution and the writing of a new constitution in 1818, Connecticut continued to be governed by a seventeenth-century document known as the Fundamental Orders of Connecticut. The Fundamental Orders, an article adopted in 1638 by the earliest settlers of the Connecticut River Valley, ordered a Christian frame of government. It claimed that the colonial government was "established according to God" based upon the teachings of the "word of God." The governor of the colony was required to "execute Justice according to the rule of Gods word" in the "name of the Lord Jesus Christ," and magistrates were required to swear a similar oath. The state would become a prime target for champions of religious freedom, such as Thomas Jefferson, who did everything they could to topple the close connection between church and state and encourage the state's growing number of religious dissenters.[11]

In the Mid-Atlantic states, where a tradition of religious freedom had existed since the English settlement of the region in the seventeenth century, state constitutions reaffirmed this commitment to religious liberty but also placed limits on who could benefit from it. In Pennsylvania, civil rights were afforded to anyone who "acknowledges the being of a God." Each member of the legislature was required by law to subscribe to a belief in a God who creates and governs the world, a God who rewards the good and punishes the wicked, and the "Divine inspiration" of the Old and New Testaments. The 1776 New Jersey Constitution noted that it would be unlawful for its citizens to pay taxes to support churches. But like Pennsylvania it limited civil rights and government participation to Protestants. New York's Constitution afforded "liberty of conscience" to "all mankind" and forbade ministers or priests from holding office.[12]

In the South, the Maryland Constitution (1776) offered religious liberty to "All Persons, professing the Christian religion," and allowed the legislature to "lay a general and equal tax, for the support of the Christian religion" that allowed individuals to direct the tax toward either the Christian congregation of their choice or toward the relief of the poor from a particular denomination. Maryland officeholders were expected to declare a belief in the "Christian religion." The South Carolina Constitution of 1778 required all "state officers," members of the "privy council," and state legislators to be Protestants. The right to vote was limited to any free white male who "acknowledges the being of a God" and believed in "the future states of rewards and punishments." The South Carolina Constitution also affirmed that the "Christian Protestant religion shall be deemed, and is hereby constituted and declared to be, the established religion of this State."[13]

The Avalon Project at Yale University is the best place to find all the original Revolutionary Era state constitutions.[14] Since many of these constitutions are long and probably too cumbersome for the average undergraduate, I usually cull the religious language from all thirteen constitutions and paste them into a document that I give to students at the start of class. I offer a brief lecture on the need for creating such constitutions and then put students into groups, assigning each group an individual state to consider. After about ten minutes or so of group work, we come together and share our findings. Students notice very quickly the differences between the states in terms of both test oaths and religious establishments. There are two essential takeaways for this exercise. First, students should see that there was no unified understanding of the relationship between church and state in the first decades of the early republic. Second, the role of religion in the state constitutions was very different and in most cases more overtly Christian than the more liberal religious clauses of the federal Constitution and the First Amendment.

In conclusion, founding fathers certainly believed religion was important to the success of the republic, but they also wanted to separate it from government.

Any analysis of this question of whether the United States was founded as a Christian nation should provide opportunities for teachers to show their students that history does not conform easily to the kinds of "yes" or "no" answers that most present-day Americans want when they ask these questions or debate it on cable news. Such lessons apply to those who doggedly defend the notion that the United States was founded as a Christian nation, and those who doggedly defend the notion that the United States was founded as a secular nation. Students should leave their study of religion and the Revolutionary Era with a greater appreciation for nuance and complexity.

ADDITIONAL RESOURCES

Carte, Katherine. *Religion and the American Revolution: An Imperial History.* Chapel Hill: University of North Carolina Press, 2021.

Fea, John. *Was America Founded as a Christian Nation? A Historical Introduction.* Louisville, KY: Westminster/John Knox Press, 2012.

Green, Steven K. *Inventing a Christian America: The Myth of the Religious Founding.* New York: Oxford University Press, 2015.

Haselby, Sam. *The Origins of American Religious Nationalism.* New York: Oxford University Press, 2016.

Kidd, Thomas. *God of Liberty: A Religious History of the American Revolution.* New York: Basic Books, 2010.

Noll, Mark A. *America's God: From Jonathan Edwards to Abraham Lincoln.* New York: Oxford University Press, 2005.

NOTES

1. Gordon Wood, *The Purpose of the Past* (New York: Penguin Books, 2008), 8; David Lowenthal, *The Past Is a Foreign County* (Cambridge: Cambridge University Press, 1986), xvi.

2. "Virginia Statue of Religious Freedom," 1786, Basic Readings in U.S. Democracy, accessed March 2, 2020, https://usa.usembassy.de/etexts/democrac /42.htm.

3. For Jefferson's commitment to religious liberty see Thomas F. Buckley, *Church and State in Revolutionary Virginia, 1776–1787* (Charlottesville: University Press of Virginia, 1977) and John Ragosta, *Religious Freedom: Jefferson's Legacy, America's Creed* (Charlottesville: University of Virginia Press, 2013).

4. See John Fea, *Was America Founded as a Christian Nation? A Historical Introduction* (Louisville: Westminster John Knox Press, 2011), 186–88, 199–202; Mary Thompson, *"In the Hands of Good Providence": Religion in the Life of George Washington* (Charlottesville: University of Virginia Press, 2008); Sara Georgini, *Household Gods: The Religious Lives of the Adams Family* (New York: Oxford University Press, 2019).

5. "March 23, 1798: Proclamation of Day of Fasting, Humiliation and Prayer," Miller Center, University of Virginia, accessed March 2, 2020, https://millercenter.org/the-presidency/presidential-speeches/march-23-1798-proclamation-day-fasting-humiliation-and-prayer.

6. Thomas Jefferson to Samuel Miller, January 23, 1808, Founders Online, accessed March 2, 2020, National Archives, https://founders.archives.gov/?q=January%2023%2C%201808%20Author%3A%22Jefferson%2C%20Thomas%22&s=1111311111&r=14&sr=.

7. This section draws heavily from Fea, *Was America Founded as a Christian Nation*, 131–33.

8. Iredell quoted in Isaac Kramnick and R. Laurence Moore, *The Godless Constitution: The Case against Religious Correctness* (New York: W.W. Norton, 1996), 38–40.

9. Aristocrotis, "The Government of Nature Delineated or an Exact Picture of the New Federal *Constitution*," 1788, in *The Complete Anti-Federalist*, vol. 3: *Pennsylvania*, ed. Herbert J. Storing (Chicago: University of Chicago Press, 1981), 205–6.

10. Massachusetts Constitution, 1780, The Founders' Constitution, at http://press-pubs.uchicago.edu/founders/print_documents/v1ch1s6.html. For a short overview of the religion clauses in the Massachusetts Constitution see John Witter Jr., "'A Most Mild and Equitable Establishment of Religion': John Adams and the Massachusetts Experiment," in *Religion and the New Republic: Faith in the Founding of America*, ed. James H. Hutson (Lanham, MD: Rowman and Littlefield, 2000), 1–40.

11. Fundamental Orders of 1638," The Avalon Project, Yale Law School, https://avalon.law.yale.edu/17th_century/order.asp; Philip Hamburger, *Separation of Church and State* (Cambridge, MA: Harvard University Press, 2002), 144–45.

12. Edwin Gaustad, *Faith of Our Fathers: Religion and the New Nation* (San Francisco: Harper & Row, 1987), 173–74.

13. Ibid., 162, 164, 168–69, 170–72.

14. The Avalon Project, Yale Law School, https://avalon.law.yale.edu/.

The Constitution and Religion in the Early Republic

DANIEL L. DREISBACH

Religion has long featured prominently in American political culture; and few topics have provoked more controversy across the broad sweep of American history than the prudential and constitutional role of religion in public life (including in public school classrooms). Many contested issues today regarding the appropriate place of religion in the public square are variations on disputes that have agitated Americans since the early republic. In the wake of independence, Americans began to reevaluate the role religion should play in their new republic. Emerging from often contentious debates were novel, distinctively American approaches to the relationships between religion and the civil state. Among the important state papers addressing religion and religious liberty in the new political order are the Massachusetts Constitution (1780), Articles II and III (Part the First); the Virginia Statute for Establishing Religious Freedom (1786); and the US Constitution's Article VI, clause 3, religious test ban, and First Amendment, nonestablishment and free exercise of religion clauses.[1] Prominent figures also contributed to discussions of this topic through their public pronouncements, such as George Washington's Farewell Address (1796).[2] These documents give insights into American conceptions of religious liberty, which are among the most innovative contributions Americans have made to political thought. Moreover, because the US Supreme Court has given great weight to history in its interpretation of these constitutional principles, students are well advised to be attentive to these seminal documents.

Among the questions Americans have asked in the past and continue to ask today are the following: What role, if any, should religion play in public life? More specifically, what is the appropriate relationship between religion and the civil state? Does the American constitutional tradition espouse a principle of church-state separation restricting religion's place in public life? Must the civil state provide protections and accommodations for the free exercise of religion? These questions require consideration of evolving definitions of key terms, such as "religion," "religious liberty," "establishment of religion," and "separation of church and state."

Although beyond the scope of this chapter, students will gain additional insights into religion's role in the new nation by examining the place of religion in the colonies. Most of the colonies had established churches, following a model known in Europe in which one church enjoyed the legal and financial support of the civil state. A number of the independent states, however, reconsidered this arrangement.

This chapter gives guidance on how to teach students about the American founders' views on religion's role in public life and, by extension, to analyze controversies today regarding relationships between religion and civil government in the American constitutional order. The chapter begins with a few observations about religion in the American founding. This is followed by a discussion of the founding generation's diverse views on and approaches to relations between religion and the civil state. A concluding section examines the specific provisions in the US Constitution pertaining to religion and church-state relationships.

A good starting point for a unit on this topic is a discussion, or even a debate, among students on several broad questions regarding religion's potential to be a beneficent influence or source of conflict in society.

- What, if anything, can religion contribute to a political society? Do student responses depend on the specific religious sect and beliefs in question (in other words, do students think some religions are more beneficial or detrimental than others to a political society)? Does the degree to which a society is religious, secular, or culturally diverse inform student responses?
- What, if any, are the legitimate restrictions the civil state may place on religious exercises and expression? Does it make a difference if religion is sponsored by the government or by a private entity? Is

there something about religious exercises and expressions in public life that suggest they should be subject to more scrutiny and restrictions by the civil state than activities and expressions that are philosophical, political, economic, or artistic in content?

Religion and the American Founding

The expansive role of religion—specifically Christianity—in the political order of the founding era reflected the religious demographics of the American people. Despite the challenges in determining the religious affiliations and commitments of eighteenth-century Americans, historians of religion have estimated that around the time of independence, 98 percent or more of Americans of European descent identified with Protestantism.[3]

Americans at the end of the eighteenth century drew on and synthesized diverse intellectual traditions in framing their political thought and institutions. Among them were British constitutionalism, Enlightenment liberalism (in manifold forms), and classical and civic republicanism. Christianity and its sacred text were also among the influences that informed the founding generation. The Bible was the most cited source in the political literature of the founding era, accounting for approximately one-third of citations. The book of Deuteronomy alone was mentioned more than any other work and was referred to more frequently than influential thinkers such as John Locke or Baron de Montesquieu.[4]

Many in the founding generation valued Christianity and the Bible for their insights into human nature, civic virtue, social order, political authority, the rights and duties of citizens, and other concepts essential to framing a new polity. There was also broad agreement that religion—specifically biblical morality—was useful for nurturing the civic virtues that give citizens the capacity for self-government. Many also saw in the Bible political and legal models—such as republicanism and separation of powers—they believed enjoyed divine favor and were worthy of their consideration. Furthermore, over the course of many generations, Americans wove into their constitutional traditions specific principles and measures said to be derived from the Bible and transmitted to the colonies by way of the English common law and customs. These included provisions pertaining to due process, double jeopardy, cruel and unusual punishment, corruption of blood, and standards of weights and measures.

Religious Diversity and the Pursuit of Religious Liberty

By the time the national Constitution was crafted in the late 1780s, a declining number of Americans supported a legally established church in their respective states, and few advocated for a national ecclesiastical establishment. The extraordinary religious diversity in the new nation meant that the establishment of a national church was practically untenable. No denomination was sufficiently dominant to claim the legal favor of the national regime, and there was little likelihood that a political consensus would emerge as to which sect or combination of sects should constitute a "Church of the United States." Nonetheless, many influential citizens, despite some Enlightenment influences, continued to believe that religion must play a public role in the polity.

Few Americans of the seventeenth and eighteenth centuries, even among those who supported disestablishment, doubted the value of a vibrant religious, specifically Christian, culture. There was a consensus that religion fosters the civic virtues and social discipline that give citizens the capacity to govern themselves. Authoritarian rulers use the whip and rod to compel social order, but this approach is unacceptable for a free people. A self-governing people, in short, had to be a virtuous people who were controlled from within by an internal moral compass, which would replace external control by the whip and rod. A moral people respect social order, legitimate authority, oaths and contracts, private property, and the like; and such civic virtue, many eighteenth-century Americans believed, was nurtured by Christian morality.

Historian James H. Hutson called this notion "the founding generation's syllogism": "virtue and morality are necessary for free, republican government; religion is necessary for virtue and morality; religion is, therefore, necessary for republican government."[5] Many founders took this one step further, arguing that religious liberty was a desirable precondition for effective republican government insofar as it unleashed religion and its beneficent influence in society.[6]

The political literature of the founding era is filled with expressions of religion's vital role in a regime of republican self-government. The idea was espoused by Americans from diverse religious, intellectual, and political traditions; walks of life; and regions of the country. No one expressed this idea more famously or succinctly than George Washington in the Farewell Address (1796): "Of all the dispositions and habits which lead to political prosperity, Religion and morality are indispensable supports." He then proceeded to cast doubt on the supposition that morality could be maintained in the absence of religion.[7] David Ramsay, a delegate to the Continental Congress and the first major historian of the American Revolution, also expressed this idea succinctly, writing in 1789: "Remember that there can be no political happiness without liberty; that there can be no liberty without morality; and that there can be no morality without religion."[8]

For this reason, many Americans of the age viewed Christianity and its sacred text as vital to their political experiments, and they gave attention to how to nurture popular religion and extend its beneficent influence in society. By the mid-eighteenth century, two distinct, conflicting schools of thought had emerged regarding how best to promote a vibrant religious culture. Benjamin Rush, a respected signer of the Declaration of Independence, said: "There are but two ways of preserving visible religion in any country. The first is by establishments. The second is by the competition of different religious societies."[9]

The first way, which was the practice in Europe and most of the colonies, was to maintain a legally established church. A common view in the colonial period was that, because religion was indispensable to social order and political happiness, the civil state must officially and legally maintain a specific church, which citizens had an obligation to support. These establishmentarians feared that a failure to establish a church with the civil state's sustaining aid would impair religion's ability to extend its influence into civil society.

In the second half of the eighteenth century, an unlikely coalition of religious dissenters, nonconformists, and moderate Enlightenment rationalists advanced a second way to nurture a vibrant religious culture. They advocated for dismantling the old arrangement of one state, one church—that is, terminating legal privileges for one particular sect or combination of sects over all others—and replacing it with a disestablished regime in which all sects were on an equal footing before the law and could compete for adherents and their support in an open marketplace of ideas. They believed the multiplicity of religious sects that would flourish in this disestablished regime would foster religious liberty as multiple sects would check any one sect from working in concert with the civil state to oppress and persecute other sects.[10] As jurisdictions abandoned ecclesiastical establishments toward the end of the eighteenth century and the start of the nineteenth century, matters regarding religious belief or disbelief and association with and support of a particular minister or religious society were left to the voluntary choice of individual citizens; and, increasingly, the civil rights and prerogatives of citizens were no longer conditioned on their religious beliefs. In this open marketplace of ideas, Thomas Jefferson confidently predicted, "truth is great and will prevail if left to herself . . . unless by human interposition disarmed of her natural weapons, free argument and debate."[11] These opponents of state churches argued that disestablishment and competition among religious sects, in the words of James Madison, resulted "in the greater purity & industry of the pastors & in the greater devotion of their flocks."[12] Disestablishment, they thought, facilitated a vibrant religious culture in which the best and purest religion would emerge; state churches (state ecclesiastical monopolies), by contrast, tended to become complacent, corrupt, and intolerant.[13]

The state constitutions and laws written following independence reveal diverse approaches to church-state arrangements. Some expressly promoted an official role for religion in the civil polity; others espoused nonestablishment, sect equality, and open competition among religious sects. This latter view ultimately prevailed in America at both the state and national levels. Encourage students to examine these differing approaches by comparing the Massachusetts Constitution of 1780, Articles II and III (Part the First) with Thomas Jefferson's Statute for Establishing Religious Freedom (1786).[14] Then consider these questions:

- What are the best arguments for and against the differing church-state approaches set forth in these documents? What are the premises and goals of the policies in these documents, and what consequences in terms of religious liberty, sect equality, and so on, might be expected if a state were to adopt one of these documents as its governing policy?
- How might the interests of a political society be served or disserved by maintaining a government-sponsored church (the "first way" described above)? Many countries around the world continue to maintain state churches. What benefits do they see in such an arrangement?
- Many in the founding generation believed religion was essential for nurturing a virtuous citizenry capable of self-government. Why did they believe that? Were they right? What other than religion is capable of nurturing essential civic virtues?

- For a more ambitious project, have students compare the "second way" discussed above, arguing for competition among religious sects in a marketplace of ideas, with Adam Smith's free market ideas in *The Wealth of Nations* (1776). Smith considered this topic in his famous treatise, which was read and discussed by Americans.[15]

Religion and the American Constitution

The national constitution framed in Philadelphia in 1787, together with the First Amendment to it, was attentive to religion's place in civic life. The Constitution shaped a distinctively American approach to church-state relations expressed in Article VI, clause 3 and the First Amendment. The first declares that "no religious Test shall ever be required as a Qualification to any Office or public Trust under the United States," and the second provides that "Congress shall make no law respecting an establishment of religion, or prohibiting the free exercise thereof."[16] The former is binding only on federal officeholders. It did not invalidate religious tests that existed under state laws. Similarly, the latter provision did not initially alter church-state arrangements and practices at the state and local levels.

The Constitution's Article VI religious test ban generated lively debate in the state ratifying conventions. Critics said it suggested inattentiveness to the vital task of selecting rulers committed to protecting and nurturing religion and morality. Once it is conceded that not all religions are conducive to good civil government and political order, then there are plausible grounds for excluding adherents of some religions from public office. Oliver Ellsworth of Connecticut, however, defended the ban, arguing that "a good and peaceable citizen" should receive "no penalties or incapacities on account of his religious sentiments."[17]

The inclusion of religious tests in the laws of many states of the era indicates some measure of support for them. Moreover, religious tests coexisted with free exercise and nonestablishment provisions in some state constitutions, suggesting that these concepts were not always viewed as incompatible. The Constitution of 1787, as a matter of federalism, denied the national government all jurisdiction over religion, including the authority to administer religious tests. There was a consensus that religion was a matter best left to individual citizens, religious societies, and state governments. Many in the founding generation, it would seem, supported a federal test ban because they valued religious tests required under state laws, and they did not want the federal regime to mandate a test that would displace existing state test oaths and religious establishments.[18]

Significantly, early state constitutions restricting public office to Protestants afforded Jews and Roman Catholics, who constituted a small minority of the population, an opportunity to offer interpretations of religious liberty and church-state arrangements that differed from prevailing Protestant interpretations. In early September 1787, for example, Jonas Phillips wrote to George Washington and members of the federal constitutional convention meeting in Philadelphia. Describing himself as "one of the people called Jews of the City of Philadelphia, a people scattered and despersed among all nations," Phillips complained that a religious test requiring officeholders to affirm belief in both the Old and New Testaments, a provision included in some early state constitutions, would deprive him of his natural and inalienable rights of conscience because it is "absolutely against the Religious principle of a Jew and is against his Conscience to take any such oath." Such measures, he further observed, do not characterize "a government where all Religious societys are on an Eaquel footing." Thus, he petitioned "the honourable Convention[,] . . . for my self[,] my Children and posterity and for the benefit of all the Israelites through the 13 united States of America," to avoid language in the new constitution that would require oath takers to "acknowledge the scriptures of the new testament to be given by devine inspiration."[19]

Roman Catholics contended with similar disabilities. In addition to explicitly limiting public office to Protestants, some states required officeholders to renounce all allegiances to any foreign prince or prelate in all matters civil or ecclesiastical. This was a barely veiled reference to the pope, apparently calculated to disqualify Catholics from holding public office. Writing anonymously to a Philadelphia newspaper the same week as Jonas Phillip's letter, John Carroll, who was later consecrated the first Roman Catholic bishop in the United States and the first archbishop of Baltimore, denounced state religious tests because they unjustly placed "the degrading mark of distrust [and] the galling yoke of inferiority" on Catholics who had shed their blood alongside Protestants in the late war for American independence. Restricting public office to "protestants alone," he noted, failed to put "every denomination of christians . . . on the same footing of citizenship" and confer on Catholics "an equal right of participation" in civic life.[20] Carroll returned to this topic in a June 1789 letter written to the *Gazette of the United States* (New York). No citizen, he wrote under the pseudonym Pacificus, should be excluded from public office or otherwise deprived of "the stipulated rights of the political society" "merely on account of their religious opinions."[21] (Religious tests were but one issue on which Jews, Catholics, and other religious minorities challenged dominant Protestant interpretations of religious liberty in the new nation.)

A number of states conditioned their support for the proposed Constitution on the adoption of amendments—including an amendment protecting religious liberty. Early in the first Congress under the Constitution, Representative James Madison proposed the following amendment: "The civil rights of none shall be abridged on account of religious belief or worship, nor shall any national religion be established, nor shall the full and equal rights of conscience be in any manner, or on any pretext, infringed."[22] Both the House and the Senate debated drafts of the amendment over the summer before the matter was sent to a conference committee that crafted the final language adopted by the House on September 24 and by the Senate the following day. This text, now known as the First Amendment, was ratified by the requisite number of states and added to the Constitution in December 1791.

Although diverse interpretations can be drawn from this text and its legislative history, there is broad agreement for several modest conclusions. First, the framers proscribed the creation of a national church like the established church in England. Congress was prohibited from conferring legal preferences or special favors on one church that are denied to others. The nonestablishment provision was not meant to silence religion or require civil government to hold all religions in utter indifference. Second, the amendment implicitly affirmed that the states retained authority to define church-state relationships within their respective jurisdictions. (This purpose was turned on its head by the incorporation of the First Amendment into the Fourteenth Amendment.)[23] Third, the amendment protected citizens from actions by the federal regime inhibiting the free exercise of religion. The free exercise guarantee, at the very least, prevented Congress from compelling or prohibiting religious worship. It affirmed a right to worship God, or not, according to the dictates of conscience, free from coercion, interference, discrimination, or punishment by the national government.

While the legislative history reveals aspects of the First Amendment's original understanding and purposes, many questions about its application remain unanswered. For example, what role, if any, does the Constitution permit religion to play in the formulation of law and public policy; or to what extent is the federal government authorized to assist or encourage religion generally; or to what extent does the free exercise provision grant a citizen an exemption from a facially neutral law of general applicability because the law inhibits the adherent's religious exercise? These questions continue to provoke debate today.

With these questions in mind, invite student to engage the following questions:

- Many states included in their post-independence constitutions and statutes provisions requiring religious test oaths for civic obligations, protecting religious freedom, and prohibiting state churches. Are these provisions compatible? What might their inclusion in the same document reveal about the definitions, scope, and applications of these provisions in late eighteenth-century political thought?
- The conference committee of the First Congress that framed the First Amendment considered the House of Representative's draft amendment, which contained three religion clauses: nonestablishment, free exercise, and rights of conscience clauses.[24] The committee removed the "rights of conscience" language from the final draft. What are plausible explanations for deleting this clause? What might this revision reveal about the original definitions, scope, and applications of these three clauses?

Conclusion

From the founding era to the present day, Americans have debated the prudential and constitutional place and role of religion in civic life. Few controversies today involving religion and public life raise wholly novel issues; indeed, many contemporary conflicts are variations on disputes that have engaged prior generations of Americans. Much debate on these matters turns on the interpretation of the First Amendment provisions respecting the nonestablishment and free exercise of religion. Significantly, the US Supreme Court has counseled that this amendment should be construed "in the light of its history and the evils it was designed forever to suppress."[25] Accordingly, reflection on religion's historical role in American public life casts light not only on the past but also on the future of relations between religion and the civil polity.

ADDITIONAL RESOURCES

Dreisbach, Daniel L. "Religion and the Constitutional Tradition." In *Religions in America, 1790 to 1945*, vol. 2 of *The Cambridge History of Religions in America*, ed. Stephen J. Stein. New York: Cambridge University Press, 2012, 26–45.

Dreisbach, Daniel L., and Mark David Hall, eds. *The Sacred Rights of Conscience: Selected Readings on Religious Liberty and Church-State Relations in the American Founding*. Indianapolis, IN: Liberty Fund, 2009.

Hamburger, Philip. *Separation of Church and State*. Cambridge, MA: Harvard University Press, 2002.

Hutson, James H. *Church and State in America: The First Two Centuries*. Cambridge: Cambridge University Press, 2008.

Kidd, Thomas S. *God of Liberty: A Religious History of the American Revolution*. New York: Basic Books, 2010.

Witte, John, Jr., Joel A. Nichols, and Richard W. Garnett. *Religion and the American Constitutional Experiment*. 5th ed. New York: Oxford University Press, 2022.

NOTES

1. These documents are readily available online. They are also reproduced in Daniel L. Dreisbach and Mark David Hall, eds., *The Sacred Rights of Conscience: Selected Readings on Religious Liberty and Church-State Relations in the American Founding* (Indianapolis: Liberty Fund, 2009), 245–47 (Massachusetts Constitution), 250–51 (Virginia Statute), 373 (Article VI, clause 3), 433 (First Amendment).

2. George Washington, Farewell Address, September 19, 1796, in Dreisbach and Hall, *Sacred Rights of Conscience*, 468–70.

3. See Eric Kaufman, "American Exceptionalism Reconsidered: Anglo-Saxon Ethnogenesis in the 'Universal' Nation, 1776–1850," *Journal of American Studies* 33 (1999): 440.

4. Donald S. Lutz, "The Relative Influence of European Writers on Late Eighteenth-Century American Political Thought," *American Political Science Review* 78 (March 1984): 189–97.

5. James H. Hutson, *Religion and the Founding of the American Republic* (Washington, DC: Library of Congress, 1998), 81.

6. By republican government, the founders meant, at least, popular government, committed to the rule of law, in which government authority is derived from the consent of the governed and exercised through representatives freely and fairly chosen by the people.

7. George Washington, Farewell Address, in Dreisbach and Hall, *Sacred Rights of Conscience*, 468; online in *The Founders' Constitution*, http://press-pubs.uchicago.edu/founders/documents/v1ch18s29.html.

8. David Ramsay, *The History of the American Revolution*, 2 vols. (London, 1790), 2:356.

9. Benjamin Rush to Granville Sharp, April 27, 1784, in *Letters of Benjamin Rush*, ed. L. H. Butterfield, 2 vols. (Princeton, NJ: Princeton University Press, 1951), 1:330–31.

10. See James Madison, Speech in the Virginia Convention, June 12, 1788, in *The Papers of James Madison*, ed. Robert A. Rutland et al. (Charlottesville: University Press of Virginia, 1977), 11:130–31.

11. "A Bill for Establishing Religious Freedom, Virginia," in Dreisbach and Hall, *Sacred Rights of Conscience*, 251.

12. James Madison to Jasper Adams, September 1833, in Dreisbach and Hall, *Sacred Rights of Conscience*, 613.

13. See James Madison, A Memorial and Remonstrance against Religious Assessments (1785), in Dreisbach and Hall, *Sacred Rights of Conscience*, 311–12.

14. See Massachusetts Constitution, *The Founders' Constitution*, http://press-pubs.uchicago.edu/founders/print_documents/v1ch16.html; Virginia, Act for Establishing Religious Freedom, *The Founders' Constitution*, http://press-pubs.uchicago.edu/founders/documents/amendI_religions44.html.

15. See Adam Smith, *The Wealth of Nations* (1776; Cannan, ed., 1904), book 5, chap. 1, part 3, article 3, which is reprinted in Dreisbach and Hall, *Sacred Rights of Conscience*, 76–79, and available online.

16. US Constitution, Article VI and First Amendment, in Dreisbach and Hall, *Sacred Rights of Conscience*, 373, 433.

17. A Landholder [Oliver Ellsworth], no. 7 (December 17, 1787), in Dreisbach and Hall, *Sacred Rights of Conscience*, 377.

18. See Daniel L. Dreisbach, "The Constitution's Forgotten Religion Clause: Reflections on the Article VI Religious Test Ban," *Journal of Church and State* 38 (1996): 261–95.

19. Jonas Phillips to the President and Members of the Constitutional Convention, September 7, 1787, in Dreisbach and Hall, *Sacred Rights of Conscience*, 374.

20. A Reader, To the Editor (dated September 1, 1787), *The Columbian Magazine; or, Monthly Miscellany* (Philadelphia, 1787), supplement to the first volume, 881.

21. Pacificus, *Gazette of the United States* (New York), June 10, 1789, 65. See generally Michael D. Breidenbach, *Our Dear-Bought Liberty: Catholics and Religious Toleration in Early America* (Cambridge, MA.: Harvard University Press, 2021), 169–80.

22. Madison, Speech in Congress, June 8, 1789, in Dreisbach and Hall, *Sacred Rights of Conscience*, 420.

23. In the mid-twentieth century, the US Supreme Court incorporated the First Amendment religion provisions into the "liberties" protected by the Fourteenth Amendment's due process of law clause, thereby making them applicable to state and local authorities. This constitutional development prohibited state laws and practices "respecting an establishment of religion" or prohibiting religious exercise. The free exercise and nonestablishment of religion provisions were incorporated into the Fourteenth Amendment in *Cantwell v. Connecticut,* 310 U.S. 296, 303 (1940) and *Everson v. Board of Education,* 330 U.S. 1, 15 (1947), respectively.

24. "Religion Clauses from House Resolution and Articles of Amendment," August 24, 1789, in Dreisbach and Hall, *Sacred Rights of Conscience,* 431, 638.

25. *Everson,* 330 U.S. at 14–15.

Religion and Westward Expansion

JOHN G. TURNER

In the spring of 1857, President James Buchanan decided to send the US Army to the Utah Territory. Since 1851, Brigham Young, the president of the Church of Jesus Christ of Latter-day Saints, had served as Utah's governor. In recent months, Buchanan had received several reports that Young and other church leaders were hostile to non-Mormon federal appointees and even had sanctioned acts of violence against non-Mormons in the territory. Several of those federal appointees urged Buchanan to replace Young with a non-Mormon governor, but they warned the president that a replacement would not be safe without a military escort. By May, Buchanan had decided to act, and in July 2,500 troops left Fort Leavenworth, preceded by their supply trains. The Utah War, a revealing chapter in the history of the American West, had begun.[1]

It is easy for teachers to be intimidated by religion in the American West. "All that most of us know and learn about American religion keeps us firmly moored in an east-to-west framework," writes Laurie Maffly-Kipp, "and the farther west we go, the less important the religious events seem to become, in part because the vast majority of us know much less about them."[2] The West is a vast space, a collection of diverse geographic areas. As historians typically define the West, it encompasses everything between the Pacific Coast and the Mississippi River, with Alaska and Hawaii lumped in for good measure. The landscapes include fertile river valleys, grasslands, mountains, deserts, arctic tundra, and volcanic islands. The peoples that have inhabited these lands over the past five centuries are just as diverse: the Sioux, the

Comanche, the Shoshone, the Aleuts, and the Hawaiians, each people with its own language and cosmology; the variety of European and Americans who came to the West as conquerors, settlers, and missionaries; the Chinese, Japanese, Filipino, and Hmong who arrived in California and dispersed to other communities across the United States. It is impossible to understand these peoples—and instances of cooperation and conflict among them—without understanding their cosmologies and the rituals by which they interacted with gods and spirits. But where to begin?

There are many excellent starting points: the interactions of *californios*, prospectors, Native and Chinese laborers, Mormon settlers, and Protestant missionaries during and following the California Gold Rush; primary sources and photographs that document the Sun Dance of Plains Indians and the Ghost Dance movement of the late nineteenth century; the variety of peoples involved in the early Pentecostal movement in California, Texas, and Kansas in the early twentieth century. In the fast-paced march of events common to surveys of American history, however, it is difficult to know when to stop and discuss topics such as Pentecostalism, Buddhism, and Mormonism.

The example of the Latter-day Saints enriches the narrative of westward expansion in significant ways. Whereas many Americans believed that part and parcel of their manifest destiny to expand to the Pacific meant a corresponding expansion of evangelical Protestantism, the Mormons—along with Catholics and Quakers—took their own religious traditions with them. On the surface, though, the results of settlement looked familiar. When the Mormons colonized the Great Basin, they conquered and displaced the Native peoples of the region. The Saints, however, soon found themselves in conflict with US officials and soldiers asserting their own sovereignty over the region. Meanwhile, the "Mormon question" brought national debates over territorial governance and popular sovereignty into sharper relief. At the same time that politicians such as Stephen Douglas called for the people of each territory to decide on slavery's legality within their jurisdiction, Democrats grudgingly conceded that the extirpation of Mormon polygamy and theocracy justified federal intervention. The subject of westward expansion, moreover, presents instructors with an opportunity to teach students about one of the most successful—and notorious—religious movements to originate in the United States. Other instructors might choose to introduce the subject of Mormonism within the context of antebellum reform or early twenty-first century politics. Mormonism, however, was a salient political issue within the United States from the mid-nineteenth through the early twentieth centuries. The Saints assumed this national importance when they migrated west, and federal officials and Mormon leaders did not fully restore peace with each other until a decade after Utah's 1896 statehood.

In 1830, Joseph Smith published the Book of Mormon, which he presented as the record of the ancient ancestors of Native Americans. That same year, he and a few followers formed what they called the Church of Christ, which they understood as the restoration of Christ's one, true church after centuries of Catholic and Protestant apostasy. Smith's followers accepted him as God's chosen prophet, who dictated revelations from the Lord, revealed ancient texts, and unveiled teachings that thrilled some individuals and repelled others. The antebellum United States had many religious innovators, but the Mormons attracted outsized notoriety in large part because they gathered together. Expelled from Missouri in 1838 by mobs, militia units, and the state's political leaders, the Mormons took refuge on the banks of the Mississippi River in a city they renamed Nauvoo. There, Smith introduced a dizzying array of new teachings and rituals, including the privilege and obligation of righteous male church members to marry additional wives. In June 1844, Smith was arrested after he, as Nauvoo's mayor, ordered the destruction of a dissident Mormon printing press. An anti-Mormon mob stormed his jail cell and shot Smith and his brother Hyrum dead.[3]

As they learn about the history of the United States, students should gain familiarity with the religious traditions of its people. Today, the Church of Jesus Christ of Latter-day Saints boasts more than sixteen million members around the world, nearly seven million of which live in the United States. Sometimes categorized as a new religion, and by others as a new branch of Christianity, Mormonism has been the stuff of Broadway musicals, best-selling exposés, and considerable theological debate. Students, therefore, should know something about Mormonism, but how best to introduce them to it? How does one talk about golden plates and angels? How does one introduce the subject of polygamy in a way that doesn't elicit chuckles or descend into voyeurism? Fortunately, there are many texts that serve as excellent introductions to these subjects. I often have students read the canonical account of Joseph Smith's history—it is scripture for Latter-day Saints—and sometimes ask them to compare it with other narratives that Smith wrote or dictated. Smith's history begins with a visionary experience in which Jesus Christ tells him not to join any of the Protestant churches that had confused him with their competing claims. I also briefly introduce students to major themes in Mormon theology by having them read or listen to "O My Father," a poem written by Eliza R. Snow (one of Smith's thirty-plus wives and later married to Brigham Young) that became a popular Latter-day Saint hymn. There are also abundant letters and diaries written by both male and female church members.[4]

While instructors should help students gain a basic familiarity with the doctrines and practices of religious movements for their own sake, Mormonism also presents students with an underexplored topic within the history of westward expansion of the United States. Brigham Young, one of Smith's top associates, gained the support of the greatest number of church members and undertook an exodus from Nauvoo that eventually led the Saints across the Rocky Mountains to the Great Salt Lake. The Saints wanted to escape the United States and settle far from other white people (nearly all Mormons were of European descent), but by the time the Mormons had reached their destination, the United States had acquired it through the Treaty of Guadalupe-Hidalgo.[5]

Two factors precipitated conflict between church leaders and the US government. Although President Millard Fillmore appointed Brigham Young as the first governor of the Utah Territory, Young and his associates did not accept the principle of separation of church and state. Young once explained that his people lived under a "theodemocracy," in which the voice of God became the voice of the people. Especially during the territory's first two decades, the Mormon people voted in lockstep, and the same men generally occupied high-ranking offices in both church and government. The church's August 1852 public acknowledgment that its members taught and practiced plural marriage also stoked tension.[6]

In June 1856, at its first national convention, the Republican Party called on Congress "to prohibit in the Territories those twin relics of barbarism—Polygamy, and Slavery." Overturning prior congressional compromises, the 1854 Kansas-Nebraska Act had enshrined Stephen Douglas's principle of popular sovereignty. The settlers of a territory could decide whether or not slavery would be legal within its bounds. Popular sovereignty quickly led to violence in Kansas and in the nation's capital. In the months before the Republican Party's 1856 convention, proslavery Missourians attacked antislavery settlers and newspaper offices in Lawrence, Kansas; South Carolina representative Preston Brooks beat Massachusetts senator Charles Sumner on the Senate floor; and John Brown, his sons, and associates murdered five proslavery settlers at Pottawatomie Creek. With Kansas bleeding, Mormon Utah might have remained an afterthought. The Republican Party, though, shrewdly linked slavery to polygamy. Democrats favored popular sovereignty for slavery. Did they also think the Mormon settlers of Utah were free to practice and codify polygamy? The Republican stance on Utah put Democrats in a bind. They did not want to defend polygamy, but they did not want to encourage federal oversight of territorial affairs. When Buchanan took office, he anticipated violence and unrest in Kansas. He did not expect the wave of reports from Utah about Mormon abuses of power and harassment of federal officials. Buchanan's decision to dispatch the US Army to Utah, however, brought about unusual if grudging bipartisan agreement. Douglas, previously a defender of the Mormons, allowed that "the popular sovereignty doctrine is not intended for Utah." Former Illinois Representative Abraham Lincoln pounced on Douglas's concession, alleging that "from the beginning . . . the doctrine was a mere deceitful pretense for the benefit of slavery."[7]

It turned out that Mormon Utah was not easily subdued. When Brigham Young and other Mormon leaders got wind of the Utah Expedition, they prepared to defend their territory against what they considered an unauthorized invasion. In mid-August, Young delivered a fiery Sunday sermon in which he promised "that the last mob has come to afflict this people that ever has come." It is a remarkable discourse and is newly available in a recently published documentary history of the Utah War. Instructors should ask students to examine the sources of Young's hostility toward the US government, identify his military strategy, and consider his views of Native people.

For years, Mormon leaders, like many other westerners, complained that the territorial system denied them basic rights of self-government. Why could they not choose their own governor? What right had Congress to review laws passed by their elected legislature? Buchanan had dispatched troops to Utah without informing its government of his accusations and intentions. Young alleged that the army would do its utmost to "break up this kingdom called Latter Day Saints." "I will fight them," he vowed, "and I will fight all hell than tamely submit to such outrageous wrong and oppression." Young knew that Utah's militia—the Nauvoo Legion, named for the Saints' settlement on the

Mississippi—could not defeat the US Army, especially if more troops came. Instead, he suggested that the Utahans could hold the expedition off for a season and then burn their settlements and retreat into the mountains. Young knew that his actions would lead to charges of treason, but he joked that "they never can hang us until they have catched us."[8]

Young had another warning. "If the United States send their army here and war commences," he asserted, "the travel must stop; your trains must not cross the continent." He explained that he had spent the last decade inclining the Indians to peace and restraining them from attacking emigrants passing through Utah. Now, he would hold them back no more. "I will say to them," he warned, "go and do as you as you please." US officials subsequently charged Young with treason. Instructors might ask students whether Young's August 1857 sermon supports the accusation.[9]

Young's discourse proved prophetic, in a way. While the army continued its march from Fort Leavenworth, Kansas, toward Utah, members of the Latter-day Saint militia, joined by some Paiutes, attacked an emigrant wagon train at Mountain Meadows in southern Utah. The reasons for the attack are not clear. Church leaders had whipped up animosity against non-Mormons—Gentiles, in Mormon parlance—and had urged Mormon communities to prepare to defend themselves against American invaders. It is also possible that the impoverished Latter-day Saints of southern Utah wanted to enrich themselves at the expense of the wagon train's livestock and other possessions. Regardless, after the initial attack, local Latter-day Saint leaders feared reprisals if the emigrants made it to California and reported the incident. They sent a messenger to Salt Lake City to ask Brigham Young how they should proceed. His response, which was to "not meddle" with the emigrants and allow them to "go in peace," arrived after local leaders decided they had no choice but to kill the emigrants. They approached the emigrants under a flag of truce and offered to protect them from further Indian attacks. If the emigrants surrendered their weapons, the Mormon militia would escort them to nearby Cedar City. The emigrants reluctantly did so, but after they started the journey, the Mormon militiamen slaughtered them. Around 120 men, women, and children died; the Mormons spared around 17 young children, who were eventually reunited with relatives.[10]

Young was correct about the US Army's inability to reach Salt Lake City in the fall of 1857. Troops had left Fort Leavenworth in mid-July, followed belatedly by the Utah Expedition's commander, Colonel Albert Sidney Johnston, and the territory's newly appointed governor, Georgia's Alfred Cumming. Young ordered his militia leaders to undertake a campaign of harassment against the strung out and poorly organized US Army. Mormon troops burnt grass to make it harder for the army to feed its horses and livestock, and they captured and torched several army supply trains and razed Fort Bridger. The expedition made it within sixty miles of its destination, but punishing early winter weather made it impossible for Johnston's soldiers to traverse the final passes and canyons.

The standoff lasted for the duration of winter. In mid-September, Young declared martial law as a response to an invasion "by a hostile force, who are evidently assailing us to accomplish our overthrow and destruction." He forbade "armed forces of every description from coming into this Territory." He further proclaimed that no one would be able to pass "into or through or from this Territory without a permit from the proper officer." In his December 1857 annual message to Congress, President Buchanan finally spoke publicly about the Utah Expedition. "With the religious opinions of the Mormons," Buchanan emphasized, "as long as they remained mere opinions, however deplorable in themselves and revolting to the moral and religious sentiments of all Christendom, I had no right to interfere." At the same time, he noted Young's proclamation of martial law and other recent acts of hostility. "This is the first rebellion which has existed in our Territories," the president concluded, "and humanity itself requires that we should put it down in such a manner that it shall be the last." In his own annual message to Utah's territorial assembly, Brigham Young argued that "Congress has not one particle more Constitutional power to legislate for and officer Americans in Territories than they have to legislate for and officer Americans in States." He saw no conflict between American republicanism and a theocracy based on the "sentiments and doctrines" of his church. The Latter-day Saints had chosen their leaders and their doctrines. For the US government to interfere with that choice was to commit "treason against itself."[11]

In the spring, as Johnston prepared to advance to Salt Lake City, the Mormons followed through on the threat Brigham Young had made the previous August. They abandoned their homes and moved south to Provo, with the intention of forcing Johnston to march his troops into a desolate city. By this point, however, Young, incoming governor Cumming, and Buchanan were all seeking to avert further hostilities. Cumming concluded that he could only govern Utah with the cooperation of Young and other church leaders. Buchanan, meanwhile, sent two "peace commissioners" to Utah with permission to pardon anyone now willing to submit to federal authority. Although Young insisted that he had no need of a pardon, he took the offer. In mid-June, Johnston's troops descended Echo Canyon and marched through a mostly deserted Salt Lake City. The next month, they settled into an encampment some forty miles from Salt Lake City, on the other side of Utah Lake from Provo. Johnston named the new post Camp Floyd after John B. Floyd, then secretary of war.[12]

The Utah War did not solve what federal officials and many other Americans referred to as the "Mormon problem" or the "Mormon question." Utah's Saints had capitulated on the army's (albeit distant) presence and on Cumming's installation as governor, but they did not accept the principle of federal sovereignty and supremacy. Less than three years later, the army abandoned Camp Floyd with the outbreak of the Civil War.

The Utah War was a struggle over federal authority, not Mormon polygamy. Most Democrats had recognized that federal action against Mormon marriage practices undercut their arguments for leaving decisions about slavery to territories. Secession, however, left the Republican Party with a strong majority in Congress, free to enact legislation against the twin relic of barbarism despised by northerners and southerners alike. The result was the 1862 Morrill Act for the Suppression of Polygamy, which also annulled the Utah legislature's incorporation of the Church of Jesus Christ of Latter-day Saints and limited to $50,000 the amount of property any territorial religious organization could own. Congress had no means of enforcing the Morrill Act, though. As long as judges impaneled juries of faithful members of the church, they acquitted anyone charged with bigamy or polygamy. Brigham Young responded to the act by marrying for the first time in seven years.[13]

It took the United States another half century to resolve the Mormon question. In the 1870s, additional federal legislation ensuring the presence of non-Mormons on juries enabled the successful prosecution of John D. Lee, one of the Latter-day Saints who orchestrated the Mountain Meadows Massacre. Following his conviction, Lee was executed at the sight of the massacre; other Mormons culpable for the massacre escaped prosecution by eluding arrest. The new legislation also enabled the prosecution of Mormon polygamists. The church appealed the first conviction to the Supreme Court, which in *Reynolds v. United States* (1879) upheld the constitutionality of federal prohibitions against plural marriage. Instructors who are interested in the history of religious freedom jurisprudence should ask students to read the portion of Chief Justice Morrison Waite's opinion that addressed Reynold's "defence of religious belief or duty."[14] Instructors could ask students how Waite's understanding of both religion and race influenced his opinion. The court held that "until the establishment of the Mormon church, [polygamy] was almost exclusively a feature of the life of Asiatic and of African people." Against George Reynolds's contention that religious duty compelled him to marry more than one wife, the court drew a distinction between "religious belief and opinions" and religious "practices." Religious beliefs did not exempt individuals from following the law of the land.[15]

The court's decision paved the way for thousands of anti-polygamy prosecutions and the passage of additional federal laws designed to eradicate the Mormon practice of plural marriage. Officials and judges jailed hundreds of Mormon men, seized church property, and refused to naturalize Mormon immigrants. The Supreme Court upheld an Idaho statute that effectively disenfranchised church members. After vowing for years to defend plural marriage as a sacred principle, in 1890 church president Wilford Woodruff (Brigham Young had died in 1877 and was succeeded by John Taylor, then Woodruff) advised church members to "refrain from contracting any marriage forbidden by the law of the land." Woodruff's declaration became known as "The Manifesto," representing a new revelation of the Lord. Quietly, the church continued to permit a small number of plural marriages over the next decade. Between 1904 and 1907, the US Senate debated whether to allow Mormon apostle Reed Smoot to retain his seat, to which he had been elected in 1903. Smoot was a monogamist, but his fellow senators questioned whether the church to which he belonged still sanctioned plural marriage and whether Mormon leaders accepted that federal law trumped revelation. When the Senate voted in Smoot's favor, it marked the end of the Mormon question.[16]

The Mormon communities of the Great Basin had offered staunch resistance to US sovereignty and expressed little interest in the churches planted among them by the "Utah missions" of Protestant denominations. At the same time, the decades-long struggle between church leaders and federal officials significantly reshaped the Latter-day Saints, who by the early twentieth century had set aside theocracy, polygamy, and their principle of gathering to Utah. When they grudgingly accepted the supremacy of the US government, the Mormons learned to act more like the Protestant churches that Joseph Smith had rejected.

ADDITIONAL RESOURCES

Blackhawk, Ned. *Violence over the Land: Indians and Empires in the Early American West.* Cambridge, MA: Harvard University Press, 2006.

Farmer, Jared. *On Zion's Mount: Mormons, Indians, and the American Landscape.* Cambridge, MA: Harvard University Press, 2008.

Graber, Jennifer. *The Gods of Indian Country: Religion and the Struggle for the American West.* New York: Oxford University Press, 2018.

Hyde, Anne F. *Empires, Nations, and Families: A History of the North American West, 1800–1860.* Lincoln: University of Nebraska Press, 2011.

Maffly-Kipp, Laurie F. *Religion and Society in Frontier California.* New Haven, CT: Yale University Press, 1994.

Rogers, Brent M. *Unpopular Sovereignty: Mormons and the Federal Management of Early Utah Territory.* Lincoln: University of Nebraska Press, 2017.

NOTES

1. The most recent overview of the Utah War is David L. Bigler and Will Bagley, *The Mormon Rebellion: America's First Civil War* (Norman: University of Oklahoma Press, 2012). An essential resource is the two-volume documentary history by William P. MacKinnon, *At Sword's Point* (Norman, OK: Arthur H. Clark, 2008–16).

2. Laurie F. Maffly-Kipp, "Eastward Ho! American Religion from the Perspective of the Pacific Rim," in *Retelling U.S. Religious History*, ed. Thomas A. Tweed (Berkeley: University of California Press, 1997), 130.

3. Richard Lyman Bushman, *Joseph Smith: Rough Stone Rolling* (New York: Knopf, 2005).

4. The canonized version of Joseph Smith's history is available at the Church of Jesus Christ of Latter-day Saints, www.churchofjesuschrist.org/study/scrip

tures/pgp/js-h/1. For the hymn "O My Father," see www.churchofjesuschrist
.org/music/library/hymns/o-my-father. On Snow's poem, see Jill Mulvay Derr,
"The Significance of 'O My Father' in the Personal Journey of Eliza R. Snow,"
BYU Studies 36 (1996–97): 85–126.

5. On the Mormon hegira, see Richard E. Bennett, *Mormons at the Missouri:
Winter Quarters, 1846–1852* (Norman: University of Oklahoma Press, 1987).

6. Patrick Q. Mason, "God and the People: Theodemocracy in Nineteenth-
Century Mormonism," *Journal of Church and State* 52 (Summer 2011): 349–75.
On the public announcement of polygamy, see Laurel Thatcher Ulrich, *A House
Full of Females: Plural Marriage and Women's Rights in Early Mormonism, 1835–
1870* (New York: Vintage, 2017), chap. 10; David J. Whittaker, "The Bone in the
Throat: Orson Pratt and the Public Announcement of Plural Marriage," *Western
Historical Quarterly* 18 (July 1987): 293–314.

7. Douglas, speech of June 12, 1857, in *Illinois State Journal (Springfield)*, June
13, 1857; Lincoln, speech of June 26, 1857, in *Illinois State Journal*, June 29, 1857.
Both articles may be accessed in the *Illinois Digital Newspaper Collections*, https://
idnc.library.illinois.edu/. See Brent M. Rogers, *Unpopular Sovereignty: Mormons
and the Federal Management of Early Utah Territory* (Lincoln: University of Nebraska
Press, 2017).

8. Young, discourse of August 16, 1852, printed in MacKinnon, *At Sword's
Point*, 1:239–43.

9. Young, discourse of August 16, 1852.

10. See Ronald W. Walker, Richard E. Turley Jr., and Glen M. Leonard, *Massacre at Mountain Meadows* (New York: Oxford University Press, 2008). For the
argument that Young and other Mormon leaders ordered the attack on the emigrants, see Will Bagley, *Blood of the Prophets: Brigham Young and the Mountain
Meadows Massacre* (Norman: University of Oklahoma Press, 2004).

11. Young, September 1857 declaration in MacKinnon, *At Sword's Point*,
1:284, 286–88; Buchanan's 1857 annual message in MacKinnon, *At Sword's Point*,
1:481–85; Young's December message in Bigler and Bagley, *The Mormon Rebellion*, 263–64.

12. On the peaceful resolution to the war, see Matthew J. Grow, *"Liberty to
the Downtrodden": Thomas L. Kane, Romantic Reformer* (New Haven, CT: Yale University Press, 2009), chap. 10; Bigler and Bagley, *Mormon Rebellion*, chap. 12.

13. Sarah Barringer Gordon, *The Mormon Question: Polygamy and Constitu-
tional Conflict in Nineteenth-Century America* (Chapel Hill: University of North
Carolina Press, 2002), chap. 2. On Young's marriage, see John G. Turner, *Brigham
Young: Pioneer Prophet* (Cambridge, MA: Harvard University Press, 2012), 325–28.

14. The case [98 U.S. 145 (1878)] is available as a .pdf from the Library of
Congress, accessed October 27, 2019, http://cdn.loc.gov/service/ll/usrep/usrep
098/usrep098145/usrep098145.pdf. See 161–67.

15. On the *Reynolds* decision, see Gordon, *The Mormon Question,* chap. 4. On the legal proceedings regarding the Mountain Meadows Massacre, see Richard E. Turley Jr., Janiece L. Johnson, and LaJean Purcell Carruth, eds., *Mountain Meadows Massacre: Collected Legal Papers,* 2 vols. (Norman: University of Oklahoma Press, 2017).

16. Kathleen Flake, *The Politics of American Religious Identity: The Seating of Senator Reed Smoot* (Chapel Hill: University of North Carolina Press, 2004).

The Bible and Slavery before the Civil War

MARK NOLL

Just before the fighting of the Civil War broke out, an anonymous New York editor published a particularly revealing book entitled *Fast Day Sermons: or, The Pulpit on the State of the Country*. Its chapters included ten sermons by Protestant ministers, from both North and South, and one by a New York City rabbi. One contributor was Henry Ward Beecher, who shared the hatred of slavery that his sister, Harriet Beecher Stowe, publicized in *Uncle Tom's Cabin*. Beecher enjoyed such a lofty international reputation that Abraham Lincoln sent him to Europe to promote the Union cause during the war. Beecher's sermon from early 1861 made a bold claim: "Where the Bible has been in the household, and read without hindrance by parents and children together—there you have had an indomitable yeomanry, a state that would not have a tyrant on the throne, a government that would not have a slave or a serf in the field."[1]

Just as bold was the exact opposite claim from James Henley Thornwell, a minister from Columbia, South Carolina, who was generally considered the South's premier intellectual. Slavery, according to this distinguished Presbyterian, was the "good and merciful" way of organizing "labor which Providence has given us." He was just as confident as Beecher about what the scriptures taught: "That the relation betwixt the slave and his master is not inconsistent with the word of God, we have long since settled. . . . We cherish the institution not from avarice, but from principle."[2]

Alongside this sharp contrast between Beecher and Thornwell, much of the nation had been battling over what the Bible taught about slavery, long before the First Battle of Bull Run began the Civil War. Today it is taken for granted by almost all religious believers that slavery is an evil condemned by God. Why was it different in the eighteenth and nineteenth centuries? Why was the Bible so important when Americans debated the morality of slavery? For another question that undercuts simplistic views of the Civil War, why did arguments from scripture defending slavery persuade so many white Americans *in the North* as well as in the South? And why did African Americans, many of whom believed wholeheartedly in the Bible, disagree so completely with the way white Americans understood the holy book?

Including the conflicts over the Bible and slavery when discussing the Civil War is a prime opportunity to urge students to grasp one of the most important reasons for historical study—the past is often very different from the present. In a way that is no longer the case, Americans of all sorts in that era (and not just churchgoers) held the Bible in very high esteem. After the Civil War, the Bible would continue to be influential, but the conflict explored in this essay helps explain why it gradually lost its wide influence.

The Bible and slavery debates leading to the Civil War can also be used to teach one of the important five *c*'s of historical study—complexity. If you can convince students that the Civil War was not simply a conflict between North and South but included much disagreement within both sections, it will be a major accomplishment. Seeing how some *northern* interpreters of the Bible *defended* slavery will go a long way to show that American history is often much more complicated than we usually think.

Teaching the Contexts

The Bible's teaching on slavery mattered to many Americans simply because the Bible mattered. Unlike the contemporary United States, with its diversity of religious communities, American religion before the Civil War was dominated by Protestants, mostly of English and Scottish heritage. Since the Reformation of the early sixteenth century, these Protestants had prided themselves on following *sola scriptture* (the Bible alone). To be sure, Protestants differed greatly over what exactly it meant to obey the Bible. But they were united in condemning Roman Catholics for diluting biblical truth with man-made traditions.

They also agreed that the King James Version gave them a superlative translation of the scriptures.

Protestants active in their churches never made up more than half of the population. Yet the crucial point is comparative. No other understanding of human life or human purpose enjoyed anything like the number of adherents who were shaped by Protestant convictions about the Bible. Here is a telling comparison: until well after the Civil War, Americans on average heard more sermons in person each year than they received pieces of mail through the United States post office. And almost all of those sermons were based in some fashion on a passage of scripture.

The King James Bible gave parents names for their children, as for 10 of the nation's first 16 presidents (4 James, 3 John, 1 each Thomas, Andrew, and Abraham) and 14 of the first 17 First Ladies (2 Martha, 2 Abigail, 2 Sarah, and 1 each Elizabeth, Rachel, Hannah, Anna, Priscilla, Julia, Rebecca, and Mary). The same translation also provided a rich resource for public speaking. Abraham Lincoln took the "house divided" metaphor from Matthew 12:25 in his 1858 analysis of national political division.[3] During the debates that led to Stephen Douglas's Kansas-Nebraska Act of 1854, antislave northern clergy called him "Benedict Arnold" from American history, but also "Pontius Pilot" and "Judas Iscariot" from the Bible. In later campaigns he was a "sinful Jeroboam," the son of Israel's King Solomon who had betrayed his father's wise legacy. For his willingness to back Douglas, President Franklin Pierce was likened to a "latter-day Ahab [an evil Old Testament king], deaf to the warnings of his Elijah [a prophet], the anti-Nebraska clergy."[4] Famously, after the assassination of President Lincoln, he was mourned as "Father Abraham," especially by liberated bondsmen and women.

Public education was only just starting in the 1820s, but when it did get moving the Bible played a central role. The rationale was set out by Benjamin Rush, a noted Philadelphia physician and signer of the Declaration of Independence: "We profess to be republicans, and yet we neglect the only means of establishing and perpetuating our republican form of government, that is, the universal education of our youth in the principles of Christianity, by means of the Bible: for this Divine book, above all others, favours that equality among mankind, that respect for just laws, and all those sober and frugal virtues, which constitute the soul of republicanism."[5] To ensure the virtue without which republics would fail, nothing seemed more appropriate than daily reading from a "nonsectarian" Bible (that is, the King James Version).

Much of what students read in the public school came from books like the extremely popular *McGuffey's Readers*, where stories from the Bible stood alongside stories of George Washington and other American heroes. William Holmes McGuffey's *Eclectic Fourth Reader*, published at Cincinnati in 1838, is available online.[6] Its table of contents lists seventeen selections from the Bible, and many of the others have a strongly religious character as well. Widely read novels such as *Uncle Tom's Cabin* and Louisa May Alcott's *Little Women* were filled with biblical references, as were some that only became popular later such as Herman Melville's *Moby Dick*. Students can sample important novels of the time to get a sense of the Bible's importance in the era. Chapter 12 in Harriett Beecher Stowe's *Uncle Tom's Cabin* (1852) begins with a quotation from scripture and includes an argument about how to interpret the passage from Genesis chapter 9 where Noah cursed his grandson Canaan. The defenders of slavery understood Canaan to be the ancestor of Africans and so a divine approval for slavery. Chapter 9 in Herman Melville's *Moby Dick* (1851) recounts a sermon preached at a seaman's chapel in New Bedford, Massachusetts. Melville's Father Mapple was more creative than most ministers of the period, but his reliance on a Bible story for the basis of his sermon was entirely typical.

To help students see similarities and differences between their context and the early Republic, ask them to think about the assumptions that function in contemporary life in the way that reliance on the Bible functioned in the antebellum era. They might want to consider the influence of particular leaders, movies, or songs. What about broad assumptions among some Americans that are called "political correctness"—or among other Americans who oppose "politically correct" opinions? The point of asking these questions is to have students think about powerful influences in American society today as a way of understanding the widespread assumption about the Bible's authority in this earlier period.

Arguments over Slavery and the Bible

Immediately after the Revolution, the national Methodist and Presbyterian churches, along with many local Baptist associations, spoke out forcefully against slavery. It seemed self-evident in light of principles from the Declaration of Independence and theology from scripture that slavery was an evil. Yet when the denominations succeeded in winning over more and more slave owners, their antislavery stance gradually faded away.

Events also played a role. Observers of aborted slave rebellions in Richmond (1800) and Charleston (1822) noted that the plotters had been inspired by the story of the Exodus from the Hebrew scriptures (or Old Testament). Immediately, defenders of slavery responded with scriptural texts justifying the institution. Then conflict over the admission of Missouri as a slave state brought biblical arguments to the floor of the US Congress. Against the assertion that "slavery was forbidden by God, in his Holy Bible," Senator William Smith of South Carolina responded on January 26, 1820, that Moses had sanctioned slavery "as a law to his holy people" (that is, to the people of Israel). Smith then read to the senators Leviticus 25:44–46, a passage that slavery defenders had already used and that would be cited in countless publications thereafter. Here is the key portion: "Moreover of the children of the strangers that do sojourn among you, of them shall ye buy, and of their families that are with you, which they begat in your land: and they shall be your possession. And ye shall take them as an inheritance for your children after you, to inherit them for a possession; they shall be your bondmen for ever." The senator added, since "Christ himself gave a sanction to slavery," there could be no doubt but that "Scriptures teach us that slavery was universally indulged among the holy fathers."[7] Smith's defense is available online.[8]

Controversy only intensified when a decade later Nat Turner led a slave rebellion in Virginia driven by his reading of the Exodus story and biblical passages predicting a new age of glorious freedom that God would institute for his suffering people. Shortly thereafter, the launch of William Lloyd Garrison's passionately abolitionist magazine, *The Liberator*, and the founding of the American Antislavery Society fueled the fire of abolitionism.

In response, Southern defenders of slavery turned even more passionately to the Bible. They first wanted to convince slave owners that the scriptures were not dangerous; correct biblical interpretation, they claimed, would make bondsmen and women into obedient slaves. But then they grew bolder and contended that God positively sanctioned the institution.

The passage from Leviticus was only one weapon in a large arsenal:

- The so-called "curse of Ham" or "curse of Canaan" from Genesis 9:25–27, where Noah after the Flood cursed his grandson Canaan for the indecent behavior of Canaan's father, Ham. Beginning in the late fifteenth century, apologists for European expansion simply made up an interpretation of this text that defined the biblical Canaan as the ancestor of Africans whom God designated perpetually for enslavement.
- Old Testament passages in which Abraham had held slaves and Moses regulated the enslavement of non-Hebrews (Genesis 17:12; Deuteronomy 20:10–11).
- The many passages from the New Testament where the Apostle Paul gave instructions to slaves how to act without ever questioning enslavement itself (I Corinthians 7:21; Colossians 3:22; 1 Timothy 6:1–2).
- Finally, from the silence of Jesus, who changed many Old Testament regulations (for example, concerning polygamy and easy divorce), but never said a word against slaveholding.

The defenders of slavery proclaimed: "Do not listen to the supposed experts, but read the Bible for yourself. If the biblical founders of your faith either sanctioned or did not oppose slavery, then those who attack slavery today must be opponents of the Bible."

But abolitionists also drew from an ample store of proof texts. Early in the century lengthy books by Alexander McLeod (*Negro Slavery Unjustifiable*, 1802) and George Bourne (*The Book and Slavery Irreconcilable*, 1816) stressed the Bible's commands against "man-stealing" found in both Testaments (Exodus 21:16; 1 Timothy 1:9–10). Their reasoning was direct: every slave owner is complicit in the kidnapping of Africans. Case closed, they were condemned as sinners.

Other opponents proposed more complicated biblical arguments. One of the most impressive came in 1810 from Daniel Coker, a founder with Richard Allen of the African Methodist Episcopal Church. Coker concentrated on Abraham's circumcision of his slaves (Genesis 17:13) to show that slaves could be incorporated into Israel and, once incorporated, enjoyed all the benefits God bestowed on his chosen people. In addition, "The Israelites were not sent by a divine mandate, to nations three hundred miles distant, who were neither doing, nor meditating any thing against them, and to whom they had no right whatever, in order to captivate them by fraud or force . . . and then doom the survivors and their posterity to bondage and misery forever."[9]

As time went on, abolitionists tended to emphasize more "the spirit" of the Bible. Many pointed to the Golden Rule as a self-evident condemnation of the system. These are Jesus's words from Matthew 7:12 — "Therefore all things whatsoever that ye would that men should do unto you, do ye even so to them: for this is the law and the prophets."

Significantly, many whites in the North, however much they disliked slavery, were not convinced. The proof from proslavery writers seemed too strong. So it was that in early 1861, Rabbi Morris Raphall of New York's Jewish Synagogue of New York City filled a sermon entitled "The Biblical View of Slavery" with close attention to the Hebrew scriptures. Raphall was convinced that the curse pronounced by Noah in Genesis 9 had consigned "fetish-serving benighted Africa" to everlasting servitude. His conclusion: "Is slaveholding condemned as a sin in sacred Scripture? . . . How this question can at all arise in the mind of any man that has received a religious education, and is acquainted with the history of the Bible, is a phenomenon I cannot explain to myself."[10]

Rabbi Raphall's sermon illustrates "complexity" of history as it actually developed. This prominent New York City rabbi had gone on record expressing his personal opposition to slavery as it existed in the United States, but because he was loyal to the Bible, he felt he could not be an abolitionist or simply condemn slavery.[11]

Only Black authors and a very few whites thought there was more to say. In a series of pamphlets from the mid-1840s, John G. Fee, founder of Berea College in Kentucky, developed a fully biblical position against slavery. It centered on race. Fee argued that if the slavery of African Americans was defended because they were less intelligent or had darker skin, the logic led on to an absurd conclusion: "The fact that one man, or race of men, may have more intellectual capacity than another man, or race of men, gives no just ground for enslaving the inferior; otherwise the most intellectual man that exists may have a right to enslave every other man—white and black."[12] Let us grant, he went on, that the New Testament never condemned the enslavement by Rome of those it conquered in Germany, Gaul, Spain, Greece, Egypt, and so forth. "What," he asked, "was the complexion of these nations?" His answer was that "most were as white or whiter than the Romans themselves."

Consequently, if "the apostles' teaching and practice sanctioned slavery, it sanctioned *the slavery of the age*—the slavery amongst which the apostles moved. N.B. THIS SLAVERY WAS WHITE SLAVERY . . . the large portion of those enslaved were *as white, and many of them whiter than their masters*" (capitals and italics in the original).[13]

Fee's reasoning closely followed what Black authors had already been trying to say. In David Walker's 1829 *Appeal to the Colored Citizens of the World*, he paid particular attention to the "Great Commission" from Matthew 28:18–20, where Christ after the resurrection sent out his followers to "teach all nations . . . to observe all things whatsoever I have commanded you." Walker challenged white readers head on: "You have the Bible in your hands with this very injunction—Have you been to Africa, teaching the inhabitants thereof the words of the Lord Jesus?" No, it was just the opposite. Americans "entered among us, and learnt us the art of throat-cutting, by setting us to fight, one against another, to take each other as prisoners of war, and sell to you for small bits of calicoes, old swords, knives, etc. to make slaves for you and your children." To Walker, such behavior was a direct contradiction of Scripture: "Can the American preachers appeal unto God, the Maker and Searcher of hearts, and tell him, with the Bible in their hands, that they made no distinction on account of men's colour?"[14]

Yet in a society where democratic practices supported a strong commitment to scripture, the only thing stronger than the scriptures was democracy itself. In the antebellum United States, racial prejudice was a democratic conviction that went deeper than the Bible. One useful exercise to suggest the back and forth that occurred when Americans battled each other over slavery with the Bible in hand is to put students into three groups: white proslavery, white antislavery, and Black Bible-readers. Pass out portions from the Bible to each:

- White proslavery: Genesis 9:25–27; Leviticus 25:44–46; 1 Timothy 6:12
- White antislavery: Exodus 21:16, 1 Timothy 1:9–10; Jeremiah 22:13
- Black Bible-readers: Genesis 17:9–14; Matthew 7:12

Ask each group to make a brief argument for why "their" passages support their position. Also ask each group to make a longer argument for why the passages used by the others do not prove what they hope to prove. This exercise can gave a taste of the intense national debates of the antebellum period. It can also indicate why in the decades after the Civil War some Americans began to question the authority that had once been given to the Bible.

Results

Protestant conflict over the Bible turned out to open space for other approaches to other sacred writings. Catholics especially, with rapidly growing numbers because of immigration, spoke up loudly. According to one Catholic paper, the *Louisville Guardian*, "the contradictory preaching from the Bible for many long years" and a society where Americans "are permitted to explain the Scriptures according to our own 'private spirit'" had led directly to the Civil War.[15] Soon Jews, adherents of other religious, and those we now call secularists also exploited Protestant weakness exposed by the division over slavery.

Among white Protestants who continued to trust the Bible, most retreated from the kind of public advocacy that had characterized strife over slavery. Most also simply forgot about the racial discrimination that came out of the Civil War as strong as it had been before. Only Black Protestants would continue to read scripture for a message of this-worldly liberation as well as eternal salvation. But hardly any in the larger society noticed their efforts—until in the 1950s and 1960s leaders such as Martin Luther King Jr. once again put the Bible effectively to use in public. The civil rights movement drew on many sources, including the abolitionist belief that the Bible demanded liberty for all.

ADDITIONAL RESOURCES

Callahan, Allan Dwight. *The Talking Book: African Americans and the Bible*. New Haven, CT: Yale University Press, 2006. (A readable, comprehensive, insightful treatment of its subject)

Genovese, Eugene D. *Roll, Jordan, Roll: The World the Slaves Made*. New York: Random House, 1972. (A pioneering exploration of the importance of the Bible for enslaved African Americans)

Mathews, Donald G. *Slavery and Methodism: A Chapter in American Morality, 1780–1845*. Princeton, NJ: Princeton University Press, 1965. (The best available study of why a white-led denomination moved from opposing slavery to tolerating it)

Noll, Mark A. *American's Book: The Rise and Decline of a Bible Civilization, 1794–1911*. New York: Oxford University Press, 2022. (With several chapters detailing the biblical arguments for and against slavery, also including documentation for why the proslavery arguments were so strong in the North)

Oshatz, Molly. *Slavery and Sin: The Fight against Slavery and the Rise of Liberal Protestantism*. New York: Oxford University Press, 2011. (Outstanding on why debates over the Bible and slavery pushed some white Protestant leaders toward liberal theology)

Tomlin, Christopher. *In the Matter of Nat Turner: A Speculative History*. Princeton, NJ: Princeton University Press, 2020. (A brilliant effort to show that Nat Turner's immersion in and dedication to scripture *preceded* his decision to revolt against enslavement)

NOTES

1. Henry Ward Beecher, "Peace Be Still," in *Fast Day Sermons: or, the Pulpit on the State of the Country* (New York, 1861), 289.

2. James Henley Thornwell, "Our National Sins," in *Fast Day Sermons*, 48, 44.

3. "'A House Divided': Speech at Springfield, Illinois (June 16, 1858)," in *The Collected Works of Abraham Lincoln, vol. 2: 1848–1858*, ed. Roy P. Basler (New Brunswick, NJ: Rutgers University Press, 1953), 461.

4. Quotations from Richard Carwardine, *Evangelicals and Politics in Antebellum America* (New Haven, CT: Yale University Press, 1993), 239, 302.

5. Benjamin Rush, "A Defense of the Use of the Bible as a School Book" (dated March 10, 1791), in John Eyten, *Our Lord Jesus Christ's Sermon on the Mount . . . Intended Chiefly for the Instruction of Young People*, 2nd ed. (Baltimore, 1810), 65.

6. William H. McGuffey, *The Eclectic Fourth Reader: Containing Elegant Extracts in Prose and Poetry, from the Best American and English Writers* (Cincinnati, 1838), https://archive.org/details/McGuffeys_Readers_The_Eclectic_Fourth_Reader_1838/page/n7.

7. *Annals of Congress, 16th Congress—First Session* (December 1819–May 1820) (Washington, 1855), 269–70.

8. If students would like to read all of Senator Smith's long speech in defense of slavery from its beginning, they can google "Annals of Congress/Library of Congress." Then click "Browse the Annals"; next click "16th 1819–21"; then click "Senate, 1st Session—December 16, 1819 to May 15, 1820; then in box "Turn to image" enter "259."

9. Daniel Coker, *A Dialogue between a Virginian and an African Minister* (Baltimore, 1810), 22.

10. M. J. Raphall, "Bible View of Slavery," in *Fast Day Sermons*, 235–36.

11. M. J. Raphall, "Bible View of Slavery," Hathi Trust, https://babel.hathitrust.org/cgi/pt?id=uva.x001126508&view=1up&seq=7. Also useful is a sermon

by Henry Van Dyke, a minister from Brooklyn who also did not like slavery but could not condemn it because of his respect for scripture. The book containing these sermons also contains several examples in which, as we would now expect, white southerners defended slavery and white northerners attacked it.

12. John G. Fee, *The Sinfulness of Slaveholding Shown by Appeal to Reason and Scripture* (New York, 1851), 5.

13. Ibid., 29, 28.

14. David Walker, *Appeal, in Four Articles; Together with a Preamble, to the Coloured Citizens of the World, but in Particular, and Very Expressly, to Those of the United States of America*, ed. Charles M. Wiltse (New York, 1965 [orig. 1829]), 42.

15. "The Bible as a Political Text Book," *Louisville Guardian*, January 26, 1861, 4–5.

What Connections Were There between Imperialism and Missionary Activity?

KIMBERLY HILL

Teaching about the connections between imperialism and the missions movement is a meaningful way to show students how context and methodology influence the history discipline. We can use some of the well-known terms related to imperialism to explain how the perception of these terms shifted dramatically in historiography and sometimes acquired religious significance. In particular, focusing on imperialism helps introduce students to the field of Atlantic history. The roles of missionaries in trans-Atlantic travel can also spark discussion about cultural norms, foreign relations, and economics. To reinforce the use of analytical skills rather than just memorization, this chapter explains themes and lesson activities that relate to late nineteenth-century and early twentieth-century topics in a United States history course.

A major challenge in the design of lower-level survey courses is the need to balance coverage of a long chronology with the need to examine details. Scholarship on the Atlantic World offers opportunities to accomplish both goals within a unique course theme. This field emphasizes social, political, and economic interactions linking the Americas with Europe and the African continent. For a "United States before 1865" course, the Atlantic World framework helps students relate facts about the New England colonies with histories of international trade through the Middle East and along the West African coast. And the implications of globalization during the twentieth and twenty-first centuries can be taught in comparison to scholarly arguments about the transformation of earlier Indigenous empires in the Americas and Africa. Teaching with an Atlantic history focus does not have to require squeezing additional lessons into a full syllabus. The key is to broaden the explanation of certain relevant names, events, and topics that already represent touchstones in the curriculum. For example, the term "civilization" can become a comparison point for discussions of politics and religion in foreign affairs.

Civilization and Christendom

Many students may enter the class unfamiliar with the names of specific missions sending agencies, denominational affiliations, or missiology techniques. But missions terminology fills the background of famous stories in American history, such as the first Thanksgiving dinner story and folklore about the Trail of Tears. We can build on the stories that tend to stick with students from previous classes and from cultural traditions. The historical context for late nineteenth-century mission work can become more evident when we define and review the political and religious ideals that made such stories important to American historical memory.

For example, a lesson on the age of imperialism can start with a survey of how students understand concepts of "civilization." A short online list can help students choose the descriptions they find compelling from options such as a geographic area or a type of behavior. Using a Google Forms chart to generate the relative percentage of responses, I trace the roots of each one to a similar expression or argument from the colonial era. Because many undergraduates think of the "civilization" process as the development and settlement of a specific region, I assign primary sources that reveal how similar reasoning supported nineteenth-century manifest destiny theory.

The 1872 *American Progress* painting by John Gast (available widely online and in textbooks) presents a visual contrast between east and west by using sunlight and twilight as metaphors. From right to left, significant innovations such as railroads and canals set the background for farmers, gold miners, and covered wagon passengers who represent the western settlers. Students notice the difference in the depictions of Native Americans shown on the far left of the painting as they seem to shrink away in fear of the spirit of Columbia in the center of the scene. Gast implies that progress entailed geographic relocation and the displacement of anything or anyone that did not conform to the symbols of American modernity on the other side of the painting.[1]

Frederick Jackson Turner's "The Significance of the Frontier in American History" speech can reinforce the historical context of manifest destiny ideals if the discussion focuses on his description of western settlers' transformations.[2] Turner described life within the American frontier as a civilizing process by which men of European ancestry reinvented their cultural traits. The first three sections describe the work habits acquired by American colonists in comparison to the lifestyles practiced by Europeans along the Atlantic coast.[3] Emphasizing the timing of Turner's speech can help students analyze the frontier term beyond the mid-nineteenth century and beyond the western territories. Turner spoke during the 1893 World's Columbian Exposition, adding an implied focus on the nation's place in a shifting world order. By reinterpreting the early history of the United States, Turner modeled a way for students to compare American geographic and cultural change with the reputations of the growing European empires.

Lessons on civilization theory and imperialism are incomplete without consideration of how missionaries helped define the term "Christendom." Historian Dana Robert identifies "Christendom" as the motivating factor in European Catholic and Protestant missions' endeavors from the sixteenth through the nineteenth centuries. In that era, the term referred to the European nations in which "church and state had close legal and ecclesiastical connections." Territorial expansion promised spiritual value for these nations through increased access to groups of people unaffiliated with recognized churches.[4] Lessons about the Congo Free State can describe the concepts of civilization and Christendom while countering perceptions of American history in isolation.

The Berlin Conference of 1884 and 1885 heightened the period of conquest known as the "Scramble for Africa." During that period, King Leopold II of Belgium concealed his commercial interests in the agricultural output of the Congo Free State with claims of opening "the Dark Continent" to civilization.[5] The literal process of missionaries and traders traveling past the coastal cities using roads, steamboats, and trains maintained by African workers factored into the civilizing process.

To incorporate the complicated roles of American Protestant missionaries to the Congo Free State within lessons on Gilded Age America, one could focus on business interests. Missionaries helped create demand for Western goods by promoting concepts of behavior-based civilization. Typical mission stations in this colony hosted boarding schools for children that required certain chores, habits, and styles of dress. For example, encouraging female students to sew their own Western-style clothes was a common way for Christian missions in the Congo Free State to reduce expenses.[6] Likewise, adult Africans associated with the missions were expected to make and use Western products. In other countries, demand for such objects became almost synonymous with Christian self-identification among the local population.[7] Scholars of the women's missionary movement between 1880 and 1920 place the popular efforts to provide Western material objects and home decorations to mission converts within the framework of "cultural imperialism."[8]

In some cases, students can trace Americans' growing awareness of consumerism through missionaries' use of objects to gain social or political influence. The lack of paved roads or railways in most of the Belgian Congo until at least 1919 meant that traveling preachers often relied on bicycles to navigate foot paths. In their social history study of colonial history in India and Vietnam, David Arnold and Erich DeWald described bicycles as key identifying features for Christian mission staff and for the agents of British and French colonial administrations.[9] Though the direction of American and European settlement within Asia and central Africa often flowed east, the methods for making those settlements distinctive were similar to the markers of western expansion featured in Gast's *American Progress* painting. Technology was associated with the moral changes promoted by international missionaries and by local evangelists.

To explain the significance of missionaries promoting bicycle use, I recommend circulating a short criticism of bicycle use published by an African American Christian in 1902. Author W. F. Fonvielle urged working-class people (and young women in particular) to avoid purchasing bicycles for fear that the increased mobility would tempt them to make immoral decisions.[10] But the practical advantages of imported bicycles placed overseas missionaries at the forefront of encouraging this freedom of movement for both male and female staff; bicycle travel was just one more means of merging ministry needs with enthusiasm for Western innovations. All missionaries did not share Fonvielle's concerns that this commercial product could be incompatible with civilized behavior.

Racial Uplift and Labor

The topics of imperialism and American manifest destiny often lead students to discussions of nineteenth-century racial prejudice. Including the actions of domestic and foreign missionaries in lessons about these topics can help expand the discussion beyond attempts to identify racism to analysis of racial ideology. For example, farm labor and vocational training came to symbolize competing interpretations of the term "racial uplift" in the US South and in European colonies on the African continent. In late nineteenth-century America, the term became popular through arguments that the success of most African Americans depended on the efforts individual Black leaders made to serve Black communities. W. E. B. Du Bois's theories about the social consciousness of African American intellectuals represent some of the best-known interpretations of uplift; he expected that higher education would enable a small percentage of the Black population to develop programs that would help the race overcome the consequences of slavery and Jim Crow segregation.[11] United States history textbooks often contrast the classical education represented by Du Bois with the industrial education at Booker T. Washington's Tuskegee Institute. Washington's 1895 "Atlanta Compromise" speech brought him fame as an accommodationist leader who would encourage hard work among fellow African Americans without challenging racial oppression publicly. His rhetoric regarding the importance of industrial education obscured the fact that Tuskegee Institute continued to offer a variety of industrial and classical course work led by African American faculty for at least six years after his famous speech.[12]

Booker T. Washington's reputation as the founder of a Black-led academic center inspired many African Christians to try to found institutes that would likewise enable academic achievement on the continent.[13] But one of Washington's white supporters, Thomas Jesse Jones of the Phelps Stokes Fund, popularized the industrial education concept worldwide by arguing that African ancestry predestined people for certain types of work.[14] Through his role as a specialist for one of the main sources of school funding in the country, Jones compelled Christian and secular educators in the American South, East Africa, and West Africa to prepare Black students for sharecropping, plantation agriculture, and domestic service. Ensuing competition between Jones and Du Bois to control the African educational narrative also caused direct consequences for African American secondary and postsecondary education.[15]

In comparison with assigned key terms or students' suggestions, either of the 1920s education reports from Thomas Jesse Jones could be skimmed as an activity designed to highlight the intersections between Protestant missionary education and the economic interests of colonial governments.[16] For a more direct approach, I recommend assigning excerpts from Jones's 1926 publication *Four Essentials of Education*. The preface by American sociologist Franklin Giddings summarizes the pedagogical points within this book and previous studies by Jones, and two of the four points involve the labor-intensive topics of agriculture and domestic science.[17] The argument that Hampton and Tuskegee Institutes represented model illustrations for the development of international religious education reinforced Jones's tendency to conflate the characteristics and capabilities of people of African descent.[18]

Human Rights and Pan-Africanism

The demand for natural resources that shaped Atlantic world history through the early nineteenth century combined with late nineteenth-century industrial education to sustain oppressive labor systems in many colonized nations. The protests of some American Protestant missionaries against colonial abuses during the early twentieth century provided an international approach to Progressivism. For example, the American Presbyterian Congo Mission helped to inspire an international human rights campaign against King Leopold II of Belgium from the 1890s until 1908. The campaign publicized the torture enforced by the Belgian king's agents in the Congo Free State rubber industry.[19] It remains significant as one of the ways that some American missionary leaders suggested that European and American colonizers needed additional civilization.[20]

Though the graphic violence might make the evidence disturbing for students, much of the missionaries' documentation about the crisis is accessible online. One could capitalize on name recognition by starting with documents that reveal Booker T. Washington's role in the Congo Reform Association. The foreign secretary of the American Baptist Foreign Mission invited Washington and author Mark Twain to support the cause.[21] Washington responded with an article praising the average

American missionary as "often a wiser councilor than the trader, or the soldier" and worthy of political influence.[22]

Students can browse visual evidence of missionaries' human rights efforts within the archival records of William Henry Sheppard, the co-founder of the American Presbyterian Congo Mission. The digitized examples from the Sheppard Papers include portraits of individuals wearing the neck chains and collars that were used to transport forced laborers to the rubber forests. There are also portraits of young men whose hands were cut off as a threat to compel others to collect more rubber.[23] As they consider that African men volunteered to testify against the Belgian authorities during the 1909 failed libel suit against Sheppard and his colleague William Morrison, students could compare these photos with Progressive Era efforts to stop the mass incarceration and disfranchisement of African Americans.[24]

Another benefit to the Atlantic history approach in lessons on imperialism is the chance to trace Pan-Africanist scrutiny of colonialism through the 1940s.[25] Pan-Africanism is often featured in Harlem Renaissance lessons through the work of Jamaican activist Marcus Garvey. His nationalist calls to claim "Africa for the Africans" and the popularity of his Universal Negro Improvement Association during the 1920s raised fears of potential revolutionary fervor within colonized African nations.[26]

But campaigns to empower people of African descent started in the United States over a century earlier through the African Methodist Episcopal Church. The denomination's universities trained some of the future African nationalists, and it drew the support of the independent Ethiopian church movement.[27] Max Yergan, one of several African American missionaries who organized the South African Young Men's Christian Association (YMCA) after World War I, continued his Pan-Africanist work decades later by cowriting a National Negro Congress petition to the United Nations.[28] The digitized version of that nine-page summary of discriminatory US policies could be skimmed during class and reviewed with questions about how it implies that Americans of African descent lived in a state of colonization.

Conclusion

The above exploration of imperialism and missions in the Atlantic World is designed to expand and complicate the concepts that many students already find familiar. It focuses on terms and names that are often introduced in a United States history survey course and suggests how those terms remained relevant to religious, political, and economic policies through the first half of the twentieth century. Analysis of different types of American Protestant civilizing missions reveals that many of these plans were shaped by the financial priorities of colonial governments and Western businesses. Evaluation of political activism in missions history also disrupts the standard east-to-west perspective by demonstrating how some ministers changed their political expectations while observing colonial life and expected to see reform among fellow Americans or Europeans as well.

ADDITIONAL RESOURCES

Abé, Takao. *The Jesuit Mission to New France: A New Interpretation in the Light of the Earlier Jesuit Experience in Japan*. Leiden: Brill, 2011.

Blyden, Nemata. *African Americans and Africa: A New History*. New Haven, CT: Yale University Press, 2019.

Cañizares-Esguerra, Jorge. *Entangled Empires: The Anglo-Iberian Atlantic, 1500–1830*. Philadelphia: University of Pennsylvania Press, 2018.

Conroy-Krutz, Emily. *Christian Imperialism: Converting the World in the Early American Republic*. Ithaca, NY: Cornell University Press, 2015.

Eltis, David. "A Brief Overview of the Trans-Atlantic Slave Trade: Empire and Slavery." Slave Voyages Consortium. Accessed April 14, 2023. https://www.slavevoyages.org/voyage/essays#interpretation/overview-trans-atlantic-slave-trade/empire-and-slavery/4/en/.

Gin Lum, Kathryn. *Heathen: Religion and Race in American History*. Cambridge, MA: Harvard University Press, 2022.

NOTES

1. John Gast, *American Progress*, 1872, in Joseph Locke and Ben Wright, *The American Yawp Reader* (Stanford: Stanford University Press, 2019), http://www.americanyawp.com/reader/manifest-destiny-2/.

2. Turner presented this talk to the American Historical Association in 1893 and published it within a 1921 essay collection. Frederick Jackson Turner, "The Significance of the Frontier in American History," American Historical Association, accessed March 9, 2020, https://www.historians.org/about-aha-and-membership/aha-history-and-archives/historical-archives/the-significance-of-the-frontier-in-american-history.

3. Frederick Jackson Turner, *The Frontier in American History* (New York: Holt, 1921; Project Gutenberg, 2007), 3–4, accessed March 9, 2020, http://www.gutenberg.org/files/22994/22994-h/22994-h.htm.

4. Dana Robert, ed., introduction to *Converting Colonialism: Visions and Realities in Mission History, 1706–1914* (Grand Rapids, MI: Eerdmans, 2008), 6–10.

5. Adam Hochschild, *King Leopold's Ghost: A Story of Greed, Terror, and Heroism in Colonial Africa* (New York: Houghton Mifflin, 1998), 42–46, 52–56.

6. Barbara Ann Yates, "The Missions and Educational Development in Belgian Africa, 1876–1908" (PhD diss., Columbia University, 1967), 113–17; Kimberly D. Hill, "Maria Fearing: Domestic Adventurer," in *Alabama Women: Their Lives and Times*, ed. Susan Youngblood Ashmore and Lisa Lindquist Dorr, 90–107 (Athens: University of Georgia Press, 2017).

7. For examples, see Uri M. Kupferschmidt, "The Social History of the Sewing Machine in the Middle East," *Die Welt des Islams* 44, no. 2 (2004), 204–5; James Nathan Calloway quoted in Angela Zimmerman, *Alabama in Africa: Booker T. Washington, The German Empire, and the Globalization of the New South* (Princeton, NJ: Princeton University Press, 2010), 144–47.

8. The phrase "Woman's Work for Woman" has been defined by Dana Robert as an evangelism process that "provided not only salvation but 'civilization,' the nineteenth-century term for social liberation, albeit in Western dress." Dana Robert, *American Women in Mission: A Social History of Their Thought and Practice* (Macon, GA: Mercer University Press, 1996), 130. Also see Peggy Pascoe, *Relations of Rescue: The Search for Female Moral Authority in the American West, 1874–1939* (New York: Oxford University Press, 1990); Jane Hunter, *The Gospel of Gentility: American Women Missionaries in Turn-of-the-Century China* (New Haven, CT: Yale University Press, 1984).

9. David Arnold and Erich DeWald, "Cycles of Empowerment? The Bicycle and Everyday Technology in Colonial India and Vietnam," *Comparative Studies in Society and History* 53, no. 4 (2011), 979–82.

10. W. F. Fonvielle, "The Taint of the Bicycle," in *A Hammer in Their Hands: A Documentary History of Technology and the African American Experience* (Cambridge: MIT Press, 2005), 102–5, accessed November 14, 2019, https://books.goo gle.com/books?id=QCbP5jYfajAC&newbks=1&newbks_redir=0&lpg=PA66&d q=A%20Hammer%20in%20Their%20Hands&pg=PA102#v=onepage&q&f=false.

11. Kevin K. Gaines, *Uplifting the Race: Black Leadership, Politics, and Culture in the Twentieth Century* (Chapel Hill: University of North Carolina Press, 1996), 9–10.

12. Angela Zimmerman, *Alabama in Africa: Booker T. Washington, the German Empire, and the Globalization of the New South* (Princeton, NJ: Princeton University Press, 2010), 53–55.

13. Andrew Barnes, *Global Christianity and the Black Atlantic: Tuskegee, Colonialism, and the Shaping of African Industrial Education* (Waco, TX: Baylor University Press, 2017).

14. Kenneth J. King, *Pan-Africanism and Education* (New York: Diasporic Africa Press, 2016) 134–35, 177–78.

15. King, *Pan-Africanism and Education*, 133–49.

16. Full text-searchable versions of the education reports from Thomas Jesse Jones and the rest of the Phelps Stokes Commission are available through the Hathi Trust digital archives. United States Bureau of Education, *Negro Education: A Study of the Private and Higher Schools for Colored People in the United States*, vols. 1 and 2 (Washington, DC: Government Printing Office, 1917), Hathi Trust, accessed November 22, 2019, https://catalog.hathitrust.org/Record/0014 50547; African Education Commission, *Education in Africa* (New York: Phelps-Stokes Fund, 1922), Hathi Trust, accessed November 22, 2019, https://catalog .hathitrust.org/Record/001066403; African Education Commission, *Education in East Africa* (New York: Phelps-Stokes Fund, 1925), Hathi Trust, accessed November 22, 2019, https://catalog.hathitrust.org/Record/001066404.

17. Franklin H. Giddings, preface to *Four Essentials of Education* by Thomas Jesse Jones (New York: Charles Scribner's Sons, 1926), viii, Hathi Trust, accessed November 22, 2019. https://babel.hathitrust.org/cgi/pt?id=mdp.3901506227677 2&view=1up&seq=5.

18. Jones, *The Four Essentials to Education*, 151–54.

19. Stanley Shaloff, *Reform in Leopold's Congo* (Richmond, VA: John Knox Press, 1970), 84–103.

20. *Protestants Abroad* by David A. Hollinger also provides rare interdenominational analysis of how American missionaries internalized their observations of European colonial policies and applied them to the United States. David A. Hollinger, *Protestants Abroad: How Missionaries Tried to Change the World but Changed America* (Princeton, NJ: Princeton University Press, 2017).

21. "From Thomas Seymour Barbour," *Booker T. Washington Papers*, vol. 8, ed. by Louis R. Harlan and Raymond W. Smock (Urbana: University of Illinois Press, 1979), 482–84, Google Books, accessed November 23, 2019, https://books .google.com/books?id=tN1isaLBtbIC&lpg=PR3&dq=Booker%20T.%20Wash ington%20Congo%20Reform%20letter&pg=PA482#v=onepage&q&f=false.

22. Booker T. Washington, "The Future of Congo Reform," *The Congo News Letter*, August 1906, 9–10. Google Books, accessed 22 November 2019, https:// books.google.com/books?id=tZUPAQAAMAAJ&lpg=PA16-IA9&ots=2Q8QhL 6Eiu&dq=Booker%20T.%20Washington%20Congo%20Reform%20letter&pg= PA16-IA9#v=onepage&q&f=false.

23. William Henry Sheppard collected this evidence while investigating the aftermath of a state-sponsored village raid in 1900. For an example, see William H. Sheppard, "Three Boys with Hands Cut Off," ca. 1900, RG 457, box 4, 835.03.18b, Pearl Digital Collections, Presbyterian Historical Society, Philadelphia, accessed November 23, 2019, https://digital.history.pcusa.org/islandora/ search/Congo%20atrocities?type=dismax.

24. See "Witnesses at the Morrison and Sheppard Trial. 13 Native Men," 1909, William Henry Sheppard Papers, RG 457, Box 3, 835.02.05g, Presbyterian

Historical Society, Philadelphia, PA, accessed 17 April 2023. https://digital.his
tory.pcusa.org/islandora/object/islandora%3A33602?solr_nav%5Bid%5D=436
debd2c62b4c1855a7&solr_nav%5Bpage%5D=0&solr_nav%5Boffset%5D=1.

25. E. D. Morel, *The Black Man's Burden* (New York: Monthly Review Press, 1969).

26. Marcus Garvey, "If You Believe the Negro Has a Soul," the Marcus Garvey and the UNIA Papers Project, University of California, Los Angeles, History Matters, accessed November 23, 2019, http://historymatters.gmu.edu/d/5124; Ira Dworkin, *Congo Love Song* (Chapel Hill: University of North Carolina Press, 2017), 154–57.

27. St. Clair Drake, "Diaspora Studies and Pan-Africanism," in *Global Dimensions of the African Diaspora*, 2nd ed., ed. Joseph E. Harris (Washington, DC: Howard University Press, 1993), 476; James T. Campbell, *Songs of Zion: The African Methodist Episcopal Church Movement in the United States and South Africa* (New York: Oxford University Press, 1995), 114–15, 250–76.

28. David Henry Anthony II, *Max Yergan: Race Man, Internationalist, Cold Warrior* (New York: New York University Press, 2006), 39–44; National Negro Congress, Petition to the United Nations, June 6, 1946, Internet Archive, accessed November 24, 2019, https://archive.org/details/NNC-Petition-UN-1946.

American Religion during the Industrial Crisis of the Gilded Age

HEATH W. CARTER

I distinctly remember dreading the Gilded Age unit in my high school United States history course. I loved stories of military heroics and longed to jump from the Civil War straight into World War I. A week or more on the Industrial Revolution—a revolution that, as far as I could tell, involved lots of railroad ties and factory lines, and exactly zero tightly fought battles—seemed designed to test the theory that yawning is contagious.

Not until my first semester of graduate school did I come to see the period differently. The catalyst was T. J. Jackson Lears's *No Place of Grace: Antimodernism and the Transformation of American Culture, 1880–1920*, a book that opened my eyes to just how crucial these years were in the shaping of the modern United States. The postbellum decades saw the full flourishing of corporate capitalism and the vast expansion of a bourgeois consumer culture, not to mention decisive shifts in Protestant theology. Lears contended, in part, that the retreat of traditional Christian beliefs about heaven and hell hastened the rise of a therapeutic society in which people were less and less loyal to anything outside of themselves. One signature of modernity, therefore, was a kind of existential weightlessness. I was captivated by the argument, which underscored the centrality of religious developments in defining the social, political, and cultural contours of the Gilded Age. I have spent the years since plumbing those depths and am excited to have the opportunity to share some of my suggestions on how to teach this material.

One overarching point that I always stress with students from the outset is that the Gilded Age was a period marked by unusually high suspense. Every age has its dramas, of course, but rarely have fundamental questions about the shape of modernity been so near the fore as they were in the late nineteenth century. The period witnessed a series of wrenching revolutions in the character of everyday life, including the rapid demise of venerable artisan cultures, as wage labor became for the first time widespread and entrenched, and as the so-called captains of industry consolidated their control over the means of production; and an astonishing reorganization of society around large cities, which often sprung up nearly overnight, with precious little planning and therefore markedly haphazard infrastructure, and which quickly became bustling centers of life for millions of migrants from far-flung domestic and international hinterlands. Religiously, these American boomtowns were ever-increasingly more plural. Diverse streams of Christianity and Judaism flourished in urban neighborhoods, as foreign- and native-born residents alike turned storefronts into spiritual centers and invested hard-won dollars into the construction of towering synagogues and gilded cathedrals, monuments to their gods, not to mention sources of community pride on this side of the veil. In places such as Homestead, Pennsylvania—long home to one of Andrew Carnegie's largest steel mills—the streets were dotted with a dazzling array of ethnically and racially inflected houses of worship. The Hungarian Reformed Church was just down the street from the Rodef Shalom synagogue; and both were within easy walking distance of St. John the Baptist Byzantine Catholic Cathedral, Park Place African Methodist Episcopal, and the Episcopal and Presbyterian churches that attracted high-ups in the Carnegie Steel Company.

In the early summer of 1892, Homestead played host to a bloody battle between steel workers and company-hired Pinkerton detectives, who traded shots on the banks of the Monongahela River. By the time the dust had settled, ten were dead, a tragic outcome to be sure, but one that was hardly unusual in the Gilded Age. The period saw an alarming uptick in labor conflict, punctuated by all-too-frequent melees in the streets, pitting indignant workers against whatever mercenary forces a hastily counter-organizing elite could muster to preserve its vision of social order. Contrary to what my high school self had assumed, industrial warfare was much more than a metaphor. And especially after the Paris Commune of 1871, which saw radical workers briefly wrest control of the French capital away from the government, the stakes of these confrontations seemed nothing less than the future of capitalism itself. This point cannot be overemphasized. Karl Marx saw what happened in Paris as the start of a worldwide proletarian uprising, and so did countless middle- and upper-class persons nervously following the course of events back in the United States. From that point forward, the specter of revolution loomed over the age.

Scholars long narrated the religious history of the period in terms of industrial crises and religious response. But that mode of interpretation missed the fact that the grassroots activists who built the labor movement and who thereby helped generate the prevailing atmosphere of crisis often had profound religious views of their own. In the immediate postbellum years many labor leaders were white evangelical Protestants, who championed longstanding artisan republican traditions over and against what they believed to be the corrosive logics of runaway corporate capitalism. Such advocates insisted on the inherent dignity of labor and took frequent resort to scripture in defense of their worldview. In 1867 one leading labor editor proclaimed in the pages of his nationally circulated newspaper, the *Workingman's Advocate*, "We assert without fear of successful contradiction, that the Gospel of Christ sustains us in our every demand."[1]

Many evangelical participants in the trade union movement had imagined that their pastors would rally to their side. But Protestant church leaders were almost universally opposed to trade unionism, a fact that held true, notably, across theological camps. The pathbreaking modernist David Swing, who was famously brought up on heresy charges in the Presbyterian church in the early 1870s, was certainly no progressive when it came to his labor politics. Like most Protestant clergy of the era, Swing fundamentally rejected the notion that the United States was a classed society. Atop his perch in a well-heeled downtown Chicago congregation, he felt fully justified in his belief that the laborer of today could become, with just a little dedication and hard work, the capitalist of tomorrow. Swing scoffed at the very notion of systemic defect in the economy. As he wrote in 1874, "The conflict between classes in the cities of our country is not a conflict between labor and capital, but between successful and unsuccessful lives."[2] And if labor's diagnosis of the problem was wrong, so was its proposed solution. Like countless Americans in the wake of Emancipation, Protestant clergy were growing more and more enamored with contract freedom: namely, the idea that one's liberty rested in one's ability to negotiate a contract for one's labor.[3] Labor's tactics—and especially the enforcement of the picket line—seemed to fly in the face of this God-given right. Such tactics proved only more galling as the movement's demographics shifted in ways that made many Protestants nervous: indeed, Catholic immigrants played increasingly prominent roles at the level of both the leadership and the rank and file as the century moved toward a close.

Catholic clergy were more likely to be rhetorically sympathetic to labor, but the American Catholic Church was hardly a dependable ally of the trade union movement during these years. The hierarchy found itself in an uncomfortable position. It was certainly conscious of the fact that its flock comprised an ever-growing majority of union members. But priests and bishops alike were also painfully aware of the church's tenuous place in a ferociously anti-Catholic society and were therefore loathe to spend whatever precious social capital they possessed in defending labor organizations that were, in some important respects, suspect. Catholic clergy were often particularly worried that trade unions would function as gateways through which the faithful might, unwittingly even, wander out of the church's fold and into the clutches of godless socialists.[4]

Thus one signature feature of the Gilded Age was a precipitous increase in class tensions within and around the nation's churchly institutions. A wonderful document for exploring these tensions with students is H. Francis Perry's 1898 article in the *American Journal of Sociology* entitled "The Workingman's Alienation from the Church." Readily available via JSTOR, the essay is a treasure trove of different kinds of primary source evidence. Perry was a Baptist minister on Chicago's South Side who hoped to get to the bottom of what he perceived to be a burgeoning national crisis. At the outset of the article he reproduced the text of a letter that he had sent out to trade union leaders and a variety of other working people, both churchgoing and not. Perry's brief missive read:

> My Dear Sir: Will you do me the kindness to give me your aid in trying to solve a vexing problem? The problem is this: Why are so many intelligent workingmen non-churchgoers? It may be that the church can be of more service to the men of its community than it is at the present time. Will you please send me an answer, within a few days, to the questions submitted?

1) What reasons would be given by your associates, who do not attend the church, for their absence from the church?

2) What remedies would you propose to bring your associates into closer touch with the church?

Sincerely,

H. Francis Perry

Responses came back from a wide range of informants, including everyone from Samuel Gompers, the head of the American Federation of Labor, and John F. O'Sullivan, president of Boston's Central Labor Union, to any number of ordinary workers.[5]

As Perry collected the replies, he loosely thematized them, but excerpts from the letters themselves formed the main substance of his article, and these should spark no shortage of interesting classroom conversations. They shed significant light, for one, on the dissenting theologies that flourished, not in the nation's gilded sanctuaries, but in its union halls and on its picket lines. One Miss Mary A. Nason of Haverhill, Massachusetts, declared, "Workingmen understand that Christianity is only another name for justice, love, and truth, and that churchianity is only another name for wrong, injustice, oppression, misery, and want. Then they take the two apart, and cheer the name of Jesus Christ and hiss the church, separating Christianity from churchianity." Driving home the point, another respondent pointedly asked, "Why should I wish to go into a $200,000 church and listen to a minister who gets perhaps $3,000 a year for preaching one sermon a week, denouncing the poor railroad man who is striking that his brother-worker should have $2 per day?" Perry understood himself merely as a reporter of such views, not as an advocate for them. In fact, he closed the article with a shot across the bow at many of his informants, asserting, "[The church] must also warn the workingman that his alienation often results from tendencies within himself rather than within the church. The Jesus who is applauded by the average workingman is a minimized Jesus Christ, a fictitious person, not the Christ of the gospels."[6]

If Perry's closing underscores the persistence of class divisions within the churches, the framing of the entire article can also serve as a launching pad for discussions of gender. It is noteworthy that his anxiety and that of countless other Christian clergy during these years was focused on working*men*'s alienation from the churches. Women have perennially outnumbered men in the pews, but from time to time, this longstanding trend provokes intense bouts of fear and consternation. The Gilded Age was one such time. Gail Bederman's essay in the *American Quarterly* probes the deeper sources of fin de siècle anxieties about churchly "feminization." She argues that changing economic structures were the prime mover. While white Protestants had embraced a feminized religious sphere in the earlier nineteenth century as a welcome counterbalance to the purportedly masculine sphere of production, the rise of consumer-oriented corporate capitalism—with its endless variety of white-collar desk jobs, none of which involved men wielding axes, ploughs, and the like—left many suddenly worried about a crisis of runaway effeminacy. It seemed increasingly, as Bederman aptly puts it, "[that] 'she' threatened to overwhelm 'him.'" To restore some semblance of balance to the gendered order of the day, movements such as the Men and Religion Forward Movement of the early twentieth century sought to get men back into church. This context is helpful for using the Perry essay to have students engage the themes of class and gender.[7]

While Christian clergy were often flat-footed in responding to the travails associated with industrialization, middle-class women showed remarkable creativity and resolve as they experimented with new approaches to urban reform. One of their most important contributions was the settlement house. Inspired by the example of Toynbee Hall in East London, the young women who galvanized this movement rejected the social distance that was par for the course in traditional charity work, opting to move into poor districts themselves and to forge collaborative relationships with local residents. While each settlement took on its own character, there were common threads. They often sponsored kindergartens, hosted cultural productions and events, served as headquarters for women's clubs and other civic organizations, catalyzed all different forms of neighborhood and municipal activism, and offered social science researchers a strategic vantage onto rapidly changing urban lifeways. By the 1910s there were more than four hundred settlements scattered across the country, with their presence most concentrated in the nation's largest cities. Depending on where you teach, you might do a little research and see if there was a historic settlement house nearby. If so, you might consider a field trip or find ways to incorporate primary sources associated with that specific house. If not, then you will find no shortage of materials online regarding Chicago's

Hull House, which was cofounded by Jane Addams and Ellen Gates Starr in 1889. Addams's *Twenty Years at Hull House* is a classic and eminently teachable text, which opens a window onto life at that particular settlement. The chapter entitled "Subjective Necessity for Social Settlements" also includes important reflections relating the impetus for the larger movement to what Addams called "a certain renaissance going forward in Christianity." As she went on to explain,

> The impulse to share the lives of the poor, the desire to make social service, irrespective of propaganda, express the spirit of Christ, is as old as Christianity itself. . . . I believe that there is a distinct turning among many young men and women toward this simple acceptance of Christ's message. They resent the assumption that Christianity is a set of ideas which belong to the religious consciousness, whatever that may be. They insist that it cannot be proclaimed and instituted apart from the social life of the community and that it must seek a simple and natural expression in the social organism itself.[8]

Addams always positioned herself as a mediating voice in a polarized society, but some settlement house workers were true radicals. If you want to venture deeper into those waters, you might assign an excerpt from Christian socialist and Wellesley professor Vida Dutton Scudder's writings. The longtime head of Boston's Denison House, Scudder penned books such as *Socialism and Character* (1912) and *The Church and the Hour: Reflections of a Socialist Churchwoman* (1917), both of which are readily available online. Part 3, chapter 2, of the former—which focuses on "The Ethics of Inequality"—is a good starting place that connects the Gilded Age to conversations that remain lively still today.

The Gilded Age was a heyday of Christian socialism more broadly. A tremendously varied cast of characters claimed to be a part of this fractious tradition. Most all of them were concerned about runaway inequality, but their solutions ran the gamut: some advocated state takeover of major industries, while others insisted that true reform happened first and foremost at the level of the individual. Happily, Christian socialists left behind a rich documentary record that allows you to explore these varieties and that translates exceptionally well to the classroom. You might, for example, assign selections from Topeka Congregationalist minister Charles Sheldon's best-selling novel, *In His Steps*, which first popularized the question "What would Jesus do?" (WWJD).

The story begins with a working-class man walking unannounced into a church, criticizing the congregation for its lack of concern for the poor, and then promptly collapsing. When the man dies a few days later, the conscience of the entire community is seared. Deeply convicted, the church's pastor challenges the members of his congregation to ask WWJD prior to every decision they make. Sheldon's novel is not a literary work of art, but it offers an exceptionally revealing window onto the mindset of reforming white middle-class Protestants at the turn of the century. The following decade Baptist pastor and Rochester Theological Seminary professor Walter Rauschenbusch published *Christianity and the Social Crisis* (1907), which quickly found a wide readership and soon enough became a touchstone of the middle-class Protestant Social Gospel. While Rauschenbusch never formally joined the Socialist Party, much to Vida Scudder's chagrin, his thundering call for the churches to become more engaged with social reform energized many Christian socialists on the ground. However, as much as Rauschenbusch was deeply concerned with economic inequality, he failed to engage racial injustice at all. Its omission in the famed social gospeler's corpus is all the more striking given that, ever since the early 1890s, Ida B. Wells had been blazing trails through reforming white Protestant circles, underscoring for anyone who would listen the horrors of lynching. Even as Wells was at the vanguard on that issue, other Black social gospelers such as the African Methodist Episcopal preacher Reverdy Ransom spoke to the already powerful intersection of class and race in northern cities. Ransom's 1896 sermon, "The Negro and Socialism," provides a fascinating contrast with Sheldon and Rauschenbusch and can be found in either the *AME Church Review* or a primary source reader.[9]

Among the most important consequences of surging reform activity at the grassroots was the emergence during this period of a new body of Christian social teachings, which by the turn of the century gained the official sanction of denominational and interdenominational institutions. One of the most significant and readily accessible examples of this is the Roman Catholic *Rerum Novarum*, a papal encyclical on capital and labor promulgated by Pope Leo XIII in 1891. The document seeks to outline a middle way between state-centric socialism and untrammeled capitalism, both of which the Vatican had come to see as unacceptable. Leo articulated a full-throated defense of private property and insisted that, in seeking full equality, socialists fundamentally misunderstood human nature. "There naturally exist among mankind manifold differences of the most important kind; people differ in capacity, skill, health, strength; and unequal fortune is a necessary result of unequal condition," he argued, going on to add, "Such unequality is far from being disadvantageous either to individuals or to the community." But if Leo objected to the excesses of socialism, nor was he content with laissez-faire economies. He argued that the state had a moral obligation to protect working people's interests, including everything from the right not to work on the Sabbath to the right to form associations, including trade unions. Arguably the most striking passage in the entire encyclical is paragraph forty-five, which significantly modified the regnant contract freedom ideology of the day in the course of outlining the case for the living wage. Leo declared:

> Let the working man and the employer make free agreements, and in particular let them agree freely as to the wages; nevertheless, there underlies a dictate of natural justice more imperious and ancient than any bargain between man and man, namely, that wages ought not to be insufficient to support a frugal and well-behaved wage-earner.[10]

For reasons already stated above, American priests and bishops long emphasized the encyclical's anti-socialist provisions almost to the exclusion of its pro-labor ones. But *Rerum Novarum* would only become more important in decades following its promulgation. A variety of American Catholic reformers throughout the early twentieth century invoked it to justify putting more and more of the church's machinery behind the fight for economic justice. By the New Deal era, the encyclical was widely viewed as a cornerstone of modern Catholic social teaching. As you introduce students to this important document, ask them to think about how it fits within Gilded Age debates about capitalism and socialism, as well as what seems most important about its commentary on workers, wages, and the moral status of labor unions.

Protestants were slower to elaborate any comparable statement, but the founding of the Federal Council of Churches (FCC) in 1908 and its near-immediate adoption of "The Social Creed of the Churches" marked a new day. Representing thirty-two denominations, both Black and white, the FCC had all the makings of an ecumenical powerhouse, and its early leaders hoped it would be an engine of interdenominational collaboration on issues of social reform in particular. Given the clergy's longstanding conservatism on such matters, the Social Creed's opening sentence was noteworthy to say the least: "We deem it the duty of all Christian people to concern themselves directly with certain practical industrial problems." It went on to declare:

> To us it seems that the Churches must stand:
> For equal rights and complete justice for all men in all stations of life.
> For the right all men to the opportunity for self-maintenance, a right ever to be wisely and strongly safe-guarded against encroachments of ever kind.
> For the right of workers to some protection against the hardships often resulting from the swift crisis of industrial change.

The list of injunctions went on, including everything from "For the abolition of child labor" to "the suppression of the 'sweating system.'"[11] It was hardly a radical platform. But then again, it represented a major departure from the views articulated by the Reverend David Swing less than a generation before. The FCC's positions would continue to evolve, and I have often found it useful to have students compare the 1908 Social Creed with the revised version published in 1932. The latter endorsed much more provocative measures, calling for "Social planning and control of the credit and monetary systems and the economic processes of the common good," as well as "Application of the Christian principle of redemption to the treatment of offenders; reform of penal and correctional methods and institutions and of criminal court procedure." The more that the FCC pushed in such directions, the more it invited criticism from its member denominations' vast conservative constituencies. The Social Creed would never be repealed, but by the time the FCC merged with other organizations to form the National Council of Churches in 1950, it was well along its way to being a historical artifact. In the years immediately following, as social Christianity's institutional movement slowed, surging labor and civil rights movements would come to the fore. And so the action moved back to the grassroots, where it had first gotten going in earnest in the Gilded Age.

ADDITIONAL RESOURCES

Cantwell, Christopher D., Heath W. Carter, and Janine Giordano Drake. *The Pew and the Picket Line: Christianity and the American Working Class.* Urbana: University of Illinois Press, 2016.

Carter, Heath W. *Union Made: Working People and the Rise of Social Christianity in Chicago*. New York: Oxford University Press, 2015.

Dorrien, Gary. *The New Abolition: W. E. B. Du Bois and the Black Social Gospel*. New Haven, CT: Yale University Press, 2015.

Drake, Janine Giordano. *The Gospel of Church: How Mainline Protestants Vilified Christian Socialism and Fractured the Labor Movement*. New York: Oxford University Press, 2023.

Evans, Christopher H. *The Social Gospel in American Religion: A History*. New York: New York University Press, 2017.

Fitzgerald, Maureen. *Habits of Compassion: Irish Catholic Nuns and the Origins of New York's Welfare System, 1830–1920*. Urbana: University of Illinois Press, 2006.

Higginbotham, Evelyn Brooks *Righteous Discontent: The Women's Movement in the Black Baptist Church, 1880–1920*. Cambridge, MA: Harvard University Press, 1994.

NOTES

1. "Liberal Christianity," *Workingman's Advocate* 4, no. 17 (November 16, 1867): 2. This editorial can also be found in Edwin S. Gaustad, Mark A. Noll, and Heath W. Carter, eds, *A Documentary History of Religion in America*, 4th ed. (Grand Rapids, MI: William B. Eerdmans, 2018): 411–12.

2. "The Labor Turmoil," *Alliance* 1, no. 4 (January 3, 1874): 2.

3. For more on the appeal of trade unions, see Amy Dru Stanley, *From Bondage to Contract: Wage Labor, Marriage, and the Market in the Age of Slave Emancipation* (Cambridge: Cambridge University Press, 1998).

4. For more on the above see Heath W. Carter, *Union Made: Working People and the Rise of Social Christianity in Chicago* (New York: Oxford University Press, 2015).

5. H. Francis Perry, "The Workingman's Alienation from the Church," *American Journal of Sociology* 4, no. 5 (March 1899): 621–29.

6. Perry, "The Workingman's Alienation," 622.

7. Gail Bederman, "'The Women Have Had Charge of the Church Work Long Enough': The Men and Religion Forward Movement of 1911–1912 and the Masculinization of Middle-Class Protestantism," *American Quarterly* 41, no. 3 (September 1989): 432–65.

8. Jane Addams, *Twenty Years at Hull-House* (New York: Macmillan, 1910): 122–24.

9. See Reverdy Ransom, "The Negro and Socialism," *AME Church Review* 13 (October 1896): 192–200. The sermon is also excerpted in Gaustad, Noll, and Carter, *A Documentary History of Religion in America*, 413–16.

10. *Rerum Novarum*: Encyclical of Pope Leo XIII on Capital and Labor," Vatican, accessed January 17, 2020, http://www.vatican.va/content/leo-xiii/en/encyclicals/documents/hf_l-xiii_enc_15051891_rerum-novarum.html.

11. "The Social Creed of the Churches," National Council of Churches, accessed January 17, 2020, https://nationalcouncilofchurches.us/common-wit ness/1908/social-creed.php.

The Prosperity Gospel in US History and Culture

PHILLIP LUKE SINITIERE

If you google "prosperity gospel" or "prosperity theology"—or if you ask Siri—the results that populate the first several pages of hits, including videos, images, and news, consist mostly of denunciations of the prosperity message as abhorrent and dangerous. Since many of the hits link to resources produced by Neo-Calvinist ministers and other Christian groups critical of the movement, the theological crosshairs that target the prosperity gospel deliver materials that decry the health and wealth message. Other results include journalistic expositions fixated on the oversized mansions in gated communities where prosperity gospel ministers live, the private jets on which they fly to preaching campaigns, or other controversies involving money, sex, or politics, most of it tied to the Christian Right. Increasingly, post-prosperity gospel memoirs offer an alternative conversion story, a narrative of individual transformation about leaving the prosperity gospel behind, about rescinding the health and wealth message.

Such digital materials often leave a binary impression of the prosperity gospel as either good or bad. Additionally, although there are brief references to Africa, Asia, or Latin America, many of these resources paint a picture that the prosperity gospel is primarily an American phenomenon. While the prosperity gospel's economic engine may still be in the United States, its global presence is a central part of its contemporary reality. Furthermore, few materials explain the prosperity gospel's historical roots, or how it has changed over time. Or how its origin points within American Protestantism tend to overshadow the prosperity gospel's expressions in other religious traditions such as Roman

235

Catholicism, especially outside of the United States. All of this makes teaching about the prosperity gospel challenging for history educators, lest the lessons traffic in one-sided thinking and become only about doctrine, only about politics, or only about castigation. The task before educators, therefore, is to interrelate these concepts, themes, and ideas into more complex and nuanced teaching about the prosperity gospel's impact and significance in American history.

From a chronological point of view, the prosperity gospel fits into US history at several important points across the last century or so. First, the prosperity gospel's origins emerged at the nexus of modernity: a transitional period in American life in the late 1800s and early 1900s that encompassed industrial change, social upheaval, and progress along with economic unrest and economic growth. Beyond the Industrial Age, the Gilded Age, and the Progressive Era, the movement's expansion after World War II connected to the attainment of postwar prosperity, the advent of the Cold War, and a new age of American internationalism coupled with expansive technological innovation through early televangelism and the proliferation of megachurches. Its relevance in the contemporary period of the twenty-first century offers lenses through which to understand the prosperity gospel's continued use of the latest technology through digital media along with the movement's intersection with conservative politics and the Republican Party. Additionally, wrapped within the prosperity gospel's historical unfolding is its embeddedness within American culture.

From a cultural perspective the prosperity gospel is perennially American: its individualistic orientation offers a message of personal improvement that promises the possibility of economic advancement and financial growth. The prosperity gospel movement's aspirational ethos is also about getting a second chance in life, which ironically is in fact a central plank of Christianity's message. Yet the purveyors of the prosperity gospel offer the possibility of a spiritual makeover more consonant with neoliberalism and today's climate of reality television steeped in neatly packaged stories of personalized transformation and seemingly instantaneous success. There always seems to be a good ending in the spiritualized version of the American Dream. These historical and cultural factors of the prosperity gospel offer teachers a variety of instructional deliverables for a US history course: the skills of historical thinking through chronology, change over time, cultural studies, and religion.

This essay offers ideas that will assist teachers and their students with obtaining a prosperity gospel literacy. Religious studies scholar Diane L. Moore defines religious literacy as "the ability to discern and analyze the fundamental intersections of religion and social/political/ cultural life through multiple lenses." This analysis includes familiarity with key writings or texts, the historical conditions that shaped religions or religious movements, and their political, social, and cultural impacts over time.[1] The overarching framework of a religious movement's social, political, and cultural significance coupled with historical development defines my approach to teaching about the prosperity gospel.

While there are countless ways to teach about its history and cultural significance, I have found it most effective in the classroom to focus on the prosperity gospel's language, its historical development over time, and its innovative use of new media. These three points of emphasis pave the way to understanding the interrelationships between the prosperity gospel and the social, political, and cultural environments in which it is practiced in US society. I adopt a nonsectarian or nontheological approach to teaching about the prosperity gospel's spiritual understanding of the world that historicizes the movement's doctrines. What follows below, therefore, are potential approaches for teaching the prosperity gospel's history and its social, political, and cultural importance across American society without spending unnecessary time delving into unverifiable transcendent claims, theological speculation, or doctrinal minutia, aspects of thought helpful to understanding the prosperity gospel but not vital for obtaining a basic prosperity gospel literacy.

Definitions

It is important to define and unpack the language of the prosperity gospel. The heavy reporting on the prosperity gospel presents a wide range of opinions and terms that offer a combination of potential clarity and confusion. Although this portion of a lesson might seem tedious for students and teachers, pursuing terminological precision and a common set of definitions generates deeper, more nuanced understanding. In turn, this process yields more probing, analytical exploration. Simply asking "What is the prosperity gospel?" or "What comes to mind when you hear the term prosperity gospel?" is a critical place to open pathways of discussion. In the classroom, I jot down student comments to these questions in a mind map format. The white board is visually dense with words, concepts, and names, which serves as a nice metaphor for the complexity of defining the prosperity gospel movement. If time permits, creating a word cloud is another useful strategy to examine its multilayered dimensions. At the end of the discussion period, I attempt to connect the dots between student responses and then wrap their thoughts together in the lesson's final segment on terminology. As a summary section I lay out the following terms as a bedrock for understanding the prosperity gospel's ideas, practices, and change over time.

I define the "prosperity gospel" as Christian teachings (primarily from Protestant, Pentecostal, and Neo-Pentecostal evangelicals) that emphasize the idea of divinely sanctioned material accumulation; the firm conviction that generative human action through thought, speech, or spiritual decree can activate or alter material circumstances or realities; the spiritualizing of material conditions that pivots on the idea of aspirational possibility.

Historically, the prosperity gospel is part of Pentecostalism and Neo-Pentecostalism. We can also trace its roots to the Holiness and New Thought movements of the nineteenth century that collectively coupled ideas of spiritual advancement with personal improvement. "Pentecostalism" refers to a movement that had its origins in early twentieth-century America at Azusa Street in Los Angeles. The Pentecostalism movement birthed new denominations such as the Assemblies of God and the Church of God in Christ (COGIC). "Neo-Pentecostal" refers to the post–World War II development of Pentecostalism, when the movement grew outside of historically Pentecostal denominations, fostered the creation of independent nondenominational agencies and organizations, and included Christians outside of Protestantism such as Roman Catholics who embraced Pentecostal religious experiences. This historical unfolding also featured Pentecostal Roman Catholics who became prosperity gospel proponents across both national and international religious networks. With respect to religious practice, the terms reflect the conviction that in either individual settings or collective assemblies of worship, God is undeniably present through the Holy Spirit, expressed not just through the words and teachings of the minister, but also through collective, communal gatherings. Individually, Pentecostals and Neo-Pentecostals describe experiences of the Holy Spirit through rapturous moments of intense prayer, speaking in tongues, or claims about visions and healings. Corporately, responses to the Holy Spirit find expression through clapping, shouting, raising hands, applause, singing, dancing, or physical touch (i.e., "laying on of hands"). Pentecostals and Neo-Pentecostals believe that the Holy Spirit prompts improvisational and spontaneous embodied movements or oral expressions.[2]

To the definitions of "Pentecostalism" and "Neo-Pentecostalism" I add that the prosperity gospel's cultural power resides in its promise to remake one's life, one's identity, and one's future. In other words, the prosperity gospel promises the possibility of a spiritual makeover, a second chance with potential implications for changes in one's internal disposition and alternations in one's external conditions. In addition, certainty is the overarching concept that drives the prosperity gospel's construct and its discourse: whether or not a favorable future for which one hopes ever arrives, faith cements the idea that God is somehow ultimately orchestrating the circumstances of one's life into a better outcome. There is also certainty associated with language: verbalizing aspirational statements or speaking Bible verses propels divine activity or influence toward the object of desire. Such verbalizing represents the linguistic mechanics of "naming it" and "claiming it" in prosperity gospel parlance.

In lessons on the prosperity gospel's history, the terms "evangelical," "evangelicalism," and "Pentecostal" require elucidation because not all evangelicals are prosperity gospel proponents, and not all prosperity gospel practitioners are Pentecostal. Furthermore, using the nomenclature of "evangelical" after 2016 requires additional specificity because of Donald Trump's relationship with conservative Christians. While a number of self-identifying evangelicals voted for Trump, not all theologically conservative Christians (including Pentecostals and Charismatics) supported his administration.[3]

The terms "evangelical" and "evangelicalism" refer to the historical religious movement that began in the early eighteenth century.[4] History shows that the movement is complex and has changed and adapted over time. While referencing evangelicalism's history in lessons on the prosperity gospel refers mostly to the post–World War II period, it is vital for students to know that the prosperity gospel's origins date to the late nineteenth and early twentieth centuries, a point I outline in some detail below. Highlighting the evangelical movement's individualist dimensions requires a discussion of shared characteristics that developed over time and find social articulation in everyday practice, such as a focus on an inward, identifiable spiritual change called a "new birth" by expressing faith in Jesus Christ; an emphasis on the Bible as authoritative for issues of both faith and practice; acknowledgment of the influence of the Holy Spirit for spiritual enlightenment, sometimes expressed through speaking in tongues; and the imperative to act on faith through evangelistic activity. In my classroom presentations I point out that the cluster of experiences, thoughts, and perspectives for some evangelicals can find a home in the hearts, minds, emotions, and actions of prosperity gospel proponents. I pair students off and assign short selections from scholarly writings on evangelicalism's history, which each group summarizes as part of a quick verbal assessment exercise. Thereafter I show a short Al Jazeera documentary on evangelicalism that presents the depth and breadth of the movement, using the video for a concluding discussion on the diversity of evangelical faith and political opinion. Given the abundance of reporting on evangelicals from US-centric media sources, presenting an international evaluation on evangelical politics offers a fresh examination of the subject.[5]

Televangelism, or the rise of religious broadcasting first on the radio airwaves and then on television, also drove part of the prosperity gospel's mid-twentieth-century expansion. At this historical juncture, some participants in the movement resisted rigid denominational lines that resulted in the emergence of hundreds of independent ministers and the creation of countless, associated evangelistic agencies (again, as part of the Neo-Pentecostal movement discussed above). Scholars have also used the label of "Charismatic movement" to describe the Pentecostalism of the post–World War II period. In this era, the prosperity gospel's impact broadened in the United States and across the world. It also became known as the Word of Faith movement, an expression animated by verbal expressions called positive confession and dubbed the "health and wealth gospel" or "name it and claim it" by critics. A belief that God's divine love is the originary trigger for healing coupled with an epistemic confidence that God will act in the world undergirds the perceived necessity of divine influence in times of spiritual, physical, or psychological need for wholeness.[6]

When teaching on the prosperity gospel I typically use historical examples and illustrations to flesh out the definitions offered above. There are several types of lessons I use to accomplish definitional clarity. First, I craft document-based lessons on Pentecostalism's early history. I use the movement's newspapers such as *Apostolic Faith* and early twentieth-century journalism from outlets such as the *Los Angeles Times* — sources that present a dramatic contrast in perspectives on Pentecostalism — to teach primary source analysis, context, and comparative interpretation. Archival repositories at Oral Roberts University and the University of Southern California provide free digital access to periodicals and magazines that offer US and international perspectives.[7] Second, providing students with reference work entries helps them grasp more specificity about how the movement changed over time. These strategies correspond to the teaching goal of obtaining a prosperity gospel literacy. Furthermore, teachers should not shy away from the potentially technical nature of a terminology discussion because such key ideas pave the way for enhanced understanding.[8]

History

   I have found that teaching about Aimee Semple McPherson's (1890–1944) life and influence allows students to connect the historical dots of the prosperity gospel's origins and explore the movement's changes over time. McPherson's story intertwines with other important aspects of religion in America (e.g., fundamentalism; see George Marsden's chapter) and illustrates the transition from Pentecostalism to Neo-Pentecostalism during the Progressive Era through World War II. Since McPherson used radio and television to present her message, this periodization of her life allows exploration of technology's role in the prosperity gospel's proliferation.

  After introducing the history of Pentecostalism and Neo-Pentecostalism in the context of the early to mid-twentieth century, I present a biographical snapshot of McPherson that emphasizes her adoption of Pentecostal Christianity and her eventual move to Los Angeles. I focus on McPherson's performance of Pentecostalism at Angelus Temple — her megachurch in Southern California — her traveling healing revivals, illustrated sermons, radio broadcasts from Los Angeles, and early television spots. This gives students a sense of Pentecostalism's public face, its relation to early twentieth-century culture wars over politics, race, and gender, and the paradox of the movement's progressive use of modern technological innovation to broadcast a conservative religious message, which continues into the contemporary era. A great pedagogical companion to my lecture is the PBS documentary *Sister Aimee*. The clips I show in class feature McPherson's voice and

carefully curated pictures and images from her promotional evangelistic tours across the country and her illustrated sermons at Angelus
Temple that employed Hollywood actors to dramatize stories from the
Bible. The documentary's website to which I direct students allows them
to linger with and analyze the visual primary sources from the video
clips, which visually enhances connections between Pentecostalism,
Neo-Pentecostalism, televangelism, and the prosperity gospel.[9]

After asking students to provide general impressions about McPherson's life and ministry, I introduce more analytical and comparative
questions. Based on the previous discussion of key terms, I ask students
to identify where and how they observe Pentecostal practice and other
aspects of the prosperity gospel in McPherson's larger story. I also ask
students to compare McPherson's engagement with Pentecostalism to
earlier developments in the movement in and around Azusa Street and
the emergence of early Pentecostal denominations (e.g., COGIC), questions designed to illustrate the process of historical thinking.

There are alternative formulations of this lesson. One is to pair my
McPherson lecture with a presentation on Neo-Pentecostal televangelist
and prosperity proponent Kathryn Kuhlman (1907–76). Like McPherson's life, my presentation of Kuhlman's biography draws connections
between her work as a female minister, her radio sermons, her claims
about divine healing (she was often called "The Miracle Lady"), and
her key place in post–World War II American televangelism, Neo-
Pentecostalism, and the broader Charismatic movement. While Kuhlman often modulated McPherson's influence on her, I explain how
Kuhlman used media to perform Pentecostal healing and to generate
the impact of religious celebrity. The extensive televised footage of Kuhlman's religious meetings available on YouTube provides a visual and
performance component with which to compare McPherson. This gives
students an opportunity to assess historical context and change over
time as they analyze manifestations of the prosperity gospel Pentecostalism before and after World War II.[10]

Technology

After students understand the prosperity gospel's historical development over time, they are can more easily grasp the movement's use of technology and its messaging across different new media
modalities. My references to technology here refer specifically to the

history of televangelism, a wide space of expression in which many prosperity gospel preachers operate. Since the history of televangelism is expansive, I cover the movement in a short lecture that provides students with a macro-level view of key events and issues and culminates with a close look at the televangelist scandals of the 1980s. In turn, this establishes a framework for examining one of the most important televangelists of the contemporary scene: Joel Osteen.

My presentation of televangelism defines the term capaciously: most broadly it has to do with religious broadcasting across both radio and television platforms. I discuss some of the earliest radio preachers who took to the airwaves in the 1920s, 1930s, and 1940s. Beyond McPherson, early figures in the movement included Pittsburgh Episcopal minister Lewis B. Whittemore, an evangelical preacher from California named Charles Fuller, a Catholic priest named Richard Coughlin from Michigan, and a Harlem-based African American evangelist named Mother Rosa Horn, whose messages rang out on her Radio Church of God of the Air. Organizations such as the National Religious Broadcasters and, later, favorable congressional legislation generated a ubiquitous presence of televangelism across the country by the 1950s that featured positive thinking proponents such as Catholic bishop Fulton J. Sheen and the wealthy New York City Protestant minister Norman Vincent Peale, along with an early prosperity gospel figure from Oklahoma named Oral Roberts. The story I unfold explains how during the next two decades the prosperity gospel found more solid broadcasting footing with the launch of formalized programming from the Christian Broadcasting Network (CBN) in the early 1960s and in 1973 the Trinity Broadcasting Network (TBN). These networks disseminated and popularized the prosperity gospel. They were also the same networks on which millions witnessed several notorious televangelist scandals of the 1980s, including those of the prosperity *Praise the Lord* ministry of Jim and Tammy Faye Bakker and Baton Rouge Assemblies of God preacher Jimmy Swaggart, both of which involved controversies related to sex, money, and power. I also point out that since religious broadcaster Pat Roberston's unsuccessful run for president in 1988 intersected with these scandals, public opinion of televangelists plummeted. For a time, many Americans came to believe that anyone preaching on television must be a conniving cheat and religious hypocrite interested only in fame and wealth.[11] I typically include more recent scandals such as that of Ted Haggard, whose lies about meeting with a male escort led to a departure from his Colorado Springs church and from a leadership position within the Christian Right. Interview clips with TV preachers from Ted Koppel's famous 1988 ABC feature on televangelism and interviews with a disgraced and humbled Haggard from Alexandra Pelosi's 2009 film *The Trials of Ted Haggard* present the movement's reception in contemporaneous moments. To better understand how this sensibility of suspicion continues into the present, I generate discussion questions about the public performances of televangelists and interviews conducted in the wake of scandals.[12]

Although the emergence of new media at the dawn of the twenty-first century did not significantly adjust popular opinion of televangelists, it did expand the digital modalities upon which they could present their message. I use Joel Osteen's "tel-e-vangelism" (using "tel" and "e" signals Osteen's expansive media ministry) as the primary illustration of this trend. The two decades prior to the publication of his first book in 2004 titled *Your Best Life Now,* which inaugurated the smiling preacher's public ministry, he worked in religious broadcasting by bringing his father's ministry at Lakewood Church to the television airwaves. He is the only TV preacher today who had a two-decade religious broadcasting career before the commencement of his tenure as a televangelist. Furthermore, I explain how the emergence of Osteen's public career in the early 2000s tracked with the rise of new media platforms such as Facebook, YouTube, and Twitter. Thus, Osteen's vast media fluency determined his signature place as a leading twenty-first century tel-e-vangelist, a point I make by pairing YouTube clips of Osteen's television sermons, transcripts of his sermons available online, and televisions interviews with scholarly analysis of Osteen's use of digital media. Instructors can select virtually any Osteen sermon clip posted on his YouTube page and pick a handful of his Tweets over time and find the two central elements in his prosperity gospel message: the importance of generating positive thoughts and the necessity of verbalizing positive words and aspirational sayings as a strategy for personal improvement.[13]

Broadening the scope of the prosperity gospel's influence on televangelism enriches historical understanding of the multilayered religious landscape. Given the online presence of so much of the prosperity gospel's recent history, classroom assessments and discussions of technology's place in the movement offer students opportunities to conduct their own historical research to gain a prosperity gospel literacy. Exploring available online materials related to the prosperity gospel, students can engage subject material in analytical, lateral fashion by literally and figuratively documenting the networks within which these religious celebrities engage and upon which they depend.[14]

Conclusion

Classroom lectures and discussions about the prosperity gospel's key definitions, the range of its historical arc, and the central role of technology in the movement position students to achieve a prosperity gospel literacy. Such literacy will provide the tools of analytic discernment for grasping the interrelationships between the prosperity gospel's ideas and practices and the social, cultural, and political conditions in which they have taken root over time. Understanding key figures in the movement, along with important catalyst moments over time, helps students understand historical facts about the prosperity gospel, why advocates have found it meaningful, and why it has been reviled. While students and teachers certainly have opinions about the prosperity gospel message, such personal dispositions in the classroom are not nearly as important as acquiring the analytical tools for more expansive historical thinking, transferable skills obtained through a prosperity gospel literacy.

ADDITIONAL RESOURCES

Bowler, Kate. *Blessed: A History of the American Prosperity Gospel*. New York: Oxford University Press, 2013.

Brown, Candy Gunther, ed. *Global Pentecostal and Charismatic Healing*. New York: Oxford University Press, 2011.

Frederick, Marla. *Colored Television: American Religion Gone Global*. Stanford, CA: Stanford University Press, 2015.

Sinitiere, Phillip Luke. *Salvation with a Smile: Joel Osteen, Lakewood Church, and American Christianity*. New York: New York University Press, 2015.

Wigger, John. *PTL: The Rise and Fall of Jim and Tammy Faye Bakker's Evangelical Empire*. New York: Oxford University Press, 2017.

Yong, Amos, and Katherine Attanasi, eds. *Pentecostalism and Prosperity: The Socio-Economics of the Global Charismatic Movement*. New York: Palgrave Macmillan, 2012.

NOTES

1. Stephen Prothero, *Religious Literacy: What Every American Needs to Know—and Doesn't* (New York: HarperCollins, 2007), 1–18; Diane L. Moore, *Overcoming Religious Illiteracy: A Cultural Studies Approach to the Study of Religion and Secondary Education* (New York: Palgrave Macmillan, 2007); Diane L. Moore, "Overcoming Religious Illiteracy: A Cultural Studies Approach," *World History Connected* 4, no. 1 (November 2006), https://worldhistoryconnected.press.uillinois.edu/4.1/moore.html.

2. Allan Anderson, *An Introduction to Pentecostalism* (New York: Cambridge University Press, 2004), 1–15, 144–65; Allan Anderson, "Varieties, Taxonomies, and Definitions," in *Studying Global Pentecostalism: Theories and Methods*, ed. Allan Anderson, Michael Bergunder, Andre Droogers, and Cornelius van der Laan (Berkeley: University of California Press, 2010), 13–29; Russell P. Spittler, "Pentecostal and Charismatic Spirituality," in *The New International Dictionary of Pentecostal and Charismatic Movements*, rev. and expanded ed., ed. Stanley M. Burgess and Eduard M. Van Der Maas (Grand Rapids, MI: Zondervan, 2002), 1096–1102. Examples of the intersections between Roman Catholicism and the prosperity gospel include Katherine L. Wiegele, *Investing in Miracles: El Shaddai and the Transformation of Popular Catholicism in the Philippines* (Honolulu: University of Hawai'i Press, 2005); R. Andrew Chesnut, *Competitive Spirits: Latin America's New Religious Economy* (New York: Oxford University Press, 2003), 64–101.

3. Tom Jacobs, "Did the Prosperity Gospel Help Elect Trump?," *Pacific Standard*, December 7, 2018, https://psmag.com/economics/did-the-prosperity-gospel-help-elect-trump; Jessica Glenza, "Paula White: The Pastor Who Helps Trump Hear 'What God Has to Say,'" *The Guardian (London)*, March 27, 2019, https://www.theguardian.com/us-news/2019/mar/27/paula-white-donald-trump-pastor-evangelicals; Meagan Day, "A Grift from God," *Jacobin*, August 10, 2019, https://www.jacobinmag.com/2019/08/megachurches-prosperity-gospel-capitalism-gene-lingerfelt-donald-trump; Drew Pendergrass, "The Televangelist-in-Chief: Trump and the Prosperity Gospel," *Harvard Political Review*, November 12, 2017, https://web.archive.org/web/20171203124753/https://harvardpolitics.com/culture/tevangelistinchief/.

4. David Bebbington, *Evangelicalism in Modern Britain: A History from the 1730s to the 1980* (London: Unwin Hyman, 1989), 2–17.

5. Other background reading includes Randall Balmer, *The Making of Evangelicalism: From Revivalism to Politics and Beyond* (Waco, TX: Baylor University Press, 2010); Randall Balmer, *Mine Eyes Have Seen the Glory: A Journey in the Evangelical Subculture in America*, 4th ed. (New York: Oxford University Press, 2006); Douglas A. Sweeney, "Evangelicals in American History," in *The Columbia Guide to Religion in American History*, ed. Paul Harvey and Edward J. Blum (New York: Columbia University Press, 2012), 122–35; Molly Worthen, *Apostles*

of Reason: The Crisis of Authority in American Evangelicalism (New York: Oxford University Press, 2013); Steven P. Miller, *The Age of Evangelicalism: America's Born-Again Years* (New York: Oxford University Press, 2014). See also "What Does It Take to Be a Real Evangelical?," *Al Jazeera*, YouTube, April 1, 2018, https://www.youtube.com/watch?v=tOV5FpMRQDo.

6. David Edwin Harrell Jr., *All Things Are Possible: The Healing and Charismatic Revivals in Modern America* (Bloomington: Indiana University Press, 1975); Kate Bowler, *Blessed: A History of the American Prosperity Gospel* (New York: Oxford University Press, 2013); Milmon Harrison, *Righteous Riches: The Word of Faith Movement in Contemporary African American Religion* (New York: Oxford University Press, 2005); Candy Gunther Brown, "Introduction: Pentecostalism and the Globalization of Illness and Healing," in *Global Pentecostal and Charismatic Healing*, ed. Candy Gunther Brown (New York: Oxford University Press, 2011), 4–6; Phillip Luke Sinitiere, "Televangelism: Television and Radio," in *Encyclopedia of Christianity in the United States*, ed. George Thomas Kurian and Mark A. Lamport (Lanham, MD: Rowman and Littlefield, 2016), 2271–78.

7. Gastón Espinosa, ed., *William J. Seymour and the Origins of Global Pentecostalism: A Biography and Documentary Reader* (Durham, NC: Duke University Press, 2014). At Oral Roberts University, see the Digitized Periodical Collection, https://digitalshowcase.oru.edu/hist_periodicals/; the Pentecostal and Charismatic Research Archive at the University of Southern California, http://digitallibrary.usc.edu/cdm/directory/collection/p15799coll14; the Consortium of Pentecostal Archives housed online by the Assemblies of God denomination, https://pentecostalarchives.org.

8. In addition to Kate Bowler's work, the following studies allow for a rich examination of history, religion, culture, class, and politics and are some of the leading scholarly sources on the subject: Joseph Williams, *Spirit Cure: A History of Pentecostal Healing* (New York: Oxford University Press, 2013); Amos Yong and Katherine Attanasi, eds., *Pentecostalism and Prosperity: The Socio-Economics of the Global Charismatic Movement* (New York: Palgrave Macmillan, 2012); Candy Gunther Brown, *Testing Prayer: Science and Healing* (Cambridge, MA: Harvard University Press, 2012). Similarly, showing a short clip from Bowler's 2014 appearance on C-SPAN's Book TV shortly after the publication of *Blessed* assists with a prosperity gospel literacy by helping students see a connection between the movement's ideas and practices. See Kate Bowler, "Blessed," *Book TV*, March 18, 2014, https://www.c-span.org/video/?318386-3/blessed.

9. See also Matthew Avery Sutton, *Aimee Semple McPherson and the Resurrection of Christian America* (Cambridge, MA: Harvard University Press, 2007). For television footage, see "Sister Aimee on Prohibition," August 9, 2007, https://www.youtube.com/watch?v=owfQomdMEqM.

10. Amy Collier Artman, *The Miracle Lady: Kathryn Kuhlman and the Transformation of Charismatic Christianity* (Grand Rapids, MI: William B. Eerdmans,

2019); Candy Gunther Brown, "Healing Words: Narratives of Spiritual Healing and Kathryn Kuhlman's Uses of Print Culture, 1947–1976," in *Religion and the Culture of Print in Modern America,* ed. Charles L. Cohen and Paul S. Boyer (Madison: University of Wisconsin Press, 2008), 271–97; Arlene Sanchez Walsh, *Pentecostals in America* (New York: Columbia University Press, 2018), 88–91.

11. Sinitiere, "Televangelism." The sensational but altogether important dimensions of the Bakker saga are worth exploring in the classroom; see John Wigger, *PTL: The Rise and Fall of Jim and Tammy Faye Bakker's Evangelical Empire* (New York: Oxford University Press, 2017).

12. "The Koppel Report: Televangelism, the Billion Dollar Pie," YouTube, May 12, 1988, https://www.youtube.com/watch?v=xNYA35TPhcQ; Alexandra Pelosi, dir., *The Trials of Ted Haggard* (HBO, 2009).

13. See Phillip Luke Sinitiere, *Salvation with a Smile: Joel Osteen, Lakewood Church, and American Christianity* (New York: New York University Press, 2015). Although Osteen is a singular figure in the prosperity gospel movement, teachers can also draw from the scholarship on African Americans in the prosperity gospel to expand prosperity gospel literacy. See Shayne Lee, *T. D. Jakes: America's New Preacher* (New York: New York University Press, 2005); Jonathan Walton, *Watch This! The Ethics and Aesthetics of Black Televangelism* (New York: New York University Press, 2009); Scott Billingsly, *It's a New Day: Race and Gender in the Modern Charismatic Movement* (Tuscaloosa: University of Alabama Press, 2008); Marla Frederick, *Colored Television: American Religion Gone Global* (Stanford: Stanford University Press, 2015); Carolyn Moxley Rouse, John L. Jackson, and Marla Frederick, eds., *Televised Redemption: Black Religious Media and Racial Empowerment* (New York: New York University Press, 2016).

14. Sam Wineburg, *Why Learn History (When It's Already on Your Phone)* (Chicago: University of Chicago Press, 2018), 150–52.

The Effects of the Fundamentalist/ Modernist Split

G E O R G E   M A R S D E N

M ost students should be familiar with recent "culture wars," or at least with some sharp political divides in America today, so the fundamentalist/modernist controversies of the 1920s can be introduced as background to understanding the role of religion in that divide today.[1]

The place to begin, I believe, is by observing that while the fundamentalist/modernist disputes involved white Protestants, most of the participants had reason to believe that the future of American civilization was at stake. Remind the students that at the beginning of the twentieth century the United States was overwhelmingly a Protestant nation, at least in the sense that almost everything was run by white Protestants. That did not mean that the United States was close to being a Christian nation in the sense that most of its leaders and citizens were practicing Christians or that its policies were largely shaped by Christian principles. The fact that white Protestants held almost all the power meant that African Americans (also mostly Protestant), Catholics, Jews, and others were discriminated against. Furthermore, much of the culture and economy was shaped by factors that had little to do with Protestantism. Even though there was white Protestant dominance, its effects were a mix of good and bad. So the impact of Christianity on the culture, although perceptible, was also limited.

Still, most serious white Protestant church people thought that the nation ought to be "Christian" in some broad sense. And even if many of the Protestant influences were superficial, there were others that were sometimes substantial in providing moral assumptions that undergirded the law. Sabbath "blue laws" that kept most businesses closed on Sundays were conspicuous examples. So were laws regarding marriage, divorce, sexual practices, and censorship. The easiest way to illustrate such Protestant influence is in the remarkable success of their campaigns to enact by 1920 national prohibition of the manufacture and sale of alcoholic beverages.

Students will not likely be familiar with the terms "modernist" and "fundamentalist," so these need some explaining. Modernists were progressive Protestants who believed that Christianity needed to be updated to meet the challenges of the modern age. Particularly, they thought, Christianity needed to adapt its views to modern science and to rapidly changing social conditions. Although modernists, sometimes known as "theological liberals," came in many varieties, they agreed that the Bible and theology were to be understood in the light of modern science, historical criticism that questioned many of the historical claims of the Bible, and modern insights into morality.

Modernists were strongest in the major "mainline" Protestant denominations of the North, such as northern Baptist, northern Presbyterian, northern Methodist, Congregationalist, and Disciples of Christ. "Fundamentalism" first became prominent as efforts in the early 1920s by theological conservatives, especially among Baptists and Presbyterians. They wanted to bring their denominations back to the "fundamentals" of traditional Protestant faith, such as the historical accuracy (or inerrancy) of the Bible and the authenticity of the miracles, including the virgin birth of Christ and his bodily resurrection from the dead. By about 1925 it became clear that efforts to purge these denominations of modernists would fail, and the conservatives either would have to fight rear-guard actions or form their own smaller denominations.[2]

It soon became apparent, however, that fundamentalism was an impulse among many diverse sorts of "Bible-believing" Protestants and extended well beyond the conflicts in major northern denominations. Much of American Protestantism had been shaped by the revivalist or evangelical tradition that emphasized the authority of the Bible and the necessity of conversion or being "born again" based on the atoning work of Christ on the cross. Such teachings remained strong in the South and in the heartlands of the North. Revivalist preachers (Billy Sunday is the best illustration from that time) rallied many ordinary Christians to oppose modernist trends in churches and many of the modern mores of the Jazz Age. By the mid-1920s fundamentalism could be viewed as a very loose collection of diverse sorts of Bible-believing conversion-oriented Protestants who were militantly opposed to modernist theology in the churches and to many modern cultural and moral trends.

Among those who did the most to organize a self-consciously fundamentalist movement, especially in evangelistic agencies and Bible institutes outside of major denominations, one of the most influential distinctive teachings was "dispensational premillennialism."[3] Dispensational teaching involved some very literalistic beliefs about what the Bible taught about Jesus's return to set up a kingdom for a literal one thousand years (millennium) on earth. Dispensationalists interpreted many current events as having been predicted in specific biblical prophesies and as showing that Jesus would return at any moment, and almost certainly within their current generation. That added urgency to soul-saving evangelism. It also had the appeal of offering a sharp critique of mainstream modern civilization. Rather than celebrating scientific, technological, and social progress as many elite groups did at the time, dispensational teachings said that the Bible showed that modern civilization was getting steadily worse and could be rescued only by the literal return of Jesus. One teaching that later helped keep dispensationalism popular is the predicted return of the Jews to Israel. So when that happened and the state of Israel was established in 1948, dispensationalists were among its strongest supporters. It is worth pointing out that dispensational teachings were the basis for two late twentieth-century bestsellers (especially among white American fundamentalists and evangelicals), Hal Lindsey's *The Late Great Planet Earth* (1970) and the Tim LaHaye *Left Behind* futuristic novel series (1995–2007).[4]

In the 1920s direct political action played at most a secondary role for most fundamentalists. White revivalist Protestants had a heritage of supporting reform movements such as antislavery and Sabbath campaigns and the temperance movement, and sometimes such impulses were revived as in campaigns for moral purity or against the teaching of biological evolution.

That impulse to use political action, however, seemed to run counter to dispensational teachings that held that modern civilization was beyond repair until Jesus returns. In fact, many fundamentalists throughout the twentieth century specifically said that churches should not get involved in politics. It was, they said, like rearranging the deck chairs on the sinking Titanic. They emphasized such points especially when they were criticizing modernist or liberal churches for embracing progressive political causes. Nevertheless, although political action was far from central to early fundamentalism, some would use it to promote specific social concerns — most notably in the anti-evolution crusade.

How is it that these two seemingly contradictory emphases coexisted not only in the same movement (fundamentalism was always a loose coalition of various militant conservatives) but sometimes in the same people? The answer is that some of the most basic impulses behind much of American fundamentalism involved deep resentments against certain modernizing trends that threatened the cultural norms of traditionalist white Protestants. Such resentments were often strong in regions such as the South or in small-town America of the North, where Protestant norms were still prominent. One way to explain their outlook is to compare fundamentalists' experience of modernization to an immigrant experience. That is, fundamentalists found themselves living in a nation in which "sophisticated" modern people were laughing at their quaint beliefs, such as the strict authority of the Bible. One side of the fundamentalist impulse was to treat modern America like a sort of Babylon and so to separate from such culture. Many fundamentalists formed their own pure churches and insisted on strict behavioral rules, such as no dancing, drinking, smoking, or card playing. Only Jesus's return would fix things. But at the same time, unlike immigrants, they were also old-stock Americans. They still were strong patriots who thought of America as a sort of new Israel that needed to be brought back to its original Christian principles. So sometimes they might turn to political action as a way to win back the culture. Fundamentalists often wavered between whether they should see America as Babylon that God would soon destroy or the new Israel that needed to be renewed.

The primary illustration from the original fundamentalist era of the impulse to restore a Bible-based society is the famous Scopes Trial of 1925. By that time a number of states, including a few in the North, had banned the teaching of biological evolution in public schools on the grounds that it conflicted with the Bible's account of creation in Genesis 1. Defenders of evolution convinced a young Dayton, Tennessee, high school teacher, John Scopes, to break the law and thus provide a test case. They secured Clarence Darrow, the most famous trial lawyer of the time, to defend Scopes. Fundamentalists countered with the even more famous William Jennings Bryan, three-time Democratic presidential candidate and campaigner against evolution, to defend the law. The trial in Dayton became a national sensation, even though the legal outcome remained ambiguous.[5]

Several points might be noted in presenting this event. First, it shows how political and other popular ideological conflict tends to oversimplify issues and to turn them into simple "either/or" dichotomies or choices. Prior to the fundamentalist era, Bible-believing Christians had been divided into a spectrum of views regarding biological evolution and the creation account in Genesis.[6] Many believed that the "days" of Genesis 1 might be very long periods of time, allowing God to use some evolutionary means for creation, even if humans were formed by a direct creative act. After the Scopes Trial in most fundamentalist and conservative evangelical churches throughout the rest of the twentieth century, such views became more rare. One of the most popular teachings, drawing on the literal interpretation that the "days' of Genesis 1 were each twenty-four hours, insisted that the earth could be no more than perhaps ten thousand years old. The arguments of "creation science" to support such views scientifically became popular after the mid-twentieth century, and in the 1980s two states, Arkansas and Louisiana, passed laws (eventually struck down in the courts) mandating that creation science be taught as a "balance" to teaching standard evolutionary views of origins.[7]

Second (and closely related), the Scopes Trial illustrates the connection between *populist* religion and populist *politics* in American life. Revivalist or evangelical Christianity is "democratic" or "populist" in that it does not depend on the authority of state or church but rather appeals directly to a popular constituency. As in popular politics, what often sells most widely are teachings that are presented as simple either/or choices. And such choices come to be highlighted as part of an ideological warfare. One of the most conspicuous traits of fundamentalists, as opposed to some conservative Christians who are more tolerant, is that fundamentalists are militant in their beliefs. They tend to use images that suggest they are engaged in warfare. Often the warfare is on two fronts: to combat modernist or liberal theology in the churches and to combat secular trends in the culture.

A third implication to point out is that the leadership of William Jennings Bryan in the fundamentalist anti-evolution crusade illustrates that the original movement was not necessarily tied to any one political party or ideology. Bryan was a quintessential populist Democrat, so most of his political views were very progressive, rather than conservative. Some early fundamentalists became involved in various, mostly local, political causes but did not have an overall political program and were not seen as a force in national politics.

In order to show students how these religious and cultural conflicts of the 1920s are still relevant to understanding the role of religion in American culture today, one will need to take the students rather briefly through the main stages of development during the intervening years. I suggest the points to highlight for each of these eras.

1925 to 1950: Fundamentalist Withdrawal and Rebuilding

The primary relevant point here is that after the Scopes trial fundamentalism as organized movements to combat modernism in the major Protestant churches and secularism in the culture at large seemed to be defeated or at least on the defensive. But, in fact, even though the major battles were subsiding, fundamentalists were regrouping and rebuilding their own ministries and institutions, mostly separate from the mainstream churches. Among those who identified most strongly as fundamentalists in the North, where Moody Bible Institute in Chicago was a leading representative institution, dispensational premillennialism and emphases on evangelistic preaching and missions were major traits. Revivalist Bible-believing Protestantism, however, had a much wider base than any one part of organized movements could speak for. In much of the South and in the heartlands of the North, it was the default religious position for many people.

1950 to 1965: A "New Evangelicalism" and Billy Graham as Part of the American Consensus

Billy Graham suddenly emerged in 1949 as America's leading evangelist and superstar religious figure. Although Graham began as a full-fledged fundamentalist, he soon identified with a less combative movement, "the new evangelicalism," that was emerging out of fundamentalism in hopes of better engaging the American mainstream. Graham himself moved away from the "separatist fundamentalism" of which he had been a part. Separatists insisted that because mainline ecumenical Protestant denominations tolerated modernists and liberals, those churches were apostate; that is, they had departed from the faith.[8] Graham recognized that despite liberal leadership in such denominations, many local churches and parishioners were traditionally evangelical, so he cooperated with such mainline churches. As a result, many of the more militant separatist fundamentalists denounced Graham. For a time, a useful distinction could be made between "evangelicals," who were more tolerant Bible-believing revivalist-minded Christians like Graham, and more militant "fundamentalists," who insisted on separation from mainline churches. At that time, it could be said, broadly speaking, that "an evangelical is someone who likes Billy Graham." Mainline liberal Christians thought he was too narrowly traditional and simplistic. Separatist fundamentalists thought he was compromising by associating with modernists. But a wide and varied swath of mostly ordinary believers found Graham's old-time Gospel to resonate with their own needs and convictions.

1960s and 1970s: Cultural Upheavals and the Counterculture

The 1950s, the era when Graham came to prominence, is sometimes known for a broad "consensus" regarding cultural and political values. Religions of all sorts flourished, and anti-communism united most Americans across political divides. By 1965 that post-war cultural consensus was beginning to fall apart. Racial tensions and protests were reaching a peak and sometimes sparking violence. The United States was beginning to get embroiled in Vietnam. Student protests were emerging. A new revolution in sexuality was underway as old standards of propriety were disappearing. All these trends accelerated in the following years, leaving the nation deeply divided between advocates of the new counterculture and anti-war sentiments and more traditionalist Americans who valued patriotism, anti-communism, and the proprieties of the heartland.

The leadership of mainline ecumenical Protestant churches, generally speaking, tried to keep up with the politically progressive aspects of these trends. They were among the leaders in supporting civil rights and were critics of the Vietnam War and of "love it or leave it" American patriotism.

Meanwhile, more conservative evangelical and fundamentalist churches tended to have constituencies that were on the conservative side of the political divide. Most of their actual political efforts tended to be localized for particular political causes, as in electing school board members to protest liberal teachings in schools, or in rallying behind especially attractive conservative candidates for office. Because of the persistence of the North/South divide, they still did not constitute an organized or recognizable national political force.

The telling illustration of this point is that in 1976, just as the North/South political divide was disappearing, evangelicalism was first recognized as a potential political force in support of the Democratic candidate, Jimmy Carter. Carter, originally a dark horse candidate, had created a small sensation by declaring that he was "born again," the most common code word for evangelicals, but not a term previously familiar in the mainstream news. *Newsweek* magazine declared 1976 "The Year of the Evangelical" as recognition of the reemergence of this large group of Americans as a potential force in American politics.

Late 1970s to Early 2000s: Emergence of Politically Organized Evangelicals and Fundamentalists and the "Culture Wars"

President Carter's Democratic Party political agenda proved too progressive for many evangelical and fundamentalist leaders. His administration was sympathetic to the rising feminist movement and toward emerging gay and lesbian concerns. It was also aggressive in enforcing civil rights legislation, thus aggravating some lingering racist resentments among white conservative political constituencies, especially in the South.

In the light of the new awareness of the evangelical political potential, Jerry Falwell and some allies organized "the Moral Majority" as a political coalition that included fundamentalists (as Falwell identified himself), conservative evangelicals, and some conservative Catholics and Mormons. This coalition, presenting itself as standing for "family values," patriotism, and anti-communism, allied itself with the Republican Party.

I do not recount the detail of the ongoing history of the Religious Right as a political movement since that topic is treated elsewhere in this volume. Nonetheless, I offer a few observations on the ongoing legacy of the fundamentalist/modernist divide of the 1920s.

During the 1920s, fundamentalist militancy had been found on two fronts: militancy versus modernism in the churches and militancy to preserve Christian civilization. Prior to the rise of the Moral Majority, this latter concern, while often seen locally or for single-issue causes such as anti-evolution, had not been a force in national politics. But fundamentalists" primary tool for changing the nation was evangelism. In fact, fundamentalists were sometimes accused of lacking social-political concerns, partly in reaction to the liberal "social gospel" on the left. Once white ethnic evangelicals of the North and South could be united politically, religious militancy helped fuel long-standing resentments and concerns. Exactly how much impact religious leaders and organizations had in mobilizing this constituency is difficult to measure, since most old-stock white ethnics of the South and northern heartland were moving (or remaining) solidly in the Republican camp regardless of whether they were church people. After 9/11 in 2001 the term "fundamentalism" faded as a self-identification for conservative evangelicals, probably because the term had been sometimes used to describe Islamic extremists. The militant attitudes associated with American fundamentalism, however, often persisted.

While politics gets the headlines, the broader ongoing impact of the fundamentalist/modernist split is in the "culture wars" that divide much of the nation concerning what should be its basic moral principles. It was said before the American Civil War that when the major denominations divided (as they did in the 1830s and 1840s), the division of the nation would follow. So when the major denominations divided in the 1920s, that helped set the course for a major cultural divide by the end of the twentieth century.

Regarding the liberal side of that divide, the mainline or ecumenical Protestant churches played a significant supporting role in promoting the more inclusive social emphases that have become standard parts of mainstream progressive outlooks. The modernist principle of adopting modern ethical insights eventually led to making social justice and inclusiveness major liberal Christian concerns. Especially since the civil rights era of the mid-twentieth century, some of the most conspicuous emphases of such more liberal Protestant churches have been for inclusion of people and groups that typically have been discriminated against in mainstream America. That has included emphases on racial justice, full equality for women, LGBT concerns, and openness to immigrants. The impact of liberal churches in the past half century promoting such concerns on the progressive side of the culture wars is hard to measure, since church leadership is probably following broader progressive trends at least as much as shaping them. Further, during the same era, the more inclusive mainline Protestant churches declined precipitously (from nearly 30 percent of the American population in the early 1970s to under 15 percent by the early twenty-first century), so their direct influence seemed clearly to be waning.[9] Nonetheless, it is plausible to argue (as has historian David Hollinger) that mainline liberal Protestants have in a sense won in the culture wars (at least in some regions) since so much of their moral agenda has moved beyond the churches into the mainstream secular culture, even while the formerly mainline churches themselves have declined.[10]

Meanwhile more conservative churches of bewildering varieties were generally flourishing in the late twentieth century, even though some erosion in memberships appeared by the second decade of the twenty-first century. One thing that would not have been predicted by most culture observers in the 1920s would be that most of American Christianity, as well as most of burgeoning world Christianity, would remain more or less traditional in their theologies and views of the Bible. In the United States most of the Protestant churches that remained traditional in theology also have had more conservative social agendas. One major exception is that most African American churches were more sympathetic to the liberal political views of the Democratic Party, even if they remained more conservative regarding views of the Bible and theology and on issues regarding personal morality and sexuality. Teachers can use that phenomenon to illustrate that it is difficult to measure the exact impact of church teachings on American cultural divides. Religious affiliations are voluntary, so religious leaders tend to accommodate their messages to the outlooks (and so too the biases, prejudices, and political loyalties) of their constituents. Thus religion tends to reinforce existing cultural and political outlooks and divides, probably more often than it creates them.

One possible question for discussion of such issues is to ask students to reflect on how Americans might help encourage people on opposite sides of the political divide and culture wars to talk and (more importantly) to listen to each other. Do social media reinforce tendencies not to listen to the other side? Where there is real dialogue and listening might religious beliefs be helpful or not helpful in such discussions? Can common traditional Protestant beliefs (such as are found in most the Bible-believing and conversion-oriented heritages of most African American Protestants and also among many conservative white Americans) be used to bring better understanding between the two groups?

ADDITIONAL RESOURCES

Carpenter, Joel A. *Revive Us Again: The Reawakening of American Fundamentalism.* New York: Oxford University Press, 1997. (The major study of mid-twentieth-century fundamentalism)

Fitzgerald, Frances. *The Evangelicals: The Struggle to Shape America.* New York: Simon and Shuster, 2019. (A general overview culminating in major attention to the rise of the Religious Right)

Hankins, Barry, ed. *Evangelicalism and Fundamentalism: A Documentary Reader.* New York: New York University Press, 2008. (For primary sources)

Hummel, Daniel G. *The Rise and Fall of Dispensationalism: How the Evangelical Battle over the End Times Shaped the Nation.* Grand Rapids., MI: William B. Eerdmans, 2023. (Deals with the many internal debates concerning classic fundamentalism's most distinctive teachings)

Marsden, George. *Fundamentalism and American Culture.* New York: Oxford University Press, 2022, 1980. (For a more detailed account of fundamentalism of the 1920s and overview of later manifestations)

Marsden, George. *Religion and American Culture: A Brief History.* Grand Rapids, MI: William B. Eerdmans, 2018. (For an overview of the religious and cultural context of the whole era)

Sutton, Matthew Avery. *American Apocalypse: A History of Modern Evangelicalism.* Cambridge, MA: Harvard University Press, 2014. (Puts emphasis on end-time teachings and political implications)

NOTES

1. I would recommend using Barry Hankins, ed., *Evangelicalism and Fundamentalism: A Documentary Reader* (New York: New York University Press, 2008), for excerpts that might be assigned or quoted from. Within the assigned readings, ask the students to reflect on how the concerns of 1920s fundamentalists differ from the concerns of conservative evangelicals they may know about today. Even though that question may invite highlighting politics, it is important to point out that in the 1920s the more central concerns of fundamentalists were about liberal theology in the churches (as in the Machen selection), the authority of the Bible (often as literally interpreted, as in anti-evolution crusades), and dispensational premillennial expectations of Jesus's imminent return to establish a literal kingdom on earth (see below).

2. See chap. 2, "The Fundamentalist-Modernist Controversy," in Hankins, *Evangelicalism and Fundamentalism,* 39–58, for more detail.

3. See chap. 3, "Dispensational Premillennialism," in ibid., 59–70.

4. Hal Lindsey's book *The Late Great Planet Earth* is available online: Internet Archive, https://archive.org/details/TheLateGreatPlanetEarthByHalLindsey/page/n1.

5. See William Jennings Bryan's anti-evolutionary speech during the Scopes Trial in Hankins, *Evangelicalism and Fundamentalism,* 84–95.

6. Hankins illustrates this point by providing two readings from James Orr and Henry Beach in chap. 4, "Evangelicals and Evolution before Scopes," in ibid., 71–84.

7. See chap. 5, "Evangelicals and Science after Scopes," in ibid., 97–116.

8. See the J. Gresham Machen selection in ibid., chap. 2 (44–52). Most separatist fundamentalists, as at Bob Jones University (where Billy Graham first went to college) were (unlike Machen) dispensationalists.

9. Robert D. Putnam and David E. Campbell, *American Grace: How Religion Divides and Unites Us* (New York: Simon and Schuster, 2010), 104.

10. David A. Hollinger, *After Cloven Tongues of Fire: Protestant Liberalism in Modern American History* (Princeton, NJ: Princeton University Press, 2015), 46–47.

How Did the Great Depression Change the Relationship between Church and State?

ALISON COLLIS GREENE

At the start of the 1930s, national and local banks failed, drought swept the South and then the West, and desperate parents across the nation left hungry children on orphanage doorsteps. It was the start of a bitterly hard decade, one that forced Americans across bounds of class, race, and region to confront the reality of poverty in their midst and to consider together how best to care for one another. The Great Depression, the New Deal, and the Second World War together transformed ordinary Americans' ideas about the world around them and their relationships to each other. This was a decade of tremendous suffering, of deep reflection on the meanings of citizenship, and of almost incomprehensibly rapid changes to public life. Yet our lessons on the 1930s most often open with breadlines and then quickly launch into a tour of the overwhelming array of New Deal programs. It may seem that there is no time and no good reason to talk about religion in this period when the state took center stage.

Present-day conversations about the legacies of the Great Depression and the New Deal have as much to do with religion as with the state, however. It is thus as essential for students to understand the religious worlds of the 1930s as it is for them to understand the era's political landscape. The relationship of Protestant, Catholic, and Jewish religious organizations to suffering people, and of religion to the state, transformed

261

during this decade. A study of the Great Depression and the New Deal through the frame of religion allows the learner to confront individual suffering and its relationship to institutional transformation. It renders comprehensible the widespread demand for a new kind of federal government and highlights some individual experiences of that transformed government. It expands our understanding of the limits and possibilities of American religions as they related to the state. To study religion alongside politics in the 1930s is to imagine this moment as it unfolded, this moment of profound fear and great possibility, this moment so unlike our own and yet so profoundly important in shaping who we as a nation have become.

What Was Life Like for Americans Who Faced Hard Times before the Great Depression?

To imagine life during the Great Depression, we must first imagine it before. What changed for ordinary Americans in the midst of the greatest economic crisis of the twentieth century? Who was comfortable during the boom of the 1920s, and who suffered? What theological, social, and physical resources had people once relied upon, and what happened to those resources when disaster struck?

One strategy for inviting students to consider these questions, and to peel away contemporary experiences of charity and welfare, is to ask students to do an exercise in imagination. This exercise in imagination focuses on the period just after the Depression began, when religious and voluntary assistance played a significant role in American life. It does not require prior knowledge and can in fact work better when students have only the present context on which to rely for answers. Once students have brainstormed for five minutes or so, discuss their responses and then explore the range of options available in 1930. Begin with a scenario something like this one:

> Imagine yourself a young adult in 1930, living anywhere you choose in the United States. You have a small farm in the country or a little shop in town or in the city. You have a family, constituted however you would like to imagine. You have always scraped by. But now prices have bottomed out, and no one is buying anything. The banks in your town have failed, and you lost your savings. You went into debt to save your farm or business, and your property has just been foreclosed. Your family is

hungry. Your spouse is dying of tuberculosis. You cannot find work. Where do you turn for help? Then where? Then where?

Students often come up with creative lists of potential resources, from which teachers can transition to a survey of the landscape of welfare and charity in the United States in 1930. Students might dig deeply into these questions through primary sources, suggested in the last section of this chapter, or teachers might offer a quick tour through the range of available options and move on.

Responses that focus on informal and familial resources often come up first, and those were nearly universal: Across the nation, Americans who had exhausted their savings and employment options would first turn to extended family, to ethnic or community resources such as mutual aid societies and fraternal orders, to their employers, or to local churches or synagogues. Inculcated in a culture that prioritized independence and labor, even the sickest and hungriest often sought work before direct assistance and loans before charity. Many men left their homes and families behind in search of work. Parents faced a choice between keeping their children at home and hungry or leaving them at orphanages, which housed indigent children as well as orphans.

Students are often surprised to learn that public funds represented the majority of assistance available nationwide. The federal government provided limited pensions to war veterans. Some states and municipalities also provided Mothers' Aid, a few dollars a month for widowed and abandoned mothers. Major cities sometimes offered a limited range of additional public welfare funds. "Outdoor relief," the term for direct cash aid to the poor, was unpopular and rarely available, even though it could often prove most effective for acute need. The only exception was Red Cross assistance, provided in the wake of national disasters.[1]

Cities and larger towns provided minimal institutional care—poorhouses for the indigent elderly, state and municipal charity hospitals and orphanages, and a range of asylums for individuals deemed "defective" or for unaccompanied adolescent girls. In many southern cities and in much of the rural United States—44 percent of the population in 1930—even these public resources were nonexistent, and those that existed were segregated by race and consistently and explicitly discriminated against African Americans and ethnic minorities.[2]

In much of the South, private welfare was the only option. Religious organizations played a key role: Jewish assistance organizations accounted for about a fourth of total private assistance nationally, Catholics for another 10 percent, and Protestant service organizations such as the Salvation Army and Volunteers of America yet another 10 percent.[3] Charity organization societies—such as Community Chests—linked Christian, Jewish, and nonsectarian organizations under one umbrella. Private agencies like these typically treated poverty as the result of personal choices rather than as a structural problem and expressed more concern about the dangers of charity than about the dangers of hunger or homelessness. As the head of the Methodist Goodwill Industries in Nashville, Tennessee, put it in 1927, "A taste of charity is as dangerous as the first shot of dope."[4]

In many rural places and some southern towns and cities, no organized welfare or charity existed. People instead relied on a patchwork of informal assistance from family, churches, and community members.[5] The famous images of Depression breadlines are striking not only because so many people were hungry, but also because so few resources to address their hunger were available: no public retirement or disability benefits, no unemployment insurance, no structures for food or medical care. There were few options for people suffering chronic need, illness, or deep poverty.

What Changes Did the Great Depression Bring, and How Did Institutions Respond?

Here, the lesson turns to the effects of the Great Depression, and a textbook-level narrative of the Great Depression, or one like that found in Erich Rauchway's *The Great Depression and the New Deal: A Very Short Introduction*, will help students get their bearings. This can work either as a short lecture or a reading assignment before students return to the scenarios they've imagined above.

Before students imagine how the world changed in the 1930s, they must first imagine what life was like on the cusp of the Great Depression. Just over a decade before, the United States had entered the First World War, and in its aftermath both the American economy and American lives shifted substantially. As production of goods grew more efficient and advertising more insistent, Americans began to take on household debt to purchase cars, radios, and goods that created an illusion of national prosperity supported by a steadily growing economy.

No one fed that illusion more than Wall Street, where financial speculation ran unchecked. At the same time, unstable farm prices produced an ongoing crisis in the countryside, and a decade of pro-business federal policy curtailed the already limited rights of labor. Nativist sentiment that celebrated white Protestantism appeared most ominously in the revived Ku Klux Klan but proved far more pervasive. While nativists attacked Catholics, Jews, and African Americans, they also pushed new immigration restrictions, passed in the form of the Immigration Act of 1924, which set quotas on immigration by national origin. In 1928, the United States largely ceased its postwar lending to countries still struggling to recover. These compounding factors meant a nation with a false sense of confidence in a world on the precipice. The series of crises that would become the Great Depression were not unpredictable, but to the majority of Americans they were unthinkable.[6]

If the Roaring Twenties narrative is inadequate to explain the economic life of Americans in that decade, the Scopes Trial is likewise inadequate to explain the dynamics of American religious life. Protestant, Catholic, and Jewish religious organizations had helped sell Americans on an unpopular world war in 1917, and in its aftermath they put their power and resources to use in institution building and political action. This time of rapid social change meant sharp divisions among Protestants over biblical interpretation, evolution, and women's roles in society (for the conflicts among Protestants in the fundamentalist/modernist controversy, see George Marsden's chapter). Yet Protestants were at the apex of their power, realized in part in the 1919 ratification of the Eighteenth Amendment, which banned the manufacture, sale, and transportation of alcohol. Catholic and Jewish institutions likewise thrived and provided some protection from nativist attacks in the 1920s. They also proved essential to the support of Americans who lived and worked in ethnic and religious enclaves. For all the handwringing about moral and spiritual decline, religious agencies were primed to grow in wealth and influence.[7]

It can be difficult to comprehend, let alone to convey to students, the sense of shock that Americans felt at a crisis that virtually no one had anticipated. The stock market crash in October 1929 was as much a symptom as a cause of the Great Depression, and even after the more broadly devastating spiderweb of commercial bank failures that escalated at the end of 1930, it seemed that the nation might recover quickly.

But environmental crises followed economic ones, and Europe's economy was also in a tailspin. Between 1929 and 1932, national income dropped by more than 50 percent. A quarter of the workforce—about 11.5 million Americans—was unemployed. Those who kept their jobs or found new ones saw their hours and wages drop sharply. The countryside proved no refuge, as farms across the nation faced unprecedented drought and crop loss.[8]

Shortly after New Year's Day in 1931, Black and white farmers outside England, Arkansas, banded together and marched into town to demand food. A record-setting drought across the western South in the spring and summer of that year had parched the cotton in the fields, and a wave of bank failures wiped out farmers' savings. Their families were starving, and Americans were stunned. Breadlines wrapped around city blocks, and farmers starved in the fields. Hunger was everywhere.[9]

Students might consult local newspapers and government documents (see below) to investigate conditions in the location they chose for the opening activity. Then ask students to revisit those resources that were available in 1930—many ceased to exist by 1932. Organizations that cared for the needy faced three simultaneous crises. First, the number of people seeking help soared. Second, donations to charities and churches plummeted, and bank failures wiped out any reserves they had. Third, widespread economic and environmental crises forced a reevaluation of the premise that poverty represented a personal rather than systemic failure. People saw their hardworking neighbors lose their homes and farms, their family members go hungry. It was hard to blame individuals for their suffering when society seemed to be collapsing.[10]

Churches and religious organizations tried to help. The Salvation Army expanded its meals operations and housed as many homeless men as its branches could accommodate.[11] But churches struggled too. Until 1933, giving to churches held steady relative to national income, but that still meant a 50 percent loss just as demands on church resources escalated.[12]

Private and nonsectarian agencies also struggled. Nationally, roughly a third of voluntary organizations present in 1929 collapsed by 1932.[13] Religious institutions and voluntary organizations lacked the capacity to withstand the crisis and help others survive too. A growing chorus of Americans from all walks of life began to shift from an emphasis on charity and individual responsibility and to demand that the federal government take responsibility for its citizens.

How Did the New Deal Change the
Relationship between Church and State?

Now the focus in the classroom shifts from individual experiences of the Great Depression to the public response to it. A textbook treatment of Herbert Hoover's response to the Great Depression is adequate for this lesson: After long insisting that private agencies and states handle the crisis, in January 1932, Herbert Hoover's administration agreed to provide emergency loans to banks and corporations and later to states and municipalities for public works projects. It was not enough. Democrat Franklin Roosevelt trounced Hoover in the 1932 election, on the promise that he would leverage the federal government to end the Depression.

As you introduce students to Roosevelt's New Deal programs—divided into the programs of 1933–34 and then those of 1935–36—it is useful to have them select particular programs to examine and then to teach one another in an expert group activity. Some guiding questions might include the following: What problem did this program address? Who was the program designed to benefit? Who did it benefit, and how? Who did it disadvantage, and in what ways? What broader social effects did the program have? In what ways might the program have changed the relationship between Americans and their government? What about the relationship between religious institutions and the state?

For a study of religion and the state, or the shift from voluntary to federal assistance, one of the most important New Deal programs was also one of the shortest-lived. Launched at the start of the first hundred days, the Federal Emergency Relief Administration (FERA) designated federal funds for employment relief and direct aid, to be distributed by city and state administrators. It was an emergency program, set to expire in 1935. FERA prohibited explicit racial discrimination, though its local administrators often found proxies for racial exclusion. FERA certified only public agencies to distribute aid, breaking with decades of overlapping public-private work.[14] Other programs of the first New Deal that students might examine for their relationships to voluntary agencies include the Civilian Conservation Corps, the Agricultural Adjustment Administration, the Tennessee Valley Authority, the Home Owners' Loan Act, the Civil Works Administration, the National Recovery Administration, and the Public Works Administration.

Across the nation, but especially in places that had offered little aid to the poor, New Deal spending dwarfed all previous contributions. In 1929, median per capita relief in the nation's largest 116 urban areas was $0.86, of which $0.16 came from private sources; by 1935, that total was $17.28 per capita, and only $0.13 of it came from private sources. For southern cities with little prior public relief infrastructure, such as Birmingham, Alabama, the shift was even more dramatic (from $0.15 per capita, all private, to $14.03 per capita, all public), and in rural America, virtually all aid was public. Yet private and religious agencies continued their own work—by 1935, they still provided more meals and beds than did public agencies, which focused on direct and work relief. The efforts of public and religious or private agencies thus proved complementary more often than competitive. There was plenty of need to go around.[15]

Ask students to stop and evaluate what this means. Did the state sweep in to take over what voluntary agencies and churches had been doing, as many public figures today have suggested? Recall that voluntary assistance had virtually collapsed, and then take a look at how religious institutions and clergy responded to the New Deal (below). Yet there is no question that New Deal programs shifted the emphasis in American life from individual suffering to collective responsibility, from private charity to public welfare—a change the Depression justified and the New Deal reinforced.

Unsurprisingly, liberal Protestants applauded FERA, as well as the National Recovery Administration, which granted workers the right to organize labor unions. Many saw both programs as a realization of the Social Creed of the Churches, a statement published in 1908 by the Federal Council of Churches (for more context, see Heath W. Carter's chapter). Catholics linked New Deal programs to papal decrees regarding social justice and workers' rights. Jews pointed to the connections between the New Deal and the teachings of Ancient Israel's prophets. Perhaps more surprisingly, conservative Protestants were just as enthusiastic: many declared that Roosevelt drew his inspiration straight from the Bible, and they declared that the New Deal would enable them to focus on evangelism.

In 1935, as he launched programs that would compose the second New Deal, Roosevelt invited responses from the nation's clergy. He asked specifically for reactions to the Social Security Act, which made provisions for the elderly, the orphaned, and the disabled; and the Works Progress Administration, which eventually created public works jobs for 8.5 million Americans. Over 30,000 clergy responded to Roosevelt's letter, with overwhelming enthusiasm. Of the first 12,000 replies, a full 84 percent approved. Clergy declared the welfare state a religious achievement, one that freed churches and synagogues to focus on supplementary care or to return to a focus on evangelism. Despite this strong measure of approval, a minority of American clergy worried that the federal government weakened the churches' hold on Americans because it strengthened secular community institutions and provided an alternative avenue for social support. Critics from the left also argued that the state continued to shore up a broken capitalist system.

Roosevelt's deepest wells of support came from the South; there his critics were primarily white people concerned that the New Deal threatened Jim Crow segregation. Although New Deal programs forbade racial discrimination in principle, in practice powerful southern congressmen crafted legislation that excluded or disadvantaged Black workers. Domestic and agricultural workers could not gain Social Security coverage, for instance, and home and farm loan programs denied Black borrowers. Black Americans petitioned for protection from racist aid administrators, sometimes with success but often to no avail. The New Deal simultaneously destabilized and reinforced white supremacy across the nation.[16]

Nonetheless, public support for the New Deal and its surviving programs remained strong long after the Great Depression ended. Expansions to social programs continued in both Republican and Democratic administrations. Lyndon B. Johnson's Great Society expanded the welfare state in more equitable ways in response to civil rights advocacy. But dissent bubbled over in those decades as well, as a coalition of corporate libertarians and white evangelical clergy fought to emphasize individual liberty and private charity over collective responsibility and the public good and worked to roll back the welfare and regulatory state.[17] Students might return to these themes from the 1930s, to questions about who benefited from various state structures and who did not, as they move into course materials on the 1940s and beyond.

Selected Resources for Teaching Religion and the Great Depression

The New Deal administration documented its every action, and its works programs also included local research, writing, and photography projects. Many of those sources are available online, and they are useful for any study of the 1930s. It was likewise a rich era for music, from Son House's "Dry Spell Blues" to the Carter Family's recording of "No Depression in Heaven," and fiction, such as Tillie Olsen's *Yonondio: From the Thirties* or Sonora Babb's *Whose Names Are Unknown*. Resources that directly address religion and church-state questions above are fewer, but the notes to this essay have prioritized the numerous introductory volumes, readable monographs, and online primary sources directly relevant to the material.

Digital primary sources readily available without subscription access include a fully searchable database of photographs from the Farm Security Administration/Office of War Information (FSA/OWI); the public papers of Franklin D. Roosevelt; and Eleanor Roosevelt's regular "My Day" column, which provided a short, approachable first-person overview of the First Lady's daily work for readers nationwide. The Living New Deal, a partnership between the University of California, Berkeley and a public service nonprofit project, provides an extraordinary set of databases of local New Deal projects, maps, oral histories, and more.[18] Students might be particularly enthusiastic about FSA/OWI images taken near where they live, as well as nearby New Deal projects they can locate on The Living New Deal maps—perhaps even as part of an in-class activity. Each of the aforementioned resources is searchable by location, giving the teacher an opportunity to bring the conversation close to home. A selection of the Franklin Roosevelt clergy letters, once available online, may soon reappear either at the Roosevelt Library website or another New Deal aggregator. Useful supplements to these resources include the United States Census, *Historical Statistics of the United States, Colonial Times to 1970*, and the 1926 and 1936 Census of Religious Bodies.[19] Local denominational and archival resources are also of interest to students and are often easy to access if local historical societies or university libraries are nearby.

ADDITIONAL RESOURCES

Ebel, Jonathan H. *From Dust They Came: Government Camps and the Religion of Reform in New Deal California.* New York: New York University Press, 2023.

Greene, Alison Collis. *No Depression in Heaven: The Great Depression, the New Deal, and the Transformation of Religion in the Delta.* New York: Oxford University Press, 2016.

Kelley, Robin D. G. *Hammer and Hoe: Alabama Communists during the Great Depression.* 25th Anniversary ed. Chapel Hill: University of North Carolina Press, 2015.

Library of Congress. Farm Security Administration/Office of War Information Black-and-White Negatives. https://www.loc.gov/pictures/collection/fsa/.

Roosevelt, Eleanor. "'My Day' by Eleanor Roosevelt: A Comprehensive Electronic Edition of Eleanor Roosevelt's 'My Day' Columns." Eleanor Roosevelt Papers Project. https://www2.gwu.edu/~erpapers/myday/.

NOTES

1. See Alison Collis Greene, *No Depression in Heaven: The Great Depression, the New Deal, and the Transformation of Religion in the Delta* (Oxford: Oxford University Press, 2016), 66–100; Michael B. Katz, *In the Shadow of the Poorhouse: A Social History of Welfare in America*, 10th anniversary ed., revised and updated (Basic Books, 1996 [1986]), 108, 213–24.

2. United States Bureau of the Census, "Population: 1790 to 1990," table available at http://aprsa.villanova.edu/files/us_population_1790_1990.pdf.

3. Emma A. Winslow, *Trends in Different Types of Public and Private Relief in Urban Areas, 1929–35* (Washington, DC: Government Printing Office, 1937), 52–56.

4. G. E. Holley, "Southern Goodwill Industries," *New Orleans Christian Advocate*, May 19, 1927, 14.

5. Greene, *No Depression in Heaven*, 66–100; Katz, *In the Shadow of the Poorhouse*, 192–204; Benson Y. Landis, *Rural Welfare Services* (New York: Columbia University Press, 1949).

6. Eric Rauchway, *The Great Depression and the New Deal: A Very Short Introduction* (New York: Oxford University Press, 2008), 8–22. Rauchway emphasizes the international dynamics that led to worldwide Depression, essential for understanding that event though not the focus of this chapter.

7. Greene, *No Depression in Heaven*, 48–51.

8. David M. Kennedy, *Freedom from Fear: The American People in Depression and War, 1929–1945* (New York: Oxford University Press, 2001), 65–69; Rosemary D. Marcuss and Richard E. Kane, "U.S. National Income and Product Statistics: Born of the Great Depression and World War II," *Survey of Current Business*, February 2007, 32–46; Rauchway, *The Great Depression*, 40–55.

9. Nan Elizabeth Woodruff, *As Rare as Rain: Federal Relief in the Great Southern Drought of 1930–31* (Urbana: University of Illinois Press, 1985), 56–65.

10. Greene, *No Depression in Heaven*, 66–98.

11. Winslow, *Trends in Different Types*, 49–59.

12. Samuel C. Kincheloe, *Research Memorandum on Religion in the Depression* (New York: Social Science Research Council, 1937), 17–30.

13. Walter Trattner, *From Poor Law to Welfare State: A History of Social Welfare in America*, 6th ed. (New York: Free Press, 1999 [1974]), 273.

14. Kennedy, *Freedom from Fear*, 150–75; Winslow, *Trends in Different Types*, 49.

15. Enid Baird, *Public and Private Aid in 116 Urban Areas, 1929–1938, with Supplement for 1939 and 1940*, Public Assistance Report no. 3 (Federal Security Agency, Social Security Board, 1942), 112–265; Winslow, *Trends in Different Types*, 49–64.

16. Greene, *No Depression in Heaven*, 101–59.

17. Kevin M. Kruse, *One Nation under God: How Corporate America Invented Christian America* (New York: Basic Books, 2015).

18. These databases are available at the following URLs: Farm Security Administration, https://www.loc.gov/pictures/collection/fsa/; FRANKLYN, http://www.fdrlibrary.marist.edu/archives/collections/franklin/; My Day by Eleanor Roosevelt, https://www2.gwu.edu/~erpapers/myday/; Living New Deal, https://livingnewdeal.org/.

19. For historical census data, see https://www.archives.gov/research/census. For historical statistics, see *Historical Statistics of the United States, Colonial Times to 1970*, Bicentennial ed., https://www.census.gov/library/publications/1975/compendia/hist_stats_colonial-1970.html . For more about the Census of Religious Bodies, see "A Brief History of Religion and the U.S. Census," Pew Research Center, https://www.pewforum.org/2010/01/26/a-brief-history-of-religion-and-the-u-s-census/.

Religion during World War II and the Cold War

MATTHEW AVERY SUTTON

In early 1939, President Franklin Delano Roosevelt warned the American people that new threats had materialized, both at home and abroad. To secure the nation and to protect against those threats, the president explained, Americans needed to redouble their commitments to their core values and especially to their religious faiths. "Storms from abroad," FDR explained during his annual State of the Union address, "directly challenge three institutions indispensable to Americans, now as always. The first is religion." Religion, he continued, "is the source" of the second two indispensable American institutions—"democracy and international good faith." Roosevelt insisted that religion had shaped the American character, laid the foundations for democratic government, and provided the hope for international peace. For the president, as for the American people, World War II was in part a crusade to protect freedom of religion at home and abroad.[1]

Yet for generations, historians of American foreign relations and especially World War II have mostly ignored the issue of religion and war even as the evidence was hiding in plain sight. In recent years, however, many teachers have recognized that if we want students to understand contemporary global religious conflict, they need to understand the roles religion played in previous conflicts. Examining religion in this era also helps explain changes in American culture and how Americans understood and crafted their own social and civic identities.

In contrast to scholars' work on World War II, religion has been more central to how historians teach the Cold War. As the United States and

Soviets launched the Cold War, President Harry S. Truman built on Roosevelt's World War II efforts. The president sought to bring together the leaders of the world's major religions and to convince them to organize against "godless" communism. The Cold War became for Americans both a fight over economic systems and a conflict over religious values. Religion became central to how American leaders and their citizens saw their role in the world in the mid-twentieth century. As such, it is essential that we incorporate religion into how we teach and how students understand the histories of both World War II and the Cold War.

World War II

When war began in Europe in September 1939, Franklin Roosevelt was ready. The American president believed that in some ways World War II was a conflict of competing religious ideologies, and he and his staff routinely framed it as such. Throughout the war, religion became a tool that the president used to motivate the American people to action; it served as a weapon that policymakers invoked to criticize US enemies; and it inspired the American people to act in ways that were both good and bad. Religion and religious commitments became central to the conflict.

A few guiding questions are central to teaching this material. It is useful to ask students, Why might religion have mattered to FDR? To the American people? Students should discuss whether there was anything unique or exceptional about Americans' religious commitments that inspired political leaders to link faith with warfare. The sources suggested throughout the essay will help them grapple with this question.

Until the Japanese attack on Pearl Harbor in December 1941, many Americans wanted the United States to stay out of World War II. As Congress, the president, and other leaders debated if or to what extent the US should intervene in Europe, the nation's religious leaders and laypeople offered numerous competing ways to understand the relationship between their faith and American foreign policy. Horrified by Hitler's persecution of racial and ethnic minorities and especially Europe's Jews, the majority of American Jews hoped that the United States would intervene. Many liberal Protestants were committed to the global, Christian ecumenical movement, which had grown dramatically in the 1920s and 1930s. Liberal Protestants in the US and Europe, such as those laying the foundations for what would become the World

Council of Churches, believed that together they could separate faith from crass nationalism and imperialism and in so doing lead the way toward establishing a universal kingdom of God on earth through a global, Protestant, church-based organization. Many had embraced pacifism and renewed their international alliances, confident that war was not the way to find peace in the modern era.

Others embraced a "Christian Realist" perspective, following the lead of neoorthodox theologian Reinhold Niebuhr, who argued that human efforts to redeem society were naive and called on Christians to get their hands dirty in the real world of politics, even if doing so meant supporting "lesser" evils or using the coercive power of the state for the ultimate good. American fundamentalists viewed the war through their understanding of biblical prophecy. They believed that time was short and that the world was madly careening toward a great cataclysm that would culminate in the Rapture of all true Christians from the earth, the battle of Armageddon, and the second coming of Christ. With Adolf Hitler methodically restricting religious freedom and persecuting Christians and Jews, Benito Mussolini seemingly planning the restoration of the Roman Empire, and a great empire rising in the East, for fundamentalists, the "last days" had clearly commenced. Like Protestants, American Catholics were split on US intervention as well. Once the United States officially entered the war, most Protestants and Catholics (with the exception of those in the historic peace churches) supported US armed intervention abroad.

After surveying the different ways in which contrasting religious ideas led to different positions on foreign policy, teachers should ask students to discuss the diversity and the complexity of American religious life. How did theological beliefs shape political beliefs? Why is it important to understand a variety of religious faiths in order to understand American history?

Roosevelt and his staff, cognizant of the many opinions in the nation's religious communities, worked hard to frame the war as one for the expansion of religious liberty. Harold L. Ickes, the secretary of the interior and a close adviser to Roosevelt, wrote an unsolicited letter to the president shortly after the United States entered the war, stating, "Formerly there were more wars for religion than for anything else and the religious conviction is a deep one." He suggested that the government lead "a carefully planned campaign . . . to explain the religious implications of this war."[2] The president had similar ideas. In 1941 he identified

Figure 1. Fundamentalists saw the war as fulfilling biblical prophecy, which shaped how they understood it in the years before Pearl Harbor. CREDIT: Courtesy of the *Sunday School Times*.

"freedom of worship" as one of four essential, universal values at the core of the Allies' cause, one of his famous "Four Freedoms." Securing freedom of religion around the world became a justification for American intervention abroad. Roosevelt's speech and Norman Rockwell's paintings of the Four Freedoms are useful sources in the classroom.[3]

The outbreak of war in Europe transformed the US relationship to the global Roman Catholic Church and especially the Vatican. FDR surmised that making the case for religious freedom could foster alliances all over the world, and there was no religious alliance he coveted more than with the pope. President Roosevelt put his vision for a Catholic alliance into action when he dispatched Myron Taylor as his "personal envoy" to the Holy See. This was a controversial move back home. American Protestants had a long tradition of anti-Catholicism, and they believed that sending a political representative to the Vatican was tacit acknowledgment of the political nature of the Catholic Church, which US Protestants saw as a violation of the First Amendment's separation of church and state. Roosevelt was not dissuaded. Always the pragmatist, he believed that if sending a delegate to Rome could help American foreign policy, he was going to do it. Students can consider Roosevelt's telegram to the Vatican and should wrestle with why this was so controversial in the 1940s, and why it is not very controversial today for the United States to post an ambassador in the Vatican.[4] What changed and why? What does this tell us about the changing place of Catholicism in American history?

Missionaries took on new roles during the war as well, serving as intelligence operatives. Roosevelt believed that having a good intelligence apparatus was essential to winning the conflict. To that end he established the nation's first independent, foreign intelligence–gathering agency working outside of the United States, the Office of Strategic Services (OSS), which evolved into the Central Intelligence Agency (CIA) after the war. More than just about any other group, American missionaries had proven language skills, knew how to build the trust of local populations, and had mastered the various geographies of the regions in which they had labored. The topic of missionary spies is a controversial one. Teachers might ask students whether American intelligence agencies should have employed (and should be employing) missionaries for clandestine work. What are the costs and benefits of using missionaries, priests, and religious activists for intelligence work?[5]

For some religious groups, however, Roosevelt's faith in "freedom of worship" seemed too limited. Religious persecution during the war affected numerous groups. Jehovah's Witnesses, members of a relatively small, apocalyptic Christian sect, faced substantial discrimination. In Germany, Hitler interned them. In the United States, they faced numerous problems because as pacifists they refused to serve in the military, and they pledged allegiance only to God, and not to the nation or the nation's flag. Adherents across the country faced assaults, regular harassment, and discrimination, which eventually led to Supreme Court cases that aimed to clarify the boundaries of the First Amendment.[6]

The flag salute cases offer an excellent opportunity for students to think about and discuss the limits of Americans' understandings of freedom of religion. Teachers might ask: What sacrifices did religious minorities make to secure rights and liberties that now benefit all Americans? Why did the flag and the flag salute become such important symbols?

Americans Jews had mostly united in their support of US intervention abroad. In mid-1942 reports began to circulate among Americans that Hitler was no longer just interning Jews but was killing them on a massive scale. Jewish groups and their allies in England and the United States implored the president to pay more attention to what was happening, but the American press did relatively little reporting on the Holocaust. Many Americans refused to believe that even someone as diabolical as Hitler was capable of something as horrible as the attempted extermination of an entire race of people. In 1944, FDR finally acted. He created a War Refugee Board to help resettle displaced war victims. Not until American soldiers arrived at and liberated Hitler's concentration camps did the true extent of the tragedy really hit the American public. Students might discuss a news article in the American press that reported on what was happening.[7]

When teaching this material, it is important to ask students to discuss what efforts the United States made to address the Holocaust. Could the US have done more for European Jews? If so, what? How did anti-Semitism at home influence how Americans understood the persecution of Jews abroad?

While the war devastated European Jewish communities and hindered the work of some US religious groups such as the Jehovah's Witnesses, others used the war as an opportunity to expand their influence. World War II marked a critical point in the evolution of American fundamentalism. Over the course of the conflict, they reversed roles with many of their theologically liberal counterparts. Fundamentalists became the voices of patriotism and American exceptionalism, while some Protestant liberals criticized American intervention abroad and the violent tactics of total war.

Popular music during the war, as well as propaganda posters, reveal how many Americans saw religion as central to the conflict. Irving Berlin's hit song "Praise the Lord and Pass the Ammunition" reveals the tight connection that some Americans made between the conflict and their faith. Posters produced by the Office of War Information, the government's wartime propaganda agency, also show how hard the government worked to frame the war as one for religious freedom. Examples are shown in Figures 2–4. Teachers should have students discuss and analyze these posters.

The Cold War

Although historians have only recently begun to take the religious dimensions of World War II seriously, they have long understood that religion played an important role in the Cold War. President Truman believed that the United States had a divine calling to oppose the Soviet Union while American leaders and policymakers felt sure that the USSR's explicit atheism made the conflict about more than competing economic systems. When teaching the Cold War, there are two key questions: Why was religion so important to the Cold War? What were the costs and benefits of framing the Cold War primarily around religious systems rather than economic systems?[8]

Stalin had long cracked down on religious freedom in the Soviet Union. Communism, in the minds of many Americans, came to mean not just anti-capitalism, but also atheism. Because American leaders believed that communists hoped to destroy religious faith throughout the world, they drew on religion as a source of inspiration in their struggle. In addition to saturating their speeches with biblical rhetoric, the president and other political leaders sought to unify Americans of all faiths in the struggle against communism. American Christians sent money to ministers behind the Iron Curtain, they broadcast sermons into communist nations, and they called for worldwide days of prayer. Most important, political leaders also sought to unify the world's Catholics, Protestants, Orthodox, and Jews together in the struggle. Truman reached out to the Orthodox churches of Greece and Eastern Europe

"THIS WORLD CANNOT EXIST HALF SLAVE AND HALF FREE"

SACRIFICE FOR FREEDOM!

Pvt. Joe Louis says...

"We're going to do our part ...and we'll win because we're on God's side"

Figures 2–4. American leaders made religion central to the nation's campaign to shape how the public understood the war. Victory was not just about defeating the Axis powers but also about securing freedom of worship around the globe. National Archives and Records Administration.

and the Vatican and its huge network of Catholics, as well as Jewish and Muslim leaders. Religious faith, or the lack thereof, became a tool of Cold War diplomacy.

At the center of the Cold War was fear of the atomic bomb and nuclear weapons. But many Americans in the early Cold War believed that their fellow citizens were not taking religion seriously enough. Lowell Blanchard and the Valley Trio translated these concerns into pop culture. They recorded "Jesus Hits Like an Atom Bomb" (1950), fretting that "Everybody's worried 'bout the Atomic Bomb, but nobody's worried 'bout the day my Lord will come when He'll hit—Great God Almighty—like an Atom Bomb when He comes, when He comes." It is often useful to bring in popular culture sources for students, which allow students to think about how history is made and the many kinds of sources historians can use as they reconstruct the past. Teachers should ask students to discuss how the prospect of total annihilation was or was not a religious topic. How might the Cold War nuclear arms race have sparked religious revival?

McCarthyism and American religious life influenced one another. Many conservative Christians supported leading anti-communist rabble-rousers. Religious leader J. B. Matthews, who worked with the House Un-American Activities Committee, published an article entitled "Reds and Our Churches" that highlighted communist fears and accused liberal churchmen of being communist stooges. Ecumenical leaders tended to see the strengths and weaknesses in both capitalism and communism, which made "Red-hunters" suspicious of them. Students should discuss why politically conservative churchmen linked liberal churches with communism. Were liberal Christians the dupes of communists? Why might some Americans think so? How might such accusations have impacted reform efforts?[9]

During the Cold War attendance at places of worship skyrocketed, enrollments at seminaries surged, and construction of new houses of worship boomed. Polling data from the period showed that the percentage of Americans who claimed church affiliation reached an all-time high of 69 percent in 1960. Even the president had fallen under the spell of revivalism. In 1952 Dwight D. Eisenhower famously declared, "Our government makes no sense unless it is founded on a deeply felt religious faith—and I don't care what it is" (he went on to acknowledge that in the United States it was Christianity). Such declarations tapped into a deep American tradition of "civil religion" that dated back to the Puritans.

Many Americans believed that the United States—like ancient Israel —was a particularly religious nation that had been divinely chosen by God to play a major part in his plan for the ongoing redemption of the world. They believed that God had destined the United States to bring Christian values (economic, political, and religious) to the rest of the world. This ideology melded perfectly with the Cold War. Congress's addition of the phrase "under God" to the Pledge of Allegiance in 1954 (to distinguish it from the "atheist" pledges of communist countries) and Congress's 1956 elevation of "In God We Trust" to the national motto further demonstrated the hold of civil religion on the American consciousness in this period. To explore this point, students should read the flag salute texts. Then the teacher can lead a discussion about the relationships among religion, patriotism, and nationalism in American history, and how the Cold War reinforced these relationships.

The most famous religious leader in the United States during the Cold War was Billy Graham, who masterfully played on Americans' Cold War hopes and fears as he built his ministry. During the 1950s, Graham held revivals in the biggest US cities and eventually around the world. He had a folksy, down-home style and delivered a simple, clear message—all people were separated from God because of their sins, and they needed to accept Jesus into their hearts. He worked hard to connect his message to current events and made much of the seeming growth of communism and the Soviet threat. Behind this simple message was an extremely sophisticated mass media empire. Graham used radio, television, film, magazines, and best-selling books to build an evangelical empire. His success gave him entrée into the world of elite politics. Beginning with Truman, he advised every president up to and including George W. Bush. While he claimed his work was nonpartisan, he nudged conservative Christians to the political right, helping establish the context from which the Religious Right would later emerge. Using the many sermons and tracts from Billy Graham that are available for students to discuss, teachers should ask how and why Graham became so important in American politics.[10]

The Cold War consensus that linked the United States with God began to unravel during the Vietnam War. Dozens of ministers, rabbis, priests, and theologians organized against the draft and against the war itself. Perhaps the most well-known critics were Daniel and Philip Berrigan. Ordained Catholic priests and teachers, the Berrigan brothers in the 1960s grew enamored with the peace movement. As the war developed, they put their pacifist beliefs into action. Their most famous protests included breaking into government offices and destroying draft cards with napalm; they also doused official government records with animal blood and red paint. Over the next few decades, they protested American nuclear policy as well. While many Americans felt nervous about US efforts abroad, the Berrigan brothers effectively used their Catholic faith to critique perceived American arrogance. Examining the Berrigan brothers allows students to discuss the importance of religious dissent in American history, and how, when, and why religious activists sometimes turn on the US government.[11]

In American history, war and religious faith have often marched together. This was, perhaps, clearer than ever during World War II, when the cause was just and the fight necessary. During the Cold War, however, as American policymakers continued to link faith to American foreign policy, many religious leaders began to wonder if they and their faith had been co-opted. Nevertheless, they knew, and our students should know, that religion was a central component of World War II and the Cold War.

ADDITIONAL RESOURCES

Herzog Jonathan P. *The Spiritual-Industrial Complex: America's Religious Battle against Communism in the Early Cold War*. New York: Oxford University Press, 2011.

Kruse, Kevin M. *One Nation under God: How Corporate America Invented Christian America*. New York: Basic Books, 2015.

Piehler, Kurt G. *A Religious History of the American GI in World War II*. Lincoln: University of Nebraska Press, 2021.

Schultz, Kevin M. *Tri-Faith America: How Catholics and Jews Held Postwar America to Its Protestant Promise*. New York: Oxford University Press; 2011.

Sutton, Matthew Avery. *Double Crossed: The Missionaries Who Spied for the United States during the Second World War*. New York: Basic Books, 2019.

Wacker, Grant. *America's Pastor: Billy Graham and the Shaping of a Nation*. Cambridge, MA: Belknap Press of Harvard University Press, 2014.

NOTES

1. Franklin D. Roosevelt, "Annual Message to Congress," January 4, 1939, https://www.presidency.ucsb.edu/documents/annual-message-congress.

2. Harold L. Ickes to FDR, January 6, 1942, box 128, President's Secretary's File, FDR Library, http://www.fdrlibrary.marist.edu/_resources/images/psf/psf 000511.pdf.

3. Franklin D. Roosevelt, "Annual Message to Congress," January 6, 1941, https://www.presidency.ucsb.edu/node/209473. The National Archives has made available Norman Rockwell's depictions of the Four Freedoms for the *Saturday Evening Post*: https://www.archives.gov/exhibits/powers_of_persuasion/four_freedoms/four_freedoms.html.

4. President Roosevelt to Pope Pius XII, February 14, 1940, Office of the Historian, https://history.state.gov/historicaldocuments/frus1940v01/d37. There are many additional documents on the US wartime relationship with the Vatican available at the FDR Library, http://docs.fdrlibrary.marist.edu/vatican.html.

5. Matthew Avery Sutton, *Double Crossed: The Missionaries Who Spied for the United States during the Second World War* (New York: Basic Books, 2019).

6. Minersville School District v. Gobitis, 310 US 586 (1940), https://www.oyez.org/cases/1940–1955/310us586; West Virginia State Board of Education v. Barnette, 319 US 624 (1943), https://www.oyez.org/cases/1940–1955/319us624.

7. The FDR Library has made numerous documents about Jewish refugees and the Holocaust available at FRANKLIN, http://www.fdrlibrary.marist.edu/archives/collections/franklin/index.php?p=collections/findingaid&id=505. One useful article is Varian Fry, "The Massacre of the Jews," *New Republic*, December 21, 1942, 816–19, https://newrepublic.com/article/118800/first-american-report-holocaust.

8. Truman makes the case for the continuing importance of religion shortly after World War II in this radio address: "Radio Address as Part of the Program 'Religion in American Life,'" October 30, 1949, https://www.trumanlibrary.gov/library/public-papers/246/radio-address-part-program-religion-american-life.

9. Fred Schwarz, *You Can Trust the Communists* (Englewood Cliffs, NJ: Prentice Hall, 1960), 174. See also J. B. Matthews, "Reds and Our Churches," *American Mercury*, July 1953, 3–13; Matthews, "Reds and Our Churches," Scribd, https://www.scribd.com/document/119007813/Reds-and-Our-Churches-J-B-Matthews.

10. Graham sermons can be accessed at the Billy Graham Audio Archives, https://billygraham.org/tv-and-radio/radio/audio-archives/. One that would be useful to discuss is "Christianism vs. Communism (1951)," https://billygraham.org/audio/christianism-vs-communism/.

11. On Berrigan, see "Religion: A Priest in Hiding Calls for Moral Revolt," *New York Times*, August 9, 1970.

Teaching Religion in the Civil Rights Movement

J. RUSSELL HAWKINS

For instructors of American history, teaching the civil rights movement of the 1950s and 1960s presents exciting opportunities and unexpected difficulties.[1] The instantly recognizable morality of the struggle makes for easy heroes and villains that can capture student imaginations. Additionally, many of the movement's flashpoints were captured by photographers and newsreels, producing vivid images and videos to complement the written histories of this period. Many of these visuals have become iconic, providing a steady supply of lessons in heroism that young students receive in the earliest years of their schooling. Elementary schools across the country tell the stories of Ruby Bridges's lonely bravery, Rosa Parks's quiet determination, and Martin Luther King Jr.'s soaring rhetoric. When villains are introduced—Bull Connor, Jim Clark, George Wallace—they are presented in the stark hues of unrepentant bigots, whose actions and motivations are as self-evidently immoral as the Black protestors' are pure. With such clear lines drawn between good and evil—and so visually accessible—student interest in the civil rights movement is rarely in short supply.

Ironically, the same qualities that make the civil rights movement so compelling for students can also make teaching the period difficult. This difficulty exists because so much of student perceptions of the civil rights movement have been shaped by problematic sources. As Americans have increasingly celebrated the movement's triumph in recent decades, popular accounts of the Black freedom struggle have exploded. More and more, students are arriving in our classrooms with an understanding of Black civil rights drawn from fictionalized Hollywood films loosely based on true stories. The effect of these popular accounts is that students view the movement as a scripted drama in which the triumph of equality for Black Americans is inevitable rather than contingent history where all outcomes are uncertain. This is no small matter. With a perspective of historical inevitability comes a cheapening of the cost of the Black freedom struggle and a flattening of the humanity of its participants. As I say, tongue in cheek, to my students each year, for many of us the civil rights movement has been reduced to three crucial moments. First, Mrs. Parks sat on a bus. Next, Dr. King gave a speech. Finally, Denzel Washington won a football championship. And with these three steps Black equality was realized.

The last step in my facetious historical accounting—the one with Denzel Washington—always elicits smiles from students. It refers to the 2000 film *Remember the Titans*, a Disney-produced movie whose inspirational message and PG rating has made its viewing a staple in schools and homes across the country. *Remember the Titans*—based, of course, on a true story—follows the court-ordered integration of T. C. Williams High School in Alexandria, Virginia, and the impact desegregation had on the school's football team. To mitigate the turmoil of forced school integration, the local school board hires a Black coach named Herman Boone (played by Washington) to help the newly integrated football team succeed on the gridiron. As depicted in the film, resistance from white players, parents, and coaches to an integrated team under the leadership of a Black coach was intense. But, as the season goes on, Black and white players begin to bond on and off the field, white parents come to embrace their children's Black teammates, and the white assistant coach eventually sees the wisdom of Boone's strategies. In true Disney fashion, the film ends with the Titans winning the Virginia state football championship in a dramatic and unexpected manner. As the credits roll, viewers are left with a sense that the Titans overcame a fractious past to usher in a unified present. Those Black and white football players were the heirs of Mrs. Parks and Dr. King, driving the final nail in the coffin of segregation. As it was for the Titans, the film not so subtly suggests, so it can be for all of us. (In a case of life imitating art, the theme from *Remember the Titans* played as Barack Obama took the stage to give his victory address in Chicago's Grant Park the night he was elected the country's first Black president.)[2]

Remember the Titans exemplifies how many students, especially those who are white, understand the civil rights movement, hinting at the challenges teaching this period present. Just as the stakes of the movie are relatively low—will the Titans win the state title?—so too do students struggle to see the deeper purpose of the civil rights movement, reducing the quests for full democratic participation, human dignity, and the end to racial terrorism—those goals that made up the the heart of the movement—to a struggle over bus seats and drinking fountains. Similarly, just as the ending of *Remember the Titans* is a foregone conclusion—it is a Disney film, after all—so too do students raised on popular accounts of the movement approach the topic with a sense of inevitability. This approach distorts both the nature of the struggle and the participants involved. After all, with the outcome certain, it is easy to caricature the cause, motives, and personalities of participants on both sides of the civil rights movement.

Ironically, one antidote to the problem wrought by the sanitized version of the civil rights history emblematic in *Remember the Titans* appears in the film itself. In one memorable scene, a white father barges into the football coaches' office demanding his son get more playing time. Unsatisfied with the coaches' response, the man hurls a racial epithet at Boone and storms out of the office. "Well, I guess we won't be seeing much of him," one of the Black coaches remarked. "I will," the white assistant coach responded. "He's on the deacon board with me." The actors in the scene laugh at the remark, and so do most audiences when they first hear it. Such a response is understandable. A church deacon displaying explicitly racist behavior sits incongruently in the minds of many Americans conditioned to see the civil rights movement as a morality tale between unadulterated good and unmitigated evil. Such conditioning is possible when we neglect the religious struggle at the center of the civil rights movement. Bringing religious conflict into their exploration of the movement can help students guard against the temptation to see the struggle in a reductionist and simplistic light.

To say popular histories of the civil rights movement neglect religious conflict is not to claim that religion itself is absent in such accounts. Indeed, religion regularly appears in popular portrayals of the civil rights movement, but only on one side of the struggle. Such depictions rightly show Black churches as staging grounds and headquarters for the movement's grassroots demonstrations, where freedom songs rang out and inspiring sermons drew foot soldiers to the cause of Black equality.

Indeed, as historians have demonstrated, it was a deep and abiding religious faith forged by shared experiences of oppression that energized so many Black civil rights activists and sustained them throughout their freedom struggle.[3] And yet, there is another story of religion in the civil rights movement, one that was on display, however briefly, in the scene with the church deacon in *Remember the Titans*.

As the push for civil rights began in earnest throughout the South in the 1950s, many white southerners—both clergy and laity—turned to their faith not to further the cause of integration but to mount a defense of their region's caste system. At odds with demonstrators meeting in Black churches to find strength to undo Jim Crow, these white Christians preached sermons, published pamphlets, and authored articles that mined nature and scripture to show God's support of segregation. Taken together, these sources constituted a theology of segregation that shaped the Christian imaginations of many white southerners, serving as the foundation for religious resistance to racial equality in the middle decades of the twentieth century. Pairing an understanding of the religious resistance to the civil rights movement with a deeper reading of the religious motivations of the movement's activists can help students better understand the stakes of the civil rights movement and clarify what animated its protagonists and antagonists alike.

Religion in Support of the Civil Rights Movement

Historian David Chappell has shown that it was "the irrational traditions of prophetic, revivalistic religion" deeply held by so many participants in the civil rights struggle that made the movement move.[4] As previously mentioned, many popular histories of the movement include depictions of Black churches whose congregational lives were central to the movement's success. As a result, students grasp the significant role religion played in support of the civil rights movement because they are primed to see it. An effective way of introducing students to religion's contribution to civil rights activism, therefore, is mapping these lesser-known religious motives onto the better-known political history of the movement. For example, most students have a vague familiarity of the bus boycott initiated when Rosa Parks defied a local segregation ordinance in Montgomery, Alabama, in December 1955. Students are likely less familiar with the speech Martin Luther King Jr. gave after the first day of that boycott at the Holt Street Baptist

Church, where Montgomery's Black citizens had gathered to decide whether to extend the bus boycott indefinitely. Providing students with King's speech—available online in both text and audio format—allows them to see how King used the Christian faith to describe the protestors and justify the struggle ahead. "Nobody can doubt the height of her [Mrs. Parks's] character, nobody can doubt the depth of her Christian commitment and devotion to the teachings of Jesus," King told the gathering at Holt Street Baptist. But it was not just Parks's Christian commitment that was unimpeachable, the young minister went on to tell the crowd; it was all of theirs. "I want it to be known throughout Montgomery and throughout this nation that we are a Christian people. We believe in the Christian religion. We believe in the teachings of Jesus. The only weapon that we have in our hands this evening is the weapon of protest," King reminded the crowd. King also urged his listeners to act faithfully in the struggle to come. "In all of our doings, in all of our deliberations . . . whatever we do, we must keep God in the forefront. Let us be Christian in all of our action."[5] In addition to seeing how King incorporated the Christian faith into this event early in the civil rights movement, students can also benefit from listening to how the crowd responds to King's address. Some of the loudest applause in his speech occurs when King talks about the Christian understanding of the inseparability of love and justice. When students hear the crowd affirming these ideas with their enthusiastic response, they can begin to understand both how spokespeople such as King framed the movement in theological terms and why ordinary Black Americans listening to King were willing to suffer for the movement's cause.[6]

When teaching courses on religion in the civil rights movement, I follow this same pattern, coupling the political manifestations of the movement—sit-ins, freedom rides, Birmingham campaign, and so forth—with the religious ideals that moved civil rights protestors to action and sustained them in their cause. The indispensable tool for this technique is *Rhetoric, Religion, and the Civil Rights Movement, 1954–1965*, edited by Davis W. Houck and David E. Dixon.[7] In their volume, Houck and Dixon have culled together 130 sermons and speeches that make overt religious justifications for Black equality, arranging them chronologically through the civil rights years. Some of the orators will be recognizable names to students; many will not. The power of this volume comes from the collection's correspondence to the major events of the civil rights movement. For instructors desiring student understanding of how significant religious ideas were to the civil rights movement, Houck and Dixon's volume is a worthy purchase.

Helping students understand the deep connection between the civil rights movement and religious motivation is only half the task. Students must also comprehend the contested nature of the religious ideals in the civil rights years. This reality is implied in one of the best-known documents produced during the civil rights struggle: King's 1963 "Letter from Birmingham Jail." King's letter is rightly widely studied as a political and moral treatise, but it is important that students recognize the intended recipients of King's letter were eight white clergy who had criticized the campaign of nonviolent direction action King was leading in Birmingham, Alabama. In his letter's closing stanzas, King draws attention to the lack of active white Christian participation in the civil rights movement. "I have heard numerous religious leaders of the South call upon their worshippers to comply with a desegregation decision because it is the law, but I have longed to hear white ministers say follow this decree because integration is morally right and the Negro is your brother. In the midst of blatant injustices inflicted upon the Negro, I have watched white churches stand on the sideline and merely mouth pious irrelevancies and sanctimonious trivialities."[8] King's letter is a condemnation of white churches' sins of omission, and having students read the letter with an eye for white culpability can prepare them to grapple with the religious gulf separating many Black and white Christians in the civil rights era. Indeed, just as religion was a motivating factor for some in the fight for racial equality, it also contributed to the resistance white Christians had toward the movement.

Religion against the Civil Rights Movement

Despite the copious religious rhetoric deployed by civil rights activists in service to their cause, not everyone was persuaded. At the same time civil rights activists were rooting their efforts in interpretations of the Christian tradition, white segregationists were waging a defense of Jim Crow segregation by appealing to competing interpretations of that same tradition. Helping students see the hermeneutical battle fought over God's purported stance on segregation adds layers of complexity to the civil rights story that is often told devoid of nuance.

Primary sources for the anti–civil rights religious tradition are not as easy to come by as those used in support of the cause. Although several important monographs on the topic have appeared in recent years, there is no volume dedicated to anti–civil rights sermons like Houck and Dixon's book.[9] As more archives are putting their holdings online, however, it is becoming easier to get sources into the hands of students to help them see the religious conflict in the civil rights movement. One of the most circulated pamphlets in the civil rights era against integration appeared shortly after the 1954 *Brown* decision. "A Christian View on Segregation," by Reverend G. T. Gillespie, serves similar purposes for students as King's 1955 sermon at the Holt Street Baptist Church. Whereas King roots support for Black equality in the Christian notion of love and justice, Gillespie offers a counterview that God, in fact, ordained racial segregation, laying out his case with clear biblical references.[10] Gillespie and King's contrasting interpretations of Christianity's perspective of racial equality, issued in 1954 and 1955, respectively, serve as helpful touchstones for the competing religious views that would surface in the years ahead.

Perhaps the best accessible primary source document to help students see the religious conflict of the civil rights movement was written by a high school senior. In 1960, the pro-segregation Citizens' Councils of Mississippi initiated an annual essay contest to award college scholarships to promising high school students. Contest guidelines declared that the essay competition was intended to, among other things, impart "the importance of maintaining Racial Integrity" to a generation of white students whose days in segregated public schools were feared to be numbered.[11]

In her 1960 winning essay, Mary Rosalind Healy discussed why she believed in the separation of the races, writing, "I know that the social exposure of one race to another brings about a laxity of principles and a complacency toward differences which can only develop into an incurable epidemic of intermarriage. This malady has but one inevitable result—racial death." Diagnosing the problem of racial integration as being the gateway to miscegenation, Healy arrived at her thesis: "Thus, I must believe in the social separation of the races of mankind because I am a Christian and must abide by the laws of God."[12]

For readers lacking knowledge of how God's laws were purportedly related to segregation, Healy provides numerous passages from the Old Testament that she believes gave her a "Biblical and historical basis for the belief that racial separation was divinely instituted." Healy's defense of racial segregation was not limited to Old Testament texts.

Citing a verse in the second epistle to the church at Corinth, Healy interpreted the apostle Paul's warnings to first-century Christians against becoming unequally yoked to apply "to color and culture as well as spirituality." Reaching the end of her exegesis, Healy concluded, "if I am to call myself Christian, I must accept God's plan of human development as well as the laws of nature established by Him."[13] The power of Healy's document for latter-day students comes from the fact that Healy likely did not arrive at these conclusions on her own accord. Instead, students can be shown that Healy's essay is a reflection of ideas she would have been exposed to in church over many years. Indeed, as demonstrated by historians of massive resistance, Healy's segregationist interpretation of the Bible parroted countless other white southerners in the 1950s and 1960s who, like the high school senior, read justifications for segregation in the pages of their Holy Writ. In addition to reflecting common religious arguments for segregation, Healy's essay is significant because it won a prize from the Mississippi Citizens' Council. The council's endorsement functions to validate Healy's ideas in the same way that the applause lines in King's Holt Street Baptist address demonstrated the welcomed reception of his ideas.

Pamphlets such as Gillespie's and essays such as Healy's can help students understand that for many white Christians across the South, religious sensibilities and segregationist thought produced a potent alloy that reinforced white resistance to civil rights in the mid-twentieth century. In so doing, students will gain an understanding of the movement that takes them away from the lessons learned from Disney films. The civil rights movement was a struggle over Black equality, to be sure. But it was also a struggle between people who held sincere beliefs about what their religion taught. By incorporating this religious conflict into the standard civil rights narrative, students will gain a deeper appreciation for the complexity of the movement, a realization that its outcome was far from certain, and a recognition that in many respects, the conflict rages on.

ADDITIONAL RESOURCES

Cone, James. *Martin & Malcolm & America: A Dream or a Nightmare.* Maryknoll, NY: Orbis Books, 1991. (Especially chapter 6)

Haley, Alex. *The Autobiography of Malcolm X.* New York: Ballantine Books, 1965. (Especially chapter 13)

Hawkins, J. Russell. *The Bible Told Them So: How Southern Evangelicals Fought to Preserve White Supremacy*. New York: Oxford University Press, 2021.

NOTES

1. In this chapter, I refer to the civil rights movement in its "classical" iteration, that is, the pursuit of racial justice defined as having occurred primarily in the American South between the 1954 *Brown* decision and the adoption of the Voting Rights Act in 1965.

2. "Obama Teams with 'Titans,'" *Los Angeles Times*, November 8, 2008, accessed October 27, 2019, https://www.latimes.com/archives/la-xpm-2008-nov-08-et-bigpicture8-story.html.

3. See David L. Chappell, *A Stone of Hope: Prophetic Religion and the Death of Jim Crow* (Chapel Hill: University of North Carolina Press, 2004); Lewis V. Baldwin, *The Voice of Conscience: The Church in the Mind of Martin Luther King, Jr.* (New York: Oxford University Press, 2010).

4. Chappell, *A Stone of Hope*, 179.

5. Martin Luther King, Jr., "Address to the First Montgomery Improvement Association Mass Meeting," December 5, 1955, The Martin Luther King, Jr. Research and Education Institute, Stanford University, accessed October 27, 2019, https://kinginstitute.stanford.edu/king-papers/documents/mia-mass-meeting-holt-street-baptist-church.

6. King, "Address to the First Montgomery Improvement Association Mass Meeting," YouTube, accessed October 27, 2019, https://www.youtube.com/watch?v=GGtp7kCi_LA.

7. Davis W. Houck and David E. Dixon, eds., *Rhetoric, Religion, and the Civil Rights Movement, 1954–1965* (Waco, TX: Baylor University Press, 2006).

8. Martin Luther King, Jr., "Letter from Birmingham Jail," October 27, 2019, https://www.africa.upenn.edu/Articles_Gen/Letter_Birmingham.html.

9. Carolyn Renee DuPont, *Mississippi Praying: Southern White Evangelical and the Civil Rights Movement, 1945–1975* (New York: New York University Press, 2013); Stephen R. Haynes, *The Last Segregated Hour: The Memphis Kneel-Ins and the Campaign for Southern Church Desegregation* (New York: Oxford University Press, 2012); Carter Dalton Lyon, *Sanctuaries of Segregation: The Story of the Jackson Church Visit Campaign* (Jackson: University Press of Mississippi, 2017); Joseph T. Reiff, *Born of Conviction: White Methodists and Mississippi's Closed Society* (New York: Oxford University Press, 2016); Ansley L. Quiros, *God with Us: Lived Theology and the Freedom Struggle in Americus, Georgia, 1942–1976* (Chapel Hill: University of North Carolina Press, 2018).

10. G. T. Gillespie, "A Christian View on Segregation," *Pamphlets and Broadsides*, University of Mississippi, accessed October 27, 2019, https://egrove.olemiss.edu/cgi/viewcontent.cgi?article=1000&context=citizens_pamph.

11. "Statewide Scholarship Essay Contest for Mississippi High School Students 1958–1959," box 32, William D. Workman, Jr. Papers, South Carolina Political Collections, University of South Carolina.

12. Mary Rosalind Healy, "Why I Believe in the Social Separation of the Races of Mankind," University of Mississippi, accessed October 27, 2019, https://egrove.olemiss.edu/citizens_pamph/93/.

13. Ibid.

Teaching the Rise of the Religious Right in the Age of Culture Wars

DARREN DOCHUK

Texas looms large in the history of the Religious Right. There, in the late 1970s, several events intensified cultural divisions in the United States and quickened a political revolution that would come to fruition in 1980. The politics of feminism and family values fanned the flames.

In 1977, President Jimmy Carter appropriated federal funds for the International Women's Year Commission (IWYC), a United Nations–endorsed counsel that planned regional conferences on women's issues at which delegates would be elected for a national forum in Houston. Although a center-right Democrat, Carter knew that for the sake of maintaining his power he had to endorse progressive Democratic causes: he pledged White House support of ratification of the Equal Rights Amendment (ERA), protections of women's reproductive rights, and generally sanctioned a feminist and gay rights platform. His willingness to channel $5 million toward the Houston forum was thus predictable.

But the furor that followed was no surprise either. By 1977, conservative activists had generated heavy opposition to the ERA. In the IWYC they identified "a front for radicals and lesbians," and in the planned Houston conference they saw the "evil that is inherent within . . . so-called women's liberation." The task before the anti-ERA movement, they asked? To show "how as Christians we must do good as the Lord commands by opposing this evil," and in more concrete terms to organize a competing "Pro-Family Rally."[1]

And so in November 1977 Houston played host to two momentous gatherings, whose differences in substance and tenor highlighted a fragmented America. The IWYC conference was held at the Albert Thomas Convention Center, downtown. There eighteen thousand supporters convened to "voice their needs and hope for the future" and pass resolutions that defended reproductive freedoms and gay rights. Meanwhile, in a suburb to the south roughly the same number of activists gathered in the Astro Arena. The "Pro-Family" participants passed resolutions that opposed abortion, the ERA, and lesbian rights. All the while they waved signs that read "IWY. International Witches Year," and "Not Gay, But Happy People—Happy Texas." "This is the most significant day in the history of our country," master of ceremonies Lee Goodman declared from the dais. "This is the day that we saved life."[2]

Goodman's claim of the pro-family conference's importance in the broad sweep of US history was exaggerated, but in terms of its significance for the rise of the Religious Right, it hit the mark. In the months that followed, Goodman's fellow culture warriors channeled the energy witnessed in the Astro Arena into an unstoppable movement. Outraged at Carter's left-wing initiatives, they grew determined to engender change. "There's got to be a strong outcry against this," one activist announced. "The executive power is not being checked." Leading their revolt was Ronald Reagan, who lambasted Carter's liberal leanings. Reagan's platform of free market economics, family values, and a hawkish foreign policy won over conservatives. Speaking before fifteen thousand Baptist ministers in Dallas during the lead-up to the 1980 election, he uttered the words that would seal this new alliance: "I know you can't endorse me . . . but I want you to know that I endorse you and what you are doing." A short time later, he and his allies won the election, the White House, and the mandate to redraw the American political landscape.[3]

Religious Biography as Pedagogy

These flashpoints in 1970s Texas serve as a useful entry into any history survey of right-wing religious politics in America. Carter's presidency was indeed a pivot in the politicization of conservative religion; beyond the politics of feminism and family values, he also stirred conservatives' ire by lobbying for environmental and energy conservation (countering the priorities of oil-rich Texans) and weakening

American military power on a global stage. At the same time, these flashpoints can also skew the history of the Religious Right by focusing on the sensational political outbursts rather than the sustained mobilization that drove its ascent. More than a knee-jerk reaction to Carter or sudden love affair with Reagan, the culture war politicking witnessed in 1970s Texas was the product of a generation of social, economic, and cultural change, the breadth of which students need to grasp when making sense of the movement that brought Reagan to power, and that still operates at the center of US politics today.

The pressing methodological question, though, is how to cover this expansive story? In semester-long courses on religion and politics in modern America one can be more deliberate in threading religion into capacious political themes and trajectories that span the entirety of the twentieth century. Yet to teach the rise of the Religious Right in one brief section of a standard history survey poses unique challenges, especially if the instructor wants to do justice to the range of motivations and imperatives that animated it, as well as to the long stages of development that it endured before seizing power in the late twentieth century. While we tend to see and portray the Religious Right as almost solely white evangelical in composition, for instance, in actuality it has long maintained a big-tent approach by welcoming under its political canopy activists from the Catholic, Jewish, and Mormon faiths. As illustrated in this chapter, since the Cold War period Catholic conservatives have served as a vanguard for right-wing political action. Also, although evangelical Protestants have often spurned them on theological grounds, Mormons too have lent a crucial hand in lobbying for school prayer and family values and decrying abortion, communism, and gay rights. Meanwhile, Zionist Jews' sustained, full-throated defense of Israel has made them key (if partial) members of the right-wing religious coalition as well; since the early 1970s, evangelicals who view the politics of the Middle East through prophetic terms have been especially eager to embrace these constituents as allies in a common fight. The test for anyone trying to teach the Religious Right, then, is manifold: how does one keep so many moving parts in this dynamic, always shifting ecumenical federation together and its historical record of political action accessible and contained?[4]

One way to tackle these challenges is to tell this broader history through the lens of religious biography. There is no shortage of illustrative characters where right-wing religion and politics are concerned, and rather than shy away from them in order to glimpse big-picture developments, I suggest foregrounding them as windows onto the more expansive political terrain. Two biographies stand out, in this regard, that allow students to zero in on the particular battles of the Religious Right in the eras of Carter and Reagan, while also gaining an understanding of the political steps that led to and followed those flashpoints. The profiles of Phyllis Schlafly and Beverly LaHaye serve yet another purpose. So often the Religious Right is portrayed as a movement run by male clerics and lobbyists, but as the profiles of these two female activists show, women drove much of the action.

Fighting for Family Values: The Catholic Politico

Both Schlafly and LaHaye can serve as launches into the family values politicking that played out in Texas and elsewhere during Carter's presidency. Schlafly was directly responsible for the Houston battle royale, and her activism and writings can provide students with clear access to the ideas and strategies that conservative Christians acted upon in the late 1970s.

Schlafly was, of course, the architect of STOP ERA, which helped kindle the Religious Right. She founded this organization after Congress's passage of the proposed Equal Rights Amendment in 1972. From that point forward, Schlafly rallied her supporters around the notion that the ERA would deprive women of their special status in the home and extant privileges, protections, and dignity as mothers in society. Gone would be protective laws against sexual assault, for instance, as well as court rulings in favor of women in child custody cases. Moreover, were the ERA to be ratified, she warned, women would be thrust into other compromising situations: equal with men, they would be forced to enlist in the military and even accept the reality of single-sex restrooms. Traditionalist in her Catholic faith, Schafly was stinging in her criticism of feminism; she described the ERA's supporters as "bitter women seeking a constitutional cure for their personal problems." As witnessed at the Pro-Family Rally in Houston, which Schafly cosponsored, that language struck a chord with the thousands of housewife activists who joined STOP ERA. Her speech to the Astro Arena crowd, a worthy teaching source in its own right, was highly anticipated, and she did not disappoint her fans when she railed against the IWYC conference for its irreligiosity.[5]

There is no shortage of written and visual materials documenting Schafly's anti-liberal discourse, though certain samples of her penned and spoken words stand out where classroom adoption is concerned. The interview of Schlafly that was published in the *Washington Star*, January 18, 1976, and her televised debate with feminist leader Betty Friedan on January 28, 1976, provide an effective match. The former lays out why Schlafly opposed the ERA and the women's movement. Here students can grapple with several questions: Schlafly claims to be work-ing on behalf of and not against true women's rights—can she be called a feminist? How do her views of gender set her apart from her feminist foes? What does she highlight as the critical dangers of the ERA and the women's movement? To what degree is she also trying to stoke fears in a way that will galvanize the conservative movement? How do her social and religious values blend with her anti-statist view of government? To get a better sense of Schlafly's political style, students can then watch her twenty-minute-long debate with Friedan, which took place on the *Good Morning America* program. In this conversation Schlafly comes across as a polished communicator, able to counter all of the best arguments Friedan can make, and do so with a disarming (for Friedan, disrupting) calm. Students can assess the degree to which they think Schlafly's class and confidence served her well when expanding her pro-family crusade.[6]

Fighting for Family Values: The Protestant Politico

Schlafly's Protestant counterpart, Beverly LaHaye, may not have been in Houston during the dueling conferences of 1977, but the political spirit witnessed there caused her to act as well.

At the time of the IWYC conference LaHaye was attending a Chris-tian women's convention in Anaheim, California. When she heard about the feminist resolutions passed in the Albert Thomas Convention Cen-ter, she became enraged. A good primary source for students is LaHaye's 1984 book *Who but a Woman?*, excerpts of which reveal her reactions to the Houston gathering and prompt lines of questioning: How do LaHaye's responses to the feminist movement compare and contrast to Schlafly's? What about her views of gender, sexuality, and womanhood? Might the differences between the two derive from religious differences, or do they share an ecumenical outlook? Who is LaHaye's intended read-ing audience, and what does she hope to accomplish with her book? As students come to see, one thing that angered LaHaye was political process: in her mind, the feminist organizers disbanded "fairness or parliamentary procedures" in order to silence conservative voices and force through resolutions in favor of the ERA, gay and lesbian rights, and "federally funded abortion on demand."[7]

Angered, LaHaye pledged to defend Christian womanhood by incorporating Concerned Women for America (CWA). Mirroring Schlafly's Eagle Forum, the other organization that Schlafly created in 1972 as a media outlet and lobbying source for conservative values, CWA quickly gained steam. By February 1980, thirteen months after its founding, CWA had established fifty-two chapters in fourteen states. By 1983, the number was one thousand local chapters in forty-nine states, with two hundred thousand members—four times the membership Schlafly could boast. That same year LaHaye moved CWA's headquarters to Washington, DC, announcing that CWA had arrived ready "to end the monopoly of the feminists who claim to speak for all women."[8]

By 1984, CWA would be a political juggernaut, yet by then LaHaye was also entrenched in other facets of the emergent Religious Right. Along with her husband, pastor Tim LaHaye, Beverly LaHaye spent the late 1970s writing for evangelical Protestants; two key publications, excerpts of which can be introduced in the classroom as a way to explore the evangelical subculture, were *The Spirit-Controlled Woman* (1976) and, coauthored with Tim, *The Act of Marriage* (1976). The latter especially serves as a window into evangelical beliefs about the fundamental differences between men and women, the basis of conservatives' opposition to feminism.[9]

Meanwhile, the LaHayes also began helping a group of pastors, led by Baptist minister Jerry Falwell Sr., coalesce political action in the Moral Majority, the organization Falwell created in 1979. The Moral Majority's mandate of 1980, which appeared in Falwell's book, *Listen, America!*, laid out the multifaceted agenda that conservatives now embraced, and as such it serves as an ideal tool in the classroom. Tim LaHaye was one of a handful of Falwell's team of ministers who met with President Carter on January 21, 1980, to question and challenge his liberal policies. Upon leaving this meeting, LaHaye led his counterparts in prayer, saying: "God, we have got to get this man out of the White House and get someone in here who will be about bringing back traditional moral values." Ronald Reagan would fit the bill.[10]

The Roots of the Religious Right

As much as Beverly LaHaye and Phyllis Schlafly can be foregrounded for the purpose of determining how Christian conservatives roused to action in the late 1970s, their biographies also hint at other dynamics in the long buildup to this moment. While the politics of feminism and family values clearly triggered the final step of Christian conservative political mobilization, the roots of the Religious Right run deeper in the annals of twentieth-century America.

LaHaye's life can give students access to two other fundamental dimensions of the Religious Right's ascent: regional change and race. After meeting at Bible college in South Carolina, Tim and Beverly married and a short time later assumed leadership of San Diego's Scott Memorial Baptist Church in 1956, with Tim as pastor. Scott Memorial quickly ballooned in size, with membership growing from three hundred to two thousand congregants and its infrastructure encompassing several programs and institutes. In their move across the country, the LaHayes illustrate the demographic shifts that made Southern California the epicenter of conservative activism in the post–World War II years. Flocking to Southern California's booming economy and suburbs, millions of migrants, many of them from the South, brought their populist evangelicalism with them and then transformed it into a political movement animated by free market and family politics, anti-communism, and anti-statism.[11]

The LaHayes provide direct links to this ascending grassroots conservatism. From their base in San Diego, they spoke out against communist influences and the liberalization of California's school campuses (Tim LaHaye's *A Christian View of Radical Sex Education*, published in 1969, serves as one example of this agenda). They also moved in political circles that overlapped with the John Birch Society, the secret anti-communist organization. The society's founding document, *The Blue Book of the John Birch Society*, authored by founder Robert Welch, provides a window into the ideas (one might ask students if these are exaggerated, even conspiratorial) that propelled the broader anti-communist movement during the Cold War years. So does Fred Schwarz's *You Can Trust the Communists (to Do Exactly as They Say)*, excerpts of which can underscore the role of religion in undergirding the anti-communist crusade. As head of the Christian Anti-Communism Crusade, Schwarz also organized "schools of anticommunism," weeklong seminars such as the one held in Southern California in 1961, which drew thousands of average citizens (and celebrities) together to learn how to thwart the Reds.[12]

Phyllis Schlafly sheds further light on the rise of political conservatism in California and the Sunbelt. Schlafly became politically active in the late 1940s; fighting communism was the impetus. Even as she raised a family of six children, the Radcliffe College graduate conducted research for Senator Joseph McCarthy, the Red-baiting firebrand. It was McCarthy who infamously announced in his Lincoln Day Address before the Ohio County Women's Club in Wheeling, West Virginia, in 1950 (a document worth analyzing in class for its stark contrast between "Communistic atheism and Christianity" as well as its bold claims) that there were fifty-seven "card-carrying Communists" in the US State Department. Schlafly believed the politician, and throughout the 1950s she provided leadership for local anti-communist and Republican groups and even invited Fred Schwarz to St. Louis for one of his first American appearances.[13]

Schlafly soon articulated a more expansive conservative ideology. That step resulted in her publication of *A Choice Not An Echo*, a book that argued for the virtues of Barry Goldwater (it sold three million copies). The book is short and concise, and portions are digestible for students as they engage Schlafly's assessment of the electoral system, the perils of liberalism, "traditional" values and libertarian principles, and the rise of the Goldwater movement in 1964. In that election year, which saw Goldwater capture the Republican ticket because of his base in Southern California, Schlafly became the voice of a new political force, one in which conservative Catholics and Protestants were locked in unity behind a singular cause.[14]

That cause was to champion Christian nationalism and fight big government, communism, secularism, and progressive cultural trends, but it was also about race, a second dimension of the emerging Religious Right on which the biography of Beverly LaHaye sheds light. The school at which she and her husband met was Bob Jones College in Greenville, South Carolina, an almost all-white school (some ethnic groups could enroll, but Blacks were not allowed) that forbade interracial marriage. Long after the LaHayes had graduated, the college continued to shore up racial segregation in the face of civil rights activism and government action. In 1970, the Internal Revenue Service (IRS) determined that "private schools with racially discriminatory admissions policies" were not entitled to tax exemption status. In 1975, Bob Jones's trustees agreed to admit Black students but not bend on interracial dating.

What followed as a result of that prohibition was a legal battle between the college and the federal government, one that placed race at the center of the Religious Right's surge in the late 1970s. In 1976, the IRS rescinded Bob Jones College's tax exemption. Bob Jones appealed the IRS decision, leading to a series of court battles that would play out over the following decade. Angered by the government's seeming encroachment on religious freedom, evangelical Protestants, including many who disagreed with the college's racial policies, rallied behind Bob Jones in hopes of swaying the courts in its favor. In 1981, the National Association of Evangelicals (NAE) produced an amicus curiae brief in support of Bob Jones; the document is a valuable teaching source, as it lays out the arguments that conservatives made at the time (and that they continue to make) against Washington's "subordination of religious belief to current notions of public policy." A second document that can be paired with the NAE statement is the opinion authored by Chief Justice Warren Burger, delivered in 1983. Insisting that government "has a fundamental, overriding interest in eradicating racial discrimination in education," Burger and the US Supreme Court ruled in favor of the IRS.[15]

But the effects of this legal battle reverberated far beyond the school and courts. One historian asserts that more than abortion, feminism, and the ERA, it was this matter of race and government-enforced desegregation that galvanized the Religious Right. Even though the IRS delivered its 1975 blow before he was in office, evangelicals would come to blame Jimmy Carter for federal action against Bob Jones and, by extension, against conservative religious institutions and independence. Jerry Falwell railed against state interference in Christian education: "In some states," he complained, "it's easier to open a massage parlor than a Christian school." To be sure, Ronald Reagan and his conservative allies claimed to be "color blind" and inclusive across all racial lines, yet in the Bob Jones case students can also see the limits of these claims and the degree to which many champions of the Religious Right in particular sought political change in 1980 not just in defense of traditional family values but in defense of white privilege as well.[16]

Post-Reagan Turns

Reagan's victory was certainly a capstone of sorts, for it marked the culmination of Phyllis Schlafly's and Beverly LaHaye's sustained political work, as well as that of a host of activists on the Religious Right. But the story of the Religious Right does not stop there, and even brief attention to subsequent thresholds can allow students to connect that recent past with our present.

Reagan's presidency would prove to be frustrating at points, but also highly rewarding for the Religious Right. Some of Reagan's key appointees (secretary of the interior and surgeon general, for instance) were devout evangelicals, and conservative activists enjoyed other Reagan-endorsed triumphs both in domestic and foreign policy. Thanks to Schlafly's tireless work, ERA proponents were stymied, and their failure to get the necessary thirty-eight states to ratify the amendment (they fell three states short) meant it died officially in 1982. Reagan's foreign policy pleased those on the right as well, evidenced by his well-received speech at the Annual Convention of the National Association of Evangelicals, March 8, 1983, during which he portrayed the world as a realm where good battled evil. He pledged to fight the Soviet Union—an "evil empire"—with all of America's military might. The transcript of the speech demonstrates how Reagan managed to hit all the right marks with evangelicals, and it can serve as an excellent source of debate with students: How does Reagan's worldview mirror that of the evangelicals in the audience? Do you think he is sincere in these stated priorities, or is he trying simply to win over the crowd? How does he frame foreign policy in moral terms, and with what benefits and costs in your estimation? While evangelicals wish he had gone farther in his support of anti-abortion and school prayer legislation and had nominated a conservative instead of a moderate (Sandra Day O'Connor) for the Supreme Court, by the end of his tenure they felt like a foundation for future inroads in Washington had been laid.[17]

In the years that followed the Reagan revolution, activists such as Schlafly and LaHaye ramped up their politicking, eager not just to win the presidency but also affect lasting change from the precinct level up to the Supreme Court. There are flashpoints that instructors can use, should they wish to guide their students through the more recent past. President George W. Bush would prove to be a favorite of conservative Christians, certainly because of his policies, which concurred with

Reagan's principles, but also because of his personal testimony. His autobiography, *A Charge to Keep*, provides a detailed account of his conversion to evangelical Christianity, as well as insight into the connections he drew between his faith and his presidency.

Presidential politics does not tell us all about the impact of the Religious Right on recent politics, however. Instructors wanting to offer their students a glimpse at its wider influence can highlight a few different dimensions. Of course there are the clerics, whose voices have gotten increasingly louder since George Bush's presidency. Angered by President Barack Obama's perceived attack on religious freedom (by imposition of Obamacare mandates for religious institutions to cover contraception, for instance), ministers such as Franklin Graham, son of famed evangelist Billy Graham, ramped up their political discourse. Immigration became a driving concern. In keeping with the Religious Right's Christian nationalist perspective and view of the United States as a chosen nation—but with more intensity, Franklin Graham argued for tougher immigration policies and a fiercer response to "foreign" threats. In the wake of 9/11 and throughout Obama's presidency, the "foreign" threat of greatest concern to him was Islam. The pairing of two documents provides students with the chance to evaluate Christian conservatives' recent and current stand on this matter. The first is an excerpt from Graham's 2002 book, *The Name*, which paints Islam as an intolerant faith and evil force. This portrayal of the world in Manichean terms should get students remembering Reagan and his 1983 speech about the "evil" Soviet Union. Why does this language appeal to religious conservatives' theological and political outlook? What is the impact on US foreign relations? How does it forestall US investment in internationalist projects such as the United Nations? An answer to Graham's call is the "Letter to Franklin Graham from the Council on American-Islamic Relations," dated August 15, 2002. The missive condemns Graham's portrayal of Islam as an evil religion and begs him to learn more about the faith in order to forge unity, not division, and break down barriers rather than erect them.[18]

Conclusion: Closed Careers and New Political Heights

Franklin Graham's political views continue to represent those of the Religious Right. With the help of other famous preachers such as Jerry Falwell Jr., the Religious Right achieved unprecedented power during the presidency of Donald Trump. In the 2016 election, 81 percent of American evangelicals voted for him, this despite some early reservations from pastors who questioned his moral standing. After his election, evangelicals became more spirited than ever in their endorsement of Trump and his attempts to legislate their social values, defend Christian America against foreign enemies, and complete a political transformation that began years before.

Phyllis Schlafly and Beverly LaHaye helped bring the Religious Right to this apex, a final reminder of the power that female grassroots activists—not just presidents and preachers—have wielded for the past half century. LaHaye wrote and spoke widely during the 1990s and early 2000s, evidence of which can be accessed on C-Span, which contains numerous videos of her speaking at Washington events, be it at a Senate Judiciary Committee hearing for the nomination of John Ashcroft as attorney general or in a salute to conservative senator Jesse Helms. These videos can help students not only understand LaHaye but also trace the evolution of conservatism in the past few decades. The online resources that appear on the Concerned Women for America's website can be applied this same way. So too those that appear on the website for Eagle Forum, Schlafly's creation. For her part, Schlafly spent this same time period writing, speaking, and lobbying for her principles. She decried gay marriage and abortion, Obamacare and open borders, liberal media and Washington "insiders," and she demanded an "America first" approach to the world. Coming full circle, in 2016 she published her twenty-seventh book, *The Conservative Case for Trump*, which had echoes of her first famous book, *A Choice Not An Echo*. Schlafly's last book hit stands a day after she passed away, leaving Trump and her peers to eulogize her as a true patriot. Upon her passing, LaHaye will, no doubt, receive the same tribute.[19]

ADDITIONAL RESOURCES

Critchlow, Donald T. *Phyllis Schlafly and Grassroots Conservatism: A Woman's Crusade.* Princeton, NJ: Princeton University Press, 2005.

Dowland, Seth. *Family Values and the Rise of the Christian Right.* Philadelphia: University of Pennsylvania Press, 2018.

Griffith, R. Marie. *Moral Combat: How Sex Divided American Christians and Fractured American Politics.* New York: Basic Books, 2017.

Johnson, Emily Suzanne. *This Is Our Message: Women's Leadership in the New Christian Right.* New York: Oxford University Press, 2019.

Sutton, Matthew Avery. *Jerry Falwell and the Rise of the Religious Right: A Brief History with Documents*. Boston: Bedford/St. Martin's, 2013.

NOTES

1. Quoted in Donald T. Critchlow, *Phyllis Schlafly and Grassroots Conservatism: A Woman's Crusade* (Princeton, NJ: Princeton University Press, 2005), 244–45.

2. Judy Klemesrud, "Equal Rights Plan and Abortion Are Opposed by 15,000 at Rally," *New York Times*, November 20, 1977.

3. Victoria Irwin, "Factions Seek Control of Family Conference," *Christian Science Monitor*, February 13, 1980.

4. On the Religious Right as an ecumenical alliance, see Neil J. Young, *We Gather Together: The Religious Right and the Problem of Interfaith Politics* (New York: Oxford University Press, 2015).

5. "Phyllis Schlafly in Houston, 1977, YouTube, https://www.youtube.com/watch?v=HLmJ9KbUCGw; for general rally proceedings, see "Pro Family Rally in Houston 1977," YouTube, https://www.youtube.com/watch?v=SpNa6BiSNFI.

6. "Interview with Phyllis Schlafly, *Washington Star*, April 18, 1976," in *The Rise of Conservatism in America, 1945–2000: A Brief History with Documents*, ed. Ronald Story and Bruce Laurie (Boston: Bedford/St. Martin's, 2008), 104. For the Schlafly-Friedan debate, see "Phyllis Schlafly Debates Betty Friedan on ERA," YouTube, https://www.youtube.com/watch?v=WncN6PWEMGo.

7. Beverly LaHaye, *Who but a Woman?* (Nashville, TN: Thomas Nelson, 1984), 24–26. For insight into LaHaye's convictions about gender politics, consider focusing on chapters 1–3 and 6.

8. Emily Suzanne Johnson, *This Is Our Message: Women's Leadership in the New Christian Right* (New York: Oxford University Press, 2019), 68, 82–83.

9. Johnson, *This Is Our Message*, 73. Tim and Beverly LaHaye's *The Act of Marriage: The Beauty of Sexual Love* (Grand Rapids, MI: Zondervan, 1976) was quite radical for its frank discussion of sex in Christian marriage. Chapters 1–3 provide a useful overview of how biology and biblical prescription mean fundamental differences between the two genders.

10. Jerry Falwell, *Listen, America!* (Garden City, NY: Doubleday, 1980). For Falwell's mandate as well as the questions submitted to President Jimmy Carter, see Matthew Avery Sutton, *Jerry Falwell and the Rise of the Religious Right: A Brief History with Documents* (Boston: Bedford/St. Martin's, 2013). LaHaye's prayer is mentioned in "Tim LaHaye Obituary," *The Guardian* (London), July 28, 2016, accessed March 6, 2020, https://www.theguardian.com/books/2016/jul/28/tim-lahaye-obituary, and is also detailed in a fascinating documentary, Calvin Skaggs and David Van Taylor, dirs., *With God On Our Side: George W. Bush and the Rise of the Religious Right* (First Run / Icarus Films, 2010), yet another valuable tool for the classroom.

11. Johnson, *This Is Our Message*, 70–71; Darren Dochuk, *From Bible Belt to Sunbelt: Plain-Folk Religion, Grassroots Politics, and the Rise of Evangelical Conservatism* (New York: W. W. Norton, 2011), xvi, xxiii.

12. A helpful excerpt from Robert Welch, *The Blue Book of the John Birch Society* (1960) is accessible at Encyclopedia.com, https://www.encyclopedia.com/history/dictionaries-thesauruses-pictures-and-press-releases/excerpt-blue-book-john-birch-society-c-1960. There is easy access to Fred Schwarz's *You Can Trust the Communists (to Be Communists)* at the Schwarz Report website, http://www.schwarzreport.org/resources/you-can-trust-the-communists-to-be-communists. Chapter 1 lays out Schwarz's view of communism and its "godless materialism." Chapter 11, titled "Program for Survival," provides students with an overview of the anti-communist agenda.

13. "Speech of Joseph McCarthy, Wheeling, West Virginia, February 9, 1950," History Matters, http://historymatters.gmu.edu/d/6456.

14. Critchlow, *Phyllis Schlafly and Grassroots Conservatism*, 68–72. Schlafly's *A Choice Not an Echo* is available online at Eagle Forum, https://eagleforum.org/about/phyllis-books/a-choice-not-an-echo-1964.html. Among the most teachable chapters are chapter 1, which outlines the argument and Schlafly's disdain for the Republican elite, and chapters 11 and 13, which celebrate Goldwater and grassroots conservative activism.

15. See "The National Association of Evangelicals Amicus Brief re: *Bob Jones University v. The United States* (1981)"; and Chief Justice Warren Burger's opinion re: *Bob Jones University v. The United States* (1983), in Sutton, *Jerry Falwell*, 61–65.

16. See Randall Balmer, *Redeemer: The Life of Jimmy Carter* (New York: Basic Books, 2014).

17. Ronald Reagan, "Remarks at the Annual Convention of the National Association of Evangelicals in Orlando, Florida, March 8, 1983," Ronald Reagan Presidential Foundation and Institute, accessed June 3, 2020, https://www.reaganfoundation.org/library-museum/permanent-exhibitions/berlin-wall/from-the-archives/remarks-at-the-annual-convention-of-the-national-association-of-evangelicals-in-orlando-florida/, and in Sutton, *Jerry Falwell*, 131–36.

18. "Excerpt from Franklin Graham, *The Name*, 2002" and "Letter to Franklin Graham from the Council on American-Islamic Relations, August 15, 2002," both in R. Marie Griffith, *Religions: A Documentary History* (New York: Oxford University Press, 2007), 602–6.

19. Beverly LaHaye's C-SPAN speeches can be accessed at https://www.c-span.org/person/?beverlylahaye. See also Concerned Women for America's extensive website, https://concernedwomen.org/. Less expansive but equally useful for past and current Religious Right politics is Eagle Forum's website, https://eagleforum.org/.

Contributors

Heath W. Carter is an associate professor of American Christianity and the director of PhD studies at Princeton Theological Seminary. He is the author of *Union Made: Working People and the Rise of Social Christianity in Chicago* (2015), which was the runner-up for the American Society of Church History's 2015 Brewer Prize. He is also the co-editor of three books: *The Pew and the Picket Line: Christianity and the American Working Class* (2016), *Turning Points in the History of American Evangelicalism* (2017), and *A Documentary History of Religion in America* (2018).

Darren Dochuk is the Andrew V. Tackes College Professor of History and William W. and Anna Jean Cushwa Co-Director at the University of Notre Dame. He teaches and writes on the history of the modern US, with focus on the intersection of religion, politics, energy, and environment.

Daniel L. Dreisbach is a professor in the School of Public Affairs at American University in Washington, DC. He has published numerous books, book chapters, and articles in academic journals on the intersection of religion, politics, and law in American public life. His books include *Reading the Bible with the Founding Fathers* (2017) and *Thomas Jefferson and the Wall of Separation between Church and State* (2002).

John Fea is a professor of American history at Messiah University in Mechanicsburg, PA. He is the author or editor of several books, including *Was American Founded as a Christian Nation?* (2011) and *Why Study History?: Reflecting on the Importance of the Past* (2013).

Alison Collis Greene is an associate professor of American religious history at Candler School of Theology at Emory University and affiliated faculty in the department of history. She is the author of *No Depression in Heaven: The Great Depression, the New Deal, and the Transformation of Religion in the Delta* (2016), and she is currently working on a book entitled *Backwater: Religion and Community in a Jim Crow Swamp.*

MELISSA FRANKLIN HARKRIDER is an associate professor of history at Wheaton College. She teaches undergraduate courses on American Indians, the Atlantic world, early American history, and European history. Her research on Native spirituality in the eighteenth and nineteenth centuries draws from oral histories, indigenous accounts, and contemporary scholarship on indigenous religious beliefs and practices. Her current book project examines the diverse responses of Cherokee communities to Christianity through a study of Cherokee narratives and Cherokee language hymns and texts.

PAUL HARVEY is a Distinguished Professor of History at the University of Colorado Colorado Springs, and the author of *Through the Storm, Through the Night: A History of African American Christianity.*

J. RUSSELL HAWKINS is a professor of humanities and history in the John Wesley Honors College at Indiana Wesleyan University. He is the author of *The Bible Told Them So: How Southern Evangelicals Fought to Preserve White Supremacy* (2021) and the co-editor of *Christians and the Color Line: Race and Religion after* Divided by Faith (2014).

KIMBERLY HILL is a historian of Black internationalism and American Christianity. She has taught at the University of Texas at Dallas since 2014 with a previous appointment at Del Mar College. Her first book, *A Higher Mission: The Careers of Alonzo and Althea Brown Edmiston in Central Africa*, analyzes how HBCUs and industrial education influenced African American Presbyterians serving as missionaries in colonial Congo. Hill earned her PhD from the University of North Carolina at Chapel Hill in 2008 and studied in South Africa through study abroad programs. She continues to research black missionaries by focusing on the efforts of YMCA and YWCA activists during the Long Civil Rights Movement.

KAREN J. JOHNSON is the author of *One in Christ: Chicago Catholics and the Quest for Interracial Justice* (2018). She serves as an associate professor of history and chair of the Wheaton College history department. Her research is on the intersection of religion and race in US history, and she works closely with future history and social studies teachers.

THOMAS S. KIDD is a research professor of church history at Midwestern Baptist Theological Seminary. Prior to Midwestern, he taught for two decades in the history department at Baylor University.

JONATHAN B. KRASNER is the Jack, Joseph, and Morton Mandel Associate Professor of Jewish Education Research at Brandeis University. His first book, *The Benderly Boys and American Jewish Education* (2011), was a finalist for the Sami Rohr Prize in American Jewish Literature, while his second book, *Hebrew Infusion: Language and Community at American Jewish Summer Camps* (2020), won a National Jewish Book Award. His current research centers around the development of Jewish all-day (parochial) schools in the United States.

GEORGE MARSDEN has taught history at Calvin College, Duke University, and the University of Notre Dame. He is the author of many books on American religious history, including *Fundamentalism and American Culture* (1980; updated third edition 2022).

JACLYN A. MICHAEL is an assistant professor of religion at the University of Tennessee at Chattanooga.

MARK NOLL is a retired historian who taught at Wheaton College and the University of Notre Dame. His books include *The Civil War as a Theological Crisis* (2006), *America's Book: The Rise and Decline of a Bible Civilization, 1794–1911* (2022), and other studies.

KEVIN M. SCHULTZ is a professor of history, Catholic studies, and religious studies, and chair of the department of history at the University of Illinois at Chicago (UIC).

ELIJAH SIEGLER is a professor and former chair of religious studies at the College of Charleston, and author of numerous articles and books, including *Dream Trippers: Global Daoism and the Predicament of Modern Spirituality* (2017), coauthored with David Palmer. He has degrees in Religious Studies from Harvard and the University of California. He teaches a variety of classes, including on Asian religions in America, American religious history, and religions of China and Japan.

PHILLIP LUKE SINITIERE received a PhD in American history at the University of Houston in 2009. Currently, he is a professor of history and humanities at the College of Biblical Studies, a predominately African American school located in Houston's Mahatma Gandhi District. Sinitiere is also the scholar in residence at UMass Amherst's W.E.B. Du Bois Center. A scholar of American religious history and African American Studies, Sinitiere's recent books include *Salvation with a Smile: Joel Osteen, Lakewood Church, and American Christianity* (2015), *Citizen of the World: The Late Career and Legacy of W.E.B. Du Bois* (2019), *Race, Religion, and Black Lives Matter: Essays on a Moment and a Movement* (2021), and *Forging Freedom in W.E.B. Du Bois's Twilight Years: No Deed but Memory* (2023).

JOHN HOWARD SMITH is a professor of history at Texas A&M University-Commerce, and the author of *A Dream of the Judgment Day: American Millennialism and Apocalypticism, 1620-1890* (2021).

MATTHEW AVERY SUTTON is the Berry Family Distinguished Professor in the Liberal Arts and the chair of the department of history at Washington State University. His most recent book is *Double Crossed: The Missionaries Who Spied for the United States During the Second World War* (2019). He is also the author of *American Apocalypse: A History of Modern Evangelicalism* (2014), and *Aimee Semple McPherson and the Resurrection of Christian America* (2007). He has written for the *New York Times, Washington Post*, and *New Republic*. In 2016 he was appointed a Guggenheim Foundation Fellow.

JOHN G. TURNER is a professor of religious studies and history at George Mason University in Fairfax, Virginia. He is the author of, most recently, *They Knew They Were Pilgrims: Plymouth Colony and the Contest for American Liberty* (2020).

ANDREA L. TURPIN is an associate professor and graduate program director of history at Baylor University. She is the author of *A New Moral Vision: Gender, Religion, and the Changing Purposes of American Higher Education, 1837–1917* (2016). Her current book project positions women as key players in the Protestant fundamentalist-modernist controversy of the early twentieth century, which served as a precursor to the contemporary culture wars.

ADRIAN CHASTAIN WEIMER is a professor of history at Providence College. She is the author of *A Constitutional Culture: New England and the Struggle against Arbitrary Rule in the Restoration Empire* (2023), and *Martyrs' Mirror: Persecution and Holiness in Early New England* (2011).

JONATHAN M. YEAGER is the LeRoy A. Martin Professor of Religious Studies at the University of Tennessee at Chattanooga. He is the author of *Jonathan Edwards and Transatlantic Print Culture,* named Book of the Year by the Jonathan Edwards Center at Trinity Evangelical Divinity School.

Index

The Harvey Goldberg Series
for Understanding and Teaching History

www.ingramcontent.com/pod-product-compliance
Lightning Source LLC
Chambersburg PA
CBHW030921150426
42812CB00046B/450